26c₁

ASSEMBLI

Rowland Purton

ASSEMBLIES

Basil Blackwell Publisher

ISBN 0–631–90412–3 Pbk

Phototypeset in V.I.P. Times by
Western Printing Services Ltd, Bristol
and Printed in Great Britain by
Billing and Son Ltd, Worcester

To SYLVIA
with thanks
for everything

Contents

Introduction

Teachers and others who have been using *Day by Day* will be familiar with the pattern to be found in this book. There is sufficient material here for a daily assembly for two years without repetition. The stories and prayers are appropriate to most school, community or national occasions.

The outlines are suitable for use in junior, middle or secondary school assemblies and will also be welcomed for use out of school by preachers and youth leaders. In addition, a glance at the comprehensive indexing will reveal that this book is a mine of information on many subjects.

The material has been arranged in themes of five so that each may be followed for a week if desired. Most of the stories can also be used independently, though there is close linkage within some themes. It is also suggested that the themes on pages 251–295 could profitably form the basis of assemblies for a whole term, thus giving a degree of continuity and an opportunity for comparison.

Many of the stories have a date association and attention is drawn to the Table of Contents by Date on page xxix. These could be used on anniversaries if desired but there is not a story for every day of the year as some of the themes do not lend themselves to this approach.

ASSEMBLIES has been prepared with the multi-racial, multi-cultural community in mind, though this does not preclude its use elsewhere. Reference is made to religions and cultures other than Christianity and the whole concept of the book is broadly based to enable as many as possible to feel that the assembly is a daily act of worship for them. Whilst the basis of the book is predominantly Christian it is not exclusively so. Prayers, for example, have been written on the whole without the concluding '. . . through Jesus Christ our Lord', which can be added if desired. Prayers of some other faiths have also been included.

It is sincerely hoped that the book will draw attention to the devotion of people of many faiths and to help in some measure to break down barriers caused by intolerance and misunderstanding. It may help to banish certain misconceptions held by youngsters, e.g. that Jewish history ended with the Old Testament. The last section of the book includes people of God other than those of the Christian religion. Throughout there is an attempt to draw attention to present day concerns as well as to highlight things that are of lasting value and to introduce important religious concepts.

THE ASSEMBLY

Each unit consists of a story, often incorporating a Bible reading. It is followed by a prayer and a suggested closing prayer or benediction. In most cases the prayers follow the theme of the story; but occasionally a prayer is one written by the person who is the subject of the story. All the prayers have been especially written for this book except where otherwise indicated. Modern English has been used except in a few of the old prayers.

The prayer supplement (pages 405ff) includes prayers suitable for the opening of worship, closing prayers and benedictions (to which reference is made at the foot of each page), prayers for the school and those for special occasions. These, together with the prayers printed after each story, form an extensive anthology of prayers on most subjects likely to be needed in school. Attention is drawn to the comprehensive prayer index.

Bible readings have been included where appropriate but no attempt has been made to include a reading just for the sake of doing so. Some readings introduce the stories; some find a place within the story; and others prove appropriate conclusions. It is suggested that the Good News Bible or another modern translation should be used. Poems and readings from other sources can also be used quite effectively.

It will be appreciated that the outlines given here do not form complete services but perhaps the second half. It is important that every service should begin on a note of praise and thanksgiving and perhaps prayers of a more general nature should come early in the service. A few opening prayers are included in the prayer section but there are numerous other sources of prayers of this kind, some of which may be included in the children's hymn books, thus enabling them actively to participate.

The participation of children should be encouraged in both prayers and readings. Services may profitably include prayers written by the children as well as responsive prayers in which all may join. It is also a good idea for older children to read the Bible passages at times but it is essential that the reading should be well rehearsed. There is nothing more liable to destroy the atmosphere of the service than a Bible reading mumbled unintelligibly and unheard by the majority of the children.

No doubt those arranging assemblies will keep in mind the need for variety, though an ordered framework is helpful and the children appreciate the security of some degree of uniformity.

Perhaps the most important aspect of assembly is the planning which is necessary if the act is to be more than a mere daily duty. An atmosphere created by the use of music, flowers and the general appearance of the hall will all help but will be of little avail if advance thought has not been given to the planning of the service.

It will be obvious, therefore, that this book should be used wisely and not just reached for at the last moment to be thumbed through for a story that has not been used lately. There should be that degree of thought and careful preparation which is necessary in all school work but even more so when bringing children before God.

ROWLAND PURTON

Acknowledgements

Prayers and quotations from various sources have been used. The pages on which the undermentioned prayers may be found are indicated in the list on pages 426–7.

The author and publishers would like to thank all who have given permission to reproduce copyright material.

The *Authorized Version of the Bible*, and the *Book of Common Prayer* of 1662, are both Crown Copyright: extracts reproduced herein are with permission.

Some of the ancient prayers for which the original sources are indicated may also be found in the *Book of Common Prayer*.

The Apostles' Creed © 1970, 71, 75 International Consultation on English Texts (page 425) is reproduced by permission of S.P.C.K.

The British and Foreign Bible Society for three prayers, quotations from the *Good News Bible* (British Usage Edition).

The Christian Literature Crusade for kind permission to use the extract from *A Prisoner and Yet* by Corrie ten Boom (page 400).

Messrs. T. & T. Clark Ltd. for the prayer from *The Qur'ān Translated* by R. Bell.

Messrs. J. M. Dent & Sons Ltd. for a prayer by John Hunter from *Devotional Services for Public Worship*.

Messrs. Gill and Macmillan Ltd. for the prayer by Michel Quoist from *Prayers of Life*.

Messrs. Hodder and Stoughton Ltd. for an extract from *The Impossible Voyage* by Chay Blyth (page 158) and for a prayer by Reinhold Niebuhr from *Uncommon Prayers* edited by Cecil Hunt.

The Lutterworth Press for five prayers from *Prayers at Breakfast* by Beryl Bye.

Methodist Publishing House for the Collect for Ash Wednesday (page 72) from 'Collects, Lessons and Psalms' from the *Methodist Service Book* 1975.

Messrs. John Murray (Publishers) Ltd. for a prayer from *A Chain of Prayer Across the Ages*, compiled by Selina Fox.

Oxford University Press for permission to use three prayers from the *Daily Service*.

The Society of Authors as the literary representative of the Estate of John Masefield for the verse from *Sea Fever* (page 129).

The Soncino Press Ltd. for the prayer from *The Soncino Talmud*

(18 volume edition): General Editor, Rabbi Dr. Isidore Epstein, B.A., Ph.D., D.Litt.

Messrs. Stainer & Bell Ltd. for permission to use one verse from *When I needed a neighbour* by Sydney Carter (Page 202), from *Green Print for Song*.

S. C. M. Press Ltd. for four prayers by Dr. William Barclay from *Epilogues and Prayers*.

The Taizé Community for the prayer from *The Rule of Taizé*, 71250 Taizé-Communauté, France: available in England through the Faith Press, Leighton Buzzard.

The Headmaster of Uppingham School, Mr. C. Macdonald, for a prayer from *Prayers in Use at Uppingham School*.

In addition to actual quotations, reference has been made to many source books and this is readily acknowledged. Every endeavour has been made to trace all copyright material and seek permission for reproduction. Should any copyright have been unwittingly infringed, the author extends his sincere apologies. Any omissions will, if notified, be gladly corrected in future editions.

The author wishes to express his appreciation to the many individuals, societies and organizations who so willingly provided information when requested. He would also like to acknowledge his thankfulness to his wife, Sylvia, for her assistance in so many ways, practical and otherwise: her constant encouragement has been invaluable.

Table of Contents by Theme

SERVICE

IN THE DAY'S WORK

GREAT PEOPLE OF GOD

FAITHFUL SERVANTS

Table of Contents by Date

Many of the stories have one or more date associations. This list is provided for those who would like to use the stories as 'anniversary' stories, though there is not one for every day. The undated stories shown at the end of each month may also be used where appropriate.

A figure in brackets indicates the alternative date association and care will need to be taken that stories are not used on both dates.

1 Our World

This is a series of twelve themes based upon everyday things, many of them familiar and some drawing attention to the needs of the present age.

Around town	*In the country*	*By the sea*
On the farm	*Everyday things*	*Animals*
Flowers	*Conservation*	*Old and new*
Resources	*Disaster*	*Safety*

Each theme consists of five topics. Many of them can be taken individually and most are complete in themselves but there is a degree of continuity in some, notably in *Conservation*, *Old and new*, *Resources* and *Safety*. There is also a link between the first two topics of *Flowers*.

If taken as themes, it is suggested that one of the earlier themes might be used as an opener for the first week of the school year.

Around town (1)

Houses and homes

Towns are places where people live. People do lots of other things in them too. They work there; they go shopping; they enjoy their recreation; they have places for entertainment or worship. There are hospitals, libraries, swimming baths, bus and railway stations and lots of other buildings. But most important for all people are their homes.

In most towns there are lots of different kinds of home. Most people probably live in terraced houses but some may have semi-detached or detached houses. Some may live in bungalows, others perhaps high above the ground in tower blocks. Some homes are quite old: others are very modern. Some people own their homes: others rent them from a private landlord or from the council.

There is an old saying that an Englishman's home is his castle. It is the one place in which people, in many lands apart from England, can shut themselves away from others and do the kind of things that they like to do. Home can be a place that is completely private or there can be an open door to welcome others. It can be a place where people are extremely happy and love one another, or it can be made thoroughly miserable by bad temper, selfishness or other forms of unpleasantness.

A town may contain houses of many kinds. What kind of *homes* they become depends entirely upon the people who live in them. Your home depends partly upon the people you live with but also upon you. What kind of contribution do you make? Perhaps these words of St. Paul should be heeded.

Bible Reading: Ephesians 4: 29–32

We thank you, God our Father, for our homes and the people who share them with us. Help us to make our homes happy by doing only those things which are good and right, considerate and helpful, showing love and respect to each other always. *Amen.*

Benediction No. 104

Around town (2)

The day's work

Early in the morning the town begins to come to life as people leave their homes to go to work. In larger towns and cities traffic becomes very congested as people flock to work during the rush hours, many of them travelling into the city from their homes on the outskirts or beyond. In the evening the rush hour begins again as people return home.

Many of these people work in offices and shops where work usually begins about 9 a.m. and finishes about 5 p.m. Many factory workers start earlier than that, some of them doing night shifts instead so that work never stops. In other jobs, too, people have to work during the night or early morning. Think of those in hospitals, bakeries, newspaper businesses, transport, police and fire services.

Many of these people really enjoy their work. It is the career which they chose for themselves and they find a lot of satisfaction in doing it well. Others may work unwillingly. They do not enjoy their work but do it because they need a job to earn the money to live on.

How well do people work for their wages? Some will always give of their best: others do as little as possible. This is nothing new. Listen to these words of St. Paul:

Bible Reading: II Thessalonians 3: 6–13

It is the duty of all people to give a fair day's work in return for the wages they receive. To do less is to rob one's employer. Some people see work differently. It is a part of the life they have dedicated to God and nothing less than one's best is good enough as an offering to God.

O God our Father, help us to see the need to do our best in any work that we do, for our own satisfaction, as our duty toward others, and as something worthy to be offered to you. *Amen.*

Closing prayer No. 77

Around town (3)

The market cross

Many towns have one day a week as market day when the town is busier than usual. In some towns there may be a livestock market at which cattle, sheep and pigs are auctioned but there are fewer of these markets than there used to be.

Market day in most towns is the day on which the market square is filled with stalls for the sale of all sorts of goods at prices lower than they normally are in the shops. The traders have to pay a fee for the use of a stall and they have to obey all the regulations of the market.

Many of these regulations are quite old and were made originally to ensure fair trading. Even the day on which the market is held may have been determined a long time ago, when market days in neighbouring towns were fixed for different days of the week so that towns did not compete with one another for the custom of the village folk.

In the market square there may be a market cross, perhaps hundreds of years old. Some are simple crosses: others are much more elaborate with a shelter beneath.

Probably the earliest market crosses were portable crosses carried by a priest who was present at the market. Certainly the cross could be a reminder to those at the market that their trading was supposed to be conducted in a manner that was in keeping with their Christian faith—fair, honest and with a right attitude toward others.

Bible Reading: I Peter 3: 8–12

Grant unto us, O God our Father, your guidance in all our dealings with others, that we may always be honest, reliable and just, known for our fairness and fit to be called the children of our Father in Heaven. *Amen.*

Closing prayer No. 60

Around town (4)

Street lighting

Most towns are brightly lit at night by lights of many kinds. There are street lights to light the way and make travelling safer, advertising lights, shop windows lit to draw attention to the goods on sale and floodlights to illuminate important buildings, to mention only some.

Travellers approaching a town see it from a distance not only because of its rows of lights but by the glow in the sky above.

Long ago towns were dark places lit only by the occasional lantern. It was not until gas lighting had been invented that street lighting became possible. The first street in the world to be lit was Pall Mall, London, on the night of 28th January, 1807. In the days of gas lighting, well on into the present century, lamplighters used to tour the streets with a hooked pole to turn the lights on and off. Nowadays with electric lighting the lights are turned on automatically and the busy streets are brightly lit.

Advertising and shop window lighting often adds a touch of colour and brightness. Some towns have special illuminations at Christmas. Seaside towns are colourfully lit during the holiday season.

Jesus Christ said on several occasions that he had come to bring light into a dark world.

Bible Reading: St. John 12: 44–48

He is the Light that brightens the way and helps people to journey in safety toward God. His light also draws attention to the ways and teachings of God. Perhaps it is appropriate, too, that some of the extra brightness in our world is at Christmas, when we celebrate his coming.

Lighten our world, O Lord, by the radiance of your presence so that we may journey in safety to your eternal kingdom; lighten our pathway by the understanding of your holy word; and brighten our lives by the power of your Holy Spirit. *Amen*.

Closing prayer No. 72

Around town (5)

Ethnic groups

We may think of towns as places consisting of buildings and streets, shops and offices, traffic and transport. These all go to make a town but we have to remember that people are more important than material things. The nature of a town depends upon the people who live in it.

Populations of towns are always changing as some people move to live elsewhere and others take their place. Many cities and towns now have communities of people whose homes were once in other countries but who, for various reasons, made their homes in Britain.

Some fled from their countries in Europe when they were occupied by an enemy. Others, including many from the West Indies and Asia came to find work at a time when they were greatly needed to help run hospitals, buses and other services. Many of their relatives and friends came later and naturally wanted to live nearby.

So today in many towns there are large communities of West Indians, Pakistanis, Cypriots and others. They have shops which sell their familiar foods and other goods—Asian clothes, tropical fruits, Halal meats and so on. They have opened their own places of worship and they enjoy the traditional customs of their differing cultures.

Perhaps the ways of some of our neighbours may seem strange. We may find it difficult to understand their customs, some of which may not be to our liking. But as long as we live in the same town we have a responsibility to try to understand each other, to show tolerance and kindness and to work together for the good of the community.

O God, Father of all people,
Give us an understanding of the ways of our neighbours;
Make us tolerant of anything we may not like
And ready to work for the good of our town,
So that we may live peacefully and happily together, *Amen.*

Closing prayer No. 54

In the country (1)

One of the best-known villages in England is Ambridge. Many people turn on their radios regularly to find out what is happening to the Archers at Brookfield Farm and to their various friends and acquaintances in the village.

Many people are surprised to learn that Ambridge does not, in fact, exist at all but is just an imaginary village invented for what was to become one of the best-known radio programmes. The story began way back in 1950. Five trial scripts were written and a group of actors gathered in studios in the Midlands to try them out on 12th May. Two days later they were recorded and two weeks later they were broadcast. Then followed months in which the B.B.C. decided whether to go ahead with the idea of 'an everyday story of country folk'.

It was eventually decided to start on 1st January 1951. One newspaper reported earlier: 'Farmer Dan Archer arrives on the Light Programme to introduce his family to Britain's housewives. But it will be no fleeting acquaintance. Farmer Dan is hoping that it will ripen into friendship. The Archers are here to stay.' And how right that was! In 1976 *The Archers* celebrated their twenty-five years and there was no sign that the programme would ever end.

Ambridge is typical of hundreds of villages to be found throughout Britain—small communities with lots of different kinds of people living in them, a few farmers, the vicar, the innkeeper, a few tradespeople, retired city dwellers, teachers, people who work in nearby towns—and all needing to work together to make theirs a happy, family community.

We thank you, O God, for all the people who make up the community in which we live. Grant that we may all work together, using our talents for the common good, and endeavouring to make it a happy place in which to live. *Amen*.

Closing prayer No. 54

In the country (2)

Often when travelling through the countryside one comes across a signpost by the side of the road with the words 'Public Footpath' inscribed on it. It is there to indicate a right of way which may have been there for many years and has been preserved by local by-laws so that people can still enjoy it today.

Many people will pass it by. We are so used to travelling along made-up roads in motor cars or on public transport that we often fail to make time to explore somewhere that is off the beaten track. It may lead through the fields, beside the hedgerows, over cliffs or through woods but as we leave the noise of the highway behind us we find ourselves in a different world—a world of peace and quietness, a world of nature to be enjoyed.

Familiar man-made noises give way to the sounds of nature, the singing of birds, the hum of insects, the rustle of leaves. There to be seen and enjoyed are the wide variety of wild flowers, fruits and berries; and there to be smelt are the blossom and maybe some new-mown hay. It is a refreshing world in which one can relax and enjoy an atmosphere that is free from all the rush and bustle of everyday life.

We can appreciate how the psalmist must have felt when he wrote of green pastures and still waters:

Bible Reading: Psalm 23

We do well to remember our need for such things so that we can be restored in body and soul in places of peace and quiet and in the presence of the Almighty God who created all this.

O God, our heavenly Father;
We praise you for the joys of the world you created;
We thank you for times of rest and relaxation;
We pray that we may make time to enjoy these things
And to know that you are near. *Amen.*

Closing prayer No. 53

In the country (3)

Finding one's way in the country is not always easy, especially when one is off the main roads and following country lanes which wind this way and that until all sense of direction is lost. Main roads are not so bad, for once on a road that has been signposted to a particular town there is not much likelihood of losing the way.

On country journeys nothing is more welcome to the stranger than the signpost standing at the road junction and indicating the direction to be taken. It can save a lot of time and energy which would have been wasted by taking a wrong turning.

Sometimes, too, a country church is a useful landmark. Many churches are built on high ground and the spire or tower can be seen from some distance even before other parts of the village become visible.

But even with these 'visual aids' one may still have some difficulty in finding one's destination. Village houses are not always marked as clearly with numbers and street names as houses are in town. Farms may be known just by their name and nothing else. The only solution is to find someone who knows the village and ask.

Life is rather like that. There are so many ways along which we can travel that it is not always easy to know the direction to take. But we do have our signpost, our scriptures, which help us to know what is God's way.

Bible Reading: Psalm 25: 1–12

In addition there are many who have found that the church has helped them find their way. And we should never be afraid to ask people who have learned the way of life for themselves.

Guide us, O God our Father as we make our journey through life. Show us the direction we should take and teach us the value of the help available through your church and from your people. *Amen.*

Benediction No. 99

In the country (4)

NATURAL POWER   *Windmills and watermills*

Dotted around the countryside are many windmills, relics of a
bygone age. Some have been restored by their owners to full
working order but many are mere shells with no sails, perhaps only
the brick tower remaining.

At one time most settlements had mills to which villagers would
take their corn to be ground. Wind power was the only power
available in many places in those days and the huge sails of the
windmills were set to catch as much wind as possible so that the
millstones would be turned. Smaller windmills were used for
draining fenland.

Where there was a river, watermills were built instead. These
had a large wheel on the outside of the building which was turned
by flowing water. Often a mill stream was constructed off the main
river and the river blocked by a staunch or gate so that the main
force of the water was directed through the mill stream. Water
wheels also provided power for many of the early factories.

Nowadays, when electric power is more reliable than wind or
water and when transport is so much easier, flour milling is done in
huge mills far from where the crop was grown. Old windmills and
watermills are no longer needed. Some have been put to other
uses: some are mere reminders of days gone by.

But old mills or new all depend upon the power provided from
outside—just as we are dependent upon the power of the spirit of
God. And just as the miller has sought to get the best possible
supply, so should we.

Bible Reading: St. John 3: 5–8

Make us obedient to your will, O God and put your spirit within us
so that our lives may be filled with your mighty power and guided
into the paths that you would have us to tread. *Amen.*

Benediction No. 100

In the country (5)

Most people enjoy the countryside. For some it is home and the place where they earn their living. For others it is a place to which they can escape from the town or city to enjoy the open spaces, the fresh air and the summer sunshine.

Country people know how important it is to care for the countryside. It is their home. People who are visiting country districts are not always as careful as they ought to be and sometimes do things which can cause harm to animals, damage to crops and annoyance to people who live there.

Litter, for example, is not only unsightly but can cause injury to animals. Broken glass can cause injury but may also magnify the sun's rays to start fire. Dogs running loose may enjoy chasing sheep—but the sheep do not enjoy being chased. Gates left open may allow animals to stray and perhaps be killed by traffic being driven too fast along narrow country lanes.

And so, to protect the countryside, ten simple rules have been drawn up, known as The Country Code, which are really just common sense. 1 Guard against all risks of fire. 2 Fasten all gates. 3 Keep dogs under proper control. 4 Keep to the paths across farm land. 5 Avoid damaging fences, hedges and walls. 6 Leave no litter. 7 Safeguard water supplies. 8 Protect wild life, wild plants and trees. 9 Go carefully on country roads. 10 Respect the life of the countryside.

Not only are these common-sense rules but they illustrate the kind of thoughtfulness that we should show to others wherever we live.

Bible Reading: St. Luke 6: 31 (*The 'Golden Rule'*)

Teach us always, O God, to respect the wishes of others and to treat them in the same way that we would like them to treat us. Make us thoughtful, considerate, kind, respectful and honest in all our ways so that others may see something of your nature in us. *Amen.*

Closing prayer No. 68

By the sea (1)

The Coastal Code

During the summer lots of people like to visit the seaside for holidays or days out to enjoy the sea and sunshine, swimming, sailing and all the other pleasures of such visits.

For many, part of the enjoyment of the seaside is to explore the beaches and cliffs, sand dunes and saltings, to see the wild creatures and plants for which the seaside is 'home'.

Some of the most fascinating shores are those rocky coasts where the receding tide leaves rock pools—water gardens teeming with wild life. There are colourful sea anemones and starfish, various seaweeds, perhaps a small crab, fish or shrimps and shellfish of various kinds. On the rocks nearby may be masses of seaweed, drying and limp in the sunshine but full of life when covered again by the rising tide.

There is always a temptation for some visitors to uproot the seaweed or disturb the life in the rock pools, to damage flowers, even to frighten seals or seabirds. Some take away live shellfish for collections when there are plenty of empty shells to be found. The wild life of the seashore is best photographed or sketched, then left for other people to enjoy. Moreover, the removal of wild life can sometimes upset the balance of nature.

To help protect the seashore, a Coastal Code has been drawn up to remind visitors of dangers to wild life by thoughtless people. Perhaps we should also remember that the world is ours to use, not to abuse, and that it is wrong to cause unnecessary suffering even to the humblest of God's creatures.

Almighty God, maker of our world and of all creatures great and small, we offer thanks for all the enjoyment we find in the world of nature. Help us to treat all wild life with respect and to be thoughtful lest we cause any unnecessary suffering or damage. *Amen.*

Closing prayer No. 83

By the sea (2)

Scripture Union (C.S.S.M.)

Perhaps when you have been on the beach in summer you may have seen or taken part in activities which have been organized for children on the beach, maybe by a team working for the Scripture Union.

Seaside missions have been enjoyed by children for over a hundred years since the first one was held on the beach at Llandudno, North Wales in 1867. It was organized by a movement known as the Children's Special Service Mission.

Most of these missions last for a couple of weeks. Each day there is a meeting on the beach with one of the leaders telling a story. There is usually some lively singing and perhaps Bible study or a quiz. All sorts of other activities take place as well. Sand modelling, treasure hunts and games all help the leaders and children to get to know each other. The leaders then tell the children what the Christian way of life means to them.

In 1960 these beach missions began using the name Scripture Union, which was the name of that part of the organization which prepared notes for daily Bible reading. The Scripture Union now has many branches, helping children and adults, producing materials for schools and Sunday schools, publishing books and pamphlets, training people in youth and community work, supporting Christian work overseas, running book shops and stalls, and answering many other needs of Christian people.

The Scripture Union is, of course, only one organization that runs beach missions. Many are planned and run by local churches for the enjoyment of visitors to their town.

We thank you, O God, for lots of things to enjoy on the beach on sunny days. Bless those who arrange things for the enjoyment of holidaymakers and especially those teams of people who help children to find enjoyment as they learn of you. *Amen.*

Benediction No. 106

By the sea (3)

Around the coasts of any country there are many ports and harbours, some large enough only for small fishing boats, others able to accommodate the largest of ships. Most have been there a long time since seamen first needed sheltered harbours. Some have grown because of a particular need. Think of the millions of people with their cars that pass through Dover, the nearest port to Europe.

Aberdeen was a port for the Norsemen over 800 years ago but it is another port which has grown very quickly in recent years because of the discovery of North Sea oil and gas and the need for a base from which to supply the rigs. Today Aberdeen Harbour is the main offshore supply base in Europe. A dozen or so supply vessels arrive in Aberdeen every day.

But wander around Aberdeen Harbour and you will see lots of other ships too. There is the passenger ferry providing an important link with the Shetland Islands. There are cargo ships unloading timber, wood-pulp, cereals, fertilizers, coal, cement and lots of other things. There are lots of fishing vessels, for Aberdeen is the largest fishing harbour in Scotland and third largest in the United Kingdom. And there are many other activities too.

It is when we think of all these things that we realize just how dependent we are upon other people for our food and our daily needs. And of course we are reminded in the Bible that we are also dependent upon God for our spiritual needs.

Bible Reading: Deuteronomy 8: 2–3

Today, O God, we come to say thank-you
For our daily food and our everyday provision;
For all who work to provide these things for us;
For everything we have that comes from you.
Give us thankful hearts, we pray. *Amen*.

Closing prayer No. 90

By the sea (4)

'Boston Sea Ranger'

On 5th December, 1977, the Lowestoft trawler *Boston Sea Ranger* was fishing for mackerel off Land's End, Cornwall. It wasn't a bad day for fishing and the hatches were open so that fish could be stowed in the fish hold.

Unexpectedly a giant wave hit the stern of the trawler, swept up the ramp used for getting the nets on board and flooded the fish hold. Within seven minutes the ship had sunk and five members of the crew of eight had been lost.

During summer months, many holidaymakers are attracted by the fishing boats in ports and harbours all round the coast. On the quays are many reminders of the fishing industry, nets spread out to dry, floats and marker buoys, crab and lobster pots and stacks of boxes in which the fish are sent to market.

The arrival of a fishing boat is just as sure to attract people, who want to see what has been caught, as it is to attract the gulls, which are always on the watch for something to eat. People enjoy watching the boat being unloaded or the brisk business of the early morning fish market.

Again, in the evening or when the tide is high, people watch as the boats head out to sea, their gear stowed neatly on deck prepared for yet another catch. How many of these people wish they could be on board themselves?

But fishermen are not just fair weather sailors. Theirs is not an easy job even in summer and it is even more difficult in wintry weather.

And people in most ports can recall the names of the men and the boats which sailed and never came back. It is the price which is paid for the silvery harvest of the sea.

Almighty God, we commend into your care and keeping all those who venture out to sea to provide us with food. Protect them from all harm and danger and grant them a safe return when their work is done. *Amen.*

Benediction No. 93

By the sea (5)

Bible Reading: St. John 21: 2–6

Those disciples of Jesus, fishing in the Sea of Galilee, knew, as most fishermen do, that there are times when the fish do not seem to be there to be caught and it is quite common to spend a wasted night if the nets happen to be in the wrong position.

Around the coast there are many people who depend on the sea for their living. Some go out in their fishing vessels for several days at a time; others put out their nets or lines each night and hope to bring in something to sell in the morning.

Often in the past, as in some far-off parts of the world today, garlands were cast into the waters as an offering to the gods of the sea, in the hope that this would ensure plenty of fish.

Today, Christian people are not concerned with the spirits of the sea but they do like to ask God's blessing upon their work. So, in many ports and harbours there are little ceremonies in which a clergyman blesses the boats and those who sail in them.

One such ceremony takes place at Hastings each year on or near 26th May. The local fishing season starts at the end of May. So, one evening a procession leaves All Saints' Church and St. Clement's Church in the old town and proceeds to the fish market, where the Bishop blesses the fishermen and offers prayers for a successful fishing season.

In other places, such as Cullercoats and North Shields, the clergy put to sea to bless the boats. It is always a good thing to ask God's blessing on one's work . . . AND to remember to say 'Thank-you' afterwards.

Bless the work of our hands, O God, and the workings of our minds so that we may do the very best that we are able; and accept our thanks for all that we have been able to achieve. *Amen.*

Closing prayer No. 57

On the farm (1)

Look around a farm in summer and you may see fine crops of wheat, barley, potatoes, turnips or other foods. Visit the same farm next year and different crops will be growing in those same fields. We call this 'crop rotation'. If the same crop were grown year after year in the same place it would become poorer and poorer because it would take all the nourishment out of the ground.

The idea of crop rotation was introduced to British farmers by Viscount Townshend (1674–1738). Until then the fields had been left without a crop every third year. 'Plant turnips', he told them. Soon he was nicknamed 'Turnip' Townshend. But those farmers who tried his methods found that they really did work.

Since then, people have learned a lot more about the soil and the millions of tiny creatures which live in it. They know what is good for each kind of crop and what is bad for it. In agricultural research establishments such as the one at Rothamstead scientists are continually at work, trying one experiment after another. How many leaves are pulled into the ground by worms in an orchard? This is just one of many investigations which would provide useful information.

Long ago people knew the importance of the sun and the rain, as the psalmist reminds us.

Bible Reading: Psalm 65: 9–13

Today scientists know that God has also provided millions of other things too which can be put to good use to provide better crops in a world in which more and more is needed to feed hungry people.

O God, sender of the sun and rain, creator of the tiniest of living things, and giver of wisdom to mankind; grant your blessing upon all who farm the land and upon those who help them to produce better crops so that people throughout the world may have good food and enough to sustain them. *Amen.*

Benediction No. 96

On the farm (2)

Robert Bakewell

If you take time to look closely at farm animals you will soon discover how well they suit the purpose for which they are kept. Some cattle with plenty of meat are reared as 'beef cattle'; others produce more milk for dairying. Sheep may be bred for wool or for meat or both. For animals with these qualities, modern farmers are indebted to Robert Bakewell, who lived at Dishley, Leicestershire over two hundred years ago.

Bakewell was an animal breeder who believed that animals could be bred to 'weigh where you wanted them to weigh'. By selective breeding he improved his animals all the time. His Leicestershire sheep were fine sheep and his prize ram earned him £1,200 in one year by hiring it out. The Dishley cattle were much better than others. Dishley horses were in great demand for ploughing and for the army.

Lots of farmers visited him to learn of his methods. Many of them thought him a little strange. He kept his animals spotlessly clean; he gave his sheep coats in bad weather; and he had a canal cut to irrigate his pastures. Strange, perhaps, but his methods worked!

Bakewell was never satisfied. He made more and more experiments which left him almost bankrupt when he died in 1795. But modern farming owes much to the man whose breeding methods are still world famous.

In today's world with so many people to be fed we have to be thankful for animals which provide food and for people who can introduce better animals into the poorer countries of the world.

We say thank you, O God,
For all those animals which provide us with food;
For people who breed them and care for them;
For stockbreeders who breed ever better animals;
And for all who are concerned with providing for the needs of
    hungry people in other lands. *Amen*.

Benediction No. 95

On the farm (3)

County Shows

One of the highlights of the year in most farming communities is the County Show at which some of the finest animals are entered in competitions to see which is awarded the prize as Champion of its class. Cows and bulls are paraded around the enclosure: other animals are judged in their pens.

Often there is friendly rivalry between farmers as they see who can collect the most of the highly coveted awards.

But the County Show is more than a competition to find the best animals. It is also an opportunity for manufacturers to demonstrate the best pieces of machinery and for seedsmen to argue the fine quality of their seed for the growing of crops. It is an opportunity for farmers to talk to each other and perhaps learn from the successes or failures that others have experienced.

A good farmer will want to take note of all these things because he wants to produce the best animals, dairy produce or crops that he can. And there is always something new that can be learned. It has been so throughout history and no doubt it will always be.

Jesus once told a parable about a very successful farmer who thought he knew all the answers but still had a very important lesson to learn.

Bible Reading: St. Luke 12: 16–21

It is a lesson that everyone might learn. No matter how successful we may be, nor how rich we may become, we are very foolish if we take no notice of God or fail to heed those lessons which he has taught us through the scriptures.

Give us wisdom, O God, to learn all we can from other people, and give us the sense to live according to your teachings so that we may enjoy the blessings of this present life and then be received into your eternal kingdom with all your faithful servants. *Amen.*

Closing prayer No. 67

On the farm (4)

AN ORDINARY FARMER   *John Limmer*

John Limmer is one of many farmers found throughout Britain, who work the land and keep some livestock. Born in north Essex on 18th August, 1907, he moved into Suffolk as a child and took on his present farm near Bury St. Edmunds in 1941.

He has been concerned mainly with dairy farming, keeping a herd of a couple of dozen cows and using some of his land to grow their food. Twice each day they were brought into the yard to be milked and the milk put in churns for the dairy. Usually, too, there were calves to be raised so that the cows would continue to produce milk. As he reached the age when people retire from work, John kept fewer milking cows but reared calves for sale.

Working with animals is a big responsibility for they cannot be left as crops in the field can. Someone has to milk the cows twice a day; someone has to care for them and call in a vet when necessary; and unless anyone else is available that someone is the farmer himself. Days off are few and far between.

But John Limmer has another responsibility too as Steward in his local Methodist Church, where he attends morning and evening worship. For him Sunday has hardly been a 'day of rest'—up early for milking, wash and change to attend church, milk the cows in the afternoon and dress once more for the evening service, then make sure that all is well with the animals before going to bed.

A busy day! But like many others who work on the land, he is aware of the handiwork of God in the world, so the opportunity to worship and say thank you to God is something he considers of very great importance.

Bible Reading: Psalm 8

We thank you, O God
For crops in the fields which provide us with food;
For cattle and sheep, and all other farm animals;
For farmers and all who work on the land;
For all the good things you have provided.
For these and every blessing, praise be to you, O God. *Amen.*

Benediction No. 94

On the farm (5)

HILL FARMING   *Shepherds and sheepdogs*

There are many places where the land is not suitable for growing crops but very useful for rearing sheep, which are quite happy to graze on mountainside or moorland where the grass is short. The hill farmers who keep these sheep sometimes have quite a large territory and the sheep may well be scattered.

To help him round up his sheep the sheep farmer or shepherd has his sheepdog which has been trained not only to round up the sheep but also to help them if in trouble. Sheep are timid creatures and will run if approached by a dog. The shepherd is able to guide his dog by calling, whistling or making signs so that the sheep may be gathered or driven by the dog.

There are several breeds of sheepdog, the most common being the collie. Shepherds are proud of their dogs and sometimes enter them in sheepdog trials where they compete against others. Such trials were first held in Wales in 1873, since when they have been held in many parts of Britain. International Sheepdog Trials have also been held since 1906, for sheepdogs are used in many lands.

Although the sheepdog may sometimes do things by himself, he is guided mainly by the shepherd who is responsible for and cares for his sheep, often spending long hours attending to their needs.

In Bible times the shepherd was regarded very highly. It is not surprising that very often the people thought of God as a good shepherd caring for his people.

Bible Reading: St. Luke 15: 1–7

We thank you, O God, that you guard your people like a shepherd, caring for their every need. Make us mindful of your presence and ready to trust you for all that we need. *Amen.*

Benediction No. 99

Everyday things (1)

Lavenham

Every year on 21st June the tenor bell in the tower of the church of SS. Peter and Paul at Lavenham, Suffolk, is rung to celebrate its birthday.

Lavenham is a fascinating village with many old buildings. At one time it was the centre of the woollen industry and very prosperous. Its church is a magnificent building and the bell, which is one of several in the tower is also outstanding. It was cast in 1625 by a Colchester bell-founder and ever since then it has been claimed by some to be the finest bell in England.

Weighing about twenty-five hundredweight (1,270 kg) it is a thin bell with a beautiful tone. Sometimes it is rung on its own. Sometimes it is one of several which are sounded to make a tune, or peal.

To make a peal a lot of practice is needed. Each bell has a long rope hanging from it. When this is pulled it turns a wheel on which the bell is mounted and so makes it ring. A team of bell-ringers is needed, with one person to each bell. The ringers must learn to sound their bells in the right order and in time if they are to sound right.

Church bells are used for a number of purposes. Often they call people to worship. This was very helpful years ago when most people did not have watches or clocks. Church bells are used on sad occasions and happy ones. A single bell tolling may indicate a death or a funeral, whilst a happy peal of bells may herald a joyful or festive occasion. Lord Tennyson wrote:

> *Ring out the old, ring in the new,*
> *Ring, happy bells, across the snow;*
> *The year is going, let him go;*
> *Ring out the false, ring in the true.*

As the bell-ringers work together to play a happy tune, O God, help us to learn the discipline of working together with others to bring joy and happiness into the world which we share. *Amen.*

Closing prayer No. 89

Everyday things (2)

'Big Ben'

How often during the day are you reminded that it is time you were doing something? 'It's time you were out of bed!' 'It's time you were going to school!'. A long time ago one of the writers in the Bible reminded his readers that there was a time for everything.

Bible Reading: Ecclesiastes 3: 1–8

Nowadays timing is much more important. We need to be 'on time' to catch a train, or see a television programme, or keep an important appointment. So we have clocks in our homes and watches on our wrists. And we need to check these often to ensure that they tell the right time.

Often people check the time by what must be the best-known clock in the world, the chiming clock of the clock tower of the Houses of Parliament at Westminster. Each hour, after the chimes, the great bell, 'Big Ben', strikes, the first stroke indicating the hour.

The present bell was installed in 1859. It was made from the bell of the old Houses of Parliament and was called 'Westminster Tom'. 'Big Ben' took its name from Sir Benjamin Hall, Commissioner of Works when the clock was made in 1858. The clock has four faces, each 23 ft (7 m) across, with figures 2 ft (0·6 m) long and minute hands 14 ft (4·25 m) long.

For most people, 'Big Ben' is a symbol of reliability. Even when the Houses of Parliament were bombed during the war, the clock, though scarred and blackened, continued to tell the time. In fact, if that clock stops it is news!

How nice it is to know people like that, who are thoroughly dependable and can be relied upon to do things at the right time!

Help us, O God, to learn when to do things and when to refrain from doing them; and help us to be thoroughly dependable at all times and in all ways. *Amen.*

Closing prayer No. 62

Everyday things (3)

WATCHES   *John Harrison*

So much of our life today depends upon our being on time for keeping appointments, catching trains or enjoying our favourite programmes of sport or on television, that most people own a watch and would never like to go far without it.

Five hundred or more years ago people could tell the time by clocks in the clock towers, and probably wished sometimes that they knew the time when no clock was in sight. Then, in 1500, a German from Nuremburg invented the mainspring and made it possible to have a portable clock. But these first 'watches' were big, heavy and not at all accurate.

Sometimes accurate timing is very important. Navigators, for example, need a very accurate time-piece for working out their true positions at sea. Many ships have been wrecked because they were not where their navigators thought them to be.

In 1714 a prize was offered for anyone who could make a very accurate chronometer, as sea going clocks are called. For many years John Harrison worked on such a time-piece. At last he made a chronometer which, on a voyage to Jamaica lasting 81 days, lost only 5·1 seconds.

Nowadays we have watches that are even more accurate than that. In the 1970s people began to use quartz crystal watches that gain or lose no more than one second per month. Even cheaper watches are reasonably accurate. We have little excuse today for not being on time, or, for that matter, for failing to use our time properly.

Help me today, my Father God,
To make good use of the time you have given me;
To give all the time I should to my work and duties;
To find time to help the people around me;
To spend time in your presence;
And to use all my time wisely and well. *Amen.*

Closing prayer No. 53

Everyday things (4)

We cannot travel far in town or country without finding a bridge of some kind. There are simple foot-bridges across small rivers or busy roads; there are bridges to carry traffic across rivers, railways and motorways; and there are high viaducts and aqueducts carrying roads, railways or canals from one side of a valley to the other.

Some bridges have been of great importance for hundreds of years. In fact, '-bridge' as part of the name of a town may well indicate the reason why the town developed in that particular place.

Other more recently built bridges may have been designed to serve a particular purpose. One of the most famous bridges in London, Tower Bridge, which was opened on 30th June, 1894, was especially built so that the bascules carrying the road could be raised to allow ships to pass into the once very busy Pool of London.

Some bridges have very interesting features. The fifteenth-century bridge over the River Ouse at St. Ives has a small chapel in the middle. There are bridges with chapels in other parts of the country too. In return for a gift, which may have been spent on the upkeep of the bridge, a priest might say a prayer for the traveller asking that he might enjoy a safe journey.

On our journey through life we may have many 'bridges' to cross—the difficulties to be faced and the decisions to be made. We would do well to remember when we come to these bridges to say a prayer, seeking God's guidance as we travel on.

Bible Reading: Psalm 16: 1, 8, 9 and 11

Guide us, we pray, O Lord, as we journey through life. In times of weakness give us strength; in decisions give us wisdom; in doubts give us faith; and as we cross our bridges grant us the inspiration of your Holy Spirit. *Amen.*

Closing prayer No. 71

Everyday things (5)

WATER

How much water do you use in a day? You may be surprised to learn that the average daily amount used per person in Britain is over 30 gallons (136 litres). Think how much is used every time you flush the toilet or take a bath. Washing and bathing alone accounts for an average of 11 gallons (50 litres) per person per day. Add water for drinking, cooking, washing up, laundry, gardening, washing the car and lots of other purposes. It is easy to see how it mounts up.

It is interesting to note that the daily average 150 years ago was only 4 gallons (18 litres). By 2000 it may well be over 50 gallons (227 litres). Usually we have plenty of water and we may be careless over its use. Anyone who has been camping and has had to carry all the water that is used will know how much more careful one is to use no more than is necessary.

Only in times of drought is there any sign of a shortage of water in Britain and on such occasions its use may be restricted. Imagine living in parts of the world where there is very little rain. When there is a drought in such places all water supplies dry up, animals die, crops fail and people starve.

Water is something we should never take for granted. It is precious. We cannot live without it.

The Bible sometimes refers to water in a different sense. Jesus called it 'living water'.

Bible Reading: St. John 4: 7–14

Jesus was talking about the Spirit of God, which is just as important for our souls as water is for our bodies. We should never neglect it.

Look down upon us, O God, and as the rain falls upon the earth to give it life and refreshment so let your Spirit fall upon us so that we may grow in wisdom and love; and with your power within us may we live full and radiant lives now and ever. *Amen.*

Closing prayer No. 68

Animals (1)

Greyfriars Bobby

Many people like to keep animals as pets and often there spring up close friendships between people and their pets. Dogs, particularly, will show great affection and loyalty toward their owners and one story of extreme loyalty is recorded in Edinburgh.

Mr. Gray, a Midlothian farmer had a shaggy terrier dog named Bobby and he took him into Edinburgh each week to market. Each time, when the gun sounded from the Castle Esplanade at one o'clock, they went to a cafe and each had a meal.

But the farmer died and was buried in Greyfriars churchyard in Edinburgh. Soon afterwards, when the one o'clock gun sounded, Bobby appeared in the cafe for some food. This happened each day until the cafe owner followed Bobby to see where he went. It was to the churchyard, where he lay beside his master's grave. There he remained, day and night, except for going to the cafe each day at one for his meal.

Hearing what was happening, some people built a small shelter there so that Bobby had protection from the very bad weather. After nine years, the City Council arrested Bobby: he had no licence. The cafe owner was also made to appear in court for harbouring a dog without a licence. But when the story was told the case was dropped. Bobby was given a special honorary licence and was free to return to the churchyard. There at last he died in 1872, fourteen years after the death of his master.

And there Greyfriars Bobby was buried, a rosebush marking his grave. A statue near the gate stands as a memorial to a very faithful little dog.

We thank you, O God for those animals which we can keep as pets and for all the enjoyment they give us. Help us to remember our responsibilities toward them so that we can look after them and care for them as we enjoy the companionship and pleasure that they give us. *Amen.*

Benediction No. 106

Animals (2)

ANIMALS IN ZOOS   *Gerald Durrell*

Many people enjoy a visit to a zoo, where they can see animals which come from other parts of the world. Some people do not like zoos because they think it wrong for animals to be kept in cages or enclosures. There are, of course, good zoos and bad ones. Some people who own zoos take a lot of care to ensure that their zoos are very well run and the animals contented.

Take Gerald Durrell, for example. Born in India on 7th January, 1925, he was interested in zoos and animals from a very early age. During his childhood his family moved from place to place in Europe and Gerald kept many kinds of wild animal as pets. In 1945 he became a student keeper at Whipsnade Zoo. Two years later he went on an expedition to collect wild animals in West Africa—the first of many to different parts of the world.

But Gerald had always wanted a zoo of his own and he wanted it to be a good, useful zoo—not just a place where animals could be looked at but where scientific records could be kept and where rare animals could be bred, where people could be educated as well as entertained.

Meanwhile he had written successful books about animals and zoos and become well known as an author. He was able to borrow some money too and he found a suitable site for his zoo on the island of Jersey. In 1958 he founded the Jersey Wildlife Preservation Trust into which gifts could be paid for running the zoo.

Today many visitors to Jersey enjoy this excellent zoo, in which great care in planning has provided fine accommodation and conditions for the animals kept there.

We thank you, O God, for opportunities of seeing the wild creatures of your creation. Give us a love and respect for all wild life and to learn about these creatures without taking advantage of them. *Amen*.

Closing prayer No. 72

Animals (3)

A very long time ago, man discovered that a lot of hard work could be done for him by using animals that were stronger than he was but which could be tamed to do certain kinds of work.

In the early days of the Bible story we can read how people used oxen, asses, camels and other animals to pull their ploughs or carry their goods. There were laws, too, which instructed how the animals should be treated. Here is one.

Bible Reading: Deuteronomy 22: 1–4

In Britain, for many years, the animal most used for heavy work has been the horse. Old prints and photographs show horses pulling stage coaches and wagons, carts and barges, working on the farm or in the town.

There are many kinds of horse, large and small. There are sleek, lithe horses for racing, elegant even-tempered horses for riding and strong powerfully built animals for the really heavy work. Of these the best known are the Shire horses, magnificent animals that have served man well. To promote this Old English breed of carthorse, The Shire Horse Society was formed, a society which celebrated its centenary on 11th July, 1978.

Today, when so much work is done by petrol or diesel engines, there are many people who enjoy seeing such horses at work, harnessed maybe to a cart or a plough. For some it may be a reminder of more leisurely times but for all it is an opportunity to admire a fine animal which is all too rarely seen these days.

Almighty God, we offer thanks for those animals which work for man and for the pleasure they give us. May those into whose care they are entrusted treat them well with care and affection. Grant us a love for all your creatures but especially those which are ours to look after. *Amen*.

Benediction No. 96.

Animals (4)

At one time there were many more animals in the world than there are now. And some species which were once common will never be seen again because none of them are left.

Some died out naturally but many have been killed off by men for their amusement or because they can get money by selling the hides or tusks.

Many of these creatures lived in Africa which became a paradise for hunters. Today in Africa there are national parks and game reserves in which animals are protected. There are also laws which make the poaching of animals or the sale of their hides illegal.

But there are other animals which have no such protection for they have no country. Their home is in the oceans of the world. For many years whales have been killed because of their market value. Whale products such as whalebone and oil can be used for many different purposes including making soap and inks for printers.

So many whales have been killed that there is a danger that some species may become extinct. Some countries have agreed that only a limited number should be killed but others have not and so the killing goes on.

There are many who believe that the killing should be stopped altogether because it is unnecessary. There are plenty of substitutes today for whale products. A 'Save the Whale' campaign was started so that people might be persuaded to act. It will be a tragedy if these large, intelligent creatures cannot be saved from the hunters who think more of money than of wild life.

Almighty God, by whose hand all things were created, grant us a love of all the wild creatures of our world. Put into the hearts of all people a desire to protect rather than to destroy, so that such creatures may be saved from suffering and live to be enjoyed by future generations. *Amen.*

Closing prayer No. 71

Animals (5)

People who keep animals sometimes find that those animals need medical treatment, for they become ill just as we do or may have accidents which cause injury. It is then that the services of an animal doctor, or veterinary surgeon, are needed.

But veterinary fees can be expensive—and there is no National Health Service for animals! Many years ago people became concerned about animals belonging to poor people who could not afford to pay for treatment. So, in 1917, they formed an organization known as The People's Dispensary for Sick Animals—better known by the initials P.D.S.A.

Today the P.D.S.A. has centres throughout England, Wales and Scotland as well as in some overseas countries. Most of the animals treated in the P.D.S.A. centres are the commoner pets but there are some unusual animals too. A recent report tells that in one year 504,724 dogs were treated and nearly half that number of cats but also 2,120 tortoises, 306 parrots, 50 monkeys, 40 horses, 5 grass snakes, 3 frogs, 2 donkeys, a peacock, a ram, a weasel and lots of other creatures too. In all the total came to 775,094.

No charge whatever is made for the treatment, though people are invited to make any contribution they can toward the cost. The services provided by the P.D.S.A. are paid for with money which is raised in all sorts of ways. There are P.D.S.A. gift shops and some people collect money, but there are also many animal lovers and people who in the past have been helped by the P.D.S.A., who send money when they can so that the free treatment of animals can continue.

Thanks be to you, O God, for those whose vision enabled the animals of the poor to be treated without charge. Bless all who work, or give, or organize so that this work may continue today. *Amen.*

Closing prayer No. 85

Flowers (1)

Francis Meilland

Most people enjoy flowers and have their own particular favourites. For many there is nothing more lovely than a rose. And there are so many varieties from which to choose in different shades of red, pink, orange, yellow, mauve and white.

When buying rose bushes, you will find that each variety has a name—given to it by the rose grower who first produced that particular rose. All the beautiful roses we have today have been cultivated by people who experimented, pollinating one rose with another and keeping careful records of the results. Some of these rose growers are world famous and none more than the Meilland family in France.

Papa Meilland had grown roses from the age of eleven and his son, Francis, was keenly interested in the roses growing on their land at Tassin, near Lyons. Francis spent every spare moment among the roses. Instead of staying on at school, he left as soon as he could at the age of fourteen so that he too could become a full-time rose grower. On 14th July, 1926, he put in his first full working day.

In the years that followed he produced many fine roses and he was in close touch with many other rose growers too. Louisette Paolino, whom he married, was the daughter of a rose grower from the South of France. In 1950, Francis founded an international organization called 'Universal Rose Selection', for creating and distributing new roses.

Francis never enjoyed good health. He died in 1958 at the age of forty-six, having given the world many new roses. When he was laid to rest on 15th June, he was surrounded by large numbers of his most famous creation—the 'Peace' rose.

Almighty God, we thank you for the flowers that mean so much to us. We recall how people have taken the wild flowers of the field to produce fine flowers for the garden. Help us to make good use of the talents you have given us. *Amen*.

Benediction No. 94

Flowers (2)

The 'Peace' Rose

In June 1939 war clouds were gathering over Europe but in the rose growing estate at Tassin all was sunshine. Rose growers from many countries were admiring the beauty of a new rose, which Francis Meilland knew simply by the code number 3-35-40.

Three months later war broke out. A small parcel of budded 3-35-40 was sent to a friend in Germany and another to Italy. The American consul from Lyons, when he left the country, took a parcel to an American rose-growing friend, Robert Pyle. None knew what name had been decided upon for 3-35-40. Francis had decided upon *Madame A Meilland*—his mother. The German grower called it *Gloria Dei* (Glory be to God). The Italian gave it the happiest of names, *Gioia* (Joy).

Robert Pyle in America was most impressed by this hardy rose with its long-lasting flowers and beautiful scent. So were his friends. They arranged a name-giving ceremony for 29th April, 1945. With war still raging in Europe and with no knowledge of whether Francis Meilland was still alive, the announcement was made:

'We are persuaded that this greatest new rose of our time should be named for the world's greatest desire—PEACE.'

By strange coincidence, on that very day, Berlin was taken. Strangely too, on the day that the American Rose Society gave its gold medal to 'Peace', a peace treaty was signed in Japan.

From a few plants, hastily sent to friends in several countries, have come millions of bushes now blooming throughout the world—*Madame A. Meilland, Gloria Dei, Gioia, Peace*—respected names for the finest of roses.

We thank you, O God, for all who have worked to produce something worthwhile, often in difficult circumstances, and who have never been satisfied with anything 'second-rate'. May we do likewise so that we are remembered as those who have always given of their best. *Amen*.

Closing prayer No. 77

Flowers (3)

Flowers can be enjoyed wherever they are—in pots or window boxes, in gardens or parks, some growing singly and others in large flower beds or ornate gardens. We use flowers in many ways. We may enjoy growing them from seed or tending them in our homes; we sometimes give a bouquet of flowers when we want to say thank-you to someone or to cheer up someone who is sad. On special occasions, such as weddings, we use flowers for bouquets and to decorate the church.

There are some places which are specially known for the flowers that grow there. People like to go to Holland or to Spalding, Lincolnshire, in springtime to see the tulips and other spring flowers.

But perhaps one of the most famous floral occasions during the year is held on the island of Jersey. The Battle of Flowers is held each year, usually on the last Thursday in July. It began as long ago as 1902 to mark the coronation of King Edward VII and has been held each year since then with the exception of the war years.

The main part of the Battle of Flowers is a procession of vehicles of all kinds—cycles, handcarts, lorries, buses—covered with millions of flowers, many of them grown especially for this event. Prizes are given for the best entries. At the end, petals are dropped on the crowds from a helicopter. Many holidaymakers plan their holidays to include this event.

Flower festivals are held nowadays in many churches. Special arrangements may be on display for several days, whilst the Sunday services are a time for thanking God for the flowers which brighten our world and mean so much to so many people.

Almighty God, we give thanks for all the flowers which give us
    enjoyment:
For the wild flowers of hedgerow, heath and woodland;
For flowers of park and garden, giving joy to many;
For potted plants to give colour in our homes;
For cut flowers; bouquets of happiness or consolation;
For those who grow, or sell, or arrange them:
Praise be to you, O God. *Amen.*

Closing prayer No. 83

Flowers (4)

Kew Gardens

It is pleasant sometimes to be able to wander in a garden where there are many different kinds of flower to be seen. It is fascinating, too, to see plants which normally grow in other countries where the climate is very different from our own.

Many cities have a botanic garden, where some plants grow in flower beds in the open air, whilst others are in specially heated glasshouses where temperatures resemble those of countries overseas.

One of the best known botanic gardens is at Kew, in London. Commonly known as Kew Gardens, its correct title is the Royal Botanic Gardens. It began as long ago as 1759, when Princess Augusta, the mother of King George III, planted a small garden. It was opened to the public in 1840 and now covers about three hundred acres of land. More than 45,000 different kinds of plant grow there.

Visitors may see tropical trees in the enormous Palm House and water plants with huge leaves in a heated pool.

But Kew Gardens is not just a place where people can enjoy looking at plants. It also has places where botanists can study. In the Herbarium and Library there is a collection of over six million dried and preserved plants as well as a large collection of pictures and books.

Much of our knowledge of the world of nature has been obtained because people have not just looked at plants but have studied them carefully and asked questions about how they grow.

And having studied them carefully, men have marvelled at the wonderful works of God's creation.

O God,
Give us eyes to see the beauty of the world of nature;
Give us enquiring minds which take nothing for granted;
Give us an understanding of how things live or work;
And so help us all the more to appreciate the world which you
have made. *Amen*

Closing prayer No. 59

Flowers (5)

Constance Spry

Have you ever wondered who is responsible for arranging the flowers used for decorating public buildings on special occasions? We often remark how beautiful they look, yet give little thought to the person who must have been responsible for putting them there.

When Queen Elizabeth II was crowned in Westminster Abbey in June, 1953, flowers were needed in the Abbey as well as along the route of the procession. The person who was responsible for planning these was Constance Spry, famous not only for her flower arranging but as the authoress of a cookery book!

Constance Spry was the daughter of a railwayman and was born in Derby, where she lived until the family moved to Ireland. She had always been fond of flowers and took a great interest in making floral displays of many kinds.

In 1929 Constance opened a small shop in London but it was so successful that she had to move into a much larger one. Her flower arrangements were so beautiful that she was asked to lecture to other people who wanted to learn the art of flower decoration.

The choice of Constance Spry to plan the coronation decorations was a tribute to her ability and a highlight in the life of one who had given a great deal of pleasure to lots and lots of people.

There were others, too, who owed their gratitude to Constance Spry, for she spent part of her life as a welfare worker amongst the poor, bringing happiness to quite a number of people.

She died in 1960, having helped in various ways to make the world a little brighter.

We are thankful, O God, for all who have helped to make the world a brighter place: for those who have created things of beauty: for those who have passed on their knowledge of such things to others; and for all who through their work have brightened the lives of others. Praise be to you, O God. *Amen.*

Closing prayer No. 84

Conservation (1)

POLLUTION   *The 'Torrey Canyon'*

On Saturday, 18th March, 1967, the super tanker *Torrey Canyon* was sailing between Lands End and the Scilly Isles when she struck the Seven Stones rocks and grounded. Salvage work to free her from the rocks proved unsuccessful and she was still hard and fast a week later when, in gale force winds, she broke her back. Another fine ship had ended her days on the treacherous rocks.

But the loss of a ship was only part of the story. The *Torrey Canyon* was one of the largest tankers then in use. She was as wide as a football pitch and as long as three football pitches end to end. And she was carrying 119,328 tons of crude oil. As the ship was wrecked the oil spilled out. Three days after the wrecking the oil slick was 35 miles long by 20 miles wide.

It was not long before Cornish beaches were covered with thick, black, stinking sludge. Oil was also driven across the channel by the winds until 90 miles of the coast of Brittany were affected. The cost of the cleaning up was immense but, in one sense, the cost to wild life was more disastrous. Probably 100,000 sea birds died and it is impossible to tell how many sea creatures were killed by the oil or by the detergents which were used to get rid of it.

Since then there have been other major tanker disasters and they have made news because of the danger from oil. But there are many other forms of pollution too. Rivers are polluted with chemicals: the air is polluted by smoke: the countryside is polluted by litter.

Nowadays governments are very concerned about pollution and its prevention. But are we careful enough ourselves? The world is ours to look after.

Almighty God, we thank you for the beautiful world in which we live and for all that there is to enjoy. Make us careful to do nothing which will spoil it for ourselves or for others. *Amen.*

Closing prayer No. 62

Conservation (2)

Forest fire!

It is pleasant sometimes to stroll through a forest, to enjoy the peaceful atmosphere that is found there, to watch for animals and birds, and to admire the trees.

Nowadays more than ever is being done to enable people to enjoy the forests. The Forestry Commission has set up Forest Parks in several parts of Britain. Many of the forests have camping sites and picnic places and there are lots with nature trails which can be followed with notes about all the interesting things to be seen.

One of the first things that visitors to forests will see are notices warning of the dangers of fire. And beside the notices there will probably be a number of beaters which can be used if necessary to beat out the flames.

Fire is the greatest danger in any forest. Once a fire has started, particularly in hot dry weather, it may burn for days defying all the efforts of firemen to extinguish it and causing thousands of pounds worth of damage. Valuable timber is lost, many small creatures lose their lives and a lovely forest becomes a charred, blackened waste.

Often such fires are caused by the carelessness of visitors—a burning cigarette end in some dried leaves, a picnic fire not properly put out, a piece of glass which magnifies the rays of the sun. And these are all things which could be avoided with a little more care.

The Forestry Commission is well aware of the need for conservation. It reasonably expects that those who enjoy the forests will be equally careful in doing nothing to spoil them.

We thank you, O God, for the pleasant forests that are ours to enjoy; for tall trees and shady pathways; for the animals, birds and millions of tiny creatures which inhabit them; and for all the people who take care of them. Make us thoughtful and careful, avoiding all that would harm or damage. *Amen.*

Closing prayer No. 88

Conservation (3)

Protection of Birds

Bible Reading: St. Luke 12: 6–7

In these few words Jesus was teaching an important lesson that God, who cares for the birds, cares even more for his children. He was using as an illustration something that was very common—sparrows sold for next to nothing in the market place.

It is something that we would not see today. It is unlawful for wild birds to be sold in our markets or shops because people have learned not only that it is unkind to imprison wild birds in cages but that many rare and interesting birds could be lost to the world forever if they were not protected.

Laws like this have been enforced because of the work of people who cared about birds. One such group, the Fur and Feather Group, formed in 1889 to protest against the use of exotic birds' feathers in the making of women's hats, became the Royal Society for the Protection of Birds in 1904. It now has a membership of over 250,000.

The R.S.P.B. has many activities. It manages nature reserves in which birds are protected; it examines the effect upon birds of pollution and various chemicals; it educates people about birds; and, as its name suggests, it protects birds in many different ways.

Nowadays many young people show a special interest in birds and in 1965 the R.S.P.B. formed the Young Ornithologist's Club. In just a few years it had a membership of over 75,000—children who, like the adult members of the R.S.P.B., are unlikely to harm birds or steal their eggs but will enjoy all the pleasures of observing wildlife.

Almighty God, Creator of all living things;
Grant us a love of all your creatures;
Keep us from harming them in any way;
Teach us how to protect and look after them;
And make us care, just as you, our Father, care. *Amen.*

Closing prayer No. 83

Conservation (4)

Some parts of the country are much more attractive than others. The scenery of mountains and lakes, forest or moorland, quiet dales or rocky coasts makes these the kind of places which people like to visit.

Some of these have been formed into National Parks so that everything can be done to preserve the beauty of these areas whilst encouraging people to use them for recreation and enjoyment.

The first National Park to be set up was Snowdonia, North Wales, on 21st January, 1935. It is one of the loveliest parts of Britain with mountains, lakes and forests. Nine other National Parks have since been established: Peak District, Lake District, Dartmoor, Exmoor, Pembrokeshire Coast, Brecon Beacons, North York Moors, Yorkshire Dales and Northumberland.

National Parks are not public property. Much of the land is privately owned but access is given to places of beauty. Visitors are expected, of course, to observe the Country Code and to respect the property of other people.

The National Parks are popular for holidays, camping, hiking, climbing and many other outdoor activities. Lots of people visit them just to enjoy the beautiful scenery.

It is in places such as these that we have the opportunity to see something of the beauty of the world in which we live, and as we do so we may remember God, who created the world and filled it with good things for his children.

Bible Reading: Psalm 36: 5–9

We look around us, O God, and see the wonders of the world you have made. Help us to enjoy your world and leave it unspoiled for others; and keep us mindful of all the many blessings which are ours to enjoy every day. *Amen.*

Closing prayer No. 87

Conservation (5)

In many parts of Britain one may come upon a notice bearing a symbol of an acorn and some oak leaves with the words 'The National Trust'. The symbol may be seen at the entrance to an old building or a fine garden, a strip of coastline or a rocky island, an area of forest or of inland waterway. So one could go on, for The National Trust is responsible for looking after many places and things that are worth preserving.

We live in a day when lots of things are changing. Old buildings are pulled down to make room for new. Open land is purchased and used for building houses or factories. Natural coastlines are developed to make holiday resorts. A lot that is beautiful is lost forever.

The National Trust was founded by Octavia Hill and others in 1895 to preserve places of beauty and historic interest. In spite of the name 'National' it is not a government department but it is a charity dependent upon the generosity and support of many people who care about Britain's heritage. Anyone who wishes to do so can become a member of The National Trust by paying an annual subscription.

Who cares what happens to the countryside and to old buildings or places of beauty? Well! Lots of people do but The National Trust is the largest of these and millions of people every year enjoy visiting the properties and areas for which it cares.

Organizations such as The National Trust do a very important work but it is up to each one of us to ensure that we look after and care for those things which are around us.

Almighty God, we praise you for our world and for the beauty of nature, for pleasant buildings and gardens, and for everything good that has been fashioned by man. May nothing we do spoil these things for others. *Amen.*

Closing prayer No. 89

Old and new (1)

Most towns and cities had their origin a long, long time ago. It is interesting to discover something of the origins of the town from the name or from old records, discovering why that particular site was chosen.

Perhaps there are the remains of a castle or town walls, a reminder of the days when the neighbouring countryside was controlled by an important nobleman who wanted protection from possible enemies. He built a castle for himself and surrounded the town with strong walls with defensive gateways.

Most of these castles and walls are now in ruins but some remain. Few can be more impressive than Caernarfon, North Wales, with its mighty fortress still looking from the outside much as it must have done hundreds of years ago.

Here it was that King Edward I of England promised the Welsh chieftains a prince who could speak neither English nor French and then presented them with his baby son who had not yet begun to speak any language. Here, too, on 1st July, 1969, amid much pageantry and celebration, Prince Charles was proclaimed the latest Prince of Wales.

Today Caernarfon has spread far beyond its ancient walls. The castle stands as a reminder of days which are past: around it are all the signs of progress. Our whole way of life is better than ever it has been but we may look forward to even better things, as this passage from the Bible reminds us:

Bible Reading: Revelation 21: 1–7

Almighty God, our heavenly Father,
We thank you for all that has come from the past:
We are grateful for all that we can enjoy today.
Help us to work for an even brighter future
And let us see the coming of your Kingdom. *Amen.*

Closing prayer No. 85

43

Old and new (2)

Ballingdon Hall

When people talk about moving house, they usually mean that they are moving from one house to another. Not so where solicitor John Hodge was concerned. When he moved house in 1972, he moved his house over half a mile up a hill.

His home was a four-hundred year old mansion, Ballingdon Hall, at Sudbury, Suffolk. It stood at the foot of Ballingdon Hill but the nearby land which had been open country was used for building houses and factories.

The Hall could not be taken apart and rebuilt because there are laws which protect old houses so that they are preserved for people of the future to enjoy. So Ballingdon Hall was freed from its foundations and some interior walls and fireplaces were removed. Then it was jacked up onto a huge steel frame with twenty-six wheels beneath it.

On 29th February, 1972, the tractors were attached to the frame but were not powerful enough to move it. It was several weeks before the Hall eventually reached its new position. People travelled from miles away to see the removal. During the Easter weekend, ten thousand people paid to visit the site and the money was used to help restore a local church.

The removal of Ballingdon Hall cost a lot of money and its restoration took a long time to complete but its owner was able to enjoy once again the open view over Sudbury and the river, and the Hall was preserved in pleasant surroundings for people of the present and the future to admire and enjoy.

We have inherited much from the past, not just buildings but sound laws, a good way of life and truc values. Such things are worth preserving.

We thank you, O God, for things from the past which are ours to enjoy and for the great heritage which has been passed on to us. Help us in turn to preserve what is good for the benefit of people of the future. *Amen.*

Closing prayer No. 89

Old and new (3)

A couple of hundred years ago, when people built factories they also had to build houses for people who came from the villages to work in the factories. Many factory owners built very small houses, sometimes back to back, which soon became slums. Such factory owners were more concerned with making money than with the well-being of those who worked for them.

But some factory owners were different. The Cadbury brothers, George and Richard, for example, were Quakers and cared very much for their workers. To them people were far more important than machinery or money.

Life for the Cadburys had not been easy and there were many times when it seemed as though their cocoa works in Birmingham would have to close down. Their fortunes changed when they learned that a new machine was being used in Holland to make much better cocoa. The Cadburys bought one and brought it to England. Soon they were making fine cocoa and chocolate, which was in great demand.

Their fortunes had changed. Now they could build a new factory. More than that, they could build new homes for their workers. The new factory and village was built at Bournville. There were houses, shops, gardens, a library and a meeting house. It was all carefully planned. Bournville was a model village, unusual in its day and an inspiration to people many years later when they wanted to plan new towns.

We owe a lot to people such as these, who had good new ideas and whose sincere beliefs made them care enough for others to want to offer them the best conditions they could.

We thank you, O God, for the example of those who have learned about you and then showed their love for you in caring for others. Help us to do likewise. *Amen.*

Closing prayer No. 81

Old and new (4)

Sir Titus Salt and Saltaire

As we look around many towns we see little sign of any planning in earlier times. Buildings were put up in any available space with little thought to appearance or convenience.

This was true of many of the industrial developments in the north of England in the early nineteenth century with the rapid growth of mills and houses for the people who worked in those mills.

But every here and there someone had a vision of something better. One such man was Sir Titus Salt, a mill owner in Bradford and the second mayor of that town in 1848. Sir Titus owned five mills in Bradford but decided that his business would be much more efficient if he had a new factory with new machinery. So he found a site four miles from Bradford on the River Aire, which was to become Saltaire—a model industrial community.

The mill at Saltaire was opened on 20th September, 1853, the 50th birthday of Sir Titus. It was the first of many buildings. Sir Titus was determined that the homes of his workers would be better than the insanitary ones in Bradford and 800 houses were built. Some had small gardens and there was a park nearby. Shops were built and public baths and wash houses. There was a school for the children who worked in the mill.

Sir Titus Salt was a Congregationalist and a new Congregational Church was built, in which Sir Titus and other members of his family were later buried.

There have been many changes since then but Saltaire remains a community to this day and a memorial to a humane, generous man.

Accept our thanks, O God, for all who have helped to build the community in which we live. Guide those who have responsibility for it today, so that they may see what is best for the people who live here and plan for the common good. *Amen.*

Benediction No. 95

Old and new (5)

It is good that many old things can be preserved, especially ancient or interesting buildings and quaint narrow streets. But quaint narrow streets, which were all right for a few horses and carts are useless for modern traffic and old buildings can sometimes prevent development.

Most old towns have been developed in some ways to make them more suitable for today's needs. What changes would you like to see in your town?

Sometimes it is possible for people to have a completely new beginning. Suppose you were planning a new town, what would you consider as essentials? Good houses? Wide streets? Open spaces? A big shopping centre? Pedestrian areas?

In recent years many new towns have been built to take some of the population away from the big cities. Several were built, for example, in open country around London. Most people think that one of the most successful of the new towns was Cumbernauld, built on a hilly site in Dunbartonshire, now Strathclyde, to take some of the population of Glasgow. Founded in 1956, it has a multistorey town centre and is so well planned that it received an award for its architecture. It claims to be the safest town in Britain, too, with road accidents less than a quarter of the average for the country. This may be due to the good designing of the roads and keeping pedestrians away from traffic.

But most town planners have to content themselves with improving what they have. The Bible also talks about a new Jerusalem, new heavens and a new earth—a time when much that we know will have changed for the better—and reminds people to be ready and prepared for God's kingdom on earth.

Bible Reading: II Peter 3: 13–14

Help us, O God, as we remember all your promises, to look for the coming of your kingdom and to prepare ourselves to live as you would have us live. *Amen.*

Closing prayer No. 78

Resources (1)

Plant a Tree

Many years ago Britain had huge areas of forest land but most has now disappeared. Some was cleared for farming and many trees felled for building. Large quantities of English oak went into the building of wooden warships—the 'Wooden Walls' of England as they were called.

It is said that Admiral Collingwood, who took command at Trafalgar after Nelson's death, was so anxious that there should always be a supply of oak that he carried acorns in his pockets and planted them as he journeyed.

In more recent times the government has taken steps to ensure timber supplies and the Forestry Commission has planted many new forests. These are mainly forests of fir and spruce which grow quickly and supply softwood timber which is in great demand.

But trees are important for other reasons than to be felled for timber. They are pleasant to look at and they provide homes for wild creatures. Many old trees have been lost in gales or through disease and so people are encouraged to plant more trees. In 1973 there was a campaign to 'Plant a Tree in '73': the following year it was 'Plant some more in '74'.

So today we look after our resources, trees that will provide timber for industry and trees that are pleasing to look at. And if we take time to study those trees and the creatures that inhabit them, we shall find that we can learn a lot from doing so.

The Psalmist in the Bible drew a lesson for life from the trees:

Bible Reading: Psalm 1

Make us, O God, to be like the trees, to send our roots deep to find the water of life and to reach upward toward the sunshine of your love, so that we may live and bear fruit to the glory of your Name. *Amen.*

Benediction No. 91

Resources (2)

North Sea Oil

One of the most important resources of the world is oil. Millions and millions of gallons (litres) of it are used for refining into petrol, fuel oil for heating and driving machinery, and for a host of other purposes.

Oil is found only in certain parts of the world and so it is necessary for people who have no oil of their own to buy from those who do have it. One of the biggest oil-producing areas is around the Persian Gulf and the Arabs have become very rich from the sale of their oil. Some countries, such as Britain, had to spend more than they could afford to buy their oil.

Then something happened which was to change the position. It was discovered that there were deposits of oil in the ground under the North Sea. The big oil companies built huge platforms from which they could drill into the sea bed to see whether any oil was there.

One of the largest oilfields to be discovered was the Forties field, discovered late in 1970 about 110 miles (177 km) east of Aberdeen. It is thought to contain between 260 and 300 million tonnes of oil. And the Forties is only one of many oilfields under the North Sea.

On 3rd November, 1975, the Queen officially opened the valve which allowed oil to flow direct from the production platform in the Forties field through a pipeline to the refinery at Grangemouth in Scotland. It was a very important day for Britain for it meant a steady supply of oil for which money did not have to be paid to another country.

But we must beware. When it is all used there will be no more from there. Such resources must not be wasted.

Help us, O God, to accept those things which are provided for our benefit or pleasure; but teach us to use all things wisely and to guard against waste. *Amen.*

Benediction No. 106

Resources (3)

F.A.O.

Do you know how many people there are in the world? There are more every minute. The number is expected to grow from about 3,000 million in 1975 to about 7,000 million in A.D. 2000. The world population is growing by over a million people every week. And all those extra people will want food!

It is difficult for people living in the prosperous countries of Europe, North America and elsewhere to realize what a hard time people have in the rest of the world. We are used to going to the supermarket or the local shop, where we buy food produced in many parts of the world. There is no one so poor that he needs to be really hungry and there is enough food for us to have an interesting variety giving a balanced diet.

As long ago as 1946 the United Nations Organization set up the Food and Agriculture Organization (F.A.O.) to look into the question of world food supplies, to see what could be done to provide more food and to educate people to employ better methods of food production. Much has been done, but people are still starving in many places.

The trouble is mainly that the people in poor or 'developing' countries have very little money to spend on what they need, whilst rich nations can afford all they require.

Food is one of the most important natural resources. Without it we die. But it is distributed unfairly and there just is not enough. As the population grows, so will the food problem unless people can learn to produce much more and truly to share what there is.

Bible Reading: Isaiah 58: 10–11

We remember, O God, the hungry people of the world and pray for all who seek to increase the amount of food they can have. Make us mindful of them and help us never to waste the food we have. *Amen.*

Closing prayer No. 75

Resources (4)

Bible Reading: St. John 21: (1 or) 7–14

Fish for breakfast! That may not be our choice but there are many times when people do enjoy a meal of fish. It may be boiled fish, smoked fish or canned fish but for many people the most popular is fish and chips, obtained easily from the local fish shop.

In Britain people eat about 41½ lbs (18·8 kg) of fish per head each year and that is small compared with Norway, where it is about 136¼ lbs (61·8 kg) per head. If the population of Britain is 56 million it means that we eat 2,324 million pounds—over one million tonnes of fish every year. And that is a lot of fish!

Where does it all come from? Fortunately fish breed in large numbers but even so there are dangers that supplies may run out because of 'over fishing'.

A few years ago much of our fish was caught in the seas around Iceland but the people of that country became worried that their fishermen would be unable to earn a living. So they said that, after 15th October, 1975, no foreign vessels would be permitted to fish within 200 miles of the coast.

British trawlers continued to fish there protected by the Royal Navy. Icelandic gunboats tried to stop them. This 'Cod War', as it was called lasted for several months. Now similar fishing limits are set around much of the coast of Europe.

All over the world the 'silver harvest of the sea' has provided many people with good nourishing meals but even food which is as plentiful as fish must be protected if supplies are to continue in the future.

O God, we thank you for our daily food and all who help provide it. Make us mindful of those who do not have enough and teach us not to be selfish or wasteful of food we often take for granted. *Amen.*

Closing prayer No. 85

Resources (5)

Friends of the Earth

It might be interesting to make a list of all the things you throw away in the course of a day or a week. Some things come readily to mind—paper tissues, sweet wrappers, empty food packets, drink cans, glass or plastic bottles and jars.

We live in what has been called a 'Throw-it-away' or 'Waste-age' society. Instead of making things which can be used lots of times, we make those which can be used once only. Drink bottles today are mostly non-returnable instead of being collected, cleaned and re-used as they used to be. The result is that we are using far more raw materials than ever in the past.

All these waste materials were once what we would call 'natural resources'—things which grew or were dug out of the earth. Some waste materials can be used again, or 're-cycled' but many are lost. Many of the world's natural resources such as metals, coal and oil are being used up very quickly. When they are gone there will be no more!

Some people are trying to do something about this. There is, for example, an international organization known as Friends of the Earth, which tries to encourage individual people and governments to look after the Earth. Our world has plenty of enemies who are slowly destroying it and it needs plenty of friends who will be more careful.

Each of us can do something, however small it may seem, to ensure that we do not waste the good things which God has given us.

Bible Reading: Genesis 1: 27–31

We thank you for our world, O God, and for your provision for our daily needs. Teach us not to waste what you have given but to use all things wisely and well. *Amen.*

Closing prayer No. 61

Disaster (1)

Mount Vesuvius

One of the most famous mountains in the world is Mount Vesuvius, overlooking the Bay of Naples in southern Italy. It is one of the tourist attractions of Italy because it is no ordinary mountain but a volcano which, long ago, destroyed the towns of Pompeii and Herculaneum which stood at its foot.

The first sign of trouble had been in A.D. 62, when great rumblings came from the mountain and the earth began to heave. Huge cracks appeared in the roads, buildings began to collapse and a reservoir broke its banks. People panicked and fled.

But Vesuvius settled down once more. People returned to the city and began rebuilding. All was well for seventeen years. People went about their business as they had before.

Then, on 20th August, 79, the earth shook once more and many people remembered what happened before. But although they were afraid they were relieved when the noises died down. Four days later disaster struck. With a loud explosion Vesuvius erupted. Molten lava poured down the mountain burying Pompeii and its inhabitants for nearly two thousand years, after which the ruins were excavated and may be seen today.

People who live near a volcano are always in some danger as people who live in many parts of the world have discovered since then. The inhabitants of Pompeii would have been wise to heed the warnings. But people so often take no notice of warnings until it is too late.

Bible Reading: St. Matthew 24: 37–39 and 42–44

Grant unto us, O God, the sense to heed any warnings we receive about people or things which could endanger or harm us; and teach us the wisdom of accepting your guidance and obeying your commands. *Amen.*

Closing prayer No. 62

Disaster (2)

Tabas, Iran

The picturesque little town of Tabas lay about 430 miles (692 km) from Teheran, the capital of Iran and on the old route to China used by the silk merchants of long ago. Mosques and temples towered above the mud-brick houses, many of them the homes of rug-weavers and farmers.

On Saturday evening, 16th September, 1978, about the time many of the 13,000 inhabitants would be having their evening meal, the earth gave one terrific heave, nearly every building in Tabas collapsed and some 11,000 people were killed.

About thirty neighbouring villages were also destroyed in the earthquake which shook buildings as far away as Teheran. The total number killed was estimated at 22,000 with many injured. It was not far from here, in 1962, that 13,000 were also killed in an earthquake.

There are some parts of the world where earthquakes are more likely to be experienced than elsewhere. This is one of them. A violent earthquake always takes the lives of many as the buildings fall and people are killed instantly or are buried beneath the rubble.

It is on occasions such as this that rescue squads and relief organizations go swiftly into action to rescue any who may be trapped, to take the injured to hospital, to provide food, water and blankets for any who survive and to give what comfort they can. These are times when people, regardless of colour or creed or of any differences they may have, are ready to work together to help those who are in distress.

Hear our prayer, O Lord, for any who suffer as a result of earth-quake or other natural disaster. Comfort the bereaved, heal the sick and injured, strengthen the faint-hearted and help the distres-sed; and upon all who seek to help grant your richest blessing. *Amen.*

Benediction No. 93

Disaster (3)

Cyclone in South India

Sometimes as we sit at home we hear the wind whistling around the house. Occasionally the wind is so strong that tiles are blown from the roofs and very occasionally houses are more severely damaged. It is difficult for us to imagine the dreadful destruction that is experienced in some parts of the world.

On 12th November, 1977, a cyclone struck the coast of South India. High winds ripped buildings apart and an 18 ft (5·5 m) tidal wave swept 3 miles (4·8 km) inland. Crops and buildings were destroyed over an area of 20,000 square miles (5,000,000 hectares).

By the time the cyclone ended, over 25,000 people had died and more than two million were homeless. About £175 million worth of crops had been destroyed. And all this was in a part of the world where people are desperately poor and millions go hungry!

Hurricanes are sometimes experienced in the West Indies and parts of America. Winds blowing at speeds of 150 m.p.h. (240 km/h) destroy buildings in their path. Huge waves break large ships from their moorings and leave them high and dry on the beach.

After the hurricane or the cyclone comes the task of trying to help people who have lost so much. Often they can do nothing for themselves and it is left to the relief organizations such as the Red Cross, Oxfam and Christian Aid, together with similar organizations from other countries, to do what they can by providing money for food, medical supplies, tents, clothing, vehicles and other necessities.

Almighty God, we commend into your hands all who suffer as a result of natural disasters [*and at this time we remember especially the people of . . .*]. Help them in their time of difficulty and distress and bless the work of all who seek to help them. *Amen.*

Closing prayer No. 75

Disaster (4)

'Oh, I do like to be beside the seaside!' begins an old song and it is echoed by lots of people each summer. But summer sunshine and winter gales present two very different pictures.

On 13th January, 1978, people were beginning to reckon up the damage along the east coast of England after high tides and 80 m.p.h. gales. Piers were smashed to matchwood; streets and houses were flooded; and ships and boats were battered.

People had begun to wonder whether this would be a repeat of the great floods of fifteen years earlier when exceptionally high tides had breached sea walls in many places and caused widespread flooding. Following these worst storms of the century, sea walls were raised and strengthened and better warning systems introduced.

But even that was not as bad as the great storm of 1703, which began on 27th November and lasted for several days during which fifteen men-of-war and hundreds of merchant ships were lost, more than 1,500 seamen drowned, the Eddystone lighthouse swept away, 4,000 oaks uprooted in the New Forest, church steeples blown down and so much damage caused that towns looked as though they had been bombarded by an enemy.

It is very pleasant to be by the sea—sometimes! And those who have experienced stormy winds and mighty seas know just how frightening those experiences can be. We recall how scared the disciples of Jesus were in a storm and how helpful they found the presence of Jesus.

Bible Reading: St. Mark 4: 35–41

Almighty God, we remember before you those who suffer because of storms and floods and especially those who have lost members of their families. Comfort and strengthen all who are distressed and grant that they may be helped by the knowledge that you are near. *Amen.*

Benediction No. 99

Disaster (5)

Every day of our lives there are many accidents in which people are killed. About most of them we hear nothing, for the death of a few people in one accident is so common that it may no longer be regarded as news.

Every so often there is a very serious accident in which many people lose their lives. The loss of life if an air liner crashes must be great because there are so many people on board. And if two 'planes are involved, and both of them 'Jumbo' jets, the results is horrific.

That was what happened on 27th March, 1977, at Tenerife in the Canary Islands. No less than 576 people were killed in what was described as the worst ever air disaster—and it took place on the ground!

Two Boeing 747 Jumbo jets, one American and one Dutch, were about to take off. The Dutch 'plane gathered speed on the fog-bound runway. As it was taking off the American Jumbo taxied into its path. There was a violent explosion; burning wreckage was scattered far and wide; nearly seventy people were lucky to escape; but the rest of the passengers and the crews died.

Nowadays, aircraft, ships, trains, buses and all passenger vehicles are thoroughly tested to ensure they are safe. Drivers, pilots and other people responsible are very well trained and tested. But however strict the tests may be there is always mechanism which can fail—and there are always people who can make mistakes.

Accidents *will* happen. We can all help to prevent others by taking care.

We thank you, O God, for all modern transport which we find so useful for our journeyings. Help all who build, or test, or drive; the navigators, the traffic controllers, and all who are concerned with safety; that they may do their work conscientiously and well, knowing that the lives of others are in their hands. *Amen.*

Benediction No. 101

Safety (1)

Bible Reading: Acts 20: 7–12

Eutychus was very fortunate that St. Paul was around and that he could do something to help. Fancy sitting in an open window anyway! It was rather foolish.

But are some of the things we do any more sensible? Are we not guilty of doing things at home and in school which are dangerous and which we would not have done if we had thought of the dangers? Have you leaned out of an upstairs window lately? Or jumped down a flight of steps? Or balanced yourself on a chair placed on a table? Or played with an electric socket?

Perhaps you do not do such things because you think of your own safety. But do you also think of the safety of others, especially old people and young children. Do you ever leave things lying on the floor for old people to trip over? Or leave handles of pots of boiling water where young children can pull them over? Or leave a fire or stove unguarded? No doubt you can think of many other such dangers too.

Every year about 7,000 people die as a result of accidents in the home and hundreds of thousands are injured, some very severely. That is more than are injured or killed in street accidents. Many of these could be prevented with a little more thought and care.

We have only one body, which has to last us a lifetime and it is up to us to look after it. St. Paul also wrote in one of his letters that the body is God's temple and we should keep it pure for him.

O God, help us to do nothing which is a danger to others; help us to take care of ourselves and keep our bodies from harm or danger; and help us to keep our bodies pure to be used for your glory. *Amen.*

Benediction No. 93

Safety (2)

Each year some interesting old cars make their way from London to Brighton in the Vintage Car Rally. The first procession of cars from London to Brighton took place as long ago as 1896. Then they were up-to-date models and they did it to prove that motor cars were reliable.

They were also celebrating the repeal of the 'Red Flag' Act under which road vehicles were restricted to a speed of 4 m.p.h. and required someone to walk in front carrying a red flag by day or a red light at night as a warning to pedestrians.

Since then there have been many Acts of Parliament to 'protect' road users. In 1934, for example, the 30 m.p.h. limit in built up areas was introduced. So were driving tests and pedestrian crossings. More recently there have been other speed restrictions and traffic regulations to try to reduce the number of accidents in which thousands of people are killed or injured on the roads each year.

Motorists taking their driving test must know the Highway Code but all road users, motorists, cyclists, pedestrians and others should also know it and remember that the rules are important for the safety of everyone. For many years children have been taught kerb drill or the Green Cross Code. Yet there are still many unnecessary accidents.

Nowadays cars are quieter and faster. Streets are busier than ever. There is no one with a red flag to warn us of on-coming traffic. We have to use our eyes, our ears and our common sense. We must always be alert to possible danger. There can be no excuse for carelessness: our lives are too valuable for that!

Almighty God, our heavenly Father,
Open our eyes to the dangers that are around us;
Keep us alert where these dangers exist;
Make us aware of all that is done for our safety;
And protect us as we try to protect ourselves. *Amen.*

Benediction No. 101

Safety (3)

IN THE WATER

There's lots of fun to be had in or on the water. People of many ages enjoy their swimming, surfing, sailing, canoeing, boating, and all sorts of other water sports and pastimes, especially during the summer months. Each year several hundred of these people enjoy the water for the last time because they are drowned and about one third of these are children.

Why? Usually because those concerned have not observed the simple safety rules that should always be remembered when taking to the water. Every summer, for example, we read of swimmers who swim out to sea only to find that they cannot get back, perhaps because they have swum on the ebbing tide. Many do not realize how strong the currents are or how powerful the waves.

Lots of people drown when they fall out of boats because they haven't taken the trouble to wear a life-jacket. Most of these are people who know that they *should* wear a life-jacket but they are careless and think that it does not matter. Or perhaps they think that they will be quite all right. It is *other* people who have accidents!

People who are wise take all the precautions that are necessary. They learn and observe all that is needed for safety in their sports. Above all they learn to swim, which is a life-saver for many when they find themselves in the water by accident.

Life has been described often as a voyage through stormy seas. We shall be wise if we seek the safe-keeping of Almighty God.

Bible Reading: Isaiah 43: 2–3a

Make us wise, O God, on our journey through life, to remember the advice and the example of those who have gone before us and, trusting in your fatherly care, overcome all temptations. *Amen.*

Benediction No. 91

Safety (4)

The Davy Lamp

Nowadays people are very concerned for the safety of people at work and many Acts of Parliament have been passed to ensure that dangers to workers are kept to a minimum. Each place of work is now entitled by law to have a safety representative who will keep an eye open for danger and report it to someone in authority.

It was not always so. It was once quite common for people to be seriously injured by machinery in the factories because there were no guards to protect them.

Some of the worst conditions were those experienced by the coal miners, who had to work in almost complete darkness because a naked light would cause an explosion of a gas called fire-damp. One man who was very concerned was the Rev. John Hodgson who worked in a mining parish near Newcastle-upon-Tyne.

Talking to Sir Humphry Davy about it led to the inventor trying to solve the problem. He designed a lamp which he thought would be safe because the wire gauze surrounding the flame would keep the gas away from the flame. He tried it with fire-damp from a bottle but the only way to be sure was to test it in a coal mine. The man who offered to risk his life to do so was the Rev. John Hodgson. It worked. Since the Davy lamp was first used on 9th January, 1816, it has saved the lives of many, as well as making working conditions so much safer.

Today most people remember the name of the inventor but few will know the name of the brave man who tried it out. Many safety devices that we know today have come to us because of the bravery and courage of those who have put them to the test.

We remember, O God, all who are concerned with the well-being of others; those responsible for framing safety laws; the inventors of safety devices and those who have tested them; and all who work for safety today. May their efforts be rewarded. *Amen.*

Closing prayer No. 70

Safety (5)

Father had finished with the very strong cleaning liquid that he had been using and wanted to keep what was left, so he poured it into a lemonade bottle and put it under the sink. His son, feeling thirsty, saw the lemonade bottle, took a quick drink from it and ended up in hospital. Father had broken two important rules. Never use drink bottles for other fluids. Keep dangerous substances away from the reach of children.

Mother needed those pills to keep her well. They were brightly-coloured sugary-coated pills and she had to take one in the morning and one in the evening. She left them on the sideboard where her young daughter spotted them while mother was upstairs. She tried one and it tasted nice. So she had another, and another until the bottle was empty. They took her to hospital too but she died.

Perhaps the pills should have been in one of the modern types of container which little children cannot open. On the other hand mother should not have been careless in leaving the pills within reach. They should have been locked away.

Nowadays there are many regulations to protect people from taking harmful medicines and warnings are often given about the dangers of drugs, pills and poisons. Yet people are careless or thoughtless and this can often result in disaster. The wonderful discoveries of medicine can be killers if misused. We cannot be too careful.

Neither can we be too careful in other things too. James likens the tongue to deadly poison.

Bible Reading: James 3: 8–10

Help us, God our Father,
To do nothing which would harm anyone else;
To say nothing that is unkind or untrue;
To avoid all that is evil and uphold what is good;
And in all things to live as you would have us to. *Amen.*

Benediction No. 104

2 Through the year

These seven themes are related to the seasons of the year. They include religious festivals, interesting customs associated with the time of year and special observances.

It is suggested that they are best taken at the appropriate season of the year, although most of the topics can be taken individually.

Winter	Early January
Shrovetide and Lent	February. Week of Shrove Tuesday
Spring and Eastertide	Week before Easter or overlapping Easter holiday
Summer	July/August
Harvest	End of September
Autumn	Early November
Christmastide	Last week before Christmas holiday

A few of the topics are related to specific days and it may sometimes be helpful to change the order within the theme. There is, however, some linkage as for example *Winter* 1 and 2, *Shrovetide and Lent* 1, 2 and 3 and also in the other themes.

Attention is also drawn to the *Table of Contents by Date* (page xxix) which gives topics related to particular seasons of the year, some of which could be used instead of those included in this section or additionally where a term begins or ends mid-week. *Christmastide*, for example, could include any of the topics on pages 108, 112, 115 or 238 to extend the theme, rearranged if felt advisable, over a week and a half.

Winter (1)

New Year and Twelfth Night

The first few days of January are traditionally days of celebration. January 6th, the Feast of Epiphany, when the Christian Church celebrates the visit of the Wise Men from the East, is the last of the Twelve Days of Christmas. It is the day when festivities end and by which all decorations should be taken down.

During the twelve days of Christmas the Old Year has passed and the New Year begun. People celebrate this with parties, especially in Scotland, where Hogmanay is a time of great festivity. It is a time when people wish each other 'Good health' and traditionally call on others.

In Scotland people go 'first-footing' and it is considered lucky if the first person to enter a house in the new year is dark-haired. Visitors are offered food and drink. An old Welsh custom, known as Mari Lwyd, took place during this time too. Singers carrying a horse's skull went from house to house. After a kind of singing competition they were invited in for cake and ale.

Wassailing used to be common in England. 'Wassail' meant 'Be whole' and was used when drinking people's health. Twelfth Night was a favourite night for wassailers, who were given food and drink after singing.

An old Somerset custom, which is still observed in places today, was to wassail the cider apple trees on Twelfth Night. Cider was thrown into the branches and guns were fired to drive away evil spirits and so ensure a good apple harvest.

We may wish health and happiness to others in the New Year, and no doubt we wish for prosperity ourselves. Perhaps we should heed some advice given by King David in one of his psalms.

Bible Reading: Psalm 34: 11–16

At the beginning of the year, O God, we look back with thankfulness upon all your past mercies. Be with us in the coming days; bless us with your presence; and help us to be all that you would have us to be. *Amen.*

Benediction No. 107

Winter (2)

Long ago, when most people lived in small villages and farmed the land, January was the time for ploughing the fields in readiness for planting crops. Once the festivities of Christmas were over, it was time to get down to some hard work.

The Monday after Epiphany (6th January) became known as Plough Monday, when people asked God's blessing on their work. On that day, a plough, decorated with ribbons, was dragged through the village by young farm labourers accompanied by two characters known as Bessy and the Clown. At various places they would stop to perform a sword dance or a short play about the battle between good and evil. In some places they would wear masks or blacken their faces and crack whips as they went.

The custom, which was just fun for many people, had once been considered a way to drive evil spirits from the ground just as wassailing the apple trees had been thought to drive evil spirits from the orchards. Prayers had once been said to the ancient gods but the Christian Church encouraged people instead to ask God to bless their work.

Nowadays, like many other old customs, the ceremony of blessing the plough has been revived in some country districts. On Plough Monday farm workers may gather round the plough whilst the vicar blesses them and the work they do. In some places this little ceremony is conducted in the church on the previous day during one of the services.

Long ago, in Old Testament times, people sought God's blessing:

Bible Reading: Psalm 67

We come before you, O God, and ask your blessing upon all the work we have to do. Help us to work to the best of our ability; teach us to be patient and diligent; and grant us wisdom and understanding. Bless us, we pray, and accept our grateful thanks for all your great gifts. *Amen.*

Closing prayer No. 76

Winter (3)

People in many parts of the world have their own special ways of celebrating New Year or looking forward to spring. When those people settle in a new country they take their customs with them and so many interesting customs have been taken from one part of the world to another.

The Chinese, for example, celebrate New Year between the middle of January and the middle of February. The date varies from one year to another because the Chinese calendar is based upon the moon. New Year is the most important and colourful of all the Chinese festivals and may last for as long as fifteen days, though usually it is kept to three or four.

Celebrations start on their New Year's Eve. Then, as midnight strikes, fire-crackers are set off and these continue throughout the festival. Streets and houses are decorated with brightly coloured lanterns, banners and flags. Lion and dragon dances are performed and special food is eaten.

Each year is given the name of an animal. 1977 was the year of the snake and 1978 the year of the horse. Others, in turn, are the sheep, monkey, cockerel, dog, pig, rat, ox, tiger, hare and dragon.

The Chinese New Year festival is an opportunity for family gathering. Presents are exchanged and the traditional greeting *Kungshi fa ts'ai* is given. The Chinese also remember their ancestors at this time and invite them to share the blessings they seek for the coming year. It is a time of great rejoicing but also one with deep religious meaning.

O God, as we rejoice over all the things which are ours to enjoy, help us to remember those who have made these things possible:

Our parents and other members of our family;
Our ancestors who planned for the future;
The leaders of our nation and community.

Accept our thanks for these and for all the blessings you have bestowed. *Amen.*

Benediction No. 97

Winter (4)

Ice skating

In the heart of winter cold winds sweep down from the north and east bringing with them the ice and snow. Blizzards sweep across the country blocking roads with drifts of snow; whole areas are sometimes isolated; and many animals suffer hardship.

But these same conditions bring opportunities for amusements which are not otherwise possible. Children enjoy making snowmen or playing with snowballs, tobogganing down the hills or sliding on frozen ponds. There are, of course, many dangers from venturing on frozen ponds, particularly from thin or melting ice, but sometimes skating is possible.

With plenty of space it is possible to attain high speeds at ice skating. The Russian Yevgeniy Kulikov set up a world record on 29th March, 1975 of 29·43 m.p.h. (47·36 km/h). Speed skating began over seven hundred years ago on the frozen canals of Holland. It was introduced to England where, in the fens of East Anglia, competitions were first held in 1814.

More spectacular to watch than speed skating is figure skating. One of the finest women figure skaters of all time was the Norwegian Sonja Henie, who first competed in the Winter Olympics when only eleven years of age. Between 1927 and 1936 she won ten consecutive world titles and gold medals in three Olympics. Becoming a film star she did much to popularize figure skating. Ice dancing is also a keenly contested international championship event.

But for most of us the fun of winter is that which we make for ourselves and we have to take care that the things we do are not dangerous to ourselves or to others.

In this season of winter, O God,
Enable us to find enjoyment in the open air;
Keep us from any form of harm or danger;
Remind us of those for whom the winter brings hardship;
And help us to help them, in your Name. *Amen.*

Closing prayer No. 54

Winter (5)

There are lots of people who enjoy winter sports such as skiing and take the opportunity of a winter holiday in the Cairngorms of Scotland, the Austrian or Swiss Alps, or Scandinavia.

Every fourth year the champions of the world gather for the Winter Olympic Games to compete in such events as Nordic skiing, Alpine skiing, Figure skating, Speed skating, Bobsleigh, Tobogganing and Ice hockey.

Perhaps the most spectacular is the Nordic ski jumping in which the competitors hurtle down a ramp at speeds of about 75 m.p.h. (120 km/h) and take off to fly through the air with a perfect poise and make a good landing.

Bobsledding has its thrills too as the two-man or four-man bobsleighs hurtle along the specially prepared course with bends and banks at speeds sometimes exceeding 90 m.p.h. (145 km/h).

It was in this event on 31st January, 1964, at the Innsbruck Olympics, that the Italian bobsleigh driver, Eugenio Monti, showed true sportsmanship. With several world titles to his credit he was expected to win the gold medal. After the first of the four runs his closest rival, the British Tony Nash broke his rear axle which could have put him out of the Games. But Monti, after his second run, took off his own axle and lent it to Nash. Nash went on to win the gold, leaving Monti to finish with only the bronze. We can imagine how popular the result was four years later when Monti won gold medals for both bobsleigh events.

Winning an event is a fine achievement but to be a good sports-man is infinitely greater. And this is true of every part of life too.

Bible Reading: Hebrews 12: 1–2

Teach us, O Lord, so to live that we may be highly regarded by those around us as we strive to be the very best we can in your service. *Amen.*

Closing prayer No. 64

Shrovetide and Lent (1)

Mardi Gras

The period of forty days leading up to Easter is known as Lent. Nowadays it is not observed as strictly as it once was, when people would fast or deny themselves luxuries and when certain activities were forbidden. The three of four days before Lent are known as Shrovetide, from the old Roman Catholic custom of being shrove or shriven, that is confessing and having one's sins forgiven.

It is hardly surprising that Shrovetide became a time when people 'let off steam' and enjoyed themselves before observing Lent.

The last day of Shrovetide was Shrove Tuesday, known in some Roman Catholic countries as Mardi Gras. This was a day when colourful carnivals and other festivities were held. These carnival ideas spread to the New World and became a great tradition in the south of the United States and in the Caribbean. The celebrations may last for two days, as in Trinidad, where they begin at 5 a.m. on the Monday and last until midnight on Tuesday.

The ancestors of the people of Trinidad came from many different countries and customs from them all go to make up the carnival, which is a gay, colourful time, with processions, steel bands, dancing, a festival of the arts and lots of other things to enjoy. Thousands of spectators gather to see the magnificent costumes and to have a carefree time. Although the carnival lasts only two days, the preparations for it will have kept people busy for a long time beforehand.

And when it is over, no doubt many will be looking forward to the next one.

We thank you, God our Father, for all the opportunities we have of enjoying ourselves, and especially those where we work together with other people. Help us to realize that we gain so much more in life if we learn how to work with others, and teach us the value of working as a team. *Amen.*

Benediction No. 97

Shrovetide and Lent (2)

Shrove Tuesday, the last day before Lent begins, used to be a day for boisterous games, some of which are still played to this day. It is also the day which is popularly known as Pancake Day, from the old custom of frying up stocks of fat, butter and eggs, which people were forbidden to eat during Lent.

One of the famous events of Shrove Tuesday is the Pancake Race, held at Olney, Buckinghamshire. There are pancake races elsewhere but none is as popular as the Olney event. It dates back to 1445, when it is said that a housewife heard the church bell while she was making pancakes and rushed to the church still wearing her apron and holding her frying pan.

Only women may take part in the race today. They must wear an apron and a hat or scarf and carry a pan containing a pancake which must be tossed three times before reaching the church. The winner receives a kiss from the bellringer and a prayerbook from the vicar.

Elsewhere there are some strange sporting events including unusual football matches. At Ashbourne, Derbyshire, one is played between the Up'ards and the Down'ards, depending upon whereabouts in the town they were born. The goals, two mill-wheels, are three miles apart. Some football pitch!

After the merriment of Shrovetide came the forty days of Lent, during which people were enjoined to think about the stories in the Bible of the events leading up to the crucifixion of Jesus. Here is one of those stories.

Bible Reading: St. Matthew 26: 6–13

O God:
Help us to think more of you than we do of ourselves;
Help us to offer you the best gifts that we can;
Help us to be of service to others in your Name;
And to you be the glory for ever. *Amen.*

Closing prayer No. 69

Shrovetide and Lent (3)

The first day of Lent is called Ash Wednesday. It is a day on which many people attend church services to mark the beginning of Lent. It used to be the custom, and it still is in some churches, for those attending the service to be marked on the forehead with ashes. It was an old Jewish custom, often referred to in the Bible, to wear ashes as a sign of sorrow.

So in Lent it has been the custom for people to express their sorrow for ways in which they may have offended God and to ask his forgiveness. Lent has always been a season for fasting as well. Fasting did not mean going without food altogether but going without certain kinds of food. Fasting was once more common than it is today. It used to be observed throughout Lent but now the Roman Catholic Church in England has only two fast days— Ash Wednesday and Good Friday.

Fasting is a kind of self-discipline. By going without certain foods or denying oneself some pleasures, one is constantly reminded why one is doing so, and in the case of Lent this is to remember God's goodness and seek to serve him better.

But as Jesus told the people of his day, fasting is not something to boast about or make a great show of: it is a very personal matter between each individual and God.

Bible Reading: St. Matthew 6: 16–18

The Collect for Ash Wednesday:
Almighty and everlasting God, you hate nothing that you have made, and forgive the sins of all those who are penitent. Create and make in us new and contrite hearts, that, lamenting our sins and acknowledging our wretchedness, we may receive from you, the God of all mercy, perfect forgiveness and peace; through Jesus Christ our Lord. *Amen.*

Closing prayer No. 72

Shrovetide and Lent (4)

The fourth Sunday in Lent, or Mid-Lent Sunday, is also known as Mothering Sunday. Nowadays it is a day when children remember and give greetings cards and flowers to their mothers, but the origin of the name for this day had nothing at all to do with mothers.

Hundreds of years ago, when Lent was very strictly observed, Mothering Sunday was the one day out of the forty when feasting and games were permitted. In those days many people lived in tiny groups of houses too small to be called villages and they worshipped in small chapels but on Mid-Lent Sunday they went to the mother-church of the parish and offered special gifts. Hence the reason for calling this Mothering Sunday.

Gradually, as times changed, and no one knows just when, people began thinking of their own mothers on this day. During the eighteenth and nineteenth centuries it was customary for servants and others working away from home to be given this day off so that they could visit their mothers and take a cake and maybe flowers. It was a family day, when the whole family went to church together and special tributes were paid to mother at the family meal.

In the Bible there are reminders that one should honour and respect parents. Here is one.

Bible Reading: Ephesians 6: 1–3

But for most people a commandment is unnecessary. Mothering Sunday is an opportunity to say thank-you to mother for all her love, care, guidance, thoughtfulness—and so many other things.

Today, O Heavenly Father, we remember with thankfulness all the blessings received from our mothers. Help us to show our appreciation by being helpful and considerate, thoughtful and kind, and by growing to be the kind of people that they would wish us to be. *Amen.*

Closing prayer No. 58

Shrovetide and Lent (5)

BRITISH SUMMER TIME   *Daylight Saving*

Every year in March, or perhaps April, the date being decided by Parliament, we are reminded that we have to put our clocks forward one hour so that we change from Greenwich Mean Time to British Summer Time. This means that instead of having so much daylight early in the morning when most people are asleep it is added on to the end of the day when people welcome the extra hour to enjoy their leisure.

The idea of changing the time like this was first put forward in an amusing essay written as long ago as 1784 but the man who did most of the campaigning to get people to accept the idea of 'Daylight Saving' was William Willett. His plan, put forward in 1907, was rejected by Parliament in 1908.

It was during World War I that several countries adopted daylight saving in order to save fuel. In Britain the Summertime Act was passed on 17th May, 1916, and on 21st May clocks were put forward one hour for the first time. It was some years later, on 7th August, 1925, that the Summertime Act made daylight saving a permanent measure and fixed the dates when it would operate each year.

There have been changes since then. During World War II, for example, we had Double Summer Time to save even more fuel. In recent years Summer Time has begun earlier, in March.

Then, when we have enjoyed our summer, the clocks are put back again at the end of October and the dark days are with us again.

It serves as a reminder of the words of Jesus about the light that he brought into the world.

Bible Reading: St. John 12: 35–36

Lighten our lives, O Lord, we pray, by the brightness of your presence and help us to walk in your light all the days of our lives so that when darkness abounds all around us we may know your love and the peace which passes all understanding. *Amen.*

Benediction No. 107

Spring and Eastertide (1)

Palm Sunday

The week before Easter is known as Holy Week because it com-memorates the events of the last week in the life of Jesus. The end of the week, when the Last Supper and the Crucifixion are recal-led, is traditionally a very solemn time but the week begins on a note of triumph on Palm Sunday, as the story of Jesus entering Jerusalem is retold.

Bible Reading: St. Matthew 21: 1–9

To celebrate this it became the custom to decorate churches with palm or willow and to carry these in procession. In England, the Sallow Willow with its large fluffy catkins is used often instead of the palm, which has to be imported. Boys used to go 'a-palming' and gather catkins to decorate their houses too because this was thought to bring good luck.

In Roman Catholic churches it is common to give small sprigs or palm crosses to the people who attend the church service. This custom has been introduced into some other churches and chapels in recent times.

There are other interesting local customs that take place on Palm Sunday. In parts of Wales the day is *Sul y Blodau*, Flowering Sunday, when flowers are placed on family graves. One pleasant custom in Hentland, Herefordshire is to distribute cakes in church after the morning service. As each cake is given the clergyman says, 'God and Good Neighbourhood', the idea being that those who have eaten together should have good will toward one another.

O God our Father, as we join together to think about those events which showed your great love for all people, may we show our thanks in our love for you and toward our neighbours. *Amen.*

Closing prayer No. 54

Spring and Eastertide (2)

The Thursday of Holy Week is called Maundy Thursday. It is a day on which the Christian Church recalls the last supper which Jesus shared with his disciples. After supper Jesus took a bowl of water and washed the feet of the disciples, a task normally done by a servant. Then he said this:

Bible Reading: St. John 13: 12–17

The name Maundy Thursday comes from the Latin word *mandatum*, meaning 'command', because Jesus then said, 'I give you a new commandment: love one another. As I have loved you, so you must love one another.'

For many years it has been the custom for the sovereign of Britain to give away money on Maundy Thursday. The money, known as the Royal Maundy, follows a custom started by King Edward III. Until 1689, the monarch ceremonially washed and kissed the feet of some poor people, in memory of what Jesus did for his disciples. The feet had previously been well washed by the Yeomen of the Laundry!

Since the reign of James II, money has been given instead. It is money specially minted for this purpose and consists of coins to the value of a penny for each year of the sovereign's age. At one time the distribution was always made in Westminster Abbey but now it is done in various cathedrals.

The clergy present at this ceremony still have linen towels on their shoulders, a reminder of the old custom of washing the feet.

Teach us, O God, not to think too highly of ourselves but to remember the lesson in humility given by our Lord, so that we may always be ready to serve one another and in doing so to serve you; through Jesus Christ our Lord. *Amen.*

Closing prayer No. 69

Spring and Eastertide (3)

Easter Eggs

Easter is the festival which recalls the resurrection of Jesus Christ from the dead. After his death on the cross on Good Friday he was laid in a tomb and a stone rolled across the opening. This is the story of what happened then.

Bible Reading: St. Mark 16: 1–8

It has always been the happiest festival of all and for many years was much more important than Christmas. It is a time when everything seems to come to life. Bare churches are decorated with flowers and the solemnity of Good Friday gives way to rejoicing. Many people like to put on new clothes for Easter if only an Easter bonnet or a new pair of shoes.

Most children expect and receive Easter eggs. Nowadays they are usually chocolate eggs. At one time they were ordinary eggs that had been decorated. The egg has always been regarded as a symbol of resurrection and new life and it is easy to see how eggs become associated with Easter.

But Easter goes back long before Christian times. The name Easter comes from Eostre, the Anglo-Saxon goddess of Spring. The hare, which was the sacred animal of Eostre, was probably the origin of the Easter Bunny, popular in America.

So the very old pagan spring customs were adopted by the Christian Church as the symbols of the resurrection of Jesus. The rejoicing over the new birth of the world at springtime became the joyful Christian festival of Easter.

Help us, God our Father, to understand something of the real message of Easter, that through the death and rising again of our Lord Jesus Christ we learn of your great love for us. May we know how he lives today in the hearts of all who love him, and find for ourselves the true joy of Easter in the presence of the living Lord. *Amen.*

Benediction No. 100

Spring and Eastertide (4)

Easter has always been a time for revelry and games. Many old customs are still observed in various parts of Britain.

Egg rolling or Pace-egging is one of these. Hard boiled eggs are taken to the top of a slope and rolled down until they break. This may have been a reminder of the stone that was rolled away from the tomb of Jesus, or it may be a continuation of a much older custom in which hard-boiled eggs were held in the hand and banged against those held by others, much as children do today with conkers. The egg that was not broken was the champion. Egg rolling takes place on Good Friday in some places and on Easter Monday in others.

Easter Monday has always been a day for games, some of them quite boisterous. At Hallaton, Leicestershire, for example, people 'scramble' for Hare Pies and then join in a bottle-kicking contest. The 'bottles' are really small casks of beer which are kicked or handled toward a 'goal', which is one of two streams about a mile apart. Today there are many Easter Monday sporting fixtures.

The Easter holiday used to last until the following week, when the Monday and Tuesday were known as Hocktide. On these days men and women would collect money for the church. Usually the men collected on the Monday and the women on the Tuesday by 'capturing' members of the opposite sex and demanding money as a toll or forfeit. Hocktide celebrations have now almost disappeared except at Hungerford, Berkshire, where there are colourful celebrations on the second Tuesday after Easter.

We thank you, God our Father, for all the opportunities we have of enjoying ourselves in sport or recreation. Teach us how to keep our bodies fit and our minds alert so that we may be happy and healthy. *Amen.*

Benediction No. 91

Spring and Eastertide (5)

FLOWERS OF SPRING   *The Bulbfields*

One of the earliest signs that spring is on its way is the appearance of the spring flowers, some of the earlier ones pushing their way through the snow and the frozen earth to give their touch of colour to the bare ground. Snowdrops and Scillas, Winter Aconites and Crocuses are some of the earlier ones before the masses of golden daffodils burst into bloom.

This is the time when some people enjoy their visits to the country, to places where naturalized daffodils bloom in the wild, where woods are carpeted with bluebells, or where cushions of yellow primroses abound.

Some places are especially renowned for the flowers that are grown there. In April and May many people go to visit the tulip fields in Holland. Others make their way to Spalding, Lincoln-shire, where the bulb fields are particularly colourful.

At Spalding one can visit Springfields, a twenty-acre garden, designed especially to display spring flowers and roses in different settings. The Springfields Horticultural Society organizes a Flower Parade each year and this is a very popular event.

Some people especially enjoy the spring flowers because they seem to be a sign that the dark dreary days of winter are behind and the pleasanter weather is near at hand. Others enjoy them because they are so easy to grow from bulbs both in and out of doors.

God has created a beautiful world, full of life and colour and it is here for us to enjoy.

Almighty God we praise you for all the joys of springtime, the flowers that bring fresh colour into the world after the bleakness of winter, and the new life being born into the animal world. Keep us mindful of all the joys of your creation and help us to appreciate these, your gifts. *Amen.*

Closing prayer No. 83

Summary (1)

> *The tall trees in the greenwood,*
> *The meadows for our play,*
> *The rushes by the water*
> *To gather every day:*

This verse of *All things bright and beautiful* reminds us of summer days when we can enjoy the countryside, the trees, the meadows and the rushes by the water. But why would people want to gather the rushes every day?

The hymn was written in 1848, when country cottages were very different from the homes we enjoy. Many had earth or stone floors and carpets were unheard of unless you happened to be rich. So people covered their floors with rushes which were soft to tread upon and certainly warmer than the bare earth.

Churches, too, had earth or tiled floors and these were also cold. So it became the custom in many places to strew the floors of the churches with rushes. These were not changed every week but would remain in place for the whole of the year. Then it was time to have a good clean out, get rid of all the old dirty rushes and replace them with new ones. Villagers would come to the church on a particular day, each carrying a large bundle of rushes to be spread on the floor.

Some of these rush-bearing ceremonies are still kept up. At Ambleside, Cumbria, for example, the ceremony takes place on the nearest Saturday to 26th July (St. Anne's Day), but instead of bundles, the rushes are made into decorative shapes and coloured with flowers. Similar services are held in other villages in the north-west and elsewhere on various dates in summer.

We have been reminded, O God, how people not only worked to bring comfort into their homes but into the house of God and how they worked together to do that. Help us to think not only of ourselves but of your work in the world and make us ready and willing to work together with others. *Amen.*

Closing prayer No. 89

Summer (2)

Well-dressing

Every year many visitors make their way in summer to certain Derbyshire villages where they can admire the beautiful well-dressings. Each village has its own day for the well-dressing, most of them in June but some in August. One of the most famous is Tissington, where there are five wells, all of them decorated on Ascension Day.

It is generally believed that the custom goes back to the year 1350 when the people of Tissington survived the Black Death because of the pure water in their wells. There was also a time of severe drought early in the seventeenth century when the Tissington wells continued to supply water.

So people gave thanks to the spirits of the waters by making an annual gift of flowers, throwing garlands and posies into the water.

Then, in 1818, for the first time, instead of throwing flowers into the water, they made them into a picture on a clay-covered board and the practice that is common today began. Today each well has behind it a large framework with a clay-covered board on which a very colourful picture is made by pressing into the clay any natural objects—flower petals, leaves, mosses, cones, bark, feathers, beans, pieces of stone—anything as long as it is natural. Tin, glass and other man-made substances are not allowed.

These large pictures of Bible stories are surrounded by colourful designs and a text from the Bible, all executed with meticulous care as a way of saying 'Thank-you' for that most valuable of God's gifts—pure, fresh water.

Accept our thanks, O God, for all your great gifts to us, especially those of food and drink, health and strength, families and friends. Help us to show our thanks not only in word but in deed, offering to you the best of our talents to be used in your service and for the benefit of our fellows. *Amen.*

Closing prayer No. 59

Summary (3)

A TOUCH OF COLOUR   *The Morris Men*

One of the colourful scenes in summer is the appearance of the Morris men, dancing on village greens or in the streets, in town squares or in other public places.

Morris dancers are always teams of men, dressed in various styles but most of them wearing hats and ribbons and having bells on their legs. Many dance with large handkerchiefs, though some still carry staves or swords. As they dance to the accompaniment of violins or accordions, they stamp and kick, causing their bells to jingle wildly. It is certainly great fun for those taking part and fine entertainment for those who watch.

At one time, as with so many things, it was a very serious business. Morris men came out in Maytime and danced their way through the village to wake up the spirits in the ground so that there would be a good harvest and to drive out those evil spirits which might be there. Hence the stamping and the bells, the staves and the swords. It is thought that the name Morris may be a corruption of 'Moorish' and mean 'pagan' but no one can be sure. Certainly Morris dancing is very old and it might have died out except that Cecil Sharp spotted the Morris men at Headington, Oxford, in 1889 and encouraged people to keep up this kind of dancing.

Now there are many groups of Morris dancers throughout Britain, enjoying various forms of dance, accompanied by characters such as the Betsy or Moll, the Fool and lots of others.

Nowadays they dance, not to drive out the spirits, but to use up their energy in a good, healthy form of exercise which gives lots of pleasure to others too.

We thank you, O God, for the enjoyment we can find in healthy exercise or activities and for the pleasures gained from watching others. Give us always thankful hearts. *Amen.*

Benediction No. 106

Summary (4)

Bank holiday

Summer is the time when we take most holidays—a time when we can get away from work and enjoy ourselves in the country, by the sea or in some foreign parts, where we can bask in the sunshine and admire the scenery.

Nowadays we accept holidays away from home as the thing to do, but this is something which has happened only in quite recent times. There have always been holidays but not as we know them. Holidays in the ancient world enabled people to take part in the seasonal festivals, some of which became the main Christian holidays.

The word holiday comes from holy day. A few hundred years ago in Britain many of these days were observed. After people had attended Mass in the morning the rest of the day was their own. These days added up to about eight weeks per year, many of them as single days. In fact a couple of hundred years ago the Bank of England was closed for no less than 33 saints' days or other festivals and anniversaries.

But times changed. Factories were built. Conditions were different. Business became important. Holidays lost working time and cost money! By 1834 the days on which the Bank of England closed had been reduced to four. The modern Bank Holiday system was introduced by Act of Parliament in 1871 but of course there have been many changes since then in people's attitudes toward holidays. We know how important it is to get away from business or work for a complete change to build ourselves up.

Jesus recognized the value of this too when his disciples had been very busy.

Bible Reading: St. Mark 6: 30–32

Help us, O God, to enjoy our holiday times, to restore our bodies in relaxation in the open air; and help us to restore our minds and spirits as we spend time in your presence. *Amen.*

Benediction No. 105

Summer (5)

For many Welsh people the highlight of the year is the Royal National Eisteddfod. Held in August, it alternates between North Wales and South Wales. The great pavilion which seats 9,000 people is erected in the Eisteddfod field and thousands of people gather from all over Wales.

The gorsedd circle, a circle of stones with an altar in the centre, is the scene of the opening ceremony. As the procession of druids and bards with various attendants arrives, the Chief Druid takes his place by the altar. One by one the druids place their hands on the great Gorsedd Sword. The Chief Druid cries out three times '*A oes heddwch?*' (Is it peace?). Each time the crowd responds, *Heddwch!*' (Peace!).

Thereafter the pavilion becomes the focal point where competitions will be held for poets, singers, harpers, choirs, bands, dancers and many others. The highest awards are the bardic crown and the bardic chair, each awarded for different kinds of poetry. Competitors for the various classes will have been practising for a long time. Success in the Eisteddfod is a great honour.

But the competitions are only part of the Eisteddfod, for many it is a chance to meet friends and enjoy the whole atmosphere. It is Welsh through and through. And those who have attended go away with special memories but with a renewed love for Wales, its language and its culture.

In Old Testament times many people found special help and inspiration in God's Temple:

Bible Reading: Psalm 48: 9–14

Almighty God we thank you for those things which stir our emotions and make us proud of the heritage that is ours. Help us to rejoice in all that you have given and send us forth from your presence renewed in our desire to serve you faithfully. *Amen.*

Closing prayer No. 58

Harvest (1)

Toward the end of summer the peace of the countryside is shattered by the sound of giant combine-harvesters moving relentlessly across the fields and gobbling up the crops of golden grain. Inside the machine the corn is threshed so the grain can be delivered into lorries and the straw discarded.

It was not always so. For thousands of years men and women harvested the crops by hand. We can read about this in the Bible:

Bible Reading: Ruth 2: 2–9

One hundred years ago in Britain horse-drawn reaping machines were just appearing. But on most farms everyone gave a hand to gather the harvest. Men would gather with their scythes and choose as their leader the tallest and most skilful reaper, who was known as 'King of the Mowers'. He wore a plaited hat, decorated with poppies and trailing bindweed, as he led the others.

The corn was then bound into sheaves which were pitch-forked onto farm wagons. Magnificent cart-horses slowly pulled the heavily laden wagons to the stackyard, then returned 'at the gallop' for another load. The last sheaf to be gathered was decorated and called the 'Maiden Sheaf'. As it was carried on the last wagon the workers shouted and sang verses about Harvest Home.

That night there was a great feast given by the farmer and his wife for all the workers and their families. It was one way of saying 'Thank-you' to those who had brought in the harvest.

Do we remember to thank those who bring in our harvest? Or to thank God who provides?

O God, our Father, we are thankful to all who have worked to give us our food and to you who sent the sun and rain to make it grow. Help us never to take these things for granted but give us grateful hearts. *Amen.*

Closing prayer No. 87

Harvest (2)

Corn dollies

When the harvest has been reaped the fields are bare. Modern farmers will often set light to the stubble that remains and plough in the ashes to help fertilize the soil for the next crop. The ploughed fields are then well prepared and good seed sown for the following year.

Long ago people wondered what happened when the harvest was reaped. They believed that there were spirits in the ground which made the corn grow; and they believed that when the corn was reaped the corn-spirit had to be kept alive until the following spring.

The last sheaf of corn, the 'Maiden Sheaf' was sometimes thought to contain this corn-spirit. In some parts of the country corn dollies were made by weaving together a few pieces of corn, sometimes resembling a woman, and decorating them with ribbon. These were then kept safely until the following spring, when the spirit was thought to return to the ground ready to produce the next harvest.

During the year there were other customs which were intended to drive evil spirits from the fields and so protect the harvest. At Hallowe'en, for example, on the night when all sorts of evil spirits were believed to be about, people lit bonfires and marched around their fields, making as much noise as they could, believing that this would frighten evil spirits away.

Nowadays we do not fear evil spirits; nor do we believe that we have to keep the corn-spirit alive. We just enjoy the old customs and we are thankful that we do not have to live under superstition and fear—as people still do in many parts of the world today.

Almighty God, we thank you for the harvest of field and orchard, for the weather which makes things grow, and for all who have learned how to grow good crops. Hear our prayer for those who do not understand as we do, that they may increase in their knowledge of your world. *Amen.*

Closing prayer No. 90

Harvest (3)

In countries of Europe and some other parts of the world people can always be sure of a harvest. It may be better in some years than in others and there are occasionally years when some crops are very poor or fail. But there is always something. The Jewish people were reminded of this long ago:

Bible Reading: Genesis 8: 22

But there are many parts of the world, particularly in Africa and Asia where nothing is certain. In these places the harvest is never good but sometimes there is none at all. To the south of the Sahara Desert in North Africa is a region called the Sahel. In the late 1960s and early 1970s there was a long period with no rain, when the earth was scorched by the burning sun and there was no harvest. It is believed that about one million people died then.

Sometimes the problem is one of having too much rain. In Pakistan and Bangladesh there have recently been floods which have swept away all the crops.

When there is no harvest there is famine, and famine means real hunger. We feel hungry if we miss one meal. Imagine having only one meal every other day—and that only a single pancake made from grain, with nothing to make it tasty, no oil, no sugar, no milk! Imagine having to go several days without food!

Some people are *always* hungry. About two-thirds of all the people in the world do not have enough of the right kind of food to eat, and that number is growing bigger every day. It is one of the big problems of the present age.

O God hear our prayer:
For all who try to improve the world's food supplies;
For all who do not have enough to eat;
For all who suffer today because of famine.
Help us to be mindful of the needs of others and not to waste food or other precious materials. *Amen.*

Benediction No. 105

Harvest (4)

Do we take our food for granted? Do we remember to be thankful to those who produce it? Or to God who sends the sun and rain?

Harvest festivals of one kind or another have been held for many, many years. The ancient Egyptians, to mention just one people, held a harvest festival in honour of a god they called Min.

Jewish people, long before the time of Jesus Christ, kept two important Harvest Festivals. The first of these was Shevuoth (*Shevōō'ot*), also known as the Feast of Weeks, or Pentecost, when the barley harvest was ending and the wheat harvest beginning. Synagogues to this day are decorated with flowers for this festival.

The second festival came later in the year. This was Sukkoth (*Sukŏt'*), commonly called the Feast of Tabernacles, or Booths. It marked the gathering of the grape harvest and dated from the days in the wilderness after the Exodus from Egypt. This eight day festival of thanksgiving is kept by Jews today, who take their meals in booths set up in their gardens.

Like people of some other religions, the Jewish people believed they should offer the 'first fruits' of their crops to God and the law laid down the way in which this offering should be made.

Bible Reading: Deuteronomy 26: 1–11

For many years Harvest Thanksgiving services have been held in Christian churches, too, when the church is decorated with fruit, vegetables and flowers as the people give thanks, not so much for food they have grown themselves but for the food which is always available in the shops.

Almighty God, we give you thanks
For food which we have grown in our own gardens;
For food which we can buy in the shops and markets;
For people who work hard to produce our food;
For all those who carry it by land and sea.
For these, and every blessing received, we praise your name, O
God. *Amen.*

Closing prayer No. 83

Harvest (5)

When one thinks of harvests it is usually of things such as wheat and barley, apples and pears, coffee and tea.

But there are many other harvests too. We may think of a harvest of seaweed! This can be an important food product for a hungry world. Or a harvest of eggs or fish.

People living near the sea are thankful for the harvest of fish. In some places there are interesting old customs such as 'Blessing the Waters', when a priest goes out in a fishing boat to ask God's blessing on the work of the fishermen. At Colchester, Essex, there is a famous Oyster Festival, to give thanks for those shellfish.

In many fishing towns and villages there are special thanksgiving services. At Seahouses, Northumberland, for example, on one Sunday in August the Methodist Church is decorated with fishing nets, ships' flags, model ships, lifebuoys and other equipment. A choir of local fishermen sings and everyone gives thanks for the harvest of the sea.

In a church in an industrial town the harvest display may not be one of fruit and vegetables but of bright shining pieces of machinery and of tools made in the local factories. Another 'harvest' service may consist of paintings, models and other works of art and craftsmanship which people have made in their leisure time.

Harvest is, after all, a time for people to give thanks for the work of their hands, whether it be in the fields, the garden, the home, the factory or on the sea and to praise God for every gift and talent possessed.

O Lord, our God, we give you thanks for every talent we possess; for healthy bodies which enable us to do a good day's work; for skilful fingers and clear vision; for brains to work things out and opportunities to use our skills. Help us to use these gifts wisely for Jesus Christ's sake. *Amen.*

Closing prayer No. 84

Autumn (1)

The last Thursday in October in the Somerset village of Hinton St. George is 'Punkie Night' when children parade with their punkies—hollowed out mangel-wurzels with a candle inside.

Elsewhere such celebrations are kept for Hallowe'en, the evening of 31st October. They may go by a different name as in Newcastle-upon-Tyne where turnip lanterns are carried on 'Dookie Apple Night'. In North America much larger lanterns are made with pumpkins.

The short period from 31st October to 2nd November is sometimes called Hallowtide. It was once the pagan festival of Samain (Summer's end), the Celtic New Year which began on 1st November. Ghosts and spirits were believed to be about and one had to beware.

The Christian Church turned this old festival into a special festival of remembrance, offering prayers for all the saints on 1st November, which is All Saints' Day, or All Hallows, and remembering the rest of the dead on 2nd November, which is All Souls' Day.

In later years it became the custom on Hallowe'en to beware not only of spirits and ghosts but witches and all sorts of other strange powers. Great bonfires, known in some parts as *teanlas*, tindles or tandles, were lit on the hilltops as people sought to drive all evil forces away from their land.

Today Hallowe'en may be a time for fun rather than fear. Few people believe in evil spirits. Christian people believe that the love of God is stronger than all other powers.

Bible Reading: Romans 8: 38–39

We remember with thankfulness, O God, the saints who have set us an example and all the ordinary folk who have served you faithfully in all ages. Help us to follow their example and to know for ourselves your might, your love and your peace. *Amen.*

Closing prayer No. 74

Autumn (2)

Gradually the lighting of huge bonfires on Hallowe'en died out. People lit them on 5th November instead! These were not fires to drive away evil spirits: they were lit by people who just wanted to enjoy making a good blaze.

If any excuse were needed it was provided by Parliament, which decreed that 5th November should be kept as a public holiday in thankfulness for the escape that Members had had from being blown sky-high by Guy Fawkes with his barrels of gunpowder stacked in the cellars below.

Guy Fawkes was arrested and, with the other conspirators, put to death. But he was not forgotten, as the old rhyme reminds us.

> *Remember, remember, the fifth of November,*
> *Gunpowder, treason and plot.*
> *I see no reason why gunpowder treason*
> *Should ever be forgot.*

So many people made their effigies of Guy Fawkes and burned them on their bonfires. Children made Guys to display on street corners, asking passers-by for a 'penny for the Guy'. The money was usually spent on fireworks and the Guy ended up in the middle of the bonfire.

Nowadays fewer people have their own bonfires and fireworks, preferring to join in special displays which are held on or near 5th November. They may not be quite as much fun as letting off your own fireworks but they save a lot of accidents that happen every year because of carelessness or the misuse of fireworks.

In all our enjoyment, O Lord, help us
To be sensible in everything we do;
To show consideration toward other people;
To be an example to young children;
To avoid any form of cruelty or harm;
To heed the good advice of others.
O Lord, hear our prayer. *Amen.*

Closing prayer No. 101

Autumn (3)

REMEMBRANCE   *Poppies*

During the early part of November, imitation poppies are offered for sale on shop counters, in clubs and by sellers in the streets. They are sold in readiness for Remembrance Sunday, the second Sunday in November, when people not only wear poppies but lay wreaths of poppies on war memorials or plant crosses in gardens of remembrance. It is done to remember men and women who died fighting for their country in two World Wars.

Why poppies? That goes back to the days of World War I, when red poppies flowered where the fighting took place in Belgium and a Canadian medical officer, Colonel John McCrae, wrote a simple verse:

> *In Flanders' fields the poppies blow*
> *Beneath the crosses, row on row*
> *That mark our place, and in the sky*
> *The larks, still bravely singing, fly*
> *Scarce heard amid the guns below.*

The verse captured the imagination of many people, including those in a new organization founded in 1921 and called The British Legion. To raise money to help disabled ex-servicemen, the Legion sold poppies. That first Poppy Day raised £106,000.

Nowadays the poppy appeal raises about £3 million. Millions of poppies and many thousands of wreaths and crosses are made in the Legion's own factory at Richmond, which employs 140 disabled men, 50 of whom assemble the poppies in their own homes.

So people buy their poppies in remembrance of those who died but also to help disabled people today.

Almighty and merciful God, we remember those who have been disabled while serving their country in the armed forces, whether in war or while on other duties. May they find help in overcoming their difficulties through the care and helpfulness of others. *Amen.*

Closing prayer No. 65

Autumn (4)

The Royal British Legion

At 11 a.m. on Remembrance Sunday people stand in silence for two minutes in churches and at war memorials to remember those who died in two World Wars. Often the services include the words of R. L. Binyon:

> *They shall not grow old as we that are left grow old:*
> *Age shall not weary them, nor the years condemn.*
> *At the going down of the sun and in the morning*
> *We will remember them.   We will remember them.*

But remembering those who died is only part of the story. There are many who think it more important to remember and help those who live and still suffer as a result of fighting for their country.

After World War I many local groups were formed to help those in need or to provide meeting places for ex-servicemen. But little groups did not have much power to help and Field Marshal Earl Haig, who had been the wartime Commander-in-Chief, suggested that they unite to form one large organization. They did and the British Legion was born. Fifty years later, in 1971, it became The Royal British Legion.

The Legion has always aimed to keep alive the memory of those who died but it is also determined to remember those who live and to offer whatever help it can to ex-servicemen and women in need. Throughout Britain and overseas there are local branches and clubs. There are homes for the old and sick, employment and seaside holidays for the badly disabled, as well as legal help and assistance of many kinds.

We will remember them! The Royal British Legion most certainly does.

Almighty God, we remember before you all who care for the disabled and those who are troubled in body or mind. Grant them wisdom, guidance, patience and a sense of satisfaction as they help those in need, for whom we also ask your blessing. *Amen.*

Benediction No. 104

ST. CLEMENT'S DAY   'Old Clem'

People of most trades and professions have their own special or patron saint, who is supposed to look after their interests. November 23rd is the day when blacksmiths have remembered their patron saint, St. Clement.

Rather disrespectfully, perhaps, St. Clement was often referred to as 'Old Clem'. Charles Dickens, in *Great Expectations*, refers to a blacksmiths' song about 'Old Clem'. 'Thus you were to hammer boys round—Old Clem! With a thump and a sound—Old Clem! Beat it out, beat it out—Old Clem! With a clink for the stout—Old Clem! Blow the fire, blow the fire—Old Clem!' No doubt the big hammer came down on the anvil each time the words Old Clem occurred.

On St. Clement's Day the blacksmiths would often have a noisy time, putting gunpowder into holes in their anvils and exploding it with sparks from their hammers. In some places they dressed a man up to represent 'Old Clem' and went out begging.

But why St. Clement as their patron saint? According to a legend (for which there appears to be no foundation) he is said to have been put to death by being tied to an anchor and dropped into the sea. And since anchors were made by blacksmiths St. Clement became their patron saint.

Very little is known about St. Clement. He was one of the earliest Popes, living about the end of the first century A.D. Some believe that he may be the Clement referred to by St. Paul in a letter.

Bible Reading: Philippians 4: 1–3

He was certainly considered a faithful servant of God and worthy to be called a saint.

We remember before you, O God, those who have been faithful servants of yours in past days and all who have helped to teach others what is good, and true and right. Thank you for these. *Amen.*

Closing prayer No. 56

Christmastide (1)

An important Jewish festival falling in December is Chanukkah. The date varies from year to year because Jewish festivals are based on the phases of the moon and thus it may fall early in the month or later.

Chanukkah is a festival which lasts for eight days and celebrates a great victory won over 2,000 years ago. The Holy Land was then under the control of Antiochus of Syria, who decreed that the Jews must not worship the Lord God. A brave fight was put up by Mattathias the priest and then by his son Judah the Maccabee ('the Hammer').

After three years Judah was successful and led his army into Jerusalem. Pagan objects were thrown out of the temple and the House of God cleansed. Only enough pure oil was found to keep the temple lamp alight for one day but by a miracle it kept burning for eight. So the festival of Chanukkah is an eight-day celebration.

In the synagogue, as well as in the home, a special eight-branched candle-stick is used. A candle is lit on the first evening and an additional one each evening until on the eighth evening all eight are lit.

As each candle is lit, prayers are recited: 'Blessed art thou, O Lord our God, who hast sanctified us by thy commandments and hast commanded us to kindle the light of Chanukkah.' 'Blessed art thou, O Lord our God, who achieved miracles for our forefathers in days of old at this season.' In the daily service a special prayer is spoken and Psalms 113 to 118 are recited. Here is one of them.

Bible Reading: Psalm 117

Almighty God, we thank you for your great love for us. We thank you for the example of your servants of old who stood bravely for the right and remained true to your holy laws. Help us also to be strong and courageous to do your will at all times and to resist all that is false, unclean or evil in your sight. *Amen.*

Closing prayer No. 71

Christmastide (2)

December 21st is celebrated in the Christian Church as the feast of
St. Thomas, one of the disciples of Jesus. It so happens that
December 21st is also the shortest day of the year. There is an old
rhyme:

> *St. Thomas Gray, St. Thomas Gray;*
> *Longest night and shortest day.*

In some places, St. Thomas's Day is the day on which people
traditionally give to charity. In Warwickshire, for example, it was
the custom for poor people to call on the farmers to collect flour
for making their Christmas bread. In return the farmers were
given a sprig of holly. This custom was known as 'a'corning' or
'Thomassing'.

Times have changed but there are still plenty of people in need
of help and the Christmas season is one of goodwill, when many
people are prepared to put their hands in their pockets or open
their purses to help those in need. We do not have to look far to
find Christmas cards that are sold in aid of a charity, stockings or
collecting boxes in shops, and all sorts of other appeals.

Christmas is also a time when people remember services that
others have given them. Boxing Day was the day in the past when
priests opened the alms boxes in the churches and gave the money
to the poor. It became the day when people gave gifts of money to
those who had been of service to them during the year—servants,
postmen, dustmen and paper-boys.

It is fitting that we should thank God for all the blessings of
Christmas by remembering what we have received and showing
our thankfulness by our generosity to others.

Bible Reading: I John 4: 11–16

Help us to remember, O God, how much you loved us to send your
Son into the world. Help us always to be thankful to you and to
show our thanks by loving others and helping those in need. *Amen.*

Closing prayer No. 68

Christmastide (3)

Christmas Tree

During the days just before Christmas, many people will be setting up Christmas trees as part of their decorations. Most of them will be decorated with coloured lights, gay ornaments and tinsel. Large trees may have gifts tied to the branches: others may have presents stowed beneath them.

Around the room will be paper and foil decorations and other things which will make the house look as gay as possible. Perhaps there will be sprigs of holly and mistletoe, reminders of a bygone age when all the decorations consisted of greenery such as holly, ivy, mistletoe, rosemary or bay. In those days too there were lots of superstitions about the greenery and when and how it should be removed.

Christmas trees were set up in Germany long ago but were not seen in Britain until certain German princesses introduced them. They became very popular after Prince Albert, the husband of Queen Victoria, had one at Windsor.

Nowadays there are few towns where Christmas trees with coloured lights are not to be seen in public squares and open spaces. Christmas visitors to London often go to Trafalgar Square to see the huge tree that stands there, a gift each year since 1946 of the people of Oslo, Norway.

It is said that once the German reformer Martin Luther compared the twinkling lights of the candles on the Christmas tree with the stars that must have shone in the sky over Bethlehem on the night that Christ was born.

Bible Reading: St. Luke 2: 8–16

Today we do not have twinkling candles on the tree but it would be nice to think that the lights, the presents and perhaps a star on top might remind us of Jesus Christ, whose birth we celebrate at Christmas.

Help us to remember, O God, that we celebrate Christmas because of the birth of Jesus Christ. May the whole of Christmas be a reminder of your great love for us. *Amen.*

Closing prayer No. 79

Christmastide (4)

Most people enjoy a good sing and Christmas provides an opportunity for us to do so as we join with others to sing the familiar Christmas carols.

Many of today's Christmas carols are hymns of praise and thankfulness. The original carols, taken from the French word *carole* had no religious associations. They were dances with singing used on joyful occasions.

Most of our Christmas carols tell part of the Bible story of the birth of Jesus. Here is one of the birth stories. No doubt you can think of several carols which refer to this.

Bible Reading: St. Luke 2: 1–7

Just before Christmas, carol services are held in most churches and chapels. One of the best known is the Festival of Nine Lessons and carols held on Christmas Eve at King's College, Cambridge. Many churches also use this service. Some have special services of 'Carols by Candlelight'.

But carols are frequently sung in the streets too. Parties of carol singers are a familiar sight just before Christmas. In the past carol singers were known as Waits. They used lanterns to light their way and sang outside houses, where they received gifts of food, drink or money for their singing. Nowadays most street carol parties go out to collect money for well-known charities. Quite a lot of money is raised in this way.

Christmas is, after all, something to sing about and our happy singing can often bring cheer to others, quite apart from the cheer we can bring to deserving causes by the money we raise.

We thank you, God our Father, for the coming of Jesus Christ into the world and for all that his coming means to us. We pray that the joy in our hearts may be passed on to others so that Christmas is a time of happiness and goodwill. *Amen.*

Benediction No. 92

Christmastide (5)

Plum Pudding and Mince Pies

Many people associate Christmas with feasting. In many homes Christmas dinner is a family occasion, often with turkey or other poultry and lots of trimmings, followed by Christmas pudding. Later in the day comes the Christmas cake, mince pies and lots of other goodies.

The feasting is an old tradition dating back long before Christmas came to be celebrated. The Romans had a winter festival called Saturnalia, which included feasting and this continued when the Christian Church decided to celebrate Christmas at the same time. In Tudor England, Christmas feasts sometimes lasted for eight or nine hours!

Served with the meat was a dish called plum porridge, consisting of meat, broth, breadcrumbs, raisins, currants, prunes and spices. It was eaten with a spoon. Later it was made much stiffer and became the Christmas Pudding which is still enjoyed today.

Mince pies were also different from ours. Originally they were oval or oblong and filled with minced meat and spices. They represented the cradle in which Jesus lay and sometimes had a figure of Jesus in them, which was removed before the Mince Pie or Christmas Pie was eaten. Later the meat in the pie became the mince-meat we know today, consisting of fruit and peel.

No doubt this year there will be many people who will feast with their families but there will also be those who will have other thoughts. In many places, Christian people will be arranging Christmas dinners in church halls to which they will invite old and lonely people. Christmas is a time to remember other people, especially those in need of help.

We remember, O God, those people who feel lonely at Christmas time and those who will not enjoy good food or family gatherings. Bless all who are able to help them and open *our* hearts so that we may do what *we* can; through Jesus Christ our Lord. *Amen.*

Closing prayer No. 52

3 For our enjoyment

These nine themes are about those things which give enjoyment in many different ways, in the world of entertainment, sport, literature, the arts and other fields.

Enjoyment	*Entertainment*	*Music*
Sport	*Out of doors*	*Poetry and books*
Art	*Craftsmanship*	*Travel*

Some of the themes lend themselves to the use of additional material. *Music* and *Art*, for example, could include aural or visual aids as appropriate. *Craftsmanship* (3) could be linked with work done in school on stained glass.

Some of the *Sport* and *Out of doors* topics may best be taken as individual seasonal stories or linked with school activities, e.g. *Out of doors* (1) Cycling related to a Cycling Proficiency course held in school.

Enjoyment (1)

Some pleasant forms of entertainment, many of them rather quaint, are those customs which have come down to us from the distant past, many of them held at the beginning of May.

On 1st May, at Padstow, Cornwall, there is the Hobby-horse festival. The 'Oss is a strange creature, his body hidden by a six-foot hoop covered by a tarpaulin. He wears a mask and a tall pointed hat. His attendants include the Teaser who carries a padded club.

The 'Obby 'Oss chases the women, catching one every now and then under his tarpaulin, which is supposed to bring her luck. From time to time he sinks to the ground as though dying, then suddenly springs to life again. By mid afternoon the procession reaches the Maypole in the market place and meets up with a second 'Oss, known as the 'Blue 'Oss' or the 'Temperance 'Oss'. Together they dance round the Maypole.

There is a rather different Hobby-horse at Minehead, Somerset, on the same day. This is the Sailors' Horse who lives on the Quayside and looks quite different from the Padstow one. May Day is celebrated in many other places with maypole dancing, crowning the May Queen and the appearance of strange characters such as Jack-in-the-Green, a man in a frame covered with greenery and representing Spring. A week later, on May 8th, there is the well-known Furry Day at Helston, Cornwall, with its dancing in the streets.

All these have their origin in ancient spring festivals and the Roman festival dedicated to Flora, the goddess of flowers and fruit.

We thank you, O God, for the many old customs and forms of entertainment which bring us pleasure. Help us to find pleasure not just in watching others but in taking part ourselves in activities where we work together with others. *Amen.*

Benediction No. 104

Enjoyment (2)

FUN OF THE FAIR   *Nottingham Goose Fair*

Lots of people enjoy a visit to a fairground, to enjoy the thrill of
the rides, the skill or chance of the sideshows, the music and lights,
hot dogs and candyfloss and all the other things that help to make
the 'fun of the fair'.

Nowadays fairs are all or mostly fun and amusement. At one
time the amusement was just a small part of a trade or business fair
at which people bought and sold all sorts of things. Such fairs were
held long ago. We can read of them in the Old Testament.

Bible Reading: Ezekiel 27: 12–24 (*or part thereof*)

Fairs were always held at the same time of year in a particular
town and sometimes were for trade in one particular commodity.
The Nottingham Goose Fair is now a fun fair but it was once a real
goose fair to which thousands of geese were driven from the
surrounding countryside to be sold on the fairground. It was
moved in 1928 from the market place to a piece of open ground
about a mile away that is known as the Forest. In the Middle Ages
it lasted for twenty-one days. Now it is just for three days, beginning on the first Thursday in October—and there isn't a goose to
be seen!

Elsewhere there are horse fairs and sheep fairs; there are hiring
or mop fairs; there are charter fairs once given a special charter, or
permission, by the king; and there are fairs with a very interesting
history to them.

Some fairs are no longer held. They were popular but became
too rowdy. We know today how the fun and enjoyment of a lot of
people can be spoiled by rowdy, nasty or selfish behaviour.

O God, help us to learn how to enjoy ourselves without spoiling
the enjoyment of others. Make us thoughtful, considerate, courteous and unselfish as you have taught us in your word. *Amen.*

Closing prayer No. 58

104

Enjoyment (3)

Steam Engine Rallies

Every summer something like a million people visit one of the steam engine rallies that are held in many parts of Britain. They go to see great iron monsters that once used the roads, steam traction engines, steam tractors, steam rollers, steam wagons and the magnificent showmen's steam road locomotives.

Years ago people were pleased to see the back of these slow, smelly, dirty, noisy machines as much cleaner and faster petrol or diesel engined vehicles took their place. But once they were no longer there people began to remember them with affection. Old engines were rescued from the scrapyards and from all sorts of odd corners where they were rusting away. They were cleaned up, painted and polished with loving care and proudly exhibited at steam engine rallies.

Behind the steam engines were the men who had ideas for using them. John Fowler, for example, who was born on 11th July, 1826, was a Wiltshire man who invented the first workable steam powered plough. He established a large engineering works at Leeds, which produced some fine steam engines.

Among these were the showmen's road locomotives which pulled trains of trailers by road from one fairground to another, there providing power for the rides and generating electricity for lighting. The last of these, the *Supreme*, No. 20223, was built in 1934. After only six years it was cut down for heavy haulage and retired in 1947. Now restored, it is regarded as the finest road locomotive ever built.

Times change; fashions change; people change. When all else changes it is comforting to recall that God remains the same.

Bible Reading: Psalm 102: 24–27

O God, from age to age the same, we remember how you have helped people in past years and we pray that you will help us in the same way today. *Amen.*

Closing prayer No. 56

Enjoyment (4)

Cecil Sharp

Bible Reading: Jeremiah 31: 3–4

From earliest times, when people have been happy they have danced and when they have wanted to be entertained they have watched others dancing. And each group of people has developed its own form of dancing. Think of the delicate body movements of India, the boisterous dances of Russia, the square dances of America and the Highland Fling of Scotland.

Each age, too, has its own form of dancing. People of old enjoyed Morris dancing or danced around their maypoles; at Queen Elizabeth's court they danced in pairs; in the nineteenth century ballroom dancing became popular; whilst more recently there have been Rock-'n'-Roll, twisting, shaking and others.

But many people still enjoy the old country dancing, danced in circles or lines, each dance having its own particular steps and formations. *Brighton Camp*, *Cumberland Reel* and many others are frequently enjoyed.

For this we are indebted very largely to Cecil Sharp, who first saw Morris Dancing at Headington, Oxford on Boxing Day 1899. He thought what a pity it would be if old dances were allowed to be forgotten. So he began collecting information about dances from many parts of the country and kept a record of all he found. He died on 23rd June, 1924, but his work is continued by the English Folk Dance and Song Society and groups of dancers, both young and old, are able to enjoy these old folk or country dances.

We thank you, God our Father, for all the enjoyment we can find in dancing and in watching the dances of others. Help us always to find enjoyment in the entertainment provided by others but teach us also the art of doing things for ourselves, using the gifts you have given us. *Amen.*

Benediction No. 105

Enjoyment (5)

THE TOWN GOES GAY   *Carnival Time*

Many towns have their carnival day when the town goes gay and lots of people enjoy all the fun and amusements provided. The streets may be decorated with flags before the day, on which the main event may be the carnival procession of floats which winds its way through the town. In pride of place on one of the floats will be the Carnival Queen, elected beforehand, together with her maids of honour.

Lots of people take part in the carnival. Local organizations, churches, business people and others decorate lorries and mount tableaux on them. Bands march in the procession; cycles are decorated; and people along the route may well collect money for some charity. After the procession there is often fun in a local park or maybe a firework display.

Carnivals are not new: they go way back into history. The ancient Egyptians had carnivals. So did the Greeks and the Romans. Carnivals were popular in Europe long ago, and they have remained so in the period before Lent. People went gay before that period of forty days when so much was not allowed.

One of the biggest carnivals to be held in Britain in recent years is the West Indian carnival at Notting Hill, London, where people enjoy many of the customs from the Caribbean, the dressing up, the steel bands and all the gaiety and laughter. In the Caribbean it is held before Lent but London weather at that time is not carnival weather and so the summer is a much better time.

An opportunity to unwind or 'let off steam' is good, and carnival time is often an excuse for doing so.

We thank you, God our Father, for those opportunities we have to really enjoy ourselves and when we can forget the business and tensions of everyday things. Help us to relax, to enjoy ourselves and in quieter moments to enjoy the peace of your presence. *Amen.*

Benediction No. 97

Ententainment (1)

Nowadays if we wish to see a play or some other kind of performance we go to a theatre, where the scenery offers an attractive
background to the acting. Some theatre companies have travelling actors and actresses who perform in schools with a minimum
of scenery.

Long ago, before there were theatres as we know them, plays
were performed by strolling players, who went from place to place,
performing in inn-yards or other suitable areas.

Christmas entertainment was often performed by Mummers.
There were several forms of the Mummers' play, with a hero such
as St. George or Robin Hood, and evil characters such as a dragon
or a Turkish knight. Usually there was a mock fight in which the
hero triumphed. No words were written down but the stories
remained much the same from year to year.

Other popular plays several hundred years ago were Mystery or
Miracle Plays. These were usually performed about Whitsuntide.
Mystery plays were on New Testament subjects and Miracle plays
were based upon stories from the scriptures or church history. The
town guilds, the organizations governing the workmen of that
time, were each responsible for a particular story. They were then
put together in a kind of pageant and performed without scenery
on a cart which could be moved from one part of town to another
or on staging built against a wall.

Although these plays belong to the past, some are still performed today at festivals, notably in Chester, Coventry and York.
They were, on the whole, simple Bible plays, rather like the
Nativity Plays performed in church halls or schools at Christmastide.

We thank you, O God, for the pleasure that is given to us by people
who act in plays or entertain us in other ways. We thank you, too,
for any talent we may have and ask that we find ways to use it for
the pleasure of others. *Amen.*

Closing prayer No. 61

Entertainment (2)

Lilian Baylis

Lilian Baylis, who was born in Marylebone, London on 9th May, 1874, was to become one of the really great characters of the English theatre.

At the age of seventeen she went with her family to South Africa but returned a few years later to help her aunt manage the Royal Victoria Hall, a theatre in London's Waterloo Road. Lilian became manager of the theatre in 1912 when her aunt died.

It was a struggle to find the money that was needed. Lilian begged from anyone she could and she cut expenses whenever possible but she was determined to make something good of the theatre, which was to become known as the *Old Vic*.

Perhaps her determination was linked with her strong sense of religion. She was a high church Anglican and always attended Mass on her way to the theatre. Perhaps it was partly her desire to give working-class people something good.

Within a few years the Old Vic had become a centre for the performance of Shakespeare's plays and opera in English.

Not content with that, Lilian Baylis bought and rebuilt the Sadler's Wells Theatre in north London, where she formed opera and ballet companies.

Lilian Baylis died in 1937 but she had laid great foundations. Her Sadler's Wells opera company was to become the English National Opera and the Sadler's Wells Ballet became the Royal Ballet. Moreover, her great love, the Old Vic became the home of the National Theatre Company from 1963 to 1976, when it left the Old Vic for the new South Bank Theatres.

We thank you, O God, for all who have given us the theatre and its many forms of entertainment; for opera, ballet and plays of many kinds; for actors and actresses with their varied talents; for musicians and dancers, and for all who design scenery or costumes. Accept our thanks, O God. *Amen.*

Benediction No. 96

Entertainment (3)

Benjamin Britten

On 7th June, 1945, the curtain was raised for the first performance of a new English opera, *Peter Grimes*, at Sadler's Wells. The cast had been working under great difficulty in war-time Britain and it took great faith to produce the opera only a month after the war in Europe had ended. But it was a huge success, a triumph for the players and for the composer, Benjamin Britten.

Britten was born in Lowestoft, Suffolk, appropriately on the feast day of St. Cecilia, patron saint of musicians, 22nd November, 1913. His musical family and his associations with the church no doubt influenced his music, much of which is for works of a religious nature.

Benjamin Britten became associated with the town of Aldeburgh where, with a friend, Peter Pears, he planned the first Aldeburgh Festival held in 1948. This has become a popular annual event.

It was in Aldeburgh church, after listening to a children's concert, that Britten decided to write something for children to sing and play in church. The result was *Noye's Fludde*, a medieval Chester Miracle Play set to music and telling the story of Noah in a moving way with many kinds of music, comedy and drama, and opportunities for the audience or congregation to join in the hymns.

Through his many kinds of music—operas, cantatas, poems set to music, music for trained choirs, music for amateurs and for children, some of it unusual but lively and inventive, Benjamin Britten has contributed greatly to the entertainment and pleasure of many people.

Almighty God, we thank you
For all that is provided for our entertainment;
For performances in which we can take part ourselves;
For those when we can sit and enjoy the art of others;
And for all who have composed or produced them.
Praise be to you, O God. *Amen.*

Closing prayer No. 55

Entertainment (4)

Punch and Judy

Some very enjoyable entertainment is that provided not by actors and actresses but by puppets. They are, of course, controlled by people and they need human voices but it is always the puppets that steal the show. Their operators are seldom seen.

There are various kinds of puppet but those most commonly used are glove puppets worked by people from below and string puppets whose movements depend upon someone above working the strings attached to their limbs. Nowadays we are familiar with many puppets which feature in television programmes. [*Refer to current ones.*]

Perhaps the most familiar puppet shows enjoyed by children are the Punch and Judy shows, for they have been around for a long while. The first recorded Punch and Judy show in London was over three hundred years ago, on 26th May, 1662. In Europe Punch was known even before that under such names as Pulcinella or Punchinello.

Punch is always popular because he is able to do such outrageous things and get away with them. He can beat his wife and throw the baby out of the window yet escape from the policeman and the hangman, thanks to the warnings that the children are encouraged to call out. There is lots of fun and enjoyment in the rough and tumble and hitting with sticks, which puppets can do but real people are not allowed to!

It is good sometimes to be able to escape into a world that is not real, as long as we remember that we have to 'come down to earth' and live as sensible people who have learned the value of keeping the rules of our community and God's world.

Thank you, God, for all those things we enjoy and especially those which help us to escape from everyday things. Teach us also to escape into your presence and find the strength we need for ordinary things in the everyday world. *Amen.*

Closing prayer No. 63

Entertainment (5)

Pantomime and Peter Pan

One very popular form of entertainment usually performed about Christmas time is the pantomime. Though not quite as popular as it once was, it often forms part of a family's Christmas entertainment.

The story of pantomime goes back a long way. The Romans had a form of pantomime in which all the characters wore masks and the whole performance was in mime—hence the name.

Nowadays the British pantomime is anything but mime. It has a traditional story running through it but the producers can make it into whatever they want it to be. Usually there is colourful scenery and costume, singing, dancing, clowning and joking. Often the audience is encouraged to take part.

One of the most popular pantomimes is *Cinderella*, regarded by many actors as a 'lucky' one. *Robin Hood* and *Babes in the Wood* are not as popular with some actors, who think them 'unlucky'. Other well-loved pantomimes are *Aladdin*, *Mother Goose* and *Robinson Crusoe*.

Another show that is popular with children is *Peter Pan*, written by J. M. Barrie and first performed on 27th December, 1904. There were people who said it would never catch on but it has proved to be a great success and is produced year after year. Countless children have enjoyed seeing Peter Pan, Wendy, Captain Hook, the flying fairies and other characters such as the crocodile with a clock inside him.

We thank you, God our Father,
For entertainment which we can all enjoy;
For people who write and produce it for us;
For actors and actresses, singers and musicians;
For clowns and all who make us laugh;
For all who bring us entertainment;
Praise be to you, O God. *Amen.*

Benediction No. 105

Music (1)

PROMENADE CONCERTS   *Sir Henry Wood*

There are lots of people who enjoy a visit to a concert hall where they can sit quietly, carried away by the music of a fine orchestra or the playing of a soloist or small group of musicians. Many towns and cities have their own orchestras and invite famous soloists to play with them. The Halle Orchestra in Manchester has been playing regularly there since 1857.

For Londoners and visitors to the capital, one of the highlights of the year is the series of Promenade Concerts given in the Royal Albert Hall. These have an informal atmosphere. People can sit in the seats or they can listen from the 'promenade', the floor in the centre of the hall, where they can stroll about, stand or, if there is room, sit on the floor.

The Promenade Concerts were first directed by Sir Henry Wood, a conductor and composer who did a lot to popularize orchestral music toward the end of last century. The first Promenade Concert was held on 6th October, 1895, in the Queen's Hall and they continued to be held there until that building was bombed during World War II, after which they were transferred to the Royal Albert Hall. Sir Henry Wood died on 19th August, 1944 but the 'Proms' are still referred to by his name and a bust of Sir Henry is displayed at the concerts.

Most of the music at the 'Proms' is played by an orchestra—a large number of musicians playing a variety of instruments under the direction of a conductor who ensures that each player plays as he should in harmony with the others to produce music that is pleasing and uplifting.

O God our Father, as we give thanks for all the instruments of the orchestra which blend to give such fine music, we pray that we may learn in this world how to play our part to the best of our ability, working in harmony with others under your direction until the world becomes a more pleasing place. *Amen.*

Closing prayer No. 90

Music (2)

OH, LISTEN TO THE BAND!   *Harry Mortimer*

There is something stirring about the music of a brass band, whether it be the sound of the band of the Salvation Army, the local band playing at a fête or the 'big sound' of one of the nationally famous bands.

Brass bands became popular over a hundred years ago, particularly in the north of England, where working men formed bands as a spare time hobby. Some of those names are household names today: Fodens Motor Works Band, Black Dyke Mills Band, Grimethorpe Colliery Band and others are composed of workers from those places.

One man who has had a great influence on brass bands is Harry Mortimer, whose father bought him a cornet in 1909 when he was seven. In later years Harry played in brass bands as well as being a trumpet player in symphony orchestras. He became band supervisor for the B.B.C. and he conducted the bands on the first night that brass bands ever played in one of the Promenade Concerts in 1975.

Nowadays many schools have their own bands and some of the most promising players are chosen for the National Youth Brass Band. Many of them and others from youth bands may also take part in the National Brass Band Championships which arouse a great deal of enthusiasm amongst brass banders.

For most bands the many competitions are important and bandsmen will play as though their lives depended upon the result. But they enjoy it! Banding is real fun for the many thousands throughout Britain who play and it provides a lot of enjoyment for supporters too.

O God, as we work for the coming of your kingdom upon earth, give us enthusiasm for our work and enjoyment in everything we do. Help us to forget ourselves and work well with others until we have done all that can be expected of us. *Amen.*

Closing prayer No. 77

Music (3)

The ambition of most recording stars or groups is no doubt to get to the top of the 'Pop' Charts and perhaps get a Golden Disc which is awarded for any recording that sells over a million copies.

Some recordings sell many more than that. One of the best selling records, if not *the* best seller, is *White Christmas*, sung by Bing Crosby and first sold in 1942. It has been estimated that it has sold over twenty-five million copies.

The song, written by the well-known American composer Irving Berlin, appeared in a film entitled 'Holiday Inn', starring Bing Crosby and Fred Astaire. Based upon the four main American festivals, there was a song for each but *I'm Dreaming of a White Christmas* was more popular than the others. Even now, after all these years, it remains one of the most popular and well-loved Christmas songs. Many artistes have sung it but the original recording by Bing Crosby is still a favourite.

Bing Crosby was one of the few singers who was able to keep on top of his profession for the whole of his life. He was a popular singer in the 1930s and he was giving concerts up to the time he died on 14th October, 1977, at the age of 73. His recordings were also still frequently being played.

Like many other popular singers, he was never regarded as a great singer in the pure musical sense. In fact he was affectionately known by many as 'Old Groaner'. But through his singing, his concerts, his film roles and his recordings he gave lots of pleasure to millions of people.

O God, our Father, we thank you
For popular music of many kinds which we can enjoy;
For entertainers of stage and screen;
For musical programmes on radio and television;
For recorded music to enjoy in our homes.
Make us appreciative of all that gives us pleasure today, and
   give us thankful hearts. *Amen.*

Closing prayer No. 87

Music (4)

Louis Armstrong was born in New Orleans in the deep south of the United States in 1900. As a boy 'Little Louie' sold coal from a coal cart until he was taken into a Waif's home at the age of twelve. It was there that his musical career began for he was given lessons on the cornet. A few years later he went to Chicago where his talents were developed and in that city, at the age of twenty-five, a Chicago newspaper advertisement billed him as 'The World's Greatest Jazz Cornetist'.

In the years that followed, Louis Armstrong, or 'Satchmo' as he was called, became world famous firstly as a cornetist and then as a trumpeter with a jazz style of his own. Many people were delighted by his playing, his rough singing voice and his cheerful personality.

Louis Armstrong was a born actor and a magnificent showman. There was nothing he loved more than to be in the spotlight, when he gave everything he had in his performance. He had all the qualities needed by a jazz musician and he used them to the full.

At his funeral in New York on 9th July, 1971, the world of jazz mourned the loss of one whose whole life had been music. One of his last 'hits' *What a wonderful world* was televised with Louis pictured against a background of flowers and wild life, his cheerful face and broad smile telling clearly that for him it was indeed a wonderful world—a world that he had enriched by his musical talent.

Bible Reading: Psalm 98: 1–6 (or 9)

What a wonderful world! It is yours, O God, for you have created it and put in it so much that is lovely for us to enjoy. We join with the whole of creation to praise your holy Name. Praise be to you, O God. *Amen.*

Benediction No. 94

Music (5)

Negro spirituals

Some of the most moving hymns and songs are those which are sung by people who are sad or troubled. We can imagine the feelings of the Jews who were captives in Babylon as we read this psalm:

Bible Reading: Psalm 137: 1–6

At the beginning of last century, the negro slaves in America must have felt much the same. They or their ancestors had been carried away from their homes in Africa: they were treated badly: they had little to hope for. Then came the Christian ministers to hold 'Camp Meetings' in tents, with the gospel message that God cared for them.

Even the liveliest of the hymns did not seem to satisfy these coloured folk with their emotional feelings and natural sense of rhythm. So they made up their own rough verses with choruses in which people would join, often shouting 'Amen' or 'Hallelujah!' Railways were then built and suggested a means of escape. We can imagine how they rose to *'De gospel train am a-comin'* with its chorus 'Get on board little children, There's room for many a more'.

Sometimes Bible stories were retold in song—songs like *Were you there when they crucified my Lord?* Sometimes there was the sense of wonder that God actually cared for them when few other people seemed to do so. Imagine how they would sing *He's got the whole world in his hands* to the clapping of hands and with a sense of joy that *they* were included in the message.

Today these negro spirituals are found in hymn books and sung by choirs—still with a lot of feeling for the message they tell.

We thank you, God our Father that you have the whole world in your hands. Grant us the joy of knowing that we are your children and that we are always in your loving care. *Amen.*

Benediction No. 97

Sport (1)

Once the fine weather comes there are many people who enjoy a pleasant game of cricket, whether it be a simple match on the village green or a first-class county match. But the matches that arouse the greatest interest are the Test Matches, especially those between England and Australia, which have been played now for over one hundred years.

The first Test Match was held at Melbourne, Australia, and was a three-day match beginning on 15th March, 1877. Australia won by 45 runs. The first Test Match in England was held at the Oval in 1880.

It was two years later, in a Test Match played in England in 1882, that the Australians won a surprising victory. The *Sporting Times* reported a mock death of English cricket and said that the ashes had been taken to Australia. From that time to this the trophy for each England-Australia Test series is 'The Ashes', which of course do not exist.

There have been many memorable people and occasions. Don Bradman (Australia) scored 5,028 runs in 52 Tests; Jim Laker (England) 'won' the 1956 match at Old Trafford by taking 19 Australian wickets for only 90 runs. They are but two.

Test matches nowadays are played between other countries too, New Zealand, India, Pakistan, the West Indies with some of the liveliest and most exciting cricket coming from the matches involving the West Indies.

One of the enjoyments of cricket is that in general it is a good, clean game and without the rowdy behaviour associated with some sports.

Help us in the game of life. O Lord,
To learn and be willing to keep all the rules;
To avoid selfishness and work in co-operation with others;
To work hard, play fairly and live cleanly;
And to realize that much is expected of us. *Amen.*

Closing prayer No. 54

Sport (2)

Many people have a favourite football team which they support. Usually it is a team which plays nearby but some teams draw supporters from long distances. There are few soccer teams which have more supporters than Manchester United, a team which draws large crowds wherever it plays.

The popularity of Manchester United over a long period is undoubtedly due in a very large measure to one man, Sir Matt Busby. He became manager of United in 1945 and had a very successful team which won the F.A. Cup in 1948.

Busby knew, however, that an ageing team could not remain on top. New young players were needed. And so he trained up some good youngsters, who became known as the 'Busby Babes' and put them in the team. They were poised for greatness when tragedy struck. On 6th February, 1958, after a cup-tie in Belgrade, their plane crashed while taking off from Munich. Eight players and three club staff were killed. Matt Busby was very seriously injured.

Some thought it was the end of Manchester United but they were wrong. Matt Busby survived to build yet a third successful Manchester United, which won the F.A. Cup only five years later and the European Cup in 1968.

Matt Busby was awarded the C.B.E. in 1958 and was knighted in 1968. In football circles he was held in great respect and described as 'Britain's finest football ambassador'. He resigned as manager in 1969.

Sir Matt Busby was a most successful manager but the success of Manchester United is also due to good players who have learned to play together under the guidance of their manager.

Help us to remember, O God, that we are members of a great team of people who must learn to live and work together: and help us to accept the guidance of your Holy Spirit so that we may know how best to do it, following the pattern set by our Lord Jesus Christ. *Amen.*

Benediction No. 101

Sport (3)

Mark Spitz

The ambition of many of the top athletes of the world is to win a gold medal in the Olympic Games, for an Olympic gold medallist can say that he is world champion in his event.

Sometimes an athlete gains more than one 'gold' but few are ever likely to equal the record of Mark Spitz, who won no less than seven gold medals for swimming in the 1972 Olympics at Munich. Four were for individual successes and the other three for team relay events. It was a remarkable achievement by a man who has been described as 'one of the all-time great swimmers—if not *the* greatest swimmer ever'.

Olympic successes were the climax of a record-breaking career. At the age of ten Mark Spitz began breaking age-group records. In all he broke 32 world records and won many other awards including the title 'World Swimmer of the Year' 1967, 1971 and 1972. After the Munich Olympics he retired from competitive swimming.

Mark Spitz had the right physique for a swimmer but he also had to train regularly for hours at a time over a period of twelve years. And he had a good coach, Sherman Chavoor, to help him.

Hear what St. Paul had to say about training.

Bible Reading: I Corinthians 9: 24–27

In life we also need determination to succeed and we have to take strict control of ourselves as we train for the future. We are also wise if we listen to our 'coach'—none other than God himself—whose words come to us in all sorts of ways.

Help us, Almighty God, to be successful in life; help us to control our minds, our bodies and our actions; help us to listen for your words of guidance and inspiration; and so make us real champions in the cause of righteousness. *Amen.*

Closing prayer No. 67

Sport (4)

GYMNASTICS   *Olga Korbut and Nadia Comeneci*

When the Olympic Games opened in Montreal in the summer of 1976, people all over the world tuned in to find out how the athletes were faring in their favourite sports or how their country was faring in the medals table.

The track and field events are always sure of a good audience both in the Olympic stadium and by viewers at home. But there were very many in 1976 who were looking forward to the women's gymnastics, for interest had been aroused in the previous Games by Olga Korbut, a young Russian gymnast who had given a sparkling performance on the beam and in other gymnastic events. In the years between the games people of many countries had enjoyed her visits and applauded her achievements.

Now they wondered. Would the Russian team win this event? Or would some of the other countries in which gymnastics had become important be able to do even better? They were soon to discover who would steal the show. It was a fourteen-year old Romanian, Nadia Comeneci, who gave such an outstanding performance on the asymetric bars that she was awarded 10 points out of 10—the first perfect score in Olympic history. And she went on to score another six perfect scores of 10. She has been described as the 'nearest thing to perfection yet seen in gymnastics'.

For Nadia Comeneci it was a climax to years of training. Born in Romania on 12th November, 1961, she began gymnastic work when she was very young and she put everything she had into her training to achieve something many would have said was impossible—perfection.

Bible Reading: James 3: 2

Help us, God our Father, to strive to be perfect, so that our lives may be lived to your glory and we may give pleasure to those around us as we become the best we can be. *Amen.*

Closing prayer No. 68

Sport (5)

Stoke Mandeville Stadium

Each summer some 1,000 athletes, escorts and officials from about thirty countries gather in Aylesbury, Buckinghamshire for the International Stoke Mandeville Games. For the athletes, coming from as far afield as Argentina and Australia, Israel and Indonesia, this is the highlight of a life-time and especially so since all are disabled, being partially paralyzed and needing wheelchairs to move around.

The idea of using sport to help the paralyzed was that of Professor Sir Ludwig Guttman, who became President of the International Stoke Mandeville Games Federation. He was the person who aroused the interest of many others which led to the founding of the Games and the building of the Sports Stadium, which was opened by the Queen on 2nd August, 1972.

There are various events familiar in the world of sport—archery, fencing, shot putting—which can be done from a wheel-chair. Weightlifting is done lying under the weights instead of standing. Swimming events take place each evening. Bowls, table tennis and snooker require skills of a different kind. And for the all-rounder there is a Pentathlon.

Some of the excitement in the Games is provided in the games of Basketball, the players skilfully manoeuvring their wheel-chairs on the field.

During the year there are other events too, such as Basketball and Archery Championships held in other countries to which teams from the United Kingdom travel. There is many a disabled person who is thankful for the encouragement received by being shown just how many things it is possible for him to do.

Hear our prayer, O God, for all who are disabled and for all those who work with them to help and to encourage. Grant to each of them courage, determination, perseverance, patience and a very real sense of your presence. *Amen.*

Closing prayer No. 58

Out of doors (1)

British Cycle Federation

Early in August 1978 cyclists from all over the world gathered in Harrogate, Yorkshire, for a very special occasion. It was just one hundred years previously, on 6th August, 1878, that two organizations had been formed in Harrogate, the British Cycle Federation to govern cycle racing and the Cyclists' Touring Club for cyclists who wanted to enjoy riding for leisure.

To celebrate the occasion there were not only some of the 'big names' of the cycling world but also many different kinds of cycle from the vintage machines to the most modern of cycles.

During the past century, great numbers of people have enjoyed cycling, and especially the opportunities for taking to the country roads for a breath of fresh air and some good healthy exercise. Today with more and more motor traffic on the roads, cycling is not as common as it once was.

It is perhaps more important than ever that those who cycle should know all about the rules of the road and should ensure that their cycles are in tip-top working order. Young cyclists are encouraged not only to keep their machines clean but to check on brakes, lights and all that aids safety. Cycling proficiency training and testing is now carried out in many schools and certificates awarded to those who are successful.

But if this is necessary for cycling, is it not equally important for other things too? Are we just as careful in looking after ourselves? Do we keep our bodies fit and in good working order? Do we keep our minds clean? And our speech? And do we seek the help of God in learning the way to travel on the highway of life?

Bible Reading: I Timothy 4: 8–10

Teach me today, O God, to keep my body fit, my mind alert, my thinking clear, my actions wise, my words clean and my life pure; and help me to keep on the road that leads to you. *Amen.*

Closing prayer No. 62

Out of doors (2)

Uffa Fox

During the summer months lots of people like to take to the water for their recreation. Some like cruising along rivers and canals or putting out to sea in power boats. Others prefer to hoist sail and make the most of the wind.

The first yacht race recorded in Britain is mentioned in Pepys's Diary for 1st October, 1661 and was a race on the Thames between King Charles II and his brother. The king won. In those days yachting was strictly for the rich.

It was only after World War I that small yacht racing really began and then clubs in various parts of the country developed their own kind of boat which made competitions difficult. Many of these boats were heavy too. But in 1928 came a new dinghy, *Avenger,* which won 53 of her 57 races in her first season. Her designer was Uffa Fox, a man whose name is greatly respected among yachtsmen. It was he, in later years who designed many different kinds of boat.

Today dinghies are not too expensive and many youngsters are able to enjoy sailing. They soon realize how important it is to take great care of their boats and to keep fit themselves. They learn how to control the boat, how to set the sails, how to make the most of the wind, how to lean right outboard to get extra speed—and how to look after themselves if the boat capsizes. And all of it adds up to a great deal of pleasure and a sense of achievement.

So in life too we learn how to look after ourselves and if we are wise we do all we can to gain for ourselves all the power of the Spirit of God, which gives a purpose and zest to life.

Grant unto us, Almighty God,
A desire to make the most of life in your service
And a willingness to prepare ourselves as best we can.
Then fill us with the powerful winds of your Spirit
To speed us on towards our goal. *Amen.*

Benediction No. 100

Out of Doors (3)

ANGLING   *Izaak Walton*

Every year thousands of people throughout Britain look forward to 16th June for that is the day, in most parts of the country, when they can take out their fishing tackle and find a quiet spot by a river where they hope to tempt fish to take a bite at their baited hook. The three months previous to this date have been the close season when coarse fishing is prohibited to allow the fish to breed.

Fishing is one of man's oldest occupations. From earliest days he has fished for food and the fish hooks of many ancient peoples have been found. One person who did much to popularize fishing in Britain was Izaak Walton. He was born in Stafford on 9th August, 1593, became Steward to the Bishop of Worcester and moved with the bishop to Winchester, where he died on 15th December 1683. His book *The Compleat Angler*, first published in 1653, is a kind of angler's text-book.

Today angling, that is fishing with a rod and line, is the sport or pastime that attracts the largest number of people. There are various forms of fishing: coarse fishing in rivers and lakes, game or fly fishing for salmon and trout, sea fishing from the shore and sea fishing from boats for the really big game fish.

But whichever kind of fishing it is, the angler knows that he needs to have his equipment in good working order and he may need an awful lot of patience before he can persuade a fish to be caught! Perhaps the disciples of Jesus learned that same need for patience when they fished for men as commanded by Jesus.

Bible Reading: St. Luke 5: 1–11

Grant unto us, O Lord, a vision of what you would have us to do in life; help us to equip ourselves for the task; and grant us patience until we have completed the course. *Amen.*

Closing prayer No. 77

Out of doors (4)

How good are you at reading maps? Do you enjoy outdoor activities needing skill and common sense? Are you athletic and fit? Do you like treasure hunting? These are the kind of things that attract people to orienteering, a sport which is becoming increasingly popular in Britain.

Orienteering began in Sweden about 1920 but it was not until 1962 that European Championships were held and 1966 World Championships.

Orienteers need to be very fit, for the course they follow is cross country, often through forest land, up and down hills, over streams and ditches. The course to be followed has been prepared by the planners who produce maps to be followed and set up check points every so often which must be found by the competitor before going on to the next. Competitors set off at intervals and set their skill against that of the course planner. Each competitor uses his own skill: it is no use following someone else because he may be going the wrong way.

Apart from the map, each competitor carries a special protractor compass to find the way, a whistle in case of emergency, a red ball-pen for marking the map and polythene bags for keeping maps and cards dry. All else that is needed is the knowledge that one must observe all the rules if one is not to be disqualified and a determination to finish the course as best one can. There is a great sense of achievement when reaching the end.

Life is rather like that too. We have our course to run; we have certain rules to keep; and we must keep ourselves fit. The Christian has his Bible as a map and compass, and prayer not just for emergency but for keeping in touch with the planner, God himself. And at the end . . . the reward.

Bible Reading: Philippians 3: 12–14

Help us, O God, to follow the course of life according to the rules which you have laid down and bring us at last to our heavenly reward. *Amen.*

Closing prayer No. 73

Out of doors (5)

National Playing Fields Association

What kind of recreation do you enjoy? Organized games such as football or cricket? Group activities such as cycling or rambling? Individual pastimes such as angling? As a member of a club, or on your own?

And whereabouts do you go for these things? Some people are more fortunate than others. They have plenty of open spaces or playing fields near their homes. Others have very few open spaces and may be dependent for their recreation upon the local park or adventure playground.

Many of those facilities which do exist have been provided through an organization known as The National Playing Fields Association, which was founded as long ago as 8th July, 1925. Since then it has raised over £2 million and has spent it on many recreational facilities including over 4,000 children's playgrounds.

Today, perhaps more than at any time in the past, people are encouraged to undertake more recreation for the good of their health, for people who take regular exercise are usually much fitter than those who do not. Recreation is very important.

But recreation can also be regarded as re-creation, a remaking or rebuilding of ourselves. This is what happens when we engage in physical activities. There is another form of re-creation, too, the rebuilding of our minds, which comes when we turn away from our usual work and think about other things which are important.

Listen to what St. Paul had to say and remember that this is just as important as keeping fit in body—if not more so!

Bible Reading: Ephesians 4: 22–24

Make us aware, O God, of our need to look after our bodies so that we may be fit for your service and to renew our hearts and minds so that we may become all that you would have us to be. *Amen.*

Closing prayer No. 78

Poetry and books (1)

NONSENSE!   *Edward Lear*

> *'How pleasant to know Mr. Lear!'*
> *Who has written such volumes of stuff!*
> *Some think him ill-tempered and queer*
> *But a few think him pleasant enough.*

Edward Lear wrote this as the opening verse of a poem about himself. We shall never know Mr. Lear because he died on 29th January, 1888, but most people are familiar with his 'nonsense' poems such as *The Owl and the Pussycat*, *The Jumblies* or *The Dong with the Luminous Nose*. Or perhaps they enjoy reciting Limericks—those humorous five lined verses beginning 'There was an old man of . . .'. It was Edward Lear who made them popular.

Lear has been described as a genius of nonsense verse, yet it was as an artist that he earned his living and through his art that he began to write verses. From the age of fifteen he earned a living by drawing, working for the Zoological Society of London, the British Museum and for the Earl of Derby, who had a private zoo. At one time he was engaged to give drawing lessons to Queen Victoria. Later, owing to ill health he travelled abroad to various parts of the Mediterranean, having given up much of his drawing in favour of landscape painting.

It was while working for the Earl of Derby that he wrote his first *Book of Nonsense* to amuse the Earl's children. Little did he know then that those same poems would give pleasure to many generations of children and to adults too.

There are lots of times when we have to be serious. It is pleasant sometimes to be able to relax and enjoy a little fun or nonsense.

Thank you, O God for all the things which we can enjoy and especially those which help us to relax when we have been busy. Grant us a sense of humour, an appreciation of simple things and thankfulness for all our blessings. *Amen.*

Closing prayer No. 55

Poetry and books (2)

BALLADS AND BOOKS   *John Masefield*

From the Apocrypha: Ecclesiasticus 44: 1–15

The heritage which we enjoy has been passed on to us by a great many people. Some are remembered: others are forgotten. Amongst these are many who have given us enjoyable stories or stirring poems. There is so much from which to choose that we can all find something which appeals to us.

Sometimes a piece of writing or a poem will paint a picture so vivid that it stirs our imagination. Take John Masefield's *Sea Fever* for example.

I must go down to the seas again, for the call of the running tide
Is a wild call and a clear call that may not be denied;
And all I ask is a windy day with the white clouds flying,
And the flung spray and the blown spume, and the seagulls
   crying.

It is almost possible to feel the wind and the spray, to hear the seagulls and to be drawn to the sea. Born near Ledbury on 1st June, 1878, John Masefield had the sea in his blood. He ran away to sea at the age of thirteen and he sailed round Cape Horn in a windjammer when only fifteen.

He left the sea whilst still a young man to work in New York and then London, where he began writing for periodicals. His *Salt-Water Ballads* (poems of the sea) was published in 1902. Other poems and books followed. In 1930 he was chosen to be Poet Laureate, the national poet, who writes poems for special occasions. Later in his life he received other honours for his books and poems. He died on 12th May, 1967.

We remember with thankfulness, O Lord, all those who have given us so much to enjoy. Especially today would we thank you for the writers of books and poems, those who are well-known and those who may be forgotten. Help us to enjoy their works. *Amen.*

Benediction No. 105

Poetry and books (3)

Beatrix Potter

There are lots of children today who enjoy reading the story of *Peter Rabbit*, just as children have enjoyed reading this story for a very long time. *Peter Rabbit* was first published as long ago as 1901 but he is even older than that for the story first appeared in a letter written to a sick child in 1893 which was illustrated with drawings of Peter Rabbit.

The writer of the letter was Beatrix Potter, who was born on 28th July, 1866. She and her brother were children of parents from rich cotton families in Lancashire. Beatrix was a very lonely child, especially when her brother went away to school. She loved animals and spent a lot of time in sketching and making water colour paintings which were very faithful to nature. It was the quality of her water colour painting as well as the stories she told which made her books so much loved by children.

Within a few years *Peter Rabbit* had been followed by *The Tailor of Gloucester*, *Squirrel Nutkin*, *Mrs. Tiggy-Winkle*, *Jemima Puddle-Duck* and a host of others. The stories were simple with a trace of north-country humour and with lots of little lessons to be learned from animals which behaved remarkably like children! (Peter Rabbit was told *not* to go into Mr. McGregor's garden. But of course he did!).

Beatrix loved to escape to the Lake District and after she married William Heelis in 1913 that became home. Most of her time was spent farming and tending sheep until she died on 22nd December, 1943, at the age of seventy-seven. She is remembered for her many gifts of land to the National Trust but also as one who has given lots and lots of pleasure to generations of children.

O God our Father, we remember lots of books that have given us pleasure. Thank you for those who wrote them, or painted the pictures, or published them, giving us so much enjoyment. *Amen.*

Benediction No. 104

Poetry and books (4)

ALICE   *Lewis Carroll*

One of the most famous books in the English language is *Alice's Adventures in Wonderland*, more commonly known simply as *Alice in Wonderland*. Nor is it only well known to English-speaking people. It has been translated into over 30 languages.

The book was written under the pen name of Lewis Carroll but the author's real name was Charles Lutwidge Dodgson. Born in Cheshire on 27th January, 1832, he attended Oxford University and stayed there as a lecturer in Mathematics.

One day he was in a boat on the river with the daughter of the dean of Christ Church College—a little girl named Alice—and he began telling a story to amuse her. It was a story of how Alice fell down a rabbit hole and had all sorts of adventures. Later he added to the story and it was published in 1865. Many children, and adults too, have enjoyed reading of strange characters such as the Queen of Hearts, the Mad Hatter and the Cheshire Cat.

A few years later he wrote a second book about Alice entitled *Through the Looking Glass* with other oddities such as the Jabberwock and the twins Tweedledum and Tweedledee. He also wrote a humorous poem called *The Hunting of the Snark*, in which the Banker, Baker, Beaver and Bellman search for this imaginary creature. There is lots of fun in it like this:

> *He would answer to 'Hi!' or to any loud cry,*
> *Such as 'Fry me!' or 'Fritter my wig!'*
> *To 'What-you-may-call-um!' or 'What-was-his-name!'*
> *But especially 'Thing-um-a-jig!'*

Although Lewis Carroll wrote books on Mathematics under his own name it was the Alice books that brought him fame. He died on 14th January, 1898.

We thank you, God our Father, for the pleasures of reading and for all the good books that we can enjoy. Give us thankful hearts for these and for every blessing. *Amen.*

Benediction No. 96

Poetry and books (5)

SEARCH FOR A PURPOSE   *Leo Tolstoy*

Count Leo Tolstoy, one of the world's most famous authors, was
born in Russia in 1828. His parents, well-to-do landowners, died
when he was a boy, leaving him a large country estate. After
service in the army he returned to his estate, where he farmed the
land and looked after the welfare of the peasants who worked
there including opening a school for the children.

There he wrote his most famous novel *War and Peace*, the story
of several families in Russia at the time of the invasion by
Napoleon in 1812. It was published in instalments from 1865 to
1869 and it was followed a few years later by another great novel,
Anna Karenina, a love story of an unhappy woman.

Tolstoy had become famous as an author but unhappy as a man.
He thought it wrong that some people should be very rich whilst
others were very poor. He believed he himself was living very
selfishly. So he gave up his writing, dressed as a peasant and began
working on the land. He read what others had to say about the
ways of life and he spoke with many people. He thought, too,
about some words of Jesus:

Bible Reading: St. Matthew 5: 38–42

This and other teachings led him to condemn violence in any form.
He did not conform with the teachings of the Christian Church. He
insisted that society would only improve when people tried to live
more perfect lives and love one another. He wrote books about
this, too.

At the age of 82 he left home to seek freedom from all worldly
cares but died a few days later on 22nd November, 1910.

Help us, O God, to find the right way to live our lives; to be
peaceable, unselfish and loving toward our neighbours; and to
strive in all things to walk in your holy ways. *Amen.*

Closing prayer No. 74

Art (1)

John Constable

Ask anyone to name some great English artists and the name of Constable will almost certainly come near the top of the list. Many of his paintings are proudly displayed in art galleries, whilst prints of such paintings as *The Hay Wain* and *Dedham Mill* hang in a great many homes.

John Constable was born on 11th June, 1776, in the village of East Bergholt on the borders of Essex and Suffolk, where the River Stour meanders through Dedham Vale. There John sketched houses and mills, horses and carts, trees and people, farming and boat-building, which were to appear in some of his famous paintings.

Like most artists, he was not recognized in his own country as a great painter for most of his lifetime. He could have become rich if he had gone to France after his most famous painting *The Hay Wain* had been hung in Paris but he preferred to remain in and paint his 'own dear England'.

Constable lived for a while in London and then at Brighton owing to the ill-health of his wife but the Suffolk countryside remained his favourite study. In later life he lectured on landscape painting and published a book of his paintings and sketches entitled *English Landscape*.

Soon afterwards, when travelling on a coach in Suffolk, he remarked to a stranger on the beauty of the countryside. The stranger replied, 'Yes. This is *Constable*'s country'. And Constable Country it still is—a fitting tribute to one of the greatest English landscape artists.

Almighty God, we thank you for works of art and craftsmanship which we can enjoy. We thank you too for any abilities which we may have and pray that we may be able to use them to create things which are pleasing and attractive to those around us. *Amen.*

Closing prayer No. 84

Art (2)

If you have ever tried to draw or paint a portrait of someone you will know how difficult it is. Not only must you make the face the right shape and have all the features right but you must also capture an expression which is characteristic of the person whose portrait it is.

To be able to paint a lifelike portrait is a special gift which few people possess. One such artist is Graham Sutherland, who was born on 24th August, 1903, and has paintings exhibited in art galleries all over the world. They are not all portraits. Sutherland is an artist of many talents.

Perhaps his greatest and best-known work is the huge tapestry which fills the wall behind the altar in the new Coventry Cathedral. Entitled *Christ in Glory*, it took him ten years to plan. Each part was sketched in detail and then enlarged so that the tapestry could be made. Measuring 72 ft × 39 ft (22 m × 12 m) it was woven at Felletin, Central France, where fourteen weavers used about 2,000 miles (3,218 km) of wool to complete it.

The design of the tapestry is modern and in keeping with the architecture of the cathedral. Some people like it but others have their doubts. But this is true of most forms of art. All people have their likes and dislikes.

Sutherland, like many artists, never wished to be tied down to a particular form of art. He could have made a fortune by doing nothing other than paint portraits but he preferred to feel completely free to paint what he wanted and to do it when he wanted to.

We give you thanks, O Lord our God
For all the beauty and colour of our world;
For those who have captured this colour in art;
For beautiful paintings in oils or water-colours;
For sketches and engravings, tapestries and prints.
For these and all we have to enjoy
Praise be to you, O God. *Amen.*

Benediction No. 95

Art (3)

Leonardo da Vinci

Among the many exhibits in the Louvre, the great Paris museum, are two of the most famous works of art in the world. One is the marble statue known as the Venus de Milo, made about 150 B.C. by an unknown Greek. The other is the 'Mona Lisa', also known as 'La Gioconda', a portrait painted by Leonardo da Vinci about five hundred years ago.

Leonardo da Vinci was a remarkable man in many ways. It is said that he was extremely handsome and so strong that he could bend a horseshoe in his hands. Yet those same hands could do some of the most delicate art work and careful drawing.

During his lifetime Leonardo da Vinci did many different things, drawing plans for rebuilding Milan, military engineering, and canal building. He was a musician and a scientist. He studied the flight of birds and drew plans for a flying machine. He explored the workings of the human body. He made all sorts of notes about his researches which were written in mirror writing from right to left which he found easiest: he was left-handed.

But it was nature which interested him most as an artist and particularly the beautiful things. He loved to paint and draw leaves and flowers, animals and birds, and beautiful people. But he was a perfectionist and many of his works remained unfinished because he could see faults which were unnoticeable to others.

Leonardo da Vinci spent the whole of his life in Italy except for the last couple of years and it was in France that he died on 2nd May, 1519, leaving behind enough works of art for him to be remembered as one of the greatest artists of all.

Almighty God, Creator of all things,
We thank you for everything of beauty around us.
Give us eyes to appreciate all lovely forms,
And a heart to love the God who made them. *Amen.*

Closing prayer No. 59

Art (4)

Pablo Ruiz Picasso

Young Pablo Ruiz showed great promise as an artist. Born on 25th October, 1881, in Malaga, Spain, he moved later to Corunna, where his father taught art. By the time Pablo was thirteen, his father was so impressed that he handed over his own artist's materials to his talented son. Pablo went on to study at Barcelona and Madrid.

Soon he was painting many different subjects, while living in a dingy room above a factory. His friends persuaded him to paint under his mother's maiden name, which was less common than his own. So he became Pablo Picasso—one of the most famous artists of the present century.

The next years were spent in France, Spain and Italy, painting still life, portraits and scenes, besides designing ballet sets and costumes. But he was developing a style of his own with figures and forms which were quite unlifelike. Some of his paintings came to be recognized as masterpieces.

Like many artists, Picasso was a man of moods and his paintings sometimes reflected his feelings. One of his famous paintings was inspired by an event during the Spanish Civil War when, in April 1937 the little town of Guernica was destroyed by bombs, killing two thousand civilians. Picasso's painting, 'Guernica', a huge canvas in black, grey and white, was a cry from the heart at what he regarded as an outrage against civilization.

Most people, at some time, feel deeply upset about something. Some, like Picasso can express their feelings in art, some in writing and others in speaking. And sometimes it takes a lot of courage to do so.

Bible Reading: St. Mark 11: 15–18

Help us, O God, to keep our eyes open and see what is happening around us; and when we see anything that is wrong, give us courage to do something about it. *Amen.*

Closing prayer No. 67

Art (5)

National Art Galleries

Most people would agree that fine paintings should be available for as many people as possible to enjoy. Some, of course, are in private collections but many are exhibited in art galleries in cities and towns all over the world.

The National Gallery in London, overlooking Trafalgar Square, was founded as long ago as 1824. It now contains over 2,000 pictures painted by many famous artists. Each is displayed very tastefully so that people can focus their attention on one picture. The National Portrait Gallery nearby has portraits of famous British men and women.

Scotland has its national art gallery in Edinburgh. The National Gallery of Scotland, which was opened on 21st March, 1859, also contains about 2,000 pictures.

Some of our art galleries came into being as a result of a gift to the nation of a private collection of paintings. Sir Henry Tate was one who did this. He was a sugar merchant who had built up a collection of 65 British paintings. He decided to give these to the nation and provide the money to build a gallery where they could be seen. So today we have, overlooking the River Thames, the Tate gallery which contains the national collection of British paintings from the sixteenth century to the present day, together with other modern art and sculpture.

Apart from the local art collections it is often very rewarding to visit exhibitions of the work of present-day artists. There are many attractive works to be seen, as well as some we might think ugly. People's tastes in art are very different.

We thank you, O God, for all the works of art which are available for us to enjoy and for the places where we can go to see them. Grant us an eye for beauty and appreciation of the creations of others. *Amen.*

Benediction No. 96

Craftsmanship (1)

STONE MASONRY *Henry Yeveley*

Have you ever looked at a great cathedral or other old building and wondered who built it? Think of the skill that must have gone into cutting and shaping the stone to make those huge pillars and the care that went into carving the stone figures and ornaments. This was the work of stone masons many of whom were masters of their trade.

If we look closely at old stone work we can sometimes find masons' marks cut into the stone. But these tell us very little about men whose work we can see but whose names are long since forgotten. One of these old stone masons of whom we do know quite a lot is Henry Yeveley, who was born about 1320 and died in August 1400.

Among some of the greater works of Henry Yeveley are the huge naves, pillars, arches and vaulting of Westminster Abbey and Canterbury Cathedral. In fact, in the cloisters of Canterbury Cathedral, there is a face looking down from the roof, which is believed to be that of Yeveley. It is thought that he designed the magnificent tomb there to the Black Prince. Certainly royal tombs and those of other people were designed by him. He even designed his own tomb in the church of St. Magnus, London.

Although Yeveley was a very clever mason himself there came the time when he was in such demand that all he could do was design the work which others would then do. And when we look at some of these huge buildings we have to admire the work of those who were able to build them without any of the equipment that builders have today. Truly the masons and other craftsmen were very skilful.

As we look at the craftsmanship of people of all ages, O God, we recall how every talent and ability has been given by you. We thank you for all beautiful craftsmanship and pray that we may be able to use our creative abilities for your glory. *Amen.*

Closing prayer No. 61

Craftsmanship (2)

Grinling Gibbons

If you have ever tried your hand at wood carving you will know how difficult it is. One slip of the knife or one miscalculation and the whole work can be spoiled, for once the wood has been cut away it cannot be replaced.

Imagine being able to carve leaves that were so delicate that they fluttered in the breeze or having the ability to carve from a piece of lime wood an imitation lace collar. The man who could do such things was Grinling Gibbons, a master wood carver who was born on 4th April, 1668, and died on 3rd August, 1721, in the Stuart period of British history.

Gibbons first came to fame when, at the age of 23 he carved *The Stoning of St. Stephen*, which is now exhibited in the Victoria and Albert Museum in London. Soon his talents were widely known and many rich people sought his services.

At that time Sir Christopher Wren was designing new churches, including St. Paul's Cathedral in London. He was introduced to Grinling Gibbons who was commissioned to carve many of the interior decorations of the new cathedral and of other churches too, including St. George's Chapel, Windsor and St. James's Church in London's Piccadilly.

Many people have since admired the work of Grinling Gibbons, who has been described as one of the greatest if not *the* greatest wood carver. It is a pleasant thought that the great talent which had been given to Grinling Gibbons was used in a very large measure for the glory of God in the beautifying of places of worship—as has so often happened through the ages.

Bible Reading: II Chronicles 2: 5–9

Almighty God, to whose glory people throughout the ages have dedicated their talents and their service, help us to recognize that all we have has come from you and should be used wisely in your service. *Amen.*

Closing prayer No. 90

Craftsmanship (3)

Visitors to churches and cathedrals will often stand and admire the stained glass windows which are made of small pieces of coloured glass, joined together with strips of lead to form pictures or designs.

The building most famous for its stained glass windows is York Minster. There in the windows of the cathedral can be seen stained glass from every century from the twelfth to the twentieth and in its 117 windows can be seen nearly half of all the stained glass from the middle ages that can be seen anywhere in Britain.

The great east window of the Cathedral is one of the largest areas of stained glass in the world. It is the work of John Thornton of Coventry and it took him from 1405 to 1408 to complete it. Christ himself is shown at the top of the window and beneath him are angels and saints. There are over a hundred panels which illustrate Bible stories from the Creation to the visions found in the Book of Revelation. Beneath that are bishops and kings.

We might ask why a man like John Thornton would spend such a long time in making one window, or why so much coloured glass was used when clear glass would let in more light.

No doubt many of the windows were made as the visual aids of their time and used to illustrate some of the Bible stories as they were told. But no doubt, too, many of them were made to beautify God's house and the craftsmanship that went into them was the work of people who wanted to offer their best to God.

God of all life, Creator of every beautiful thing, and Giver of every talent of art and craftsmanship; accept our thanks for everything that man has created for the joy of his fellows and the glory of God; and enable us to make the best possible use of all that you have given us. *Amen.*

Closing prayer No. 89

Craftsmanship (4)

Josiah Wedgwood

Josiah Wedgwood was the thirteenth son of a potter living in Burslem, Staffordshire. Some might say 'unlucky thirteen'. Perhaps in some ways they might be said to have been right. His father died when Josiah was nine and he had to be taken away from school. Two years later he caught smallpox which affected his knee and left him a cripple in constant pain for twenty-two years. Then he had his leg amputated and in those days there were no anaesthetics to kill the pain.

Yet there are other ways in which Josiah might be regarded as lucky. He was blessed with the determination to overcome his difficulties; and he had a skill and talent for pottery that was far greater than most potters had.

Whereas many were content to make ordinary pots, Josiah was always experimenting with new ideas, different colours, a variety of glazes and exciting new designs. Soon people took notice of his wonderfully artistic designs. Until then all beautiful pottery was from other countries and was expensive. Josiah Wedgwood changed that.

Orders for his pottery came so fast that he had to extend his workshops and he ensured that they were kept clean and tidy. Everything about Wedgwood's work had to be first-class. His designs and tints were not copied from other potters but from observation of nature. He established his business in the Etruria works, around which he built a village, school and chapel.

Josiah Wedgwood died on 3rd January, 1795. In his lifetime he was honoured by being appointed Queen's Potter. His greatest memorial is in the pottery that still bears the name Wedgwood, that during two hundred years or so has given pleasure to so many people.

O God, Creator of all that is beautiful, we say thank you for those who have created works of craftsmanship and beauty, giving pleasure to the many people who see or handle them. *Amen.*

Benediction No. 97

Craftsmanship (5)

Sir Giles Gilbert Scott

Several very well-known buildings were designed by the architect Sir Giles Gilbert Scott, who was born on 9th November, 1880. He was the grandson of another famous architect, Sir George Gilbert Scott, whose work had been mainly concerned with the restoration of church buildings, including Westminster Abbey and the cathedrals at Ely, Hereford, Salisbury and Gloucester.

It is not suprising, therefore, that Giles was also interested in church architecture. When architects were invited to draw up plans for a new cathedral at Liverpool, Giles entered the competition and was successful in having his plans chosen. At the time he was only 22½ years of age. The building began in 1904 and was completed in 1978. It was after the consecration ceremony in 1924 that the architect was knighted.

But Scott was not only a church architect: he drew up the plans for many public buildings. One was Battersea Power Station beside the Thames, a London landmark which was built 1927–1933. He also produced the designs for Cambridge University Library (1933), the Bodleian Library, Oxford (1941) and the new Waterloo Bridge across the Thames which was completed in 1945. By the time he died on 8th February, 1960, Sir Giles Gilbert Scott had designed fine buildings in several cities.

But Battersea Power Station and Liverpool Cathedral had something else in common. Battersea provided much of the electric power needed by London. Liverpool Cathedral is a power house of a different kind, for through it and the people who serve in it the power of God helps people to grow in faith and to live fully.

Bible Reading: Romans 1: 16–17

Let the power of your Holy Spirit come into our lives, O God, so that we may be guided to know the truth of the gospel and inspired to live life fully in your love and service. *Amen.*

Benediction No. 101

Travel (1)

ROADMAKING   *John Metcalf*

We are so used to good roads and comfortable travel that it is difficult to imagine what it was like to travel with no proper roads and when a journey across country would take days instead of hours.

It was only a couple of hundred years ago that people turned their thoughts to making good roads in Britain and suprisingly one of the great road builders was a man who was blind.

John Metcalf was born at Knaresborough, Yorkshire, on 15th August, 1717. At the age of six he caught smallpox and, though he recovered, was left blind. Yet Blind Jack was to become a legend. He could do all the things that other boys could. He climbed trees and rode horses. Later he learned to play the violin, he served with the army, he drove wagons and he did some smuggling.

But despite his blindness Jack knew the countryside around his home town and frequently guided travellers across the lonely moors. When a stretch of road was to be made up between Knaresborough and Boroughbridge, Jack won the contract. It was such a good road that he was asked to build others.

He laid firm roads across marshy ground; he designed bridges and parapets; and often he was seen tapping the road with his staff, listening intently and testing the surface to ensure that it was sound. No shoddy work was allowed to pass. Other famous road-builders such as Macadam and Telford learned from his methods.

Jack was over seventy when he made his last road. Then he bought a farm which he ran until his death on 26th April, 1810, at the age of ninety-two.

O God our Father we pray that you will show us what we ought to do. Help us to lay firm foundations and to build on them, using all the talents which you have given us and never being content unless we have done our best. *Amen.*

Closing prayer No. 82

Travel (2)

Highway robbery

Bible Reading: St. Luke 10: 25–37

This familiar story was told to demonstrate good neighbourliness but it also reminds us of the dangers of travel in the time of Jesus. They are, of course the dangers that have faced travellers ever since. It is not uncommon even today to read in our newspapers of people being 'mugged', attacked or having their property stolen even in our city streets.

Sometimes in history the highway robbers have been portrayed as rather glamorous characters, especially the highwaymen who held up the stage coaches, stealing valuables from the men and kisses from the ladies. Claude Duval, who came from France in the 1600s, is one of whom various tales of gallantry are told, but he was caught and hanged in 1669—the fate of many a highwayman.

Perhaps the most famous of all highwaymen was Dick Turpin who spent much of his time on the road out of London through Epping Forest. The story of his famous ride to York on Black Bess is often told, though it is probably a story that belongs to a different highwayman. Dick Turpin certainly made his way to York and worked under a different name but justice caught up with him and he was hanged there for horse stealing on 7th April, 1739.

Glamorous the highwaymen may seem as we read of some of their exploits and adventures but they were, after all, no more than common thieves, taking by force things which belonged to other people. There is no justification whatever for robbery in whatever form: highway robbery, burglary, shoplifting and theft are all evil.

Almighty God, we pray that you will grant safe journeying to all who travel; and to those who would steal give instead a desire for honesty and good neighbourliness so that all may feel secure and enjoy peace of mind. *Amen.*

Benediction No. 101

Travel (3)

Pneumatic tyres

Travelling in stage coaches and other horse-drawn carriages a century and more ago was far from comfortable. Their wooden wheels with iron tyres clattered along the cobbled streets of the towns and only the springs of the carriages prevented the passengers from feeling every bump in the road.

Yet when R. W. Thompson drove through the streets of London on 10th December, 1845, it was different. His ride was quieter and smoother. He had made some hollow tyres for the wheels of his carriage by sticking strips of canvas together. He called them pneumatic tyres, because they were filled with air. It seemed such a good idea but no one was very interested and the idea was forgotten for over forty years.

It was in the 1880s that John Boyd Dunlop, a Scottish veterinary surgeon who was working in Ireland, became weary of travelling on bumpy roads and began experimenting. His idea was to use air-filled tyres made not of canvas but of rubber and he tried out his invention on his ten-year-old son's tricycle. It worked. So he set up in business to make tyres—the first Dunlop tyres.

There had been solid rubber tyres for some time, following the discovery by the American Charles Goodyear of the way to make reliable rubber goods. Dunlop's invention of pneumatic tyres was to be the beginning of a revolution in road transport.

Since then other inventions have resulted in stronger, safer, more reliable tyres, which give greater comfort and make driving safer. We owe our comfort and safety to many people.

We thank you, O God, for the comfort that we can enjoy on our journeyings today, for those whose inventions have made it possible, and for those who still seek to make more improvements today. Make us thankful for all our blessings. *Amen.*

Benediction No. 95

Travel (4)

Bible Reading: Isaiah 40: 1–5

In his vision of the future Isaiah spoke of levelling the ground to make a highway for the coming of the Lord. Perhaps you have watched the giant earth moving machines at work preparing for today's motorways so that there are no steep hills or sharp bends.

It was on 2nd November, 1959, that the first section of the M1, Britain's first motorway, was opened. By 7 p.m. the same day over 13,000 vehicles had used it, many motorists anxious to sample the joys of fast travel without many of the hazards of ordinary roads.

In Britain the M1 was a novelty. Other countries had motorways many years before. Italy had the first, the *autostrade* in 1925: Germany had *autobahnen* soon afterwards.

The M1 was just a beginning. Since 1959 a motorway network has been constructed and further motorways are planned so that all the major cities are linked by a road system which is fast and comparatively safe, provided that people use the motorways sensibly, observing the traffic rules and slowing down when it is advisable to do so.

Sometimes it is pleasant to leave the highways for the byways, to travel on more scenic routes and enjoy the pleasures of the countryside but, when needing to travel quickly from one place to another, there is nothing to beat the motorway.

Perhaps we might still heed those words of Isaiah today. There are many obstacles and hazards to be faced in life and if we can but help to remove some of them we shall be making God's world a pleasanter place—a highway for our God.

Help us, O God, to make this world a better place, by doing what we can to remove those obstacles which cause others to stumble on their journey through life; and grant us a safe journey on that highway which leads to your eternal kingdom. *Amen.*

Closing prayer No. 73

Travel (5)

Transatlantic balloonists

On 17th August, 1978, a balloon landed in a cornfield sixty miles north of Paris and three exhausted balloonists stepped out of the gondola to be surrounded immediately by an excited crowd. It was the end of a journey that men had dreamed of for a hundred years, the first transatlantic crossing by balloon.

The three American balloonists, Ben Abruzzo, Max Anderson and Larry Newman in their craft, *Double Eagle II*, had travelled over 3,000 miles (4,800 km), not only the first Atlantic crossing but the longest ever balloon flight. Their flight of 139 hours 10 minutes was also the longest time men had spent in the air.

There had been many anxious moments. In Mid-Atlantic the wind dropped but began to blow more strongly again. Off Ireland the balloon plummeted down and nearly all the ballast had to be thrown out to stop it. Neither was it very comfortable. They were buffeted by the wind and nearly frozen at the high altitude. The small gondola was cramped and uncomfortable. But it was a challenge that had been attempted unsuccessfully by many before them and for that alone it was worth it!

Nowadays few people would choose to travel by balloon. We have comfortable jet planes with every convenience for air travel, luxurious liners for travel by sea and modern coaches for land travel, all of which are pretty reliable for getting us to our destinations. A balloon is dependent entirely upon the wind blowing in the right direction.

Life is rather like that. Nothing is certain. But we can launch ourselves and depend upon the power of the Spirit of God to carry us to our final destination.

Lift us up, O God, by your mighty power, and grant that we may trust our lives to the guidance of your Holy Spirit believing that you can help us on our way through life. *Amen.*

Benediction No. 107

4 Use of talents

A series of seven themes illustrating the ways in which people have used their various talents in creation, exploration, invention and leadership, some for the benefit of mankind and some for the glory of God.

World of music   *Challenge of nature*
Science and invention   *Engineering and construction*
Astronomy   *Space travel*
Leadership

Most of these are topics which stand on their own, although there is some continuity in the themes of *Astronomy* and *Space travel*.

World of music (1)

Arturo Toscanini

Some of the finest music is played by a full orchestra consisting of a large number of musicians. Many of them play stringed instruments such as violins or cellos. Others play brass, woodwind, percussion or other instruments of which there are many kinds.

Before playing, the musicians try out their instruments to make sure they are in tune. Each has his own music so that he knows when to play his particular part. But the most important man in an orchestra has no instrument. He is the conductor, who ensures that the musicians not only play together but produce the right tone and effect.

There have been many world-famous conductors but one who has been called 'the greatest conductor of his time' was Arturo Toscanini. Born at Parma, Italy on 24th March, 1867, he showed great talent for music as a child. In 1894 he was given his first appointment as a conductor.

Toscanini was a difficult man to work for. He demanded perfection always, just as he demanded perfection of himself. His talent for music was so great that he could pick out the notes of a tune that he had heard only once. Or he could take up his conductor's baton and conduct an orchestra at a moment's notice. His talents were put to good use, for many people all over the world were very moved by his conducting.

In life we might remember that we need to be in tune with other people. That is something we can do ourselves. But we have also to look to the conductor to help us to work together. That is God—and *he* demands our very best response.

Show us, God our Father, how to be in tune with others; and teach us to look to you for guidance so that, working willingly with others we may bring harmony into the world. *Amen.*

Benediction No. 102

World of music (2)

SONG WRITER   *Irving Berlin*

One might reasonably think that a man who was to become one of
the world's most famous songwriters would need to be able to read
and write music. Yet the man who became the richest composer of
this century could do neither. In fact his is one of the great rags-
to-riches stories.

Israel Baline was born on 11th May, 1888, the eighth son of a
very poor Russian-Jewish rabbi who had emigrated to America.
But young Israel had a talent for writing songs and he did so under
the name of Irving Berlin. And when Irving Berlin wrote a song
there was usually something catchy about it so that lots of people
began singing it or humming the tune.

Perhaps you know a rousing little march called *Alexander's
Rag-time Band*. That was one of his earlier compositions dating
from before World War I. Undoubtedly his best-seller is *White
Christmas*, which has sold 113 million records and nearly six
million copies of sheet music. He has also written music and songs
for a number of succesful shows such as *Annie Get Your Gun* and
the music for films.

Although Irving Berlin became rich himself, others also benefited from his work. The Scout movement has received over a third
of a million pounds from his anthem *God Bless America*. Many
singers, too, have earned quite a lot of money by singing his songs.

But many would say that the greatest value of his songs, and he
wrote about a thousand of them, is the great pleasure that they
have given to millions of people. Irving Berlin had a talent for
music and he used it well.

We thank you, God our Father, for those with a talent for music
who have used that talent to bring pleasure to millions of people.
Help us to know that every talent we are given is a gift to be used
and to be used wisely. *Amen.*

Closing prayer No. 89

World of music (3)

Jenny Lind

Johanna Maria Lind was born in Stockholm, Sweden, on 6th October, 1820. As Jenny Lind she was to become one of the greatest singers of her time, known even to non-musical people all over the world.

It was in opera that she began her singing, appearing for the first time in Stockholm in 1838. The purity and naturalness of her singing was outstanding and many went to hear her. After singing in many cities on the continent she came to London in 1847. It was reported then that London went mad about the 'Swedish Nightingale' and it is by that name that she has been remembered.

Two years later she withdrew from opera but still sang in concerts. In 1883 she left the stage to become a success in singing oratorios. From that year until 1886 she taught at the Royal College of Music, London. Jenny Lind, who had become a British subject in 1859, died at Malvern, Worcestershire on 2nd November, 1887.

One of the qualities for which Jenny Lind will always be remembered is her readiness to do little things to bring joy to others. One remembers, for example the story of how she took shelter in a house just before a Manchester concert. The old lady, not knowing Jenny Lind, said that many people were looking forward to the concert but she could not go herself because she was too old. And so Jenny Lind, in that humble home, sang some of her finest songs for the old lady.

But that, of course, is the sign of true greatness. And some of the greatest joys are those which come when we do something unexpectedly to bring happiness to other folk.

Help us, O God, to make the most of the talents you have given us but to remember that they are your gifts to be used in your service to bring joy to the lives of others and glory to your holy Name. *Amen.*

Closing prayer No. 52

World of music (4)

Yehudi Menuhin

Yehudi Menuhin's parents were Russian Jews living in New York and it was there that he was born on 22nd April, 1916. Before long his parents moved to San Francisco and there Yehudi grew up. When he was four years old he began learning to play the violin and took to it remarkably well.

When he was only seven years old, in 1924, Yehudi caused a sensation by playing the violin solo in Felix Mendelssohn's Violin Concerto with the San Francisco Orchestra. There was no looking back. Yehudi Menuhin had become a fine violinist in his early years and he was to be recognized as one of the greatest violin virtuosos of the twentieth century. He toured widely, often accompanied by his sister who played the piano.

It would have been easy to let success go to his head and to have become aloof or self centred but Yehudi Menuhin was determined that his music should be used to give pleasure to as many people as possible. During World War II he travelled to many places to give concerts to servicemen, giving over five hundred concerts.

Then, when the war was ended, he travelled throughout Europe giving concerts and donating the greater part of his income from these to help people in need.

In 1959 Yehudi Menuhin moved to London and, four years later, opened the Yehudi Menuhin School, a boarding school for musically gifted children, at Stoke d'Abernon, Surrey. He was awarded an honorary KBE (Knight Commander of the British Empire) in 1965, an honour worthy of a great musician and a kindly man.

Help us, God our Father, to develop those talents which you have given us and then to use them humbly for the benefit of others, finding for ourselves the joys that abound in your service. *Amen.*

Closing prayer No. 84

154

World of music (5)

Cliff Richard

'Who is number one in the Charts this week?' 'Who is on the way up the Top Twenty?' Common enough questions among young people. Some of the names of the singing stars or groups are familiar: others are new. Most of the stars of a few years ago are no longer there but there are some who don't fade out of the picture.

Cliff Richard is one. He had his first 'hit' in 1958 and during the next twenty years was in the Top Twenty over fifty times. As a teenager he had made up his mind that pop music would be his life and he set out to achieve this.

But it was after the death of his father in 1961 that Cliff began thinking seriously about religion. Many people helped him and he committed his life to God in the Christian faith. His most exciting moment was when he stood with the evangelist, Billy Graham, in the packed stadium at Earls Court in 1966 and declared his Christian faith.

There were rumours that he was giving up pop singing. He took a course in Religious Knowledge and found lots of work to do in the church and with young people. He made two films for Billy Graham; he wrote a book *They way I see it* about his beliefs; he spoke out against evil practices; and he gave gospel concerts. But he carried on singing, giving pleasure to the young and the not-so-young.

Cliff Richard had decided to show that Christianity can have its place in one's normal work and that talents given are talents which should be used. With his large audiences and popular singing he has probably done more to help others than if he had changed his way of life. Jesus once told a man that he could witness much better where he was known.

Bible Reading: St. Mark 5: 18–20

Help us to know, O God, what you would have us to do, show us how and where, and make us bold to tell others of all that you have done for us. *Amen.*

Closing prayer No. 71

Challenge of nature (1)

CLIMBING MOUNTAINS   *Chris Bonington*

A mountaineer was once asked why he must climb a particular mountain and his reply was simply, 'Because it is there!' Many people like to face up to a challenge and will go to great lengths to achieve an objective, especially if it is something that has never been done before.

For many years Mount Everest, the highest mountain in the world, was the greatest challenge. No one had reached the summit until the British expedition under Sir John Hunt did so in 1953. But there was still a challenge and that was to climb the South West face of Everest, the steepest and highest mountain face in the world.

In the autumn of 1972, Chris Bonington, one of Britain's outstanding mountaineers, attempted to conquer the South West Face but he was defeated by wind and extreme cold. When he returned he said that he would never attempt it again.

Chris Bonington was a very successful rock climber. He began climbing at the age of sixteen, was the first to climb the Old Man of Hoy, a rock stack in the Orkneys, and the first Briton to climb the North Wall of the Eiger in the Alps. In 1960 he had reached the summit of Annapurna II in the Himalayas.

But the challenge of the South West Face of Everest remained and, when the opportunity arose for a further attempt in 1975, Chris Bonington led the expedition.

On 24th September, 1975, two of the party reached the summit. Doug Scott and Dougal Haston were not the first to do so: a Chinese expedition had planted a flag on top during the previous year. But they had done what they set out to do. They had faced up to a challenge and had conquered.

Help us, O God, to face up to the challenges of life. Give us a vision of what must be done, a determination to win through, and courage to overcome all obstacles until we reach the goal. *Amen.*

Closing prayer No. 101

Challenge of nature (2)

EXTRAORDINARY ACHIEVEMENTS   *Norman Croucher*

Most people would agree that climbing a mountain is difficult and reaching the summit of the Eiger in the Swiss Alps is quite an achievement. To conquer the Eiger with only artificial legs would seem an impossibility, yet, on 7th September, 1972, Norman Croucher did just that at his third attempt on the mountain.

As a boy Norman had enjoyed rock climbing in his native Cornwall and he was a fine athlete until a tragic accident occurred at the age of nineteen when, after tumbling down a railway embankment, he had both legs cut off below the knee by a train.

Norman was determined to make the best of a difficult situation and could not wait to get his artificial legs. When he did he began climbing trees and rocks and engaged in lots of other activities which he found very painful at times but was nevertheless determined to master. Soon he was climbing small mountains.

But he needed to build up his strength for the big ones. So, in 1969 he decided to do a sponsored walk for Oxfam from John o' Groats to Lands End. He succeeded in walking the 880 miles in three months and he raised well over £1,000.

It was in the following summer that Norman began climbing the Alps and then two years later he conquered the Eiger. But he has conquered mountains of a different kind too. Jesus once spoke of having faith that could remove mountains:

Bible Reading: St. Matthew 17: 14–20

Norman Croucher had faith in himself; he showed many people just what a disabled person can do; and he has given great encouragement to many people who are disabled to do things for themselves.

Hear our prayer, O God, for all who are disabled in body that they may find the encouragement they need to succeed in leading a full and enjoyable life. *Amen.*

Benediction No. 93

Challenge of nature (3)

Chay Blyth, a Scotsman from Hawick loved adventure and a challenge. He served for several years in the Parachute Regiment but first made a name for himself when, in 1966, he and Captain John Ridgway rowed across the Atlantic in 92 days. Two years later he sailed single-handed to South Africa as part of a round-the-world race but he was forced to give up, much to his disappointment.

It was a chance remark of his wife Maureen that set Chay off on his epic adventure. 'Why not sail round the world the *other* way?' Sailing ships had always sailed from West to East, getting the full advantage of winds and currents. To sail round the world from East to West meant a constant battle against both. And no-one had done it single-handed. People said it was impossible.

In a specially built yacht *British Steel* he set sail on 18th October, 1970, southward through the Atlantic, round Cape Horn, across the Southern Ocean to South Africa and then northward in the Atlantic. At times he was becalmed; at others he was battered by gales and high seas. Equipment, including the self steering gear, was smashed. At last, on 6th August, 1971, he stepped ashore after 292 days at sea. The impossible voyage was not, after all, impossible.

Later, Chay Blyth wrote, 'Ten months in solitude in some of the loneliest seas of the world . . . gave me a new awareness of that power outside man which we call God. I am quite certain that without God's help many and many a time I could not have survived to complete my circumnavigation. I hope that I have brought home a new humility in my approach not only to other men, but to all living creatures.'

O God, when things seem to us to be impossible, help us to be aware of your presence and to know that you can give us the courage to go on. *Amen.*

Closing prayer No. 64

Challenge of nature (4)

PROVING A THEORY   *Thor Heyerdahl*

Thor Heyerdahl, who was born in Norway in 1914, became very interested in natural science and in the study of where races of people originated.

As a young man he went to live in the Marquesas, a group of islands in the Pacific Ocean. On some Pacific islands he found stone heads and carvings similar to some found in South America. He began to wonder. Could the ancestors of these island people have been Indians from South America? If they were, they would have had to make the journey on rafts made from balsa wood, for that was the kind of craft used by the Indians of a thousand years ago.

Heyerdahl studied the construction of such rafts. He studied and plotted the effects of wind, tide and currents across the Pacific. He believed his theory was right and so he set out to prove it.

In 1947 he built a balsa wood raft, which he named *Kon-tiki* after the Polynesian Sun-god and, on 28th April with five companions, he set sail, believing that his journey would take 97 days. It was an adventure requiring courage. The raft might become water-logged and sink. They might die of hunger or thirst, be attacked by giant octopuses or capsized by a whale.

But, on 7th August, they reached one of the islands, proving that the Polynesians *could* have originated in South America. In 1970, to prove another theory, Heyerdahl sailed with a crew of seven from Morocco in Africa to the West Indies in *Ra-2*, a papyrus reed-boat of a type used by the ancient Egyptians.

Much of our knowledge of things today has come to us because people like him have set out to prove what they believe, sometimes at great risk to themselves.

O God, give us active minds to work things out for ourselves and give us patience as we try to find out whether we are right. *Amen.*

Closing prayer No. 77

Challenge of nature (5)

BENEATH THE SEA   *Jacques-Ives Cousteau*

When man had climbed the highest mountain, sailed the seven seas, penetrated the deepest jungle and explored from Pole to Pole there remained one part of the world very largely unexplored—the world beneath the sea.

In the ocean depths it is a very dark world inhabited by strange creatures: in warm coastal areas it can be a beautiful world with coloured coral, gently moving plant life and brightly coloured fish. Today many people enjoy exploring this underwater world, skin diving and breathing under water with the help of an aqualung.

The aqualung was developed in 1943 and used by frogmen who attacked enemy shipping below the water. One of those who developed it was Jacques Cousteau. Born on 11th June, 1910, he spent the earlier part of his life as an officer in the French Navy but he became very interested in underwater exploration and he developed many kinds of equipment which could be used to observe the creatures of the oceans as well as special chambers in which men could live under the water for many days at a time.

In 1951 he began to explore the oceans of the world in his ship *Calypso*. He studied the habits of marine animals and fish and wrote many books about them. He took many photographs and made films about the oceans. His television series, 'The Undersea World of Jacques Cousteau' brought into many homes something of the wonders of that part of the world which many would never see.

It also reminded people of the need to take care lest by carelessness or thoughtlessness this beautiful world and its inhabitants might be harmed.

Thank you, God, for those who have explored the seas, sometimes at great risk to themselves, to record that part of your creation. May their observations increase our knowledge of our world and make us appreciate it all the more. *Amen.*

Closing prayer No. 83

Science and invention (1)

Thomas Alva Edison

If one were to ask who was the world's greatest inventor, one would receive various answers but no doubt the name of Thomas Alva Edison would come near the top of the list. By the time he died at the age of eighty four on 18th October, 1931, he had patented one thousand three hundred inventions. And of all these the one most widely used is the electric light bulb.

It was on New Year's Eve 1879 that guests to a party in Edison's laboratory were amazed to find the place lit with strings of electric light bulbs—an invention that many scientists had thought to be quite impossible.

Edison had very little education. He was only in school for three months. Otherwise he learned from his mother. But he was the kind of person who was always curious and wanting to know why or how things happened. He first worked at selling newspapers and sweets on a train and he used the baggage car as a laboratory. He learned about and became an expert in wireless telegraphy. Several of his inventions were concerned with better methods of sending messages.

Edison found himself a place where he could have his laboratory at Menlo Park, New Jersey, U.S.A. He soon became known as 'The Wizard of Menlo Park'. It was there that he developed the electric light bulb, made a phonograph or gramophone, improved the design of telephones, planned ways of taking and showing moving pictures—the fore-runner of today's cinema and film industry.

There is no doubt at all that the world owes a great deal to Thomas Alva Edison.

O God our Father, we remember with thankfulness all those everyday things which mean so much to us. We thank you for all who have used their talents in invention or discovery. May we never take these things for granted but have grateful hearts. *Amen.*

Closing prayer No. 89

Science and invention (2)

Alexander Graham Bell

There are few inventions that have been more useful than the telephone and for this we are indebted to Alexander Graham Bell. He was born in Edinburgh on 3rd March, 1847 but much of his experimenting was done in the United States of America. His family had moved to Canada in 1870 and to Boston two years later.

Bell was a well educated man with a great interest in language. In Boston he founded a school to train teachers of the deaf. He had thought of making a machine to help deaf people to hear and his experiments on this led to the idea of sending speech by electricity.

On 15th February, 1876, Bell applied for a patent for his invention, only just ahead of others who had been carrying out similar experiments. On 10th March, in a Boston boarding house, Bell was able to speak to his assistant who had a receiver in the cellar.

But that was only the beginning. Then came the job of making and marketing telephones—and people were slow to want to buy them. There were also many lawsuits to be fought against others who wanted to cash in on the new telephones. Bell won them all. He became a very rich man and bought himself a fine country house in Nova Scotia, Canada. There he settled down to work on further inventions.

After a visit to his native Edinburgh, where he was given the freedom of the city, he returned to Nova Scotia. There he died two years later on 2nd August, 1922. His greatest memorial—the telephone—can be found in homes and offices throughout the world.

Almighty God, we say thank you for all those inventions which have helped to make life easier or more comfortable for us; and for all whose work made them possible. Keep us mindful of our blessings and give us thankful hearts. *Amen.*

Benediction No. 105

Science and invention (3)

HOVERCRAFT   *Christopher Cockerell*

What can travel over land or water, can carry people or cargo and needs no port or airfield? The answer is a hovercraft, one of the most useful of modern transport inventions, especially when one considers that the land does not have to be smooth as for a wheeled vehicle. Hovercraft can travel over very bumpy ground and ditches or cross rivers without needing bridges.

A hovercraft travels on a cushion of air. As there is no friction it can travel very fast. This cushion of air is formed by a powerful fan blowing air downwards. This air is held in place between the hull or body of the hovercraft and the ground or water by a flexible apron which hangs all round the hull.

The idea of hovercraft was considered over a hundred years ago but it was not until 1955 that the British engineer Christopher Cockerell discovered how to make it work. He did so by experimenting with the blower from an electric hair drier and some empty tins. In 1958 he was able to get help from the government and in 1959 the first man-carrying hovercraft appeared.

Nowadays there are quite large hovercraft on cross-channel ferry services. There are also air trains—the invention of a French engineer, Jean Bertin. They also travel on a cushion of air but on a track and can gain speeds as high as 300 m.p.h. (480 km/h).

No doubt these ideas will be developed still further and become more widely used in the future.

Almighty God, we thank you for those people who have used their talents to invent or to discover useful things. Help us to use whatever gifts you have given us to do things which are useful; and help us to live our lives in such a way that they will be of use to you for the growth of your Kingdom on earth. *Amen.*

Closing prayer No. 84

Science and invention (4)

Sir Robert Watson-Watt

Robert Watson-Watt, a Scotsman, was born at Brechin, Angus, on 13th April, 1892. As a boy he always regarded science as fun. As he grew older he became interested in electrical engineering and radio-telegraphy. Then, during World War I he became a 'weather man'.

In the years that followed he did some very important work on atmospherics—those noises which often interfere with radio broadcasts and reception. On 1st December, 1927, he was appointed Superintendent of the Radio Research Station at Slough. By this time his work was well-known and people turned to him for advice.

One of the most important things he did, and that for which he will mainly be remembered was to discover how to detect and locate aircraft by radio methods. He transmitted a radio wave which bounced off the aircraft and returned, showing up on a receiver as a spot of light.

This became known as RDF (Radio Direction Finding) but it has since become known as RADAR. This was of particular value during World War II, when enemy aircraft could be detected before they came into sight. RADAR had many other uses as well.

In peacetime, too, RADAR has proved of great value to navigators of ships and aircraft, who can work out their own positions as well as those of others whom they are unable to see. Sir Robert Watson-Watt, who was knighted in 1942, has deservedly received various honours for his valuable work.

Today, O God, we have been thinking about someone who showed how to find things which could not be seen, and we are thankful for his work. You, too, remain hidden from our sight but we know that we can find you through our prayers and our meditation and we say a special thank-you for those who have shown us the way, above all your Son, our Lord Jesus Christ. *Amen.*

Benediction No. 103

Science and invention (5)

Streptomycin

If we are not well we may see the doctor, who prescribes some medicine that we then obtain from a chemist. In the chemist's shop are all manner of medicines and drugs, some of which anyone can buy and others whch are only available if a doctor prescribes them.

There are liquids to be swallowed, pills and tablets of many shapes, sizes and colours, powders, ointments and other medications. Some will cure illnesses in a short time: others may correct something that has gone wrong in a person's body and must be taken for the rest of that person's life.

Some medicines have been known and used for hundreds of years but many have been developed only in recent times. Large numbers of chemists and medical scientists are continually working to find new drugs, which must be tested most thoroughly before being used.

Every now and then there is an outstanding discovery. In 1939, for example, an American professor, Selman Waksman, began to test tiny growths in the soil to see whether any of them could be used to fight the germs which cause disease. Four years later, he had discovered how to use a tiny microbe, which can be developed through various stages into a white powder called Streptomycin. This is widely used today as an antibiotic, that is a drug which fights disease. In some cases it can be more effective than penicillin.

Professor Waksman could have become very rich from the money he received as a result of his discovery but he gave it instead to establish an Institute where microbes could be studied. He was awarded a Nobel Prize for Medicine in 1952.

We thank you, O God, for all the medicines which are available to cure our illnesses, and we thank you for all those who have worked patiently to find and develop new cures. We commend to you all who research today, that their work may help build a healthier world. *Amen.*

Closing prayer No. 65

Engineering and construction (1)

Abraham Darby

Just outside the new town of Telford, Salop, lies a piece of land that is of great historical interest. Spanning the River Severn is an old iron bridge, which gives its name to the nearby village—Ironbridge.

People come from all over the world to admire the two-hundred-year-old bridge and nowadays, too, to visit the Ironbridge Gorge Museum with its many relics of the old iron industry of Coalbrookdale and the surrounding area.

Iron has been used for thousands of years and we can read of its use in the Bible.

Bible Reading: Joshua 17: 17–18

Some people had iron chariots but iron was used mainly for tools. It could not be made cheaply in large quantities.

For that we are indebted to Abraham Darby, who arrived in Shropshire from Bristol in 1708. He it was who discovered how to smelt the iron by using coke instead of charcoal and built a blast furnace which produced iron for pots and pans, ornamental gates, iron frames, machinery and lots of other uses.

Abraham Darby died on 20th March, 1717 and the work was continued by his son of the same name. It was Abraham Darby III who built the iron bridge. Their memorials are simple tombstones in the nearby Quaker burial ground but they are remembered as hard-working men of God who used their talents to help to build the modern world.

Almighty God, Creator of the world, who gave us a world filled with minerals and natural resources to be used for the benefit of mankind, we thank you for all these things and for those who have used their talents to put these resources to good use so that we have so much to enjoy today. Give us thankful hearts we pray. *Amen.*

Benediction No. 94

Engineering and construction (2)

THE CRYSTAL PALACE   *Joseph Paxton*

Prince Albert, the consort of Queen Victoria, had the idea of holding an exhibition in London, where British goods could be displayed for foreign buyers to see.

To house the exhibition in 1851, a huge glass building was erected in Hyde Park. It was called the Crystal Palace and was a most unusual piece of engineering, rather like a large greenhouse. And that was what it was, a large version of a greenhouse which had been built on the Duke of Devonshire's estate at Chatsworth, Derbyshire.

Surprisingly, the man who designed it, Joseph Paxton, had begun life a very poor man in a family so poor that he had to be brought up by an elder brother. Then he was apprenticed to a gardener and became very interested in plants.

Joseph left for London to work for the Horticultural Society and, at twenty-four, became a foreman in their garden. Now the Duke of Devonshire was the President of the Horticultural Society and he recognized the talents of the young gardener. He appointed him to take charge of his estate at Chatsworth and there is no doubt his choice was a wise one.

Often Paxton travelled with the Duke and he made many changes on the estate. In 1854 he was elected a Member of Parliament for Coventry.

Joseph Paxton died on 8th June, 1865, but his great creation, the Crystal Palace, lived on. After the Great Exhibition ended, it had been moved to a site in South London, where it was opened by Queen Victoria in 1854. There it remained until it was destroyed by fire on 30th November, 1936.

Almighty God we thank you for all the creative gifts you have given to man; for active minds and capable hands. Help us to develop our gifts to create things which are attractive and useful. *Amen.*

Closing prayer No. 61

Engineering and construction (3)

     Charles Pearson and John Fowler

We are quite familiar today with complaints that there is too much traffic using the streets of London and that something *must* be done about it. It is nothing new. People were saying the same thing in 1837 when Queen Victoria became queen, but then they were talking about horse-drawn traffic instead of cars and buses.

It was in that year that a London solicitor, Charles Pearson, had a bright idea. Why not build a railway underground to carry passengers? People laughed. Others thought it would be a disaster. But Pearson would not be put off, even though it was seventeen years before Parliament agreed to its construction.

The engineer largely responsible for it was John Fowler, a Yorkshireman who had already worked on overhead railways. He set to work on the first part of the London Underground—a section of the Metropolitan line between Paddington and Farringdon Street.

It was not a tube or tunnel as we know it today but a cutting which was later covered over in places. It was, however, the first underground railway in the world and there was great excitement when the first section, $3\frac{3}{4}$ miles of it, was opened on 10th January, 1863. The rush for seats was so great that there was no hope of boarding the train that day at any of the intermediate stations.

There was great praise, and rightly so, for John Fowler and his engineers, but for Charles Pearson who had battled for the railway for nearly twenty-five years there was barely a mention. People soon forget!

We thank you, God our Father, for people who have had good ideas and have refused to be discouraged by others. May we never be discouraged from doing what we believe to be the right thing. *Amen.*

Closing prayer No. 77

Engineering and construction (4)

TRANSATLANTIC CABLE *Lord Kelvin*

In Kelvingrove Park, Glasgow, there is a monument to Baron Kelvin of Largs, a man who is recognized as one of the great scientists of last century.

Born in Belfast on 26th June, 1824, Kelvin was educated at the Universities of Glasgow and Cambridge. He also worked in the University of Paris before becoming a professor at the University of Glasgow from 1846 until he retired in 1899.

Kelvin put his scientific knowledge to very good use and patented some 70 inventions, several of which bear his name. Many of his inventions were to do with ships and the sea. He invented the first magnetic compass that was almost free from the effects of iron in the ship. He produced a machine which could foretell changes in sea level at ports.

One work which brought him fame was that of electrical engineer in charge of the laying of the first transatlantic cable for passing messages between Europe and America. There had been several unsuccessful attempts to lay a cable but Kelvin showed how it could be done. So the cable was laid between Ireland and Newfoundland using the famous steamship *Great Eastern* and the work completed on 27th July, 1866.

Lord Kelvin, who became internationally famous as a scientist, was a very talented man and he used those talents to contribute much that has been of lasting value to mankind.

Bible Reading: Proverbs 2: 1–6

Almighty God, Giver of every good and perfect gift, we thank you for those who have used the gifts you have bestowed for the benefit of mankind. Grant unto us the wisdom to recognize our special talents, the ability to develop them fully, and a readiness to use them in the service of others. *Amen.*

Closing prayer No. 89

Engineering and construction (5)

Benjamin Baker

Spanning the River Forth at Queensferry are two huge bridges, each one a masterpiece of engineering. The old and better known of the two, the Forth railway bridge, when it was opened on 4th March, 1890, was the largest bridge in the world. It is no longer that but it remains different from other bridges.

It was the brainchild of Benjamin Baker, an engineer with considerable experience in railway and bridge building. He had the difficult task of designing a bridge to carry the railway one third of a mile (0·5 km) across a deep river and high enough to allow ships to pass beneath.

To do this he designed steel towers each 343 feet (104·5 m) high, one on each shore and one on an island in the river. From these a steel framework was built from shore to shore, using fifty thousand tonnes of steel.

For many years all other traffic had to cross the river by ferry until the new Forth road bridge was built. The building of this began on 21st November, 1958 and the bridge was opened in 1964. This is a suspension bridge with a tall tower on either shore. The bridge is 1½ miles (2·5 km) long and, at the time of building, was the largest suspension bridge in Europe and the fourth largest in the world.

Yet for all the grace of the new it is the old bridge which still captures the fascination of most people. After nearly a century of service it stands a great tribute to its designer, Sir Benjamin Baker, one of the largely forgotten engineers whose talents benefited people of their time and many thousands since.

Almighty God, we praise you for the natural wonders of our world and for all those man-made wonders which have been so useful to so many people. For those who gave these things, praise be to you, O God. *Amen.*

Benediction No. 96

Astronomy (1)

Have you ever looked at the stars on a clear night and wondered how many there are? There are, in fact, 5,776 stars visible to the naked eye but you will not see them all at once. The stars are grouped in galaxies. Our galaxy, the Milky Way, contains something like one hundred thousand million stars. And the Milky Way is only one of millions of galaxies.

How big is the universe? How far does it reach? Again the figures are too big for us really to be able to understand them. Our sun, for example, is 93 million miles (149 million km) away, and that is very close. Miles or kilometres cannot be used for measuring space distances because those distances are too great. So distances in space are measured in light years—that is the distance light travels in one year, nearly six million million miles (9·5 million million km).

The nearest star to Earth is 4·28 light years away (25 million million miles) (over 40 million million km); the furthest edge of the Milky Way is 120,000 light years away; and we know of nebulae, possibly star clusters, which are more than 100 million light years away!

It is quite beyond our comprehension. We are indebted to many people who have helped us to understand something of the vastness of the universe of which our world is such a tiny, tiny part.

Yet the Bible reminds us that the God who created all these things is the God who cares for and strengthens his people.

Bible Reading: Isaiah 40: 25–31

Almighty God, great Creator, we marvel at the vastness of the universe and the wonders of the whole of creation; but we marvel even more that you love and care for us. Accept our thanks for all your gifts and give us grateful hearts. *Amen.*

Closing prayer No. 86

Astronomy (2)

In the ancient world, especially in Egypt and Babylon, there were many people who studied the stars and learned quite a lot about them. The prophet Isaiah obviously thought very little of the Babylonians!

Bible Reading: Isaiah 47: 13–15

Were these astrologers or astronomers? Astrologers are people who predict events by the movement of the stars. Astronomers are those who make a scientific study of the stars and we owe a lot to these ancient astronomers.

Many of their findings were wrong. We would not expect them to be able to make accurate calculations about something as complicated as the universe. The oldest document we have is that of Eudoxus (409–356 B.C.) who believed everything revolved round the earth. Other people produced different theories in the centuries which followed.

About A.D. 140, Ptolemy, a Greek astronomer living in Egypt, published a book of his findings with a catalogue of stars, but it was the work of Copernicus which was of really great importance. He calculated in the fifteenth century that the earth and other planets revolved around the sun.

From then onwards there were many great astronomers. One of the greatest was Tycho Brahe. Born on 14th December, 1546, he set up an observatory in his native Denmark, where he kept accurate records of stars and planets. He was able to produce a catalogue of 777 stars and this without a telescope. Telescopes had not then been invented. After his death on 24th October, 1601, in Prague, his assistant, Johannes Kepler, worked out the movements of the planets.

We give thanks, O God, for all those whose studies of the stars have helped us to understand the universe and show us something of the wonders of your creation. *Amen.*

Benediction No. 98

Astronomy (3)

Sir Isaac Newton

Of all the scientists in the course of history few, if any, have been greater than Sir Isaac Newton, who was born the son of a farmer near Grantham, Lincolnshire.

Newton is probably best remembered for his explanation of the laws of gravity. His interest was aroused when, sitting in a garden, he saw an apple fall to the ground. 'Why did it fall in a perpendicular line to the ground?' he asked himself.

The answer, he decided, must be that the earth pulled the apple to itself. He put his theory to good use in astronomy and space too. Gravity would explain why the moon was held on its course round the earth: it was a combination of the speed of the moon and gravity.

It was Newton, too, who, in 1668, built the first reflecting telescope. By using a mirror to reflect the image of the stars it was possible to see far more than with the ordinary optical telescope.

These are only two of Newton's discoveries which were of value to astronomy. He also discovered how white light can be divided into the colours of the spectrum as seen in a rainbow. He was a very clever mathematician too.

Yet for all his brilliance, Newton was always ready to acknowledge his indebtedness to those who had gone before and paved the way for his work. He said, 'If I have seen further than most men it is by standing on the shoulders of giants.'

Sir Isaac Newton died on 20th March, 1727, at the age of 84 and was laid to rest in Westminster Abbey.

We thank you, Almighty God, for all the abilities with which we can discover those things we need for life. We acknowledge with thankfulness the work of people who have helped our understanding. Help us to benefit from all knowledge. *Amen.*

Closing prayer No. 78

Astronomy (4)

Some people have become famous in the history of astronomy for having found out how things work in the universe. Others are remembered especially for the discovery of a particular heavenly body.

One of these latter was Edmund Halley, the first man to explain what a comet was and the kind of path it travelled. One particular comet, Halley's Comet, was named after him. He studied it when it appeared in 1682 and calculated that it would appear again in 1758. It did. Its two appearances this century are 1910 and about 1986.

Halley was appointed Astronomer Royal in 1720 and he held that position until his death on 14th January, 1742.

A few years before Halley died, William Herschel was born in Germany (15th November, 1738). He came to England from Hanover as a musician but he became interested in astronomy and it is for this that he is remembered. He made his own telescopes so that he could discover the distribution of the stars in the Milky Way.

It was Herschel who discovered the planet Uranus on 13th March, 1781. Even more important was his study of the stars over a period of nearly fifty years, which resulted in his explanation of the movement of the sun and stars in space, facts which greatly increased man's knowledge of the universe. Sir William Herschel died on 25th August, 1822, leaving his son, Sir John Herschel to continue his researches.

We can imagine the immense amount of work, the faithful recording and patient study that was needed by men such as these.

Almighty God, our heavenly Father, we remember the work and the study of those who have enabled us to know more about our universe and are thankful for the knowledge they have given us. Help us also to study heavenly things so that we may know more about you and your ways. *Amen.*

Closing prayer No. 59

Astronomy (5)

Telescopes and observatories

One of the most important discoveries in the history of astronomy was the telescope which enabled men to see far more stars than ever they could with the naked eye. Galileo (1564–1642) was the man who first made a telescope suitable for astronomy. Later Sir Isaac Newton made the reflecting telescope with which people could see much more.

The largest telescope to be made for use in Britain was one with a reflecting mirror 98 inches (2·5 m) in diameter for the Royal Greenwich observatory at Herstmonceux, Sussex. But this is small compared with the huge 200 inch (5 m) reflecting telescope at Mount Palomar Observatory, California (opened 3rd July, 1948) and the even larger Russian 6 metre (236·2 inch) telescope on Mount Semirodriki in the Caucasus mountains (1976).

It is doubtful whether a larger one will ever be built. The cost of these is enormous and the present ones can be used for photographing objects which are millions of light years away from the earth.

Nowadays, too, we have large radio telescopes which are able to explore space using radio waves. The huge steerable radio telescope at Jodrell Bank Cheshire belongs to the University of Manchester and was completed in 1957. Its 260 ft (79 m) bowl has a range 1,000 times better than the best optical telescope. The world's largest radio telescope is non steerable and has a 1,000 ft (305 m) dish spanning a natural crater in Puerto Rico.

So man has used his talents to better his knowledge not only of the universe but of the whole of creation. The wise man also does what he can to increase his knowledge of God the Creator, too.

Bible Reading: Proverbs 3: 17–22

Grant unto us, Almighty God, a quest for knowledge about our universe and about you, and wisdom to understand those things which we learn. *Amen.*

Closing prayer No. 63

Space travel (1)

Wernher von Braun

Today we are familiar with news of rockets carrying spacecraft to head for the moon or beyond, yet the development of rockets is quite recent in the history of the world. One man who was very largely responsible for their development and became one of the world's leading authorities on rockets and space travel was Wernher von Braun.

Von Braun was born in 1912 in a part of Germany which is now in Poland. He experimented with rockets from an early age and was largely responsible for the German V2 rockets of World War II. Toward the end of the war he was imprisoned for refusing to co-operate with the Nazi leaders and, in 1945, with other scientists, surrendered to the United States army.

From that time he worked in America, becoming a United States citizen in 1955. When rockets were needed for America's space programme it was von Braun's team which developed the four-stage Jupiter rocket used for launching the first American space craft and, later, the Saturn rockets used to put the first man on the moon.

Von Braun was responsible for planning some of the American space programme in NASA (National Aeronautics and Space Administration) and he served as President of the National Space Institute which gives publicity to the American space programme. He died on 16th June, 1977.

Astronauts may land on the moon or be involved in complicated manoeuvres in space and receive a lot of publicity but they would be unable to do any of this without the work of scientists such as Wernher von Braun.

Today, O God, we remember the people who have used their talents to do wonderful things in the world of science and invention. Grant that such work may continue and that mankind may benefit from their labours. *Amen.*

Benediction No. 92

Space travel (2)

Into orbit

Once people had discovered how to send rockets into space, the next step was obviously to put something into orbit round the earth. This meant lifting a spacecraft high enough to be held in place by the earth's gravity and making it fast enough to travel round the world without dropping.

The first spacecraft to go into orbit was the Russian *Sputnik I*, which was launched on 4th October, 1957. A second spacecraft, *Sputnik II* carried a passenger, a dog named Laika. It was also a Russian astronaut, Yuri Gagarin, who made history by becoming the first man to orbit the earth. Man's journeys into space had begun.

It was soon realized that there were many uses for space. Artificial satellites, or man-made 'moons' could be made to go into orbit round the world and be very useful. Some of the first were communications satellites, used to 'bounce' radio waves, or like Telstar, launched on 10th July, 1962, to relay television programmes between Europe and America.

Weather satellites have proved very useful for sending weather information back to earth and navigation satellites have been used to help navigators to find their true positions. There are also spy satellites which can be used to send back military information.

Once a new discovery has been made, scientists can usually find all sorts of uses to which it can be put.

Many satellites depend upon batteries and are only of use whilst the batteries last. There are dozens of useless satellites still in orbit round the world.

O God, we live in a complicated world with so many things that we cannot really understand even though we know how useful they are. May those who do understand put these things to good use. *Amen.*

Benediction No. 107

Space travel (3)

From earliest times people have been fascinated by the moon. Ancient peoples regarded the moon as a goddess. All sorts of tales are told about the man in the moon or that the moon is made of cheese. And instead of saying that something is impossible people have said that it is like reaching for the moon.

But suddenly reaching for the moon was not impossible and people were able to discover whether or not the moon was made of cheese! If man could orbit the earth, what was to stop him travelling to the moon?

There were many things to do first. The right kinds of rocket had to be developed. Suitable space craft were needed. Photographs had to be taken all round the moon. Soft landings had to be made by unmanned craft. Both Americans and Russians played their part. Then, in 1968 came the first moon flight when three American astronauts circled the moon and returned. Many scientists had combined to use their talents to bring the moon within reach.

Now the stage was set for man to make a moon landing. Neil Armstrong was the first man to set foot on the moon on 21st July, 1969, followed a few minutes later by 'Buzz' Aldrin. It was a great historic occasion.

There was much to do and to be seen but the two astronauts took the opportunity to spend a short while in saying thank you to God in the best way they knew by eating bread and wine in a simple service of Holy Communion.

Bible Reading: St. Luke 22: 14–20

Accept our thanks, O God, for all those people who have used their talents to make it possible for men to reach the moon. Thank you, too, for those with the courage to venture into the unknown. Grant us, in our own lives, to take advantage of the works of others, to go forward with courage, and to remember to say thank-you. *Amen.*

Closing prayer No. 85

Space travel (4)

When we hear of people travelling into space it may seem a simple thing for them to do, yet there are very many preparations necessary before any space flight. Those who are to travel in space must undergo a lot of training to make sure that their bodies can adjust to all the conditions they are likely to meet.

Special pressurized space suits must also be worn to counteract the effect of the sudden speeds of take-off. Space suits have also to be worn by astronauts working outside their spacecraft because of dangers from radiation and from tiny particles of space dust.

Astronauts have also to get used to weightlessness. Because there is no gravity everything floats in the air instead of dropping to the floor. Normal movements become impossible. They must also be familiar with all their equipment because once in space they are on their own except for radio links with earth.

Then there are lots of other things to be worked out in detail. Food and drink are essential and so are toilet arrangements. Exercise and recreation are equally important.

One of the natural developments in space was the space station. This is a large satellite orbiting the earth. It may be sent into space in sections and put together there. Both Russians and Americans have sent up space laboratories in which men can work for a month or more before returning to earth.

No doubt we shall hear a lot more about the use of space in the years to come.

Almighty God, Creator of all the worlds and things which remain unknown to mortal man, help us to look after our world and the space around it, so that nothing may spoil it for us or for those who come after us. *Amen.*

Benediction No. 94

Space travel (5)

Many people enjoy science fiction stories of journeys into space and visitors from other planets. They have pictured what Martians might look like and have designed huge space ships.

Is it ever going to be possible for men to travel to other planets or beyond? Only time will tell. In the meantime scientists have been using their talents to discover more about these planets.

This exploration began on 28th November, 1964, when the Americans launched *Mariner IV*, which took photographs of Mars after a journey lasting nearly eight months. On 2nd December, 1971, a capsule carried on another spacecraft, *Mars 3*, made the first soft landing on Mars. It sent back a lot of information, but no pictures of Martians!

Venus is the next nearest planet. Back in 1967 a Russian space probe *Venera IV* was sent there to feed back information about the planet's atmosphere.

Pioneer X went even further. Launched on 2nd March, 1972, it passed Jupiter one year and nine months later, sending back information about that planet. Then it sped on and on and is probably still travelling somewhere, the first man-made object to leave the solar system.

Perhaps one day man will be able to travel to the planets but he will need a large craft and plenty of food. A journey to Mars and back would take over a year. And Mars is our nearest neighbour.

As we think of journeys into space we marvel at the progress man has made but we marvel even more at the vastness of the universe and the mighty power of God who created it.

Bible Reading: Psalm 148: 1–6 (or 14)

O God, great Creator, we praise you for the wonders of your creation; for the vastness of the universe, sun, moon and stars. Yet even more we praise you that you who can create such big things can care for little things like us. *Amen.*

Benediction No. 103

Leadership (1)

IN TIME OF NEED   *Franklin D. Roosevelt*

In 1932 the United States of America was in a mess. Millions of people were out of work; many were starving; banks were closed; people were losing their homes and businesses; and gangsters were defying law and order.

That was the year that the Americans were electing a new President. It was a little surprising that the man who was chosen was crippled. Yet Franklin Delano Roosevelt had fired the imagination of the American people by his declaration, 'I pledge you, I pledge myself, to a New Deal for the American people.'

Roosevelt was a very able man. Born of a rich family descended from Dutch settlers, he had been in politics for many years. Up to 1920 all had gone well and it seemed as though he was all set to become President. Then, after a cold dip on a hot day he was struck down with infantile paralysis (polio), which left the lower half of his body useless. By constant exercise, bathing in hot springs and the encouragement of his wife, Eleanor, he began to walk with the aid of crutches and leg irons.

As President he was equally determined to get his country out of the mess it was in and he was so successful that he was re-elected in 1936. It was during this time that war broke out in Europe. In 1940 he was elected for a third term—the first president ever to be so—and in 1944 a fourth! But by this time he was a very frail man. The strain of the presidency, added to his physical handicap began to tell. On 12th April, 1945, he died.

Roosevelt was a very gifted man—and he used those gifts to the full for the benefit of others.

Bible Reading: Romans 12: 4–8

We thank you, O God, for those gifts which you have given us. Help us to discover what our special gifts are and how we should use them for the benefit of others and in your service. *Amen.*

Closing prayer No. 64

Leadership (2)

Jomo Kenyatta

No one can be quite sure when Jomo Kenyatta was born, save that it was somewhere about the middle of the 1890s in a simple hut in a Kikuyu village in Kenya.

Kenyatta learned of two ways of life. His grandfather, a medicine man, introduced him to the old tribal ways and customs. But Kenyatta also attended a Church of Scotland mission school and was baptized into the Christian faith.

Between the two great wars there was unrest in Kenya. White settlers arrived in large numbers and so did many Indians. The Kenyans felt they were being pushed out of their own land. Kenyatta travelled to other lands—Germany, Russia, Britain—learning all the time and teaching others about the Kikuyu.

After World War II he returned to Kenya and became a leader. He was accused of taking part in a rising, known as Mau-mau, against the white settlers and was imprisoned, though it was found later that false evidence had been given.

In 1960 it was agreed that Kenya should have its own government. On 12th December, 1963, it became independent and a year later Kenyatta became President, remaining in office until his death on 22nd August, 1978.

Kenyatta was determined to make Kenya a multi-racial nation. In a famous speech he said; 'There is no society of angels, whether it is white, brown or black. We are all human beings, and as such we are bound to make mistakes.' He urged that there should be forgiveness on both sides and that everyone should work together for the good of Kenya so that people of various races and beliefs could live together.

Bible Reading: Romans 12: 17–21

O God, as we look around we see many whose colour, beliefs and way of life are different from our own. Help us to remember that none of us is perfect but we should learn to live together in love. *Amen.*

Closing prayer No. 80

Leadership (3)

DICTATORSHIP   *Adolf Hitler*

Bible Reading: II Timothy 3: 1–5

Paul warns of unpleasant people. There have been many of these but few who have affected the lives of more people than Adolf Hitler, ruler of Germany from 1933 to 1945.

It is strange that a man who loved children and animals could be responsible for the death of millions of people and cause untold suffering to millions more. In some ways his story is one of amazing success; in other ways it is one of dismal failure.

Adolf Hitler, son of a customs officer and born on 20th April, 1889, saw service in the German army during World War I. At the end of the war he was out of work and wondering how Germany could become powerful again. He formed a political party called the National Socialist German Workers' Party, or Nazi party.

Hitler discovered that he had great powers of leadership and was able to persuade men to follow him. His speeches roused people to action. In 1933 he persuaded President Hindenburg to appoint him Chancellor (Prime Minister). When Hindenburg died in 1934, Hitler took over the presidency too and became known as the Führer, dictator of eighty million people.

He began a reign of bullying and terror. Those who opposed him were imprisoned or killed; millions of Jews and others were put to death in concentration camps; weaker nations were over-run by his armies; and much of the world became involved in World War II.

But success turned to failure. As Germany was on the verge of defeat in 1945, Hitler took his own life on 30th April. So died a man who had no regard for God or man and gained a reputation as one of the most evil men in the world.

We thank you, O God, for the freedom we enjoy in our land today. We pray for people in lands where there is no such freedom and ask that the leaders in those lands may be guided into better ways for the benefit of their peoples. *Amen.*

Closing prayer No. 55

Leadership (4)

Dag Hammarskjöld

In 1953 the United Nations Organization had a new Secretary-General, whose job involved meeting with some of the most powerful leaders in the world and sometimes persuading them to do things which they would not have wished to do.

The new Secretary-General was a forty-eight year old Swede named Dag Hammarskjöld. His father had served the Swedish government well and Dag decided to do likewise. He held several important posts before taking office in the United Nations.

The Secretary-General normally has to take instructions from the Security Council or the General Assembly where the representatives of countries meet. Dag Hammarskjöld believed there were some things he should do himself if it would help to bring peace. He could be a kind of leader in making peace.

In the years that followed he achieved a lot. He worked to get better understanding between the United States and Russia; he secured the release of American airmen imprisoned in China; he helped solve the crisis when war broke out over the Suez Canal. Many people acknowledged Hammarskjöld as a great leader: others criticized him.

In 1961, Hammarskjöld flew to the Congo, in Africa, where there was fighting. He wanted to meet the leaders himself. On 17th December he flew to meet one of them but his plane crashed and he was killed. After his death he was awarded the Nobel Prize for Peace for his efforts to bring peace to the Congo.

We are thankful for such people, and we recall some words spoken by Jesus:

Bible Reading: St. Matthew 5: 8–9

Bless, O God, the efforts of all who work for peace, that we may enjoy peace in our world. Put into the hearts of all people a willingness to work together, to be tolerant of the views of others and to avoid anything which would offend; through Jesus Christ our Lord. *Amen.*

Closing prayer No. 70

Leadership (5)

Betty Williams and Mairead Corrigan

When we think of leaders, we probably think first of kings or prime ministers who lead nations. But there are other kinds of leader too. On 10th October, 1977, it was announced that the 1976 Nobel Prize for Peace had been awarded to two women who thought of themselves as ordinary people doing what they ought to do.

Betty Williams and Mairead (*Maree'ad*) Corrigan were housewives living in Belfast, Northern Ireland. For some years there had been violence because some people wanted to get their own way by force, shooting and bombing. British soldiers had been trying to keep peace but extremists on both sides had so much hatred in their hearts that they did not mind whom they killed.

One day in August 1976 a terrorist getaway car hit and killed three children aged eight, two and six weeks. People everywhere were shocked. The aunt of the three children, Mairead Corrigan and Betty Williams, herself a mother of four children, decided they would do something. They formed the Ulster Peace Movement.

In spite of threats from terrorists they demanded peace. They were ill-treated and abused but became even more determined. They spoke at rallies and they organized marches. Soon they had thousands of followers.

When the award was announced, Mairead said, 'Nobel was the man who invented dynamite. We hope to change things without dynamite. We haven't brought peace to Northern Ireland yet—but if we've managed to save just one life I'm extremely happy.'

St. Paul gave this advice on the right kind of attitude to life, which many people would do well to remember:

Bible Reading: Colossians 3: 13–16.

We thank you, God our Father, for all who work to bring peace to the world. Grant that people everywhere may learn that force and violence do not bring peace but that tolerance, forgiveness and love must be shown to all. Teach us how to live by love; through Jesus Christ our Lord. *Amen.*

Closing prayer No. 66

5 Ourselves and others

The twelve themes in this section deal with relationships, attitudes, service to others, caring and co-operation, particularly as regards man and his fellows.

Helping others	*Seeing a need*
Caring	*Medical matters*
For those at sea	*Services to the community*
Government	*Rights and relationships*
Attitudes	*Use of riches*
Working together	*Faithfulness and loyalty*

Each of the themes can be taken as a unit and some, particularly *Rights and Relationships*, may best be taken in that way as there is continuity within the theme. Most, however, can be taken independently.

Helping others (1)

Tichborne Dole

There have always been poor people in the world and there have always been people who have wanted to help them. Here are some words from the Jewish Law:

Bible Reading: Deuteronomy 15: 7–11

Money or goods given to the poor is sometimes called a Dole and there are some interesting customs in parts of Britain concerning such gifts.

In Hampshire, for example, on 25th March each year, the villagers of Cheriton and Tichborne share the contents of a huge bin containing thirty hundredweights (1·5 tonnes) of flour.

This began some eight hundred years ago, when Lady Mabella Tichborne, who was on her death-bed, asked her husband, Sir Roger, to give some land, the produce of which could be used to help the poor.

Her husband must have been a strange kind of man, for he took a burning stick from the fire and said he would give as much land as his wife could encircle whilst it was still burning. Lady Mabella was carried out of the house and managed to crawl round $23\frac{1}{2}$ acres (9·5 hectares) on her hands and knees. This land, still known as The Crawls, produces the flour for the Tichborne Dole.

In other parts of the country there are distributions of money, bread or other food. Many are given during Lent but at Bideford, Devon, a loaf of bread and half a pound of butter is given on 1st January to anyone over sixty years of age. At Winchester, travellers calling at the Hospital of St. Cross are given the Wayfarer's Dole, a small square of bread and a drink of ale.

All these and other old customs remind us of the thoughtfulness of people in the past, and they serve to remind us to consider the poor people of our own time.

We remember before you, O God, any who are poor and needy and we ask your blessing upon all who help them. Help us always to be mindful of the needs of others and to offer such help as we can. *Amen.*

Closing prayer No. 70

Helping others (2)

Near the city of Leningrad in the U.S.S.R. is the island of Kronstadt. A century or more ago, when Leningrad was known as St. Petersburg, a young priest was appointed to work in St. Andrew's Cathedral on the island. He soon found that many of the people on the island were petty criminals and down-and-outs who had been sent there from St. Petersburg, where they were not wanted.

So began a lifelong work for Father Ivan Sergiev among the people society did not want. Beggars, drunkards, crooks and scoundrels were not the pleasantest of people but to Father Ivan they were God's children.

Each day he visited the shacks where they lived; he helped the destitute, he nursed the sick; he comforted the distressed. He discovered that he had a gift of healing and was able to cure many people who had serious illnesses.

Soon his work became widely known. People from all over Russia sent him letters and money. Each day he used the money to feed up to a thousand poor people. He built workshops, a school, an orphanage and a church. About four o'clock each morning he went to the cathedral. The great building holding about five thousand people was always filled and often the service lasted until noon, after which he went visiting until late at night.

Father Ivan died on 2nd January, 1909, having spent his life being a good neighbour to those who desperately needed one. In 1970 in the Russian Church he became St. John of Kronstadt.

The Bible tells how Jesus became a friend to those whom others did not want to know.

Bible Reading: St. Matthew 9: 9–12

Almighty God, we ask your blessing for those in need:
For the poor and needy, the hungry and homeless;
For the sick and suffering, the sad and lonely;
For all who feel unwanted by others.
Bless all who help them; for Jesus Christ's sake. *Amen.*

Closing prayer No. 66

Helping others (3)

CHILDREN IN NEED   *National Children's Home*

A little over a hundred years ago there were thousands of home-less children roaming the streets of London. They slept wherever they could find shelter. They were ragged, shoeless, filthy, hungry and wild. Many stole to get food or were employed by rogues such as Fagin in the story of Oliver Twist.

To most people these children were a nuisance but there were some who wanted to help them. One, Rev. Thomas Bowman Stephenson, a Methodist Minister, thought of a way of helping a few. With the help of two other young men, he opened a small home in Lambeth for destitute children on 7th July, 1869.

But Dr. Stephenson had bigger ideas and a dream of being able to help many more. Moreover he was ready to work hard to achieve his ideas. He did not want large institutions for the children but family homes in small houses. His work grew into the large organization known today as the National Children's Home.

Since Dr. Stephenson opened his first home, over fifty thousand children have been members of the National Children's Home 'family' which, at any time, numbers over four thousand. Most live in their small family units with house parents and attend local schools but there are also handicapped children needing special care and attention. Help is offered in many other ways too.

The National Children's Home has an ever open door: no child in need is turned away. But to do this a huge sum of money is needed each year. The N.C.H. depends very much upon gifts from lots of organizations and individual people if it is to continue to help many children who need love and care today.

[*Details could be given of any local money-raising venture.*]

Father God, we remember those less fortunate than we are and especially children who are in need. Bless the work of the National Children's Home and others who care for children. May their work continue and money be found to meet their needs. *Amen.*

Closing prayer No. 75

Helping others (4)

A READY CHAMPION   *Jack Ashley*

Bible Reading: St. Matthew 15: 30–31

People in this story brought friends to Jesus because he could help in their time of need. Often the best people to offer sympathy or a helping hand are those who have experienced problems themselves. One prominent person to have done so in recent years is Jack Ashley, Member of Parliament.

Jack was born on 6th December, 1920, in a poor area of Widnes. On leaving school he became a labourer and a crane driver. But Jack was determined to get on as well as possible. At the age of twenty-two he was a Trade Union official and the youngest member of his Borough Council. Two years later he won a scholarship for working men to attend Ruskin College, Oxford. He also attended University at Cambridge.

On 31st March, 1966, he was elected Member of Parliament for Stoke-on-Trent South and appeared set for a very successful Parliamentary career. Then disaster struck! He caught a virus infection which left him totally deaf.

His first thoughts were that he would have to give up his work. But why should he? He was not one to give in. With the help of his wife he learned to lip read. Then he returned to a totally silent House of Commons, where the Speaker referred to him as 'the bravest Member of Parliament'.

As the only totally deaf member of any parliament in the world he faced many problems and had to make a great effort to overcome his disability. Soon he became known as the M.P. who was the champion of the disabled. He battled for compensation for children deformed because their mothers had taken a drug called thalidomide. His writings and appearances on television, as well as in parliament, have highlighted the problems of others. Jack Ashley has fought his own battle and those of many others too.

We remember before you, O God, people who are disabled, the crippled, the deaf, the blind and all who suffer in body or mind. May they find help, comfort and encouragement through the love and thoughtfulness of others. *Amen.*

Closing prayer No. 68

Helping others (5)

The Samaritans

Bible Reading: St. Matthew 27: 3–5

Judas couldn't live with what he had done and there was no one to help him, so he took his own life. Every day there are people who feel so depressed about something that they do not want to go on living. Some commit suicide. Others may decide to jump off buildings but are persuaded not to do so by someone who cares enough to help.

Sometimes people in despair make a telephone call. A voice answers, 'The Samaritans—can I help you?' The call may last a long time, or the caller may be persuaded to meet the Duty Samaritan at the local headquarters. There the person with the problem is befriended and helped. It may be a chat over a cup of tea or it may be the first of many meetings. It may be the means of saving someone from suicide.

The Samaritans were started by Rev. Chad Varah on 2nd November, 1953. For years he had been concerned about people and their problems but wondered how people would know how to contact anyone willing to help. Then he was appointed Rector of St. Stephen Walbrook in the heart of the city of London and this church was to become the headquarters of The Samaritans.

Once the work became known, people volunteered to help in their spare time. In time it was these people who were answering the telephone and offering help, whilst Chad Varah was busy organizing branches elsewhere, some in other lands.

Today there are very many local branches of The Samaritans and between them they receive over a million telephone calls in the course of a year. Since the Samaritans were formed their befriending has saved thousands of lives in Britain alone and many people have been thankful for the help received.

O God our Father we remember before you those people who find life difficult and cannot find an answer to their problems. Bless those who try to help and grant them wisdom, patience, understanding and wise counsel. *Amen.*

Benediction No. 99

Seeing a need (1)

Bible Lands Society

In the centre of Jerusalem is Rawdat-El-Zuhur—'Garden of Flowers'. It is in fact a school and the 'flowers' are some of the poorest and neediest children of Jerusalem who have been given a new chance to 'bloom'. Begun in 1952, the school now has 230 children aged between four and twelve.

Also in Jerusalem, on the northern side of the city is the Mary Lovell Home in which some 35 blind girls are taught. It was founded in 1895 by Mary Jane Lovell. One of her blind pupils, Miss S. Ketchijian, later became Principal of the school.

Some miles away in Bethlehem is Helen Keller House, named after that great woman who was blind, deaf and dumb, who not only conquered her own difficulties but was a great help and encouragement to others.

Helen Keller House is the centre in the Holy Land for the work of the Bible Lands Society, which accepts responsibility for the two schools already mentioned as part of its 'work of comforting and healing the sick, blind, poor and homeless in the Holy Land'. The Society dates back to 3rd July, 1854, when it was formed to work in Turkey. Later it spread to the Turkish Empire, which then included the Bible Lands and became the Bible Lands Missions' Aid Society in 1893. It found many needs, just as Jesus did in his day.

Bible Reading: St. Luke 6: 17–19

So Christian people today, drawn from many different churches, offer help to missions of many kinds at work in the Bible Lands. The Society receives its money from gifts and also from the sale of its familiar carol sheets, Christmas cards and other materials.

Hear our prayer, O God our Father, for all who are sick, poor, needy, or homeless and today especially for those in the Bible Lands. Bless the work of all who would help them. *Amen.*

Closing prayer No. 75

Seeing a need (2)

'SAVE THE CHILDREN'   *Eglantyne Jebb*

Eglantyne Jebb, an English teacher who had been compelled to give up teaching because of ill-health, was horrified. She had been working to help children in Eastern Europe who had been left homeless because of war. World War I had run its course and some thirteen million children were in desperate need, many of them starving. The city of Vienna was almost a death camp.

'We must do something,' she declared. 'We will start a 'Save the Children Fund' and collect a thousand pounds for the starving children of Vienna.' That was in April 1919. Almost unbelievably, when just one year had passed she had raised £4,000,000.

Soon the work had spread to other parts of Europe and to South America, famine relief in Russia, war orphans in China and so on. Today its work is bigger than ever and more demanding.

Eglantyne Jebb was never satisfied that enough was being done. Five years before she died in 1928 she had prepared her 'Children's Charter'. It included such things as 'The child must be protected . . . cared for . . . given the means for normal development . . . the hungry fed, the sick nursed, the handicapped helped, the orphan sheltered . . . and so on.

Eglantyne Jebb was a sincere Christian woman. No doubt she remembered what Jesus had said about the children:

Bible Reading: Mark 10: 13–16

But she also knew that the way of Jesus is not just of receiving but of giving—giving one's talents and life in the service of others.

And so her Children's Charter concluded, 'The child must be brought up in the consciousness that its talents must be devoted to the service of its fellow men.'

Hear us, O God, as we remember suffering children throughout the world; make us thankful for our many blessings and willing to express our thanks in our service toward others. *Amen.*

Closing prayer No. 69

Seeing a need (3)

Cheshire Homes

Leonard Cheshire was full of confidence. Everything seemed to have gone right for him. He had done well at school; he had been much decorated as an officer in the Royal Air Force during World War II and towards its close had been one of two Englishmen to witness the dropping of the second atomic bomb on the Japanese city of Nagasaki; he had plenty of energy; but he found himself looking for a real purpose in life. It was not that he was looking for Christian service: he had decided for himself that there was no God.

He tried going into business but it failed. It was then that he went to see Arthur Dykes who was in hospital dying of cancer and with no home or friends. Cheshire took him to his home at Le Court and looked after him himself. He found that Dykes had something to offer him too, for Dykes was a man for whom religion meant much. Cheshire came to realize that there was a God after all and that God had shown him how he should spend his life. Le Court should be a home for people with no hope of recovery.

It was just a beginning. Before long Leonard Cheshire was looking for other homes. He started a second home in huts on an airfield in Cornwall and before long there were others in various parts of Britain. Now there are over fifty Cheshire Homes in Britain besides many in other parts of the world, most of them for permanently handicapped people who can be taught to do some things for themselves and for the benefit of the community.

Today Leonard Cheshire is in contact with people of many colours, creeds and religions, all of whom are working to help those who cannot help themselves.

Today, Father, we remember people who suffer in many ways and need the help of others. We pray for your blessing on all who look after them and ask that if we see some need ourselves we may be ready to follow their example. *Amen.*

Closing prayer No. 65

Seeing a need (4)

The Shaftesbury Society

Think of many of the reforms which took place last century to give better conditions for people and one name is sure to come to mind—Shaftesbury.

Born Anthony Ashley Cooper on 28th April, 1801, he inherited the title Earl of Shaftesbury on the death of his father. By the time he died, on 1st October, 1885, he had done more than anyone else to help the poor and needy. In Parliament he introduced the laws to give better conditions in factories and mines, to prevent the use of climbing boys to sweep chimneys, and various others to help those who could not help themselves.

But Shaftesbury probably did as much, if not more outside Parliament than he did within. It was a time when the poor were really poor and could do nothing to help themselves. Many people, like Shaftesbury, were trying to express their Christian faith in service to these needy people. Children were taken from the gutters and taught in little schools which became known as 'Ragged Schools'. It was in 1844 that these schools joined to form 'The Ragged School Union' with Shaftesbury (then Lord Ashley) as President—a position he held for 41 years until his death.

What was more natural after his death than that The Ragged School Union should change its name to 'The Shaftesbury Society'? And under that name it still works today to help those in need. It is still very much concerned with children, with homes and schools and holidays. It has schools for physically handicapped children and holiday centres for disabled. It provides homes for elderly and handicapped people. And in its mission-centres and elsewhere it demonstrates the Christian love and compassion which was the basis of all Lord Shaftesbury's work.

Hear our prayer, O God, as we remember the people of our day who are in need; the very poor, the severely handicapped, the elderly, the lonely and all in distress. Bless all those who help them. *Amen.*

Closing prayer No. 66

Seeing a need (5)

The Salvation Army

Whenever people think of organizations that are ready to offer a helping hand there is one name which springs immediately to mind—The Salvation Army. In fact, for a long time it has been known as 'the Army of the helping hand'.

From the time that the movement was first formed over a hundred years ago the Salvation Army has always kept an eye open for human needs and has then done something about them. One of the earliest needs was to provide food. William Booth, the founder, saw little point in talking to hungry people about God and so he fed them first. When he saw down-and-outs sleeping out of doors he opened shelters for them.

Now throughout the world the Salvation Army has many schools, hospitals, orphanages, old people's homes, holiday homes, training centres and a whole host of other means of helping people. It also has a well-organized missing persons branch through which people can be put in touch with members of their families. People often say, 'Where there's need there's The Salvation Army.'

But to think of the Salvation Army just as a social welfare organization would be very wrong. It does these things *because* it is a Christian movement which seeks to bring people to know God. It is certainly concerned with bodily needs but the Salvation in its name is a reminder that its chief concern is to save the souls of people by bringing them to know Jesus Christ.

Bible Reading: Romans 10: 8b–13

Help us, O God, to be aware of the needs of those around us, to offer a comforting word or a helping hand; but show us also how to live so that our words our deeds and our whole lives may point others to you. *Amen.*

Closing prayer No. 81

Caring (1)

Not so cuckoo!

An interesting bird is the cuckoo, well known for the way in which it lays eggs in the nests of other birds and leaves them to bring up the young bird when it hatches out. Once she has laid her egg, the cuckoo takes no further interest in it.

Most birds and mammals are very different from that. They look after their young, ensuring that they are well fed and trained, often guarding them very protectively from harm and danger. People are like that too. Think of all that has been done for you since you were a baby and you will realize what a lot of care you have had. The care of parents for children is often taken for granted. In fact we think something is very wrong when we hear of parents who do not care.

Long ago in ancient Greece boys in Sparta were taken from their parents to be brought up by the state. This has happened in some modern states too but most societies recognize that the children with the best start in life are those who have caring parents. Nor is it just parents. Think of all the other members of the family who care. Then there are neighbours, friends, teachers and others, all of whom care for us. Most of us are surrounded by caring people.

Of course it is a two-way process. It is up to us to care for them too. There are often times when we should be caring for or caring about the folk around us.

We recall, too, that we have a heavenly Father who cares for his children. As the Bible reminds us, God cares for us. Do we care for him and for his Kingdom?

Bible Reading: St. Matthew 6: 25–34

We thank you, God our Father, for those who have cared for us from our earliest days and especially for your care and love. Help us to show our thankfulness by caring for others. *Amen.*

Closing prayer No. 54

Caring (2)

Help the Aged

Bible Reading: Genesis 27: 1–10

So Isaac, who was old and blind, was deceived into giving his blessing to the wrong person, which upset him. He was, however, fortunate in having his family around him at the end of his life. There are many old people who live alone and have no family to care for them. At present, one householder in six in Britain is a pensioner living alone.

For many the house where they live is their family home and they do not wish to leave it to move into an old people's home. Yet they can be very lonely. Sometimes they are ill and have no one to look after them or have an accident and are unable to call for help. Many do not look after themselves properly; they do not trouble to prepare suitable food; and they fail to keep themselves warm. Such things cause the death of many old people each year.

Nowadays there are lots of people who are trying to care for old folk. In 1962 an organization was set up and called 'Help the Aged'. Each year it collects millions of pounds which is spent in providing housing, centres where old people can meet to work or enjoy themselves, and in lots of other ways which enable elderly people to have more comfort and care both in Britain and overseas.

Perhaps its most important work is to make many people aware of the need to care for the old and to find ways of doing something about it. Old people can sometimes prove difficult and even unthankful of offers of help, but there are many who are very appreciative even of little kindnesses.

We commend into your hands, O Father God, the old, the lonely, the unwanted and the uncared for. Bless all who work for their comfort and well-being and grant that we may help in any way we can. *Amen.*

Closing prayer No. 75

Caring (3)

It may not be too difficult to care for people we love and those we know, even though it may take a lot of our time and patience. How far are we able to care for people we find difficult, dirty, diseased or what some people call 'unlovable'? Remember how Jesus treated an outcast of his day:

Bible Reading: St. Mark 1: 40–45

One night seventeen-year-old Sally Trench was on her way home from a visit to the country. On the benches of London's Waterloo Station were lots of scruffy old men and women, many smelling of alcohol. Her Christian instinct was to do something, so she sat between two of them, offered them cigarettes and tried to talk to them. They were two of the hundreds of methylated spirit drinkers and other drop-outs who live rough in London.

Sally decided that this was an opening for her to do something worthwhile. Each night she took out flasks of coffee, bandages and other things that would bring comfort and help. Then she learned of a minister, Rev. M. Peake, who had opened his church in Ladbroke Grove as a refuge for such men. She went there, willing to give a helping hand and offer friendship.

Often it was a thankless labour of love. Some did not respond; some even attacked her. But there were the rewarding moments. One man, whom Sally had cared for whilst he was very ill, opened his eyes, smiled and said, 'Gal, you're the first person who's ever loved me.'

But Sally wasn't doing this for thanks or reward. It was a service of love and caring in the name of God.

O God, Father of all, we remember the outcasts and drop-outs of this world and we thank you that there are those who do care for them. Make us ready to care even for those who seem unpleasant. *Amen.*

Closing prayer No. 66

Caring (4)

When I needed a neighbour were you there, were you there?
When I needed a neighbour were you there?
And the creed and the colour and the name won't matter,
Were you there?

There are many circumstances in which people may be in need of a neighbour and are thankful for whatever help is offered, no matter by whom. We hear sometimes of people taken ill at home for whom help comes after someone has noticed that the milk has not been taken in all day. There are many people who have been thankful for a good neighbour.

For most of us the neighbours are the people who live near us, for these are the ones we are most likely to be able to help. They may not be the easiest people to get on with. Some may not be very pleasant; some are old and crotchety; and some may even have been unkind to us. Yet these may be the ones who are most likely to need our help. In the parable Jesus told, the neighbour to the man who fell among thieves was a Samaritan, an enemy: and Jesus said, 'Go and do likewise.' Do we care?

Caring for neighbours may mean offering to do little jobs for them. It may mean keeping an eye open for anything that may appear to be wrong. It may sometimes be as simple a matter as being kind or considerate, treating them as we would like to be treated ourselves. If we really care there will be endless opportunities to be a good neighbour.

But whatever we do, let it be for the sake of others and not so that we may be praised for what we have done.

Bible Reading: St. Matthew 6: 2–4

Teach us to be good neighbours, O God:
Make us aware of the needs of those around us;
Show us any ways in which we can be helpful to them;
Fill us with a spirit of kindliness and love;
And accept our service as an offering to you. *Amen.*

Closing prayer No. 58

Caring (5)

A grateful leper

Do we really appreciate the many things done for us by people who care? And do we remember to show our appreciation or say thank-you?

Bible Reading: St. Luke 17: 11–19

Dr. Howard Souster, Medical Secretary of the Overseas Division of the Methodist Church tells this story:

'I was visiting the Leprosy Research Hospital at Karigiri, South India. The Director of the Institution, a skilled Indian Christian Leprologist, had introduced me to the staff outside the door of the main building. One of them came forward and garlanded me, as is the delightful custom in India.

Then, quite unrehearsed, a leprosy patient shuffled up to me on feet which had just stubs of toes, holding between his knuckles a beautiful red rose. As he was about to present it to me it fell to the ground. Seeing that he had no fingers on his hands but stubs of knuckles I quickly bent down to pick it up. The Director more quickly restrained me.

I straightened up and the poor little man bent down himself and with his stubs of fingers gathered up the rose from the dusty path, pricking himself on a thorn as he did so, and compressing it between his two knuckles handed it to me. The drop of blood dropped off his hand on to mine but his face bore an expression of triumph and delight in completing his presentation. He had been given new hope. This was his gratitude.'

The leper showed appreciation of the care he was being given. Dr. Souster felt very humble: this Christian medical work was so worthwhile.

A small token of appreciation or a word of thanks can mean such a lot!

Accept our thanks, O God our Father, for all you have done for us and for every blessing received. Help us also always to show our appreciation for the care shown us by others by offering our words of thanks and deeds of kindness. *Amen.*

Closing prayer No. 87

Medical matters (1)

HOSPITALS   *Mildmay Mission Hospital*

Today when we think of hospitals we picture large buildings with
wards full of beds, operating theatres and out-patient clinics,
skilled doctors and nurses and everything else that is necessary for
making sick people well.

The word 'hospital' comes from the same source as 'hospitality'—the friendly reception of guests by a host. Hundreds of years
ago hospitals or hospices were places where travellers were welcomed and, if sick, were looked after. They were mostly founded
by people who saw the care of others as a means of service for God.

Even in fairly recent times hospitals have been founded by those
who wanted to do something for people in the name of God. It was
a little over one hundred years ago that Rev. William Pennefather
turned his attention to the poor people in one of the most squalid
areas of London on the borders of Shoreditch and Bethnal Green.
A Mission House was set up with a base for a doctor and a few beds
for serious cases. A few years later the first Mildmay Mission
Hospital was opened.

But Mildmay was more than a hospital: it was a Mission. Its
doctors and nurses, all dedicated Christians, were anxious to heal
the sick but also to put people right with God. And so it has
continued. The words on the hospital crest read, 'He sent them to
preach and heal the sick', a reminder of Jesus's words to his
disciples:

Bible Reading: St. Matthew 10: 1 (or 5)–8 (or 10)

The Mildmay Mission Hospital is now part of the National Health
Service but the texts on the walls are a constant reminder of that
other healing work which is done for the love of Jesus Christ.

Send forth your servants through all the world, O God, to bring
healing of body and soul so that your people may know the
comfort, the strength, the love and the peace of our Lord Jesus
Christ. *Amen.*

Benediction No. 97

Medical matters (2)

ENGLAND'S FIRST!   *Elizabeth Garrett Anderson*

On 9th November, 1908, Britain's first woman mayor was elected at Aldeburgh, Suffolk. She was Elizabeth Garrett Anderson who, as Elizabeth Garrett, had first gone to live in Aldeburgh as a child.

But this was not her only first. From the time she had listened to Dr. Elizabeth Blackwell, who had qualified in America to be the world's first woman doctor, Elizabeth Garrett had determined to be the first woman doctor in England.

But it seemed impossible. No one wanted a woman as a medical student. She worked in a hospital and studied in the evenings but no college would examine a woman and so she could not qualify. Then she applied to the Society of Apothecaries for permission to take their examinations. She passed and her name was entered on the Medical Register.

So Elizabeth Garrett, the first woman doctor in England opened a Dispensary for Women in London. Soon she learned that the University of Paris was opening its medical schools to women. She took the examinations in French and became the first MD of that University.

She then married a Mr. Anderson but her work continued. She started a medical school for women; she enlarged her dispensary which became the New Hospital for Women; and she campaigned for equal rights for women in medical study and examinations.

She continued much of her medical work even after she had retired to Aldeburgh, where she died in 1917. Her hospital in London was then renamed the Elizabeth Garrett Anderson Hospital, a fine memorial to a great medical pioneer.

Almighty God, we remember those who have worked hard in the past to break down barriers of prejudice and short-sightedness so that people have been able to develop and use their talents for the healing of others. Thank you for them and for all doctors and nurses today. *Amen.*

Closing prayer No. 65

Medical matters (3)

National Health Service

Most, if not all of us, have had the experience of going to see the doctor if we are not well or the dentist if our teeth need treatment. We may have had to spend time, perhaps a long time, in hospital with the services of highly qualified doctors and the most expensive equipment. Then, at the end we have gone home without having to pay anything for it all.

Well! That is not quite correct. We have had to pay something because all this treatment is provided by the National Health Service and people pay something every week out of their salary or wages as National Insurance contributions.

Illness has always been a source of worry to people. Often people have had to put up with their sufferings because no one could cure them. Here is one story we find in the Bible.

Bible Reading: St. Luke 8: 42b–48

That woman was fortunate. She had spent all her money to get well but then she met Jesus. There have been many people, and there are in some countries today, who just cannot afford to pay for a doctor, or who come out of hospital with a bill for thousands of pounds.

In Britain the National Health Service came into operation on 5th July, 1948. It is not perfect. We still have to pay for some things and we sometimes have to wait for treatment if it is not too urgent. But although some people complain about this, there are many who are only alive today because of the National Health Service and many who count themselves fortunate to live in a country which has such a valuable medical service.

We thank you, Almighty God, for the National Health Service which provides for our physical needs; for those who planned it and for those responsible for it today. Make us thankful for such blessings. *Amen.*

Benediction No. 93

Medical matters (4)

FLYING DOCTOR   *John Flynn*

One of the most famous medical services in the world is the Royal
Flying Doctor Service of Australia. It serves that part of the
country which Australians call the 'outback'—land which is
mainly a hot dry area of plains and desert with isolated homesteads
and small townships.

It was to this part of Australia that John Flynn came in 1912 as a
young Presbyterian minister of the Australian Inland Mission, an
organization which sought to minister to the needs of people living
in these small homesteads.

These ministers travelled mainly on horseback. They also had
some medical knowledge in case it was needed. The Mission also
had clinics with nursing services.

But it was not enough. In case of emergency these medical
services could be too far away. But how could these people call for
help? The break-through came when an electrical engineer produced a pedal radio which generated its own electricity. In 1928
John Flynn set up the first radio base and began to supervise the
distribution of the pedal radio sets in the outback. A doctor was
engaged and an aeroplane was hired. On 15th May, 1928, the first
patient was treated by the Flying Doctor.

Today the Service helps thousands of people every year. Some
are visited by the Flying Doctor: many more consult the doctor by
radio and receive instructions as to the treatment they should
have. John Flynn died in 1951 but he is remembered with affection
by many who have been helped by the organization he started.

Almighty God, we remember with thanks those who have
pioneered medical services around the world and all who continue
their work today. Bless all who treat those who are sick in body,
mind or spirit. Comfort all who suffer and let your healing hand be
upon them. *Amen.*

Benediction No. 95

Medical matters (5)

THE CONQUERING SPIRIT *Mary Verghese*

Mary Verghese, whose father was a landowner in Cochin, India, was pleased when she was accepted as a medical student at the Vellore Christian Medical College. Then she learned that she would have to treat lepers and she was horrified at the thought of contact with that disease. Mary, however, had great strength of character and conquered her fear, becoming a most promising student.

In time she became a house-surgeon and knew that this was to be her life's work. Then on 30th January, 1954, disaster struck. A car in which she was a passenger overturned in an accident and her back was broken. It seemed that her career was in ruins.

But Mary was told that something could be done. An operation on the lower spine would mean that she would be confined to a chair but she could still use her hands for surgery.

So Mary had the painful operation and spent the long months of recovery in learning more about leprosy. Then she returned to the hospital and began to perform operations on hands and feet that she was able to make useful again.

Life was not easy. Mary had a considerable amount of pain and she had to travel in her wheelchair first to Australia and then to New York to take further examinations before taking up a senior position in the hospital.

The story of Mary Verghese is one of courage and a conquering spirit. Yet she has never wanted to be regarded as a heroine or a shining example—rather as a surgeon who is still able to use her talents and her knowledge to help those suffering from leprosy.

Almighty God, we come to you because you know us for what we are and what we can make of ourselves. Help us to overcome any doubts or fears so that we may grow up to be of some help to others to the glory of your holy Name. *Amen.*

Closing prayer No. 84

For those at sea (1)

Bible Reading: Acts 27: 39–44

One of the dangers facing those who go to sea is shipwreck, fortunately not as common now as it was in the days when all ships relied upon sails and the wind. Some parts of the world have especial dangers and few more so than the coast of Cornwall and the Isles of Scilly, which have claimed many victims.

It used to be doubly dangerous, for those who escaped the sea might not escape the local people who thought it their right to plunder any wrecks. An old prayer of the Scillies went, 'We pray, thee, O Lord, not that wrecks should happen, but that if any wreck should happen, thou wilt guide them into the Scilly Isles for the benefit of the inhabitants.'

Nor did some local people mind killing if it were necessary. One of the worst disasters happened on 22nd October, 1707, when the British Fleet struck the rocks. The flagship *Association* and three other ships were lost with over 2,000 officers and men drowned. The Admiral, Sir Cloudesley Shovell, reached shore alive but was killed for his emerald ring!

Sometimes, too, wreckers would light false beacon lights and sailors, thinking they were sailing a safe course, would be driven onto the rocks.

Such stories belong in the past but shipwreck is always with us. Even huge ships with modern equipment may be wrecked because of foul weather, engine failure or human error.

Hear our prayer, O God, for all who sail the seas on business or for pleasure. Keep them safe from the force of the wind, the violence of the sea and from all hidden dangers; and bring them in safety to the harbour where they would be. *Amen.*

Closing prayer No. 81

For those at sea (2)

The Lifeboat Service

When shipwrecks do occur there are always those who are willing to risk their lives to save those in danger. All around the coasts of Britain there are lifeboats of the Royal National Lifeboat Institution. This is an organization which is supported entirely by voluntary contributions, not from government funds.

The lifeboatmen themselves, with the exception of the engineer, are all volunteers doing all sorts of jobs until the maroon sounds and they drop everything to man the lifeboat.

Many a time lifeboatmen face danger: some lose their lives. On 27th October, 1953, the Arbroath lifeboat put to sea in a full gale to answer a distress signal. The search was unsuccessful and as the lifeboat tried to re-enter harbour a huge wave capsized her. Six of the crew lost their lives.

The spirit of lifeboatmen is summed up in the words of James Haylett, former second coxswain of the Caister lifeboat. In 1901 the boat capsized with the loss of nine crewmen including his two sons. At the age of 78 he had dashed into the surf and rescued two men. At the inquest it was suggested that the boat may have been returning after abandoning its mission. The old man stoutly replied 'Caister life-boatmen *never* turn back.'

And that is the spirit that has kept the lifeboat service going, together with the other air and sea rescue services which operate around the coasts.

We remember with thankfulness, O God, the work of the Royal National Lifeboat Institution and the men who man the lifeboats, the air-sea rescue services, the coastguards and all concerned with saving life at sea. Grant them courage in the face of danger, success in their missions, and a safe return at the end. *Amen.*

Closing prayer No. 75

For those at sea (3)

Many a sailor has welcomed the sight of a warning light which has guided him clear of a hidden danger. Long ago people used to light fires or beacons on nearby cliffs or maybe set up other warning signs. Often a group of monks, concerned for the well-being of others, kept a warning fire ablaze.

You may have read the poem by Robert Southey about the Inchcape Rock. Legend tells how a local abbot put a warning bell on the rock but it was removed by a pirate who was himself wrecked and drowned on that spot later because there was no longer a warning.

The Inchcape or Bell Rock lies off the East coast of Scotland eleven miles (17·7 km) from Arbroath. This huge rock, some 1,400 feet (427 m) in length is hidden beneath the water at high tide. Here in 1806 the famous Scottish lighthouse engineer, Robert Stevenson, began building the Bell Rock Lighthouse.

It was a difficult and dangerous task. All the stone—over 2,000 tonnes of it—had to be carried by boat and then on a special railway built on the rock itself to the site of the lighthouse tower. Each piece was interlocking and the tower was bound with iron rings. The light began operating on 1st February, 1811.

And there the Bell Rock Lighthouse stands to this day in spite of many batterings by stormy seas, a tribute to its builder and a guiding light that has been welcomed by many a sailor.

In the Bible Jesus is referred to as a Light sent by God.

Bible Reading: St. John 1: 6–9

O God, as we remember with thankfulness the lights that guide sailors to their havens, we recall how Jesus, the Light of the World, was sent to show us the way to our Father. May we accept his guidance and be thankful. *Amen.*

Benediction No. 102

For those at sea (4)

Corporation of Trinity House

Most people are familiar with the lighthouses and lightships around our coasts but these are only some of the safety measures which are provided. Look in the sea itself and you will find lots of buoys of various shapes and sizes each marking a channel into harbour or warning of some hidden danger. Watch a ship as it approaches a port and you may see a pilot clamber aboard to guide it safely in.

These are just some of the services provided for sailors by an organization usually referred to as the Corporation of Trinity House. It was originally a Guild of Mariners which did a lot of good work in helping seamen, including those in need because they were sick or elderly. In 1514 King Henry the Eighth gave a Royal Charter to this guild to 'train pilots and come to the relief of shipping', and the first 'Master' was appointed on 20th May.

Before 1836 lighthouses had been privately owned and the owners were entitled to collect tolls from passing ships but in that year Trinity House became responsible for all lighthouses around the English coast.

The Corporation of Trinity House has its Headquarters near the Tower of London. It is run by a body of people including a Master and Elder Brethren, a reminder of the days when it was formed as a guild. They are responsible for its work of licensing pilots, maintaining lights and buoys, and helping mariners in many other ways too.

We remember, today, O God, all who are concerned with the needs and the safety of others, especially those who sail the seas. We pray for all who work in dangerous or difficult conditions that they may find joy through their service to others. We ask your blessing upon them and upon their work. *Amen.*

Closing prayer No. 70

For those at sea (5)

COMMUNICATION   *Samuel Morse*

From time to time ships are in distress at sea. Perhaps the engines have failed, the cargo has shifted or the ship has sprung a leak. There may have been a collision, a fire or an explosion. Help is urgently needed. Rockets may be fired to attract the attention of other ships or one of the international distress signals, S-O-S or M-A-Y-D-A-Y, may be sent by ship's radio in the Morse Code.

The Morse Code takes its name from Samuel Morse, an American who was born on 27th April, 1791. He had been interested in electricity before travelling to Europe and spending much of his life as an artist. It was on a ship travelling back to America that he heard one of his fellow passengers give a talk on electro-magnets.

This made Morse think. This could be a way of sending messages quickly. He worked out a scheme of short and long signs—the 'dots and dashes' of the Morse Code—which could be used to send letters of the alphabet. This scheme was later improved by his partner, Alfred Vail, to give us the Morse Code as we know it.

In later years the Morse Code became widely used for sending messages and, with the discovery of wireless-telegraphy there seemed no limit to where messages could be sent. It has been of particular value to those at sea.

Samuel Morse hoped that his code might help to bring peace to the world but that was wishful thinking. He died on 2nd April, 1872 but his Code lives on and has brought help to a great many people.

We remember today, O Lord, how important it is for us to be able to get in touch with others and we are thankful for those who have given us the means of doing so. Help us to learn the value of communicating with you and teach us the arts of prayer and meditation. *Amen.*

Benediction No. 106

Services to the community (1)

LIBRARIES   *Melvil Dewey*

Bible Reading: Proverbs 3: 13–17

From a very early age we realize how important it is for us to learn things, to gain wisdom and understanding. Some things we learn from other people: others we learn from books. We discover too how much enjoyment we can gain from reading. There are so many different kinds of book.

Unfortunately we can never have all the books we would like to have. They would cost far too much. No doubt we prize a few books that we can call our own and we are thankful that we have libraries from which to borrow all the others we need for pleasure or for study.

With so many books in a library it is important to have some method by which they can easily be found. Most libraries now have all the non-fiction books classified by a number, so that all the books on a subject have the same number: 599 for mammals, 796 for sports and so on. This is known as Dewey Decimal Classification. It was invented by Melvil Dewey, a famous American librarian who became the Director of New York State Library from 1889 to 1906.

Melvil Dewey died on 26th December, 1931 but he will always be remembered by people who have found his system so helpful when looking for books.

We have to be thankful today as well to the people in the past who thought it a very good idea to provide lending libraries so that we can enjoy so many books without having to pay to borrow them.

We offer our humble thanks, O God,
For all those books which are ours to enjoy;
For authors and publishers who gave us these books;
For libraries where we can borrow the books we need, and for
    librarians who help us to find them;
For the greatest book of all, in which we learn of you.
May we study, learn and increase in knowledge and wisdom, to
    the glory of your holy name. *Amen.*

Closing prayer No. 78

Services to the community (2)

THE POLICE   *P.C. Paul Cady*

Late in the evening of 5th October, 1978, Police Constable Paul Cady was in a Panda car with his co-driver in Camberley, Surrey, when they saw an articulated lorry tractor strike a car. When they drove up behind, it backed into and damaged their car. The lorry tractor then damaged another Panda car before hitting several cars and a motor-cyclist.

When the lorry was almost halted by traffic, Paul Cady jumped out of his car and tried to enter the lorry cab. But the driver reversed suddenly, then swung round with the 22-year-old policeman hanging on until he was crushed against another car. The driver was later arrested but Paul was in hospital with serious injuries to his legs. It was a brave act by a keen young policeman trying to do his duty.

We have policemen to keep law and order, to apprehend law-breakers and to try to safeguard all people and property. All too often we hear of policemen who are injured in the course of their work, sometimes at the hands of criminals but also sometimes by people who are being prevented from causing trouble for others.

Policemen have many different duties and a very responsible job to do. Some of their duties may be unpleasant, though very necessary: others give a lot of pleasure, especially when the policemen know that they are helping people. They like to feel that all law-abiding citizens will regard them as friends.

Today, if we compare our police forces with those of many lands, we realize how fortunate we are. We have many good reasons for respecting them and being thankful for them.

Help us, O Lord our God, to be law-abiding citizens, doing only those things which we know to be right and helping all whose duty it is to keep law and order in our land. *Amen.*

Closing prayer No. 57

Service to the community (3)

We are all familiar with the sight of fire engines racing along the street, sirens sounding and blue lights flashing. Traffic pulls to the side of the road to allow the appliances, to give them their correct title, to pass and reach the fire as quickly as possible.

If we are wise we make sure we know how to call the fire brigade if we need to do so. Speed is always important. As soon as the alarm is received at the fire station, the men scramble on to their appliance and race to the fire. In towns and cities they expect to be at the fire within a few minutes.

But on Monday 14th November, 1977, and in the weeks that followed there were no red fire engines on the roads. The firemen had gone on strike for better pay and conditions. Emergency services were set up, using old green fire engines manned by soldiers and volunteers but they could not do all that the firemen would normally do.

Some people thought the firemen were right to go on strike; others thought they were wrong. The firemen believed it was the only way they could get what they thought they should have. Duty firemen stood outside their stations with placards and collected the names of people who supported them.

But in some special emergencies they gave a helping hand. The firemen at Poplar in east London took some equipment in their own cars when police told them that fire had broken out in a hospital and old people were in danger. Elsewhere firemen took ladders to rescue people trapped in high buildings.

It is when the firemen are not available that people realize what important work they do. The efficient fire service is something we often take for granted.

We thank you, O God, for the firemen who often risk their lives to protect life and property. Shield them when in danger; grant them courage and wise judgement; and bless them in their work. Teach us to be careful so that we do not cause fires and give them extra work to do. *Amen.*

Closing prayer No. 62

216

Services to the community (4)

AMBULANCE   *Ambulance Brigades*

Bible Reading: St. Luke 5: 17–20 (or 25)

These men in the time of Jesus were anxious to get help for their friend who was unable to walk, so they did the only thing they could, each of them holding a corner of his mattress and carrying him between them.

Nowadays if we have a friend who is in need of help we telephone for an ambulance to come for him, or in an emergency we can dial 999 and expect the ambulance to be on the spot within minutes.

Today we would find it difficult to imagine having no ambulances but until quite recent times the only way of carrying sick or injured people was on a stretcher or in a cart. The first ambulance wagons came into use at the end of the eighteenth century, about 200 years ago, when the French used horse-drawn ambulance wagons to carry their wounded from the battlefields.

It was not until 1878 that the Knights of St. John organized the first civil ambulance brigade. The Society not only provided ambulances but trained people in first aid so that treatment could be given on the spot when necessary. This led to the formation of ambulance corps or brigades in all parts of the country.

In 1946 the National Health Service Act placed responsibility for ambulance services on Local Authorities but bodies such as the St. John Ambulance Brigade and the British Red Cross continue to provide a useful service too. Today's ambulances are also fitted with special equipment which may help keep a person alive until he reaches hospital.

Our ambulance crews have saved the lives of many.

We thank you, Almighty God, for all who are concerned with the saving of life and the relief of pain, remembering especially the men and women of the ambulance services and the work they do. *Amen.*

Closing prayer No. 65

Services to the community (5)

VETERINARY SURGEON   *James Herriot*

Animals, like people, are sometimes taken ill and need the attention of a doctor. The animal doctor is often referred to as a 'Vet', which is an abbreviation for Veterinary Surgeon.

Some veterinary surgeons have their practices in towns, where many of their patients will be the pets which people keep in their homes—dogs and cats, budgerigars, hamsters, rabbits and other small mammals and birds. These are usually taken to the surgery for treatment but may sometimes be kept there for a few days if necessary.

Vets who work in country districts often have to treat much larger animals such as horses and cows, though of course there are many smaller animals in the country too. Often the vet is called out to a farm, many miles from his practice, sometimes at night, in order to treat an animal that is sick or has injured itself.

One of the best known vets is James Herriot. That is not his real name but the name he uses when he writes books. He was brought up in Glasgow and attended the Glasgow Veterinary College, where he qualified as a veterinary surgeon. Then he went to work in North Yorkshire, where he has worked ever since, with the exception of war service in the Royal Air Force.

His books, including *All Creatures Great and Small*, *Let Sleeping Vets Lie*, and *If Vets Could Fly* are popular reading. James Herriot tells some humorous stories about his adventures with animals in the Yorkshire Dales . . . and about some of their owners too! They are amusing tales drawn from a very busy life of caring for animals.

Thank you, God
For all the creatures you have made;
For those that are ours to look after;
For all the enjoyment they give to us.
Thank you, too, for vets to attend to them,
And for all who help us to care for them. *Amen.*

Closing prayer No. 87

Government (1)

One building usually on the list of visitors to London is the Palace of Westminster or Houses of Parliament. Its clock tower with 'Big Ben' is a familiar sight. Some visitors are taken inside for a conducted tour or are able to sit in the public gallery to watch Parliament at work and listen to the debates.

The main chambers of the Palace of Westminster are the House of Lords and the House of Commons. The Members of Parliament who meet in the House of Commons are those elected by people from every part of Britain to represent them in the running of the country.

Every country must have some person or persons responsible for making decisions. In some countries one man has all the power. He may be known as a dictator. In Britain no one person has such power: our parliament is called a democracy. The leader of the government, the Prime Minister, is one of a team of ministers known as the Cabinet, who must have all their decisions approved by a majority of all the Members of Parliament.

Anyone who wishes can read of all the proceedings of Parliament in a book called Hansard. Now we can all listen if we wish to broadcasts which have come direct from the House of Commons since Question Time was first broadcast on 3rd April, 1978.

Members of Parliament make many decisions which affect us all. Sometimes we may not like those decisions but we have to accept them because they have been made by our elected representatives.

Hear our prayer, Almighty God, for those in positions of authority in our land; for the Queen and her Ministers, for all elected Members of Parliament, and for all who advise them; and grant that we may be governed wisely and well. *Amen.*

Closing prayer No. 64

Government (2)

Some of the ways of Parliament may seem a little old fashioned, even strange until we understand why things are done in a particular way. Often there is a historical reason which Members of Parliament like to remember.

Each November there is a great show of pageantry when the monarch goes to open the new session of Parliament. The Queen arrives in the state coach with her escort of the Household Cavalry. Before this the cellars will have been searched by the Yeomen of the Guard, as has been done since Guy Fawkes tried to blow up king and parliament in 1605.

The Queen is not allowed in the House of Commons but sits enthroned in the House of Lords and sends for the Members of Parliament. The royal messenger, Black Rod, knocks three times one the door of the House of Commons, which is opened then slammed shut again. This is because, on 5th January, 1642, King Charles I went to the House of Commons to arrest five Members. Today's ceremony allows M.Ps. time to 'escape'—though it is doubtful whether any would need to do so!

Each day's session begins with the Speaker's Procession into the Commons. The mace is carried in and placed in front of the Speaker as a symbol that Parliament is in session. There is then a certain way of doing everything and the Speaker ensures that everyone obeys the rules of the House.

There are many people today who enjoy all the pageantry that is associated with the British parliament and many more who recognize the value of this type of parliament with its freedom, won in the past and jealously guarded today.

Bible Reading: Romans 13: 3–4

We thank you, O God, for the heritage that is ours; for the pageantry and colour of state occasions; for our parliament and all that it stands for; and for the freedom we enjoy. Keep us ever thankful. *Amen.*

Benediction No. 98

Government (3)

The Ballot

Anyone who wishes to do so can stand for election as a Member of Parliament. All that is required is that a sum of money has to be laid down as a deposit, which is lost if the candidate does not get enough votes. This is intended to deter anyone who has no chance of being elected.

Most candidates at an election are members of one of the main political parties and are chosen by those parties. Nowadays the two main political parties are Conservative and Labour but there are many others too, Liberal, Scottish and Welsh Nationalist, Communist and National Front, to name but a few.

The party which has the most members elected is normally the one which forms the government of the country and its leader becomes Prime Minister. Each party believes that it knows the best way to govern the country and tries hard in the days before the election to persuade people to vote for its candidates.

All the parties can do is to persuade. They can never force anyone to vote for them for the voting is in secret. On the day of the election each voter goes to the polling station where he is given a paper showing the names of all the candidates. He takes it into a booth where no one can see what he is doing, puts a cross against the name of the person for whom he wishes to vote, folds his paper and drops it into a slot in a sealed box. This paper will be one of thousands that are counted to see who is elected.

We have to learn to make wise decisions.

Bible Reading: Joshua 24: 14–15 and 21–24

O God our Father, we have many decisions to make in life and we ask you to guide us as we make up our minds what we believe is right. Help us then to be true to those beliefs and to you. *Amen.*

Closing prayer No. 62

Government (4)

Councils and councillors

Just as it is important to have a body of people to govern the country, so it is essential to have bodies of people responsible for parts of the country. Each county, city, borough or parish into which the country is divided has its elected councillors.

On city and borough councils the leader is the Lord Mayor or Mayor. In Scotland he is known as a Provost. Other councils have a Chairman. Councillors are elected by secret ballot in the same way that Members of Parliament are. Many candidates in the local elections are chosen by the big political parties and the elected councils are usually Conservative or Labour depending upon which has the most councillors elected.

The council has many responsibilities such as Finance (money), Housing, Education, Libraries, Highways, Parks. There is a committee of councillors and others to look after each of these and lots more besides. Some councillors serve on several of these committees. They are very busy people, sometimes working every evening of the week and maybe during the day as well.

Local councillors are not paid to do this as Members of Parliament are. Their work for the community is given freely because this is a kind of service that they like to offer to try to make their part of the country as pleasant as they can for all who live in it.

We are thankful to people who do give their time freely in this and other ways for the benefit of others. We can show our appreciation by being good citizens and looking after all that which is provided for us.

Hear our prayer, O God, for the community in which we live and for all who have responsibility for its government. May they be guided into making wise decisions that will be of benefit to all. *Amen.*

Closing prayer No. 51

Government (5)

The Suffragettes

Who can vote in a parliamentary or local election? Today it is anyone over the age of 18, whose name appears on the register of electors and who is not disqualified through being a criminal or mentally ill.

It was not always so. At the beginning of the present century only men could vote and there were certain women who thought this most unfair. Some of them became determined to do everything they could to get votes for women.

Their leader was Mrs. Emmeline Pankhurst, ably supported by her daughters, notably Christabel. They called a meeting in 1903 and planned what they should do. They spoke at meetings and on fairgrounds but knew that much more was needed. It was after a political meeting in Manchester on 13th October, 1905, that Christabel and her friend were arrested and imprisoned when they refused to pay the fine.

Many other imprisonments were to follow. The women, who became known as Suffragettes, were often in the news. Some chained themselves to railings; some broke windows and did other damage to draw attention to their cause; and one was killed trying to catch hold of the king's horse in the Derby race of 1913.

After many years of action by Suffragettes and the part played by women in World War I, women over 30 were given the vote in 1918. Ten years later anyone over 21 was allowed to vote. Now the age limit has been reduced to 18.

The right to vote was obtained only after a hard struggle. It is the responsibility of every citizen today to ensure that it is not wasted.

Today, O God, we remember those who worked hard to get votes for everyone. Help us as we grow to learn all we can so that we can become responsible citizens able to make wise decisions concerning the government of our land. *Amen.*

Closing prayer No. 56

Civil rights (1)

John Brown

Most people have enjoyed singing about John Brown:

> *John Brown's body lies a mould'ring in the grave*
> *But his soul goes marching on!*

But who was John Brown? He was a man who hated slavery and wanted all people to be free. In his day, over a hundred years ago, there were many negro slaves in the Southern States of America. Some had been brought from Africa: others were the descendants of slaves. They had no freedom and were the property of their owners, some of whom treated their slaves very harshly. A slave had no rights at all.

Some people had been trying to get the slaves freed by peaceful means but they had not been successful. John Brown believed he could only succeed by violent means. He took some slaves from their owners by force and then helped them to escape to Canada.

Then he decided to organize a slave rebellion. But he needed guns and so, with a few others, he overcame the guards at an arsenal at Harper's Ferry, Virginia. Local people became alarmed and trapped the raiders in the building. They were captured and put on trial. John Brown was found guilty of murder and treason and was executed on 2nd December, 1859.

But to those who disagreed with slavery he became a hero and the famous marching song was composed in his honour. John Brown had the right ideas about slavery and freedom but tried the wrong way to do something about it.

Help us to remember, O Lord our God, that all people are your children, created in your likeness and equal in your sight. Keep us from thinking too highly of ourselves or from looking down upon others, and show us how to live together in love and friendship because we know that you love us. *Amen.*

Closing prayer No. 69

Civil rights (2)

A RIGHT TO BE FREE   *Abraham Lincoln*

Abraham Lincoln, who became President of the United States of America in 1860, was very troubled about slavery. He had seen it for himself and he did not like what he saw. He was sure that all men and women should be free.

Soon after he became President, war broke out between the Northern States which opposed slavery and the Southern States where the slaves worked. This Civil War, which lasted for four years was eventually won by the North. During this time, on 1st January, 1863, a law, known as the Emancipation Proclamation, freed every slave throughout America.

Lincoln hoped that every negro slave would be able to receive the same treatment as the white Americans but many people thought otherwise. Lincoln himself was assassinated on 14th April, 1865. In the following year a Civil Rights Act was passed which guaranteed the rights of all U.S. citizens regardless of colour. But it was not easily enforced.

Gradually local laws were passed in the South. They were called 'Jim Crow' laws, after a negro stage character. They separated black and white people with schools for black children and others for white. White people could travel in the front seats of buses; black people had to sit behind. They were kept apart in restaurants, hospitals and other places. The law of the land said that all were equal, but they certainly were not.

Only in the Christian Church did many of them feel free because they were children of God.

Bible Reading: Galatians 5: 1

O Lord our God, we thank you for the freedom which is ours to enjoy and especially for the freedom to come to you and talk with you. Hear our prayer for those who do not know freedom as we do and give them the comfort of knowing your fatherly love. *Amen.*

Closing prayer No. 51

Civil rights (3)

Martin Luther King was born on 15th January, 1929, in Atlanta, Georgia, where his father was a Baptist minister. In time he became a Baptist minister too.

He never forgot his experiences as a child when he was made to feel inferior because he was black and he was reminded of this many times in Montgomery, Alabama, where he became the pastor of Dexter Avenue Baptist Church. But matters came to a head on 1st December, 1955, when a black woman was arrested for not giving up her seat on a bus to a white woman.

Martin Luther King persuaded the black people not to use the buses in protest. After many incidents, the United States Supreme Court ruled that segregation on the buses was wrong. On 21st December, 1956, black and white travelled together.

It was just a beginning. Demonstrations were held in other towns. Dr. King thought there should be one organization dealing with all demonstrations and, on 15th February, 1957, The Southern Christian Leadership Conference was formed. Other leaders were also church leaders and they agreed that all their demonstrations should be non-violent.

The movement adopted an old cotton-workers' hymn, *We shall overcome*, which was sung wherever there were marches or people demonstrating peacefully for their rights. And overcome they did in many ways. They overcame a lot of pride, hatred, prejudice and other attitudes which keep people apart when they should be living happily together. One remembers the words of St. Paul:

Bible Reading: Colossians 3: 8–14

Help us, O God, to take a good look at ourselves and see whether there are things about us which hurt or offend other people. Take from us all pride, envy, hatred, anger, spiteful deeds and hurtful words. Help us to act as true children of our heavenly father. *Amen.*

Closing prayer No. 60

Civil rights (4)

'I have a dream . . .'

One of the most impressive marches by the Civil Rights campaigners in the United States was held on 28th August, 1963. Two hundred thousand people marched to the Lincoln Memorial in Washington, where they heard Dr. Martin Luther King deliver a great speech which included the following words:

'I have a dream that one day this nation will rise up and live out the true meaning of its creed: "We hold these truths to be self-evident, that all men are created equal."

'I have a dream that one day on the red hills of Georgia the sons of former slaves and the sons of former slave owners will be able to sit down together at the table of brotherhood. . . . I have a dream that my four little children one day will live in a nation where they will not be judged by the colour of their skin, but by the content of their character.

'. . . When we allow freedom to ring from every town and every hamlet, from every state and every city, we will be able to speed up that day when all God's children, black men and white men, Jews and Gentiles, Protestants and Catholics, will be able to join hands and sing in the words of the old Negro Spiritual, "Free at last! Free at last! Great God Almighty, we are free at last".' In the following year the Civil Rights Act of 1964 was passed by Congress. Things had begun to happen but much still remained to be done. We have only to read in our newspapers what is happening in many of the countries of the world, where people are not free and many suffer at the hands of others.

Hear our prayers, O God our Father
For all who live in lands where there is no freedom;
For those who suffer for what they believe;
For people, even today, who are little more than slaves;
And for ourselves, that we may ever be thankful for our many
    blessings and have grateful hearts. *Amen.*

Closing prayer No. 65

Civil rights (5)

Prize for Peace

In the summer of 1964 it was announced that Dr. Martin Luther King had been awarded the Nobel Prize for Peace because he had been able to keep his followers non-violent. Without his leadership there could well have been much violence and bloodshed.

It was probably no surprise to many that Dr. King decided that the prize money—a considerable sum—should be divided amongst the organizations involved in the Civil Rights campaign. He said it was not intended for him personally but as 'a tribute to the disciplined, wise restraint and majestic courage of gallant negro and white persons of goodwill who have followed a non-violent course in seeking to establish . . . a rule of love across this nation of ours.'

Martin Luther King was loved by millions and respected by many more. But it was inevitable that he would be hated by some and treated as a trouble-maker by others. Remember the sufferings of St. Paul who was regarded as a trouble-maker in his day.

Bible Reading: II Corinthians 11: 21b–27

Dr. King likewise was often roughly handled, arrested on trivial charges and, on several occasions imprisoned. Once he was stabbed and once stoned but the climax came on 4th April, 1968, in Memphis, Tennessee, when he was shot dead.

Dr. Martin Luther King died at the age of 39 but his work went on. Throughout the world there are those who will not rest until all people have equal rights and freedom to enjoy them.

We thank you, God our Father, for all those who have dreamed of better things and have worked hard to make their dreams come true. May we, too, try to make the world a better place by our concern for the well-being of others. *Amen.*

Closing prayer No. 67

Attitudes (1)

NO, YOU CAN'T!   *Alexander Solzhenitsyn*

It would be too much to expect that we could do whatever we liked. It would, of course, be quite impossible. No doubt as children we have often been told, 'No, you can't!' There are usually very good reasons, too. Sometimes adults have to be told, 'No, you can't!' if their actions might be harmful to others.

Fortunately we are free to do almost anything we wish as long as it is within the law. The laws of Britain and some other lands allow a lot of freedom. In some parts of the world many people are imprisoned because of things they have said or written, because they have battled for justice, or, in some cases, because of their religious beliefs. This is nothing new.

Bible Reading: Acts 12: 1–5

Alexander Solzhenitsyn, a famous Russian author was one of many millions to be sent to a slave labour camp, living in awful conditions for eight years. He had wanted to feel free but was told, 'No, you can't!' In 1970 he was awarded a Nobel Prize for Literature but was refused permission to go to receive it.

But he was more fortunate than many who have been refused permission to leave their country. On 13th February, 1974, he was expelled from the U.S.S.R.—free to act as he wished: free to attend a service to thank God.

As we give thanks for our freedom today, let us ensure that we do not deny other people the right to speak, believe and practise what *they* believe to be right.

Almighty God, we thank you for the freedom that is ours to enjoy. Teach us that with such freedom there is always responsibility to avoid anything that would hurt or offend others. *Amen.*

Closing prayer No. 51

Attitudes (2)

THEY'RE DIFFERENT!   *Trevor Huddleston*

When Trevor Huddleston arrived in South Africa in 1943 he found a land that was very different from his native England. His posting was as a missionary to Sophiatown, an area of Johannesburg where many black people had their homes. Some lived in the most appalling slum conditions but some had managed to make pleasant little homes for themselves.

The government and most of the white people in South Africa looked down on the black Africans. They regarded them as people who were different and should therefore be treated differently. They were to be kept apart from white people by laws known as *apartheid*.

Under the apartheid laws the black Africans had to carry a pass wherever they went. Without it they could be imprisoned. When they wanted to take certain jobs or do things that white people did the answer was often, 'No.'

Trevor Huddleston worked in Sophiatown for twelve years. Then, on 10th February, 1955, the police moved into Sophiatown. The people were moved out and their homes were torn down. Trevor Huddleston sat down and wrote a book, *Nought for your comfort*, which was to shock the world.

But people in South Africa and elsewhere still treat the black people in the same way; just as the black people of East Africa turned out the Asian families and people all over the world shun their neighbours who may be of a different race from themselves just because 'they're different'.

And if we tend to judge others by their outward appearance, remember God's words to Samuel:

Bible Reading: I Samuel 16: 7

Help us, O God, in all things to look beyond the outward appearance and to see all people for what they are—children of God. *Amen.*

Closing prayer No. 52

Attitudes (3)

There are some people who are always boasting or letting others know how clever they are, or think they are. Do you know people who always insist that *they* are right and will not listen to others?

Some of them, of course, are not as knowledgeable as they think and insist that they are right even when they are wrong. We may call them pig-headed. On the other hand those who *are* always right we tend to regard as big-headed. We must guard against being like that: big-heads are never popular! We find that this is true of some people when talking about religion. They are so sure they are right that they insist others must be wrong. Such people we call bigots. Certain religious sects have a very bigotted outlook. They believe that they alone know the way to God and that everyone who is not one of their number has no chance of eternal life. Here are some words of St. Paul.

Bible Reading: Romans 12: 1–3

'Don't think too highly of yourself!' People are invited to seek the will of God and then to have faith to believe. And whatever our religious beliefs may be we cannot prove that they are right. Nor can we say that other people are wrong if they see things differently. All we can do is to pray that we may be guided into right thinking and then live sincerely according to those beliefs.

We must beware of being bigotted or intolerant of the beliefs of others. We should be able to say kindly, 'You have a right to your opinions, but this is what I believe.' Most people respect a person who is ready to speak out for what he believes if he has a tolerant attitude to others.

Help us, O God, not to think too highly of ourselves but to remember that all our knowledge comes from you. Help us to know what to believe, to have faith to accept it and courage to proclaim it. *Amen.*

Closing prayer No. 80

Attitudes (4)

There are two little phrases which are too seldom used. The first is
'I was wrong' and the other 'I'm sorry'. Often, on reflection, we
know that we made a mistake and yet we are too proud to admit it.
An apology costs nothing yet is not easily given. We have to be big
enough to swallow our pride.

A story tells how Dr. Aggrey, a leading West African Christian,
once said something that hurt his wife in the presence of her sister.
He realized it was wrong but could not bring himself to apologize.
After a sleepless night he decided to say, 'I'm sorry', when they
were alone. But even that would not be enough, he thought. He
had spoken in front of her sister; therefore he must apologize in
front of her sister too. It was difficult but he did it and proved
himself a bigger man for having done so.

Often an apology and an admission of fault can go a long way
toward putting things right. The Bible reminds us that this is also
true in our relationship with God. We must be ready to confess our
faults and to ask for forgiveness.

Bible Reading: I John 1: 8–10

A prayer that is often used in church services is the General
Confession. It includes these words: 'We have left undone those
things which we ought to have done; and we have done those
things which we ought not to have done . . .'

In admitting, or confessing, that we have done wrong, we not
only bring ourselves nearer to God but we remind ourselves what
we are really like and this makes us more ready to change any
wrong attitudes that we may have.

We confess, O God, that we have not always been all that we might
have been. We have hurt others by our words and our deeds; and
we have not always been faithful to you. Forgive us, we pray, and
help us to grow to be true children of God. *Amen.*

Closing prayer No. 57

Attitudes (5)

LOVE YOUR ENEMIES   *Ernest Gordon*

It may be difficult to forgive people who have done us a wrong. It is probably even more difficult to love them too. Yet this was what Jesus taught.

Bible Reading: St. Luke 6: 27–28 and 32–36

Love your enemies! Ernest Gordon was to remember these words of Jesus in 1945. World War II had just ended and he was on his way to freedom after being a prisoner of the Japanese for three and a half years.

Captain Gordon of the Argyll and Sutherland Highlanders had been captured and taken into the jungle where prisoners were made to build the notorious bridge over the River Kwai. There in Changi prison camp he and his fellow prisoners suffered in many ways. Some were brutally treated; their conditions were foul; and many died.

But whilst one could understand it if these men hated their enemies, there were some who felt pity rather than hatred. In the horror and despair of that camp new thoughts about God came to them and their Christian faith grew.

It was whilst they were on the train to freedom that Ernest Gordon and others saw a train full of injured Japanese soldiers who were in a very bad state. Without hesitation they went to help them and give a little comfort.

'But they are enemies!' he was told by someone who could not understand. They were also men and they needed help. Jesus had told a story of a Samaritan who helped an enemy who was injured, and he said. 'Go and do likewise.' Ernest Gordon and his fellow ex-prisoners were doing just that.

O God our Father, grant us
The love which is always ready to forgive;
The love which is always eager to help;
The love which is always happier to give than to get.
And so grant that living in love, we may live like Jesus. *Amen.*
                    Dr. William Barclay

Closing prayer No. 70

Use of riches (1)

John D. Rockefeller was born on 8th July, 1839, the son of a 'quack' doctor who travelled around selling patent medicines. He died on 23rd May, 1937, having become the richest man in the world. He gave away over five hundred million dollars and still had many millions left.

Even as a boy John had learned that money lent could earn more money in interest. He also had a good head for business. With money he earned and some from his father he went into business with a partner, buying and selling all sorts of things and making a profit by the end of the year.

Just then people were taking an interest in oil which could be found in the Eastern United States. John went into business in Cleveland, Ohio and then formed a company with a man who had discovered a cheap way of refining the oil to make petrol. This company became known as Standard Oil of Ohio.

It was not long before Rockefeller had bought up many other companies too, so that Standard Oil became a huge organization. Rockefeller became very rich but was upset because lots of people, perhaps jealous of his success, suggested that he was a rogue who may have used sharp practices to gain his wealth. He was particularly upset because he was a devout churchman who had always been most anxious to do business in a fair and proper manner.

However, once such suggestions are made, people keep on referring to them and it was over forty years before Rockefeller's name was considered respectable, by which time he had given away a fortune. At the time of his death he had come to be known as a great and generous man.

Bible Reading: St. Matthew 7: 1–2.

Guard us, O God, from judging others;
Help us never to jump to hasty conclusions;
Teach us never to listen to or pass on idle gossip;
Restrain us from saying anything hurtful or unkind;
Make us more mindful of our own failings than of the faults in
   others and help us to put ourselves right so that we may be
   true children of our Father God. *Amen.*

Closing prayer No. 60

234

Use of riches (2)

FOR RESEARCH *Lord Nuffield*

When William Morris was a boy his ambition was to be a surgeon but he decided instead to be an engineer. When he left school he became apprenticed to a cycle maker. He was so successful that he asked for higher wages but his employer refused.

So William Morris made an important decision. In future he would work for no one but himself. He opened his own business, The Morris Cycle Shop, in High Street, Oxford. Soon he was not only making a profit from building cycles but by making motor-cycles and repairing cars.

But William Morris wanted to make motor cars. Henry Ford was doing so in America. Why shouldn't William Morris do so in Britain? Before long his factories were turning out thousands of Morris cars. He bought up other companies which were making parts for his cars and soon controlled a huge industry.

By the time he was fifty-three he was a very rich man and able to give away a lot of money, much of it to the University of Oxford. For a man who had once thought of being a surgeon it is not surprising that many of his gifts were for medical research, one to develop penicillin, one to build iron lungs for polio victims, a gift of £2 million to Oxford University for medical research, and help for blind people in Central Africa.

In 1934, partly for his work in the motor industry and partly for his generosity, he was given the title Viscount Nuffield, the name given to Nuffield College, Oxford and to the Nuffield Foundation, which still finances research programmes.

Lord Nuffield died on 22nd August, 1963, having given away some £30 million, contributed greatly to medicine, learning and research, and having gained great satisfaction from doing so.

Bible Reading: St. Luke 6: 38

O God, our Father, help us to give what we can to others—a cheery word, a helping hand, some of our time and energy, something perhaps that we value; and help us to know that the more we give the greater our blessing will be. *Amen.*

Closing prayer No. 61

Use of riches (3)

Jesse Boot

Jesse Boot was very interested in the bottles and jars on the shelves in his father's shop. They contained all sorts of medicines, ointments and pills which could be obtained from plants. These herbal cures were ones which people had used for hundreds of years and which are still used today.

When he was only thirteen years of age he ran his father's shop in Nottingham. But he was also very interested in the new medicines which were being made and he spent his spare time learning all he could about them. Then he was ready to open a chemist's shop of his own.

Jesse was a hard worker. All day until late in the evening he worked in the shop. Then he had the books to do. But he was a man of ambition and he saved all the money he could so that he could buy a second shop. As soon as he was able he bought another, and another, and another. . . . Nowadays there are few towns which do not have a branch of Boot's the Chemist—the largest chain of chemist's shops in the world.

Jesse was helped by his wife who encouraged him to have sections in his shops for other things too, such as stationery, art, photography, libraries and restaurants. Factories were built where drugs could be made. Jesse Boot was a very rich man.

But he kept on working, even though his health suffered. It was not that he needed the money for himself. He had other ideas. By the time he died in 1931 he had given away a very large amount of money to provide much of the land and buildings of the University of Nottingham.

Bible Reading: II Corinthians 9: 6–7

Almighty God, we thank you
For healthy bodies and active minds;
For curiosity and a desire to find out;
For schools and colleges where we can learn;
For teachers and all who help in our studies.
Help us to find satisfaction in our achievements and to know
the joy of using our gifts for others; and to you be the glory.
Amen.

Closing prayer No. 90

Use of riches (4)

Howard Hughes

On 5th April, 1976 one of the richest men in the world died. His name was Howard Hughes and he was a multi-millionaire. Born in Houston, Texas, he inherited a tool company from his father in 1924 and this gave him the money he wanted for other things.

He was very keen on flying, piloted his own aeroplane, took part in air races, formed his own aircraft company, planned and built aircraft and bought a controlling interest in Trans World Airlines. Sometimes he tested aircraft himself and once narrowly escaped death when his aircraft crashed.

Hughes was also interested in film-making and produced some films which were very successful. He was extravagant, even reckless in his spending, but then he could afford to be. He had far more money than he needed for himself.

But having money does not bring happiness in itself. Nor can it buy the most important things in life. People who think too much of riches often get a wrong set of values.

Bible Reading: St. Matthew 6: 19–21

Howard Hughes could buy many things but he couldn't buy a happy home, for example. That depends upon other things such as love and consideration for one's partner.

Far from being happy, he spent the latter part of his life in fear of illness and death. In the 1950s he shut himself away from all but his 'bodyguards'. For all his wealth, Howard Hughes died at the age of seventy-one ill, lonely, friendless and afraid, a sad reflection on the wrong attitude to life.

Help us, O God, to be more ready to give than to receive, more thoughtful in our personal relationships, and more willing to be of service to others, so that we may find for ourselves the happiness that money cannot buy. *Amen.*

Closing prayer No. 58

Use of riches (5)

Often we find that someone's name is used to describe a particular kind of person. If we call someone a Judas we mean he is a traitor or betrayer. A young lover may be called a Romeo after the Shakespearean character.

It is quite common to refer to someone as a Scrooge if he is a miser or skinflint. Ebenezer Scrooge was not a real person but a character in *A Christmas Carol* by Charles Dickens, which was published in 1843 and has remained popular. Scrooge was a man who thought only of himself and of how much money he could make or save.

But this does not bring happiness. The Bible has a story of a rich man who was very troubled.

Bible Reading: St. Mark 10: 17–22

This young man appeared to have everying going for him. But he didn't want to give away his riches and he went away sad.

In the story *A Christmas Carol* Scrooge was also troubled when three ghosts appeared to him and showed him his past, present and future. He realized that he had been wrong and changed into a generous kind-hearted man.

So when we call someone a Scrooge we are only thinking of the man before he changed his ways. Reputations can often be misleading. Scotsmen are said to be mean, but most of them are not. Jews have a reputation for being interested only in getting money, but most Jews are very generous people.

We must take care not to misjudge others by what we may have heard and we must also learn the important lesson that keeping everything for ourselves never brings real happiness.

Help us to remember, O God, that all we have is a gift from you and should be used wisely and sensibly. May we learn how to be generous with our possessions and in the giving of ourselves so that we may find true happiness. *Amen.*

Closing prayer No. 76

Working together (1)

Scouts and Guides

There are some things that we like to do on our own but there are
some that are much more interesting if done together with others.
Lots of children and young people have very much enjoyed
belonging to one of the youth organizations, Scouts, Guides or one
of the Brigades, where they not only do interesting things with
others but learn a lot of useful things besides.

The Scout movement owes its origin to Lord Baden-Powell. He
was an army officer who had seen service in India and many other
places but who became famous for his defence of Mafeking during
the Boer War in South Africa. It was there that B-P, as he became
known, learned many useful tips.

In 1907 he arranged to hold a camp on Brownsea Island, Poole
Harbour, for 25 boys. The experiment was so successful that he
decided to launch a movement for boys based on open air life, on
scouting and observation and on the study of nature. As a hand-
book he wrote *Scouting for Boys*.

The first Scout troop was formed on 24th January, 1908. Soon
there were many others. Half a century later there were $5\frac{1}{2}$ million
Scouts and 3 million Guides, the sister organization that had been
started for girls.

Lord Baden-Powell held the title of Chief Scout of all the World
until he retired in 1937 at the age of eighty. Many boys and girls
who have enjoyed their time as Scouts or Guides, or in the junior
sections, Cubs and Brownies, owe much to Lord Baden-Powell.

Help us, O God, to know the pleasures of working together in
organizations or clubs where we can learn from the experiences of
others and enjoy being members of a team. Teach us to be good
learners, willing givers and loyal members, offering all that we are
able for the benefit of the team. *Amen.*

Closing prayer No. 90

Working together (2)

Every summer lots of people make a journey to the small island of
Iona off the west coast of Scotland. Some go as tourists, for this is
the island on which St. Columba settled on 12th May, 563 and
from which his monks took Christianity to most of Scotland and
the north of England.

Others go to Iona to work and join together in fellowship and
worship. They are members of The Iona Community, an organization set up by the Rev. Dr. George Macleod in 1938. At that time
Dr. Macleod was minister of a church in Govan, Glasgow, one of
the worst hit places in Britain in 'the hungry thirties'. How could
he preach to hungry, hopeless people? He remembered some
words in the Bible.

Bible Reading: James 2: 14–17

He wanted people who would dedicate themselves to doing something practical about people's problems. So the Iona Community
was born. Ministers leaving college would join the brotherhood
for two years, spending three summer months on Iona and then
working in places where there was a special need. Craftsmen and
other laymen would also spend part of summer working on Iona
and then going back to their normal employment.

Together the craftsmen and ministers rebuilt the ruined abbey
church: together they planned ways of extending their work. Many
others became interested in what was being done and today there
are thousands of Friends of The Iona Community, people of many
different denominations of the Christian Church who follow certain rules of discipline in prayer, in giving, and in practical Christian service.

Teach us how to live for you, O God:
Make us regular in our prayers and in our worship;
Make us generous with our money and our talents;
Make us mindful of the needs of those around us;
And let us serve others in your Name, for your sake. *Amen.*

Closing prayer No. 72

Working together (3)

Eurovision

When you switch on your television set you will often see news items or sports programmes which have been or are being filmed in other countries. Many of these will be seen in countries throughout Europe at the same time but with the commentary in the language of those watching.

These programmes come through Eurovision, the organization through which international co-operation is made possible. It began on 13th February, 1950, when the European Broadcasting Union (EBU) was formed by twenty-three nations of Western Europe and the Mediterranean area, mainly to exchange information and ideas about television.

In those days each country had its own system and programmes produced in one country could not be received in another. Then, in 1952, British and French engineers produced a box with lots of intricate wiring, which could convert programmes from one system to another. Eurovision was now possible and was 'born' on 6th June, 1954 when the first programme, direct from Montreux was fed into the network and relayed to member countries.

The EBU does not make any programmes itself. It is like a large distribution centre, relaying programmes from one country to others and working with television networks from all over the world to show international events such as the Olympic Games, the World Cup or Space projects. The cost is shared so that countries with a lot of viewers pay a much larger share than the smaller nations with few viewers. In this way everyone can benefit from the service provided.

It is one way today in which co-operation between a number of nations has proved possible and useful.

Almighty God, we thank you for the various ways in which the nations of the world have learned to work together and so help one another. Grant that throughout the world man may learn how to work with his neighbours and live in peace. *Amen.*

Benediction No. 92

Working together (4)

The Christ of the Andes

It was Easter Day and the people of Buenos Aires in Argentina went to the cathedral expecting the usual Easter message. But Bishop Benavente preached mainly about peace. To many people it came as a surprise because everyone was talking about war—war with their neighbouring country, Chile, over some lakes and land high in the Andes mountains on the border between the two countries.

Many people disagreed with the bishop but some thought he was right. One who was pleased to hear what the bishop had said was Bishop Java of Chile. Of course it was wrong and un-Christian to fight about such things. And so he travelled up and down his country also calling for peace.

As more and more people took notice of the two bishops, the governments too decided to talk and they invited King Edward VII of Britain to sort out their problem, which he did. They agreed that this would be the best way to sort out future problems.

Now in one of his sermons, Bishop Benavente had said, 'I should like to see Christ standing between the two peoples, guiding and leading them.' A woman named Angela de Costa remembered that and raised the money to build a huge statue of Jesus Christ and set it up on one of the mountain peaks. On 13th March, 1904, the people of both countries gathered for the unveiling ceremony and heard the prayer 'that these mountains may crumble into dust before the peoples of Argentina and Chile break the peace which, at the feet of Christ, they have given their word to keep.'

And so the statue *The Christ of the Andes* stands today as a symbol of peace and a reminder of those who worked many years ago to keep the peace.

Almighty God, help us when we disagree with others to know that fighting will not necessarily solve our differences but that we should seek peace and learn to live and work peacefully together. *Amen.*

Closing prayer No. 55

Working together (5)

Prayer for Unity

Remember the story of the great big enormous turnip? It grew so large that the man who planted the seed could not pull up the turnip that grew. So he called his wife but together they couldn't do it. They had extra help from the boy . . . and the dog . . . and the cat . . . and the mouse. As the mouse added his strength the turnip came up and the mouse said, 'I did it!'

But did the mouse do it? It was the combined effort of everyone that made it possible. It was too much for any of them to do alone. So we find in so many things that we just cannot succeed on our own. We have to work together with other people. It is not the goal-scorer who wins a match but the team working together that enabled him to score. No individual can make a school into a good school: it is dependent upon everyone working to that end.

So it is with the Christian Church, too. For many years the various denominations worked separately sometimes with little thought for what others were doing. Then various leaders began to suggest working together. The whole Christian Church could do far more than each little section of it. It had an enormous job to do!

Bible Reading: Ephesians 1: 6–10

So today there is a World Council of Churches and there are similar councils in many countries. In Britain every year there is a Week of Prayer for Christian Unity beginning on 18th January when people from many churches pray together. And since this enormous task is God's work in the world, what could be more appropriate than working together with God, united by the power of his Holy Spirit.

Hear our prayer, Almighty God, for the work of your Church throughout the world. May your people work together, guided by your Spirit, until the whole world has learned and accepted your ways. *Amen.*

Closing prayer No. 89

Faithfulness and loyalty (1)

People who have a loving family and good friends are very fortunate. There are often times when love and friendship can help us in our difficulties and there are times when we can help others immensely if we will stand by them.

The Bible has a story of Naomi and her two daughters-in-law, all of whom had been widowed. Naomi wished to return to her homeland and suggested to Orpah and Ruth that they leave her. Orpah did but not Ruth. Hear part of the story:

Bible Reading: Ruth 1: 15–18

It must have meant a lot to Naomi to know that Ruth wished to be loyal to their family friendship. Do we feel loyalty to our family? Especially when things are difficult? And are we just as ready to be loyal to our friends when things go wrong?

Aesop told a fable of two friends who vowed to stand by each other no matter what happened. Suddenly a bear appeared, whereupon the more agile of the two climbed up a tree. The other dropped to the ground, pretending to be dead. The bear sniffed at him and walked away.

Trying to make light of it, the one who had been up the tree smiled and said, 'It looked as though that bear was whispering in your ear.'

'He was,' came the reply. 'He told me I should never trust a friend who ran away when I was in trouble.'

There is an old proverb, 'A friend in need is a friend indeed.' Few things are more important in life than to be faithful and loyal to our family, to our friends and to our God.

Help us, O god, to appreciate all the love and friendship that is shown to us by our families and our friends; and help us to be loyal to them even when it may cost us something to do so, just as we pray that they will be loyal to us. *Amen.*

Closing prayer No. 67

Faithfulness and loyalty (2)

LOYALTY TO PROFESSION   *Sister Dora*

Many people do their work only because they have to earn a living. Others are so dedicated to their work that they give everything they have to it, forgetting themselves if it means they can help others.

Some who are most loyal to their profession are doctors and nurses, who often have the lives of others in their hands. One such person was Dorothy Pattison, or Sister Dora, whose work in Walsall is remembered with gratitude and is commemorated by a statue which stands there.

Even as a young girl in Yorkshire she had cared for an old lady who was very ill and had been told to stay away from home for a while so that she did not bring infection home to the other children. Then she became the village schoolmistress but this did not give her the satisfaction she wanted.

At the age of twenty-two she joined the Sisterhood of the Good Samaritans and was given the name Sister Dora. A few years later she was sent to the Samaritans' hospital in Walsall, where she worked among men, young and old, who had received serious injuries in the factories, foundries and mines.

There Sister Dora worked very long hours and gave all she had. She became so skilled that she amazed some of the doctors. She was greatly loved and respected for her work. In 1865 she was given charge of a new hospital, where she did a wonderful job. For the two years before she died in 1878, she nursed smallpox patients and others with infectious diseases. Truly Sister Dora was a great woman, who gave the utmost loyalty to her profession and great love where it was needed.

We thank you, O God, for all who are dedicated to their work and especially those who are committed to the service of others. Help us to equip ourselves for life so that we may find satisfaction in our work and offer all our work as a gift to you; through Jesus Christ our Lord. *Amen.*

Closing prayer No. 58

Faithfulness and loyalty (3)

Charles de Gaulle

There have been many outstanding Frenchmen during the present century but there is one name that stands out from the others, Charles de Gaulle—a man who was passionately fond of his country and who probably did more than any other for his country during his lifetime.

Born in Lille on 22nd November, 1890, de Gaulle was brought up in a devout Roman Catholic household with a military background. He decided to become a soldier and proved to be a very able one. He foresaw the problems which led to World War II but people took little notice of his warnings.

In 1940 he left France just before it fell to the German armies and he set up the Free French Forces in Britain. His enthusiasm was catching and many Frenchmen who had escaped from France joined him. Throughout the war years he was recognized as the leader of the free Frenchmen. When France was freed he returned to Paris to a tumultuous welcome by more than two million Parisians.

The General retired. In 1947, he announced that he would come out of retirement 'to help carry on work that remains to be done for France'. But eleven years were to pass before the people of France demanded that he should do that work. It was in 1958 that the President of France and leaders of political parties asked him to form a government. He was soon the President of France, which office he held until 1970 when he retired. A few months later, in November, 1970, he died.

People had varying views of de Gaulle—soldier, statesman, hero, obstinate, able, powerful. He was all of these and many more . . . for France!

We thank you, O God, for all the blessings of this our land; for the heritage which is ours to enjoy; for freedom, liberty and justice. Grant to our leaders wisdom, to all our people a sense of responsibility, and to us a desire to grow up as loyal citizens. Hear us and help us. *Amen.*

Benediction No. 94

Faithfulness and loyalty (4)

Chief Khama

Bible Reading: St. Matthew 7: 13–14

There is a choice in life. One can go the way that most people go and be one of the crowd. Or one can choose to 'go it alone' and stand up for what is right, which is a much harder thing to do, especially when people around are hostile.

Young Khama was the son of Chief Sekhome of the Bamangwato people in that part of southern Africa now known as Botswana. As a boy he had met David Livingstone and he had been fascinated by this fearless white man. As a young man he went to stay with a neighbouring chief who had become a Christian after listening to Livingstone. Khama decided that this was the way for him too.

Khama took a firm stand against all the things he believed to be wrong and his father became very angry when Khama would not follow the old tribal customs or take part in some of the festivals. More than once his father tried to kill him. But the tribe respected Khama and chose him to be chief of the Bamangwato in 1872.

As chief, Khama determined to get rid of some of the evil around him, especially drunkenness. He told the white traders who sold alcoholic drinks to the Africans that they should leave the country and he forbade his own people to get drunk. He went into battle against witchcraft and superstition. In his fifty years as chief he stood firm for what he believed and he did much for the good of his people.

Khama died in February, 1923, having remained loyal throughout his long life to his Christian ideals.

Help us, God our Father
To make up our minds as to what things are right;
To try all our lives to do only those things;
To remain faithful even though we may stand alone;
And to know the strength of your Holy Spirit. *Amen.*

Closing prayer No. 60

Faithfulness and loyalty (5)

Bishop Berggrav

Eivind Berggrav was born in Stavanger, Norway, in 1884. He was a clever boy and attended university in Oslo before going abroad to study. Returning to Norway in 1909 he became a teacher before deciding in 1919 to be a clergyman. People soon came to love and respect Pastor Berggrav, who seemed to understand their problems.

Ten years later he became a bishop in the Norwegian Church, serving in the far north of Norway, where he worked amongst the Lapps with their reindeer herds and with fishermen in small coastal villages.

In 1937 he returned to the capital city to be Bishop of Oslo. By this time he was well-known, not only in Norway but in many other countries too, for he had begun working with leaders of churches in other countries to form a World Council of Churches, where Christian leaders could work together.

Before the Council could meet, World War II had broken out. German armies occupied Norway but the bishop would not co-operate. When told not to preach in the cathedral on Easter Sunday, he announced that he would do so. He was thereupon taken to a lonely cottage and held prisoner there until war ended in 1945.

The rulers may have prevented him from preaching but they could not stop his words reaching people in churches throughout Norway. Bishop Berggrav was faithful to his calling as a bishop and as spiritual shepherd to the Norwegian people.

Once released, Bishop Berggrav was able to continue his work in the Church and for the World Council of Churches. He died in 1959 but is remembered as a hero in Norway and as a faithful servant of God.

O God, we thank you for the example set by those people who have given themselves into your service and have remained faithful in times of difficulty. Help us to follow their example so that we may be true to ourselves and to you. *Amen.*

Benediction No. 91

6 Religion and worship

This large section on religion and worship serves as an introduction to many beliefs, creeds, religions, sects and denominations and will be very helpful and necessary in a multi-racial community.

It may be subdivided into two. The first nine themes are probably best taken as a complete unit, occupying the whole of one term and being taken in the order in which they are printed.

Finding out   *Fear or faith*   *Hinduism*
Buddhism   *Judaism*   *Christianity*
Islam   *Some other beliefs* *Religion and life*

Visual aids and religious signs or tokens can be very beneficial.

The other themes are associated with worship, religious life and practice and are not as closely linked as those in the earlier part. Some will best be taken as complete themes

How people worship   *Where people worship*
Cathedrals   *Monasteries*
Some Christian churches   *More Christians*
The Sabbath   *Prayer and meditation*
Make a joyful noise   *Hymns we enjoy*
Sacred writings

In some of these themes there is reference to the practices of people of religions other than Christian to give a greater overall concept of the approach to God.

Finding out (1)

HOW AND WHY?

Most of us are quite used to asking questions and hoping that someone will give us the answer. How do you do these sums? Why doesn't this toy work? Why does my knee bleed when I cut it? What makes the wind blow?

These are simple questions to which an answer can be given. But there are other kinds of question that are more difficult to answer. How did the world begin? Is there a god or more than one god? What is God like? Is God good or evil? Kind or stern? Revengeful or loving?

To questions like these no one can give you a definite answer. All people can do is to tell you what *they* believe. And those beliefs will vary from person to person and from country to country according to what people have been taught or what they have decided for themselves.

Questions about how things work are what we might call scientific questions. All the knowledge that we have today about our world, about nature, about the weather, about medicine, about engineering and a host of other things, has come to us because people have thought out answers to difficult questions and have then proved their theories.

Religion is based partly on things we know but partly on things we believe but cannot prove. That is why there are so many different religions in the world and why we cannot say that one religion is right and others are wrong. All we can do is to make up our own minds as to what we believe and then be true to those beliefs.

We soon discover that we owe much to a great many people of the past and the present.

O God, we know that people think of you in many different ways. Help us to learn from others, to decide what is right, and to stand by our beliefs. Guide us in our thinking and give us wisdom in our seeking after you. *Amen.*

Closing prayer No. 80

Finding out (2)

Many thousands of years ago, people knew very little about the world and the forces of nature. They knew that there were many things that seemed much more powerful than themselves and often they were afraid of these things.

Every day the sun rose in the morning, travelled across the sky and disappeared in the evening. When it came it brought light and heat. People in many parts of the world regarded the sun as a god. The Egyptians called him Ra. The Incas and Aztecs of America were sun worshippers.

The moon was also regarded as a god—or more frequently as a goddess because it was more gentle than the sun. There were also the gods of thunder, and rain, and those which made the crops grow.

People also believed in many kinds of spirit. There were, they believed, spirits which lived in trees, in rocks, in wells and in rivers. Pieces of wood or stone that were of an unusual shape or colour were thought to contain spirits and these were sometimes taken home so that those spirits could help them against 'evil spirits'.

Evil spirits were thought to bring trouble or illness. We can read of evil spirits in the Bible in the stories of Jesus. Here is one.

Bible Reading: St. Luke 4: 33–37

We can imagine how frightening it must have been for people to believe in all these spirits and gods. They were most anxious to avoid doing things which would anger the spirits and would offer them gifts of one kind or another in the hope of pleasing them.

We thank you, O God, that our knowledge today has taken away the fear of evil spirits. We remember those people in many parts of the world who still live in fear of evil spirits and pray that they may learn how to find peace of mind. *Amen.*

Benediction No. 98

Finding out (3)

MANY GODS OR ONE   *Good and evil*

Most people in the ancient world believed in many gods and goddesses, all of whom had some hand in the way in which the world worked. The ancient Egyptians believed in over two thousand gods but regarded some as far more important than others.

A very important god in farming lands was the one who made the crops grow, whereas the Eskimo thought more of the goddess Sedna, who lived under the ice and provided him with fish and seals. Warlike people like the Vikings thought highly of warlike gods.

One thing that was noticed by most ancient peoples was that there was a lot of good in the world but also a lot of evil. They thought, therefore, that there must be good gods and evil ones. The 'good' god of the Babylonians was Marduk and the 'bad' goddess was Tiamat. They were always fighting. When the world was alive in spring and summer Marduk was winning but later, when the world died in autumn and winter it was Tiamat's turn to win.

But while many people believed in lots of gods some began to believe in only one. To the Hebrew people there was only one 'True and Living God'—but he was *their* God and they saw nothing wrong with other people worshipping different gods.

The Hebrew people believed that evil was caused by Satan, who had rebelled against God, ever since then, Satan, or The Devil, has been considered by many people as the enemy of God. There is a story in the Bible of the way in which the Devil tempted Jesus to do wrong.

Bible Reading: St. Luke 4: 1–13

Almighty God, help us to guard against all forms of evil and to resist the temptation to do wrong. Teach us to trust in your almighty power and to know that you can guard our thoughts and guide our actions so that we can be like you in all our ways. *Amen.*

Closing prayer No. 74

Finding out (4)

Cave Paintings

On 12th September, 1940, five boys from Montignac in France decided to look inside some caves at Lascaux. Inside was an amazing display of stone-age art, paintings on the cave walls which may have been there for one hundred thousand years.

Paintings similar to these have been found in a number of caves, many of them showed pictures of animals having a spear in them. These were not painted because these ancient people liked painting but rather as a kind of magic. They believed that if they painted an animal with a spear where it would kill, it would help them when they were out hunting to kill an animal which they needed for food and clothing.

A similar kind of magic took the form of dancing, when the dancers would wear horns and pretend to be the animal to be killed. Such customs may still be found among primitive people today.

People of olden times, and in many parts of the world today, have looked to one man to perform the magic which was needed for their tribe or community. We frequently call such a man a witch-doctor. Although able to do many things that others could not do, the witch-doctor was not a magician but a man who had learned many things that others had not learned such as how to cure illnesses by using plants and how to forecast the weather. Some of the things he could do must have seemed like magic to people who could not understand how he did them.

But for most people, the magic of the witch-doctor was something that would persuade the spirits or the gods to help them. It was part of their religion.

Grant unto us, O God our Father, a knowledge of yourself and your holy ways so that we may trust you for all things and know that you will help us, for you care for us. *Amen.*

Closing prayer No. 86

Finding out (5)

From earliest times, people have looked for someone who could help them in their thinking about gods or spirits, to obtain help from such spirits and perhaps to do what might be regarded as miracles.

The person to whom they would go would be the wise man, or witch. The name witch merely meant a wise person and could be a man or a woman. Often the things the witches did could not be understood and people believed they had special powers given to them by God.

Then people thought that if witches could get help from God, perhaps they could get help from the Devil as well. The result was that witches became very unpopular and feared by many people who believed that the witch could cast a spell on them or curse them so that some evil befell.

But for people in many parts of the world who wanted to know about God, the person to whom they would turn would be the holy man, the sage who had thought things out and could speak words of wisdom or the seer, who could perhaps understand things better than other people and often spoke messages which he had received from God. Such men were greatly respected and even kings would turn to them for advice.

One of the most important seers of Old Testament times was Samuel. This reading shows how he told the people what was required of them.

Bible Reading: I Samuel 12: 14–16

It was through men like this that people came to understand what God and their religion required of them.

We thank you, O God, for people through whom you have shown yourself and whose teachings have helped us to follow in your ways. Grant us your continued guidance and help so that we may be true children of our Father in heaven. *Amen.*

Closing prayer No. 85

Fear or faith (1)

Amulets and mascots

Do you know of anyone who carries a lucky charm or who wears a St. Christopher? A lucky charm is something which is supposed to bring good luck to the person who has it. A St. Christopher is worn because he is the patron saint of travellers. Or perhaps you know a house which has a horseshoe over the door, which is supposed to keep evil away from the house.

Nowadays we take little notice of these things but once upon a time they were of great importance. Imagine living in days when people believed in all kinds of evil spirits, or who thought that there were lots of witches who would cast spells, or who were afraid of what the Devil might do. If you heard of anything which was supposed to give protection from these things, no doubt you would be very anxious to obtain one for yourself.

There were lots of amulets, what some might call 'lucky charms', which were supposed to give protection. Apart from horseshoes, other things of iron were believed to give protection and so were certain trees and plants. Stones of a particular shape or colour were believed to have magical properties. And the brass symbols on the harness of a horse were supposed to protect the animal from evil.

To us it may seem strange that people should believe that simple things like a piece of iron could protect them. But we live in a day when people know so much about so many things that we no longer believe in things having magical powers.

Of course, there have always been people who have preferred to trust in God and believe that He is all the help they need. Hear the words of the psalmist in Old Testament times.

Bible Reading: Psalm 121

Almighty God, in whom people through the ages have placed their trust, look down upon us in your love, keep us from harm and danger, free us from fear and anxiety, and grant us a sense of your presence. *Amen.*

Benediction No. 99

Fear or faith (2)

Are you superstitious? Many people admit that they are about some things. Others say that they are not, yet still observe these old beliefs without thinking or just in case there is something in them after all.

Would you walk under a ladder, for example? Some people refuse to do so in case something falls on them! Others are superstitious because it was said to be unlucky to walk under a ladder. A ladder leaning against a wall made a triangle. The three sides reminded them of God—God the Father, the Son and the Holy Spirit. To walk through the triangle was like walking through, or being disrespectful to God, and that, they believed, must be unlucky.

Many of the old superstitions arose from beliefs about God and the Devil, together with the idea that nothing must be done to displease one or the other or there would be trouble. Most of the early thoughts that people had about God were that, somehow or other, he had to be pleased.

Paul, when he visited Athens, found that people were very superstitious and wanted to be safe. They believed in many gods but thought they might have missed one, and so they made an altar 'to the Unknown God'.

Bible Reading: Acts 17: 22–29

People who are not sure of themselves may well be superstitious, but people who have a strong belief in God find it quite unnecessary. They believe that God is always able to help them.

Almighty God, there are many things we do not know and many that we cannot understand. In our doubts and difficulties, help us to know that you are our God and Father, the Creator and ruler of everything that surrounds us, and the one into whose hands we can safely commit ourselves today and all our days. *Amen.*

Benediction No. 90

Fear or faith (3)

SACRIFICE

One of the earliest stories in the Bible tells how two brothers, Cain and Abel, offered sacrifices to God. Cain, who grew crops, brought some of his produce: Abel, who kept animals, made a sacrifice of some of his animals. This was their way of saying Thank-you for a good harvest.

They were doing what people in every part of the world have done since the earliest of times in making a special offering to God. Some thought that if God had been good to them they should make a sacrifice, or perhaps he would not be so good to them next year. Sometimes, when things went wrong, people believed that the gods were angry and they made sacrifices to try to win the forgiveness of the gods.

Sacrifices would have been of little use unless they were costly and so people offered the best they could to their gods. It was the first of the harvest, or the best of the animals, even the firstborn of their children. In the Bible we read how Abraham thought he should offer his only son as a sacrifice to God, but God showed him another way instead. Here is part of the story.

Bible Reading: Genesis 22: 9–13

Human sacrifice was once very common. In many countries children were sacrificed. Saxon warriors were sometimes thrown overboard as a sacrifice to the sea-god. The Aztecs of Central America sacrificed all those they captured in battle and many of their own people too.

Christians believe that the final sacrifice was made by God himself, when he sent Jesus Christ to take away people's sins. In return, people should sacrifice themselves by giving all they have in the service of God and their fellows.

Accept, O God, the sacrifice of ourselves, our time, our energy, our abilities, our skills and our talents, so that our whole lives may be lived for your glory and in the service of others in your Name. *Amen.*

Closing prayer No. 84

Fear or faith (4)

IDOLS AND ALTARS

When people wanted to make sacrifices to their gods they went to a holy place to do so. Some of these holy places were ones where something important had happened in the past which people associated with their gods.

Often these holy places were known as High Places, because that was what they were. Lots of people believed that the higher they were the nearer to god they must be. So the high places where people offered their sacrifices were often to be found on hill tops.

Some ancient peoples built temples which towered high above the earth with the place for sacrifice at the top. The temple used by the Babylonians when they sacrificed to their god was a high building called a Ziggurat.

The sacrifices were offered on an altar. The earliest altars were probably mounds of earth or piles of stones. In the Old Testament we can read how Abraham built altars to God in various places as he travelled.

Bible Reading: Genesis 12: 5–8

Sometimes an image, or idol, of the god being worshipped was set up near the altar. It may have been carved from wood, cut out of stone or made with gold or silver. But for people like the Hebrews, who believed in one God, who could not be seen, such idols were unneccessary.

Today altars are found in many places of worship. They are no longer used for blood sacrifice, but as the centre of certain acts of worship and many of them are very beautifully made.

Hear us, O God, as we bow before you in worship. We cannot see you as we see those who are around us but we ask for faith to believe that you are near and we pray that you will accept our lives, a living sacrifice offered to our God. *Amen.*

Closing prayer No. 64

Fear or faith (5)

In the very distant past people offered their own sacrifices to their gods but as religion became more organized and special places of worship were built it became the custom to have priests to be responsible for looking after the temple and offering the sacrifices.

In most religions the priests became very important and powerful. All sacrifices had to be made by the priest on behalf of the people and the priest alone could say whether an animal brought for sacrifice was good enough. Certain rituals, such as sprinkling the blood of the animal were performed by the priests. In some countries the chief priests or high priests became the rulers.

Some people still believe that it is necessary to approach God through a priest but in many religions a priest is not necessary. Muslims offer their own prayers to God. Christians believe that Jesus Christ laid down his life as a final sacrifice and became the only High Priest through whom people could come to God.

Sacrifice and fear was no longer needed. Instead people were advised to have faith to believe that they can speak with God himself in the name of Jesus Christ.

Bible Reading: Hebrews 10: 19–22

So the role of the priest has changed. In the Christian Church he leads people in worship and helps them to understand God. In some churches he is not called a priest but a pastor or 'shepherd', who helps people to know for themselves a God who cares for his people.

O God, our Father, help us to know you as a God who cares. May we accept the guidance of those who have found you for themselves and learn to live by faith, trusting in your love. *Amen.*

Benediction No. 98

Hinduism (1)

One very old religion is Hindu, the religion of India. The name Hindu is a form of the name Indus, the great river of north-west India. It was here about four thousand years ago, that conquering people known as Ayrians settled, later spreading to other parts of India. Their religion was expressed in a large number of hymns, chants and prayers which, after a long time, were written down and became known as the Vedas.

In common with many other religions, the Hindu religion had many gods and stories were told about them. There were, for example, Varuna the sky-god and Agni the god of fire. Many of these gods needed to be pleased, it was thought, and sacrifices were offered to them.

So there grew up a group of people known as Brahmins who acted as priests and became the most important class of people. They added new writings to the Vedas, which were called Brahmanas. These laid down rules for offerings and ceremonies.

Between two and three thousand years ago some very important writings were added to the Hindu religion. They were called Upanishads. Upa-ni-shad means 'near-down-sit'—an invitation to learn from the great teachers.

Among the new ideas was one that there was a great spirit or soul, known as the Brahman, which existed beyond this world.

Hindus believe the Brahman has appeared on earth many times in the lives of great people. Some Hindus accept that Jesus Christ was one appearance of the Brahman but not the *only* incarnation of God as Christians believe.

Bible Reading: Hebrews 1: 1–3

A prayer from the Hindu Vedas:
Hear this call of mine; be gracious unto me this day,
Longing for help I cry to thee.
Thou, O wise God, art Lord of all, thou art the king of earth
    and heaven;
Hear and reply with prosperity.

Closing prayer No. 52

Hinduism (2)

For people of Christian, Jewish or Muslim faiths who believe in one God, it is not easy to understand how people like Hindus can have so many. When they worship they call upon the names of many gods and they have many images of these gods.

Many of their beliefs go back to the Vedas but others were introduced in the Upanishads. At that time they came to believe in a creator-god called Brahma, who had two other personalities as Vishnu the preserver and Siva the destroyer. Vishnu and Siva are gods worshipped by a great many Hindus.

Vishnu is one god who is said to have come on earth on several occasions. One of the most famous of the Hindu writings, the Bhagavad-Gita ('Song of the Lord') tells how he appeared as Lord Krishna.

Although the Hindus have many gods, they may also believe in the one God-spirit known as Brahman. When they pray in front of their images many of them are thinking of the spirit they cannot see. And when they address their prayers to the various gods they may remember the words of Lord Krishna in their writings: 'Whichever god you pray to, it is I who answer the prayer.'

There is no rule in the Hindu religion which lays down what a person believes about God. The command to the Jews was to worship only one God:

Bible Reading: Exodus 20: 1–6

Christians and Muslims have the same kind of belief but not so the Hindus. A Hindu may believe in only one god, or more than one, or all of them, or he may believe in no god at all.

Only two things are required of a Hindu. One is that he should seek the truth. The other is that he should practice harmlessness, which means more than doing no harm. You can harm a person simply by failing to help him!

Help us, O God, to seek the truth about you so that we may be able to understand your ways and live according to your teachings. Help us, too, to seek the good of all people and love them as ourselves. *Amen.*

Benediction No. 107

Hinduism (3)

REINCARNATION AND SALVATION

One important belief that came from the Hindu writings is that of reincarnation. That means that a person may return to this life many times. The belief is that every living creature has an *atman* (soul) which is trying to escape from this world.

After death the soul returns to life in a better or worse state according to the way the previous life has been lived. A bad person might return as an animal: a good person may return to a higher class of life. After many rebirths the soul may escape to salvation, or to *Nirvana* (a state of bliss).

At one time it was believed that the only way to salvation was through knowledge, but other ways were also found. One was *karma*, the way of works, so that if people did many good works they could be saved. Another was *Yoga*, a strict control of body and mind.

The simplest way is the 'way of devotion', which is possible for anyone. People dedicate themselves to one of the gods such as Vishnu and Siva. About two hundred million Hindus worship Vishnu, the preserver.

Sometimes there is an outward sign that a particular god is worshipped. Hindu women, and men on important occasions, have a sign called a *tilaka* between their eyebrows. A red, white or black spot simply indicates that the wearer has been blessed, but a mark of a different shape may indicate a devotion to Vishnu or Siva.

So for the Hindu there are various paths to salvation, unlike the Christian belief that God sent Jesus Christ into the world to save those who believe in him.

Bible Reading: St. John 3: 14–17

Help us, O God, so to order our lives that they may become the best that we can make them. Teach us the truth about yourself and help us to remain faithful to what we believe. Show us the way of salvation and bring us at last into your eternal kingdom. And to you, O God, be all praise and glory. *Amen.*

Benediction No. 103

Hinduism (4)

Long ago, Hindus believed that people fell into four classes or *castes*. The highest was the Brahmin (priest), then the Kshatriya (warrior or nobleman), the Vaishya (peasant) and the Shudra (slave). Only the first three could take part in the Hindu religion: slaves were outside it.

In time this developed into over two thousand castes besides many who had no caste at all and were called 'untouchables'. The great Hindu leader Mahatma Gandhi helped to change that so now all Hindus may worship in the temples.

For the Hindu worship and prayer are important. When he steps out of bed he says a prayer as his foot touches God's earth. At the end of the day he says another special prayer, and there are many others during the course of the day.

In his house a Hindu has a room set aside for worship. This may have a small shrine or shelf with an image of a god or a picture of a saint. He will say prayers and make offerings of food or other objects. In the Gita Lord Krishna says: 'If one of earnest spirit sets before me with devotion a leaf, a flower, fruit or water, I enjoy this offering of devotion.' These acts of devotion are normally performed three times a day.

Most Hindu worship is carried out in the home but there are many temples for worship and where great festivals are held during the year in honour of the various gods. Music and dancing are important aspects of worship.

Many Hindus make a pilgrimage to Varanasi (Benares) to bathe in the sacred waters of the River Ganges. Bathing is a mark of purification and Hindus bathe before any religious ceremony.

For the Hindu daily life and religious observance go hand in hand. One cannot be separated from the other.

Almighty God, help us to remember that you are present with us at all times. May we remember you through the day and praise you for every blessing received. *Amen.*

Benediction No. 102

Hinduism (5)

Hinduism was not founded by one person but was revealed through a large number of sages or wise men who added greater knowledge or new thoughts to what people believed up to their time. Most of these teachers remained Hindus but some branched off to form a religion that was a little different.

One such person was Vardhamana, who lived from 599 to 527 B.C. He was given the title Mahavira (Great man) and his followers are known as Jains. Jains have nothing to say about God and they do not accept the Vedas as being inspired by a god. They seek truth and have such a deep respect for all living creatures that they sweep the path in front of them lest they tread on an ant. They even wear scarves across their mouths so that the creatures in the air are not disturbed by their breathing.

Another who broke away from Hinduism was Gautama, the Buddha, who formed the Buddhist religion. Some of the really great teachers were thought to have been more than just men. Many believe, for example, that the last time the Brahman, the God-spirit, came to earth it was in a Hindu saint, Sri Ramakrishna, who lived in Bengal during the nineteenth century.

Some people who have become wise in their religion are given the title *Pandit*. They are usually Brahmins. Others who become learned and teach are called *gurus*. People sometimes turn for help to the holy men, the *sadhus*, who have given their whole time to devotion to God so that they can become saintly. A holy man who is thought to have gained complete control over himself is sometimes known as a *swami*.

These men may all be able to help others in their religious life but every man is expected to do all he can to improve himself so that he can one day reach Nirvana.

We thank you, Almighty God, for all the means by which we can learn of you, the holy books, the teachings of others and the example of the saints. Help us to learn from these and so grow nearer to you day by day. *Amen.*

Benediction No. 98

Buddhism (1)

One of the world's largest religions is Buddhism, founded by Gautama, The Buddha, about five hundred years before Christ. Siddhartha Gautama was the son of the ruler of a small kingdom near the Himalayas to the north of India. Living in a palace he had every luxury and was protected from the world.

When he was twenty-nine he went outside the grounds and began to realize how much suffering there was in the world. He went from one Hindu teacher to another to see if one could explain the problem of suffering but none could.

He tried fasting until he became very ill but that proved nothing. Then he sat beneath a tree to think. This tree has since become known as the Bo-tree or 'tree of enlightenment' for it was here that Gautama became a Buddha, or enlightened one—someone who had learned the answers.

The problems of suffering, he believed, could be cured by having the right attitudes to life, summed up in his teaching, The Noble Eightfold Path. This included seeking truth and resolving to keep to it; right speaking, actions and correct living; and right attitudes through practising meditation.

The Buddha believed there was a Middle Path between greed and fasting. If the Middle Way were followed it would give clear vision, wisdom, peace and enlightenment. He believed, as Hindus do, that one may return to this life several times and that one finally reaches the state known as Nirvana, leaving this world for ever but continuing to exist somewhere else. The Middle Way would lead to this.

Gautama, the Buddha, died when he was over eighty years of age and passed into Nirvana.

Help us, O God, to learn the way that we ought to live. Show us what is the truth and help us to keep to it. Teach us to live good lives that will cause no offence to others, and bring us at last into your eternal kingdom. *Amen.*

Benediction No. 102

Buddhism (2)

Dhiravamsa

Buddhism is different from most religions in that it is not the worship of a god or gods but a way of improving oneself by good living and meditation. In the years after the Buddha lived, different forms of Buddhism developed.

In South-east Asia, it took the form of Therevada Buddhism, sometimes called Southern Buddhism. There the people are happy to leave much of the meditating to the monks, the Sangha, who meditate in the great monasteries. The peasant people enjoy their festivals when they deck large statues of the Buddha with flowers and regard him almost as a god.

It was in such a village in Thailand that Dhiravamsa was born in 1935. At thirteen he attended a temple festival and was singled out by an elderly temple monk, who spoke to him about Buddhist teachings.

From then on Dhiravamsa attended the temple, learning the arts of meditation until he was old enough to attend the Buddhist University at Bangkok and study the Buddhist writings.

In 1966 Dhiravamsa was appointed chief monk of a temple in London. Soon afterwards he opened a meditation centre at Hindhead, Surrey and ran study courses in America and Canada too.

In 1971 he ceased to be a monk. He felt that because he wore the monk's robes it made him seem different from other people and might be a barrier to those he wanted to help. His teachings have helped many people to meditate themselves and to find new attitudes and contentment.

People of many religions have learned that there is a great deal to be gained by sitting in silence and thinking about good things, or about God.

We bow before you, O God, and ask that in the quietness we may meet with you. Take from us all worries and anxieties and grant us peace in our minds. So may we live full and happy lives, and to you be the glory. *Amen.*

Benediction No. 106

Buddhism (3)

Chogyam Trungpa

Chogyam Trungpa was born in Tibet in 1938 in a small village where his father was a farmer. One day some monks came to the village. They had been sent to look for a boy in a particular house in the village because they believed he was someone special.

Buddhists believe in reincarnation, that is that when a person dies he returns to this world to begin a new life. During the previous year, the lama, the head of a group of monasteries had died. The monks were looking for the baby in whom the lama had returned.

So Trungpa, at the age of one, was taken to the monastery where, a few months later, he was enthroned in the presence of about thirteen thousand monks from Eastern Tibet—the eleventh reincarnation of the lama. So began a life of study until, at the age of eleven, Trungpa took his vows.

The people of Tibet follow a form of Buddhism known as Mahayana Buddhism. This has more holy writings than other forms of Buddhism and there is a belief in holy beings, something like gods, who can help people. Mahayana Buddhists do not just seek things for themselves but have a compassion for all forms of life.

In 1959 Chinese Communist soldiers invaded Tibet. Many monasteries were destroyed: many lamas were tortured and killed. The Dalai Lama, the spiritual ruler of Tibet fled and made his home in India. Chogyam Trungpa, at the age of twenty, with other lamas, escaped over the mountains into India but he then settled in Britain. He set up the first Tibetan Meditation Centre in Dumfriesshire, Scotland, and later, in the 1970s, centres in America.

Mahayana or Northern Buddhists pray, meditate and study the scriptures to improve themselves, to save others and to find the truth.

Teach us, O God, to pray, to study our scriptures and to learn what is right so that we may improve ourselves, help others, and serve our God. *Amen.*

Benediction No. 98

Buddhism (4)

The Three Baskets

The main sacred writings of Buddhists are known as the Three Baskets (Tri-pitaka). Perhaps you have seen pictures of people forming a bucket-chain, passing buckets of water from one to another when there is fire to be put out. In eastern lands, earth for building is often passed in the same way but in baskets. So the Three Baskets are the means of passing Buddhist teachings from one to another.

The First Basket is concerned mainly with rules for the monks. The Second Basket is the teaching basket, which contains, among other things, the main beliefs of the Buddha and his followers. The Third Basket contains long explanations of the teachings found in the Second Basket.

The Teaching Basket includes the birth stories, which tell how Gautama had various lives, as a bird, animal and man before his 'enlightenment'. Another book, The Way of Virtue, is a book of moral teachings which many Buddhists learn by heart.

At first, no doubt, these teachings were passed on by word of mouth. There is no trace of any written word until several hundred years after Gautama died.

Some Buddhists have many other books, the Northern Buddhists in particular. One of the greatest is the Lotus Scripture, in which the Buddha offers to save all those who have faith in him. It is called the Lotus Scripture because the Lotus flower is a symbol used for the Buddha and his teachings.

Other Buddhists have discarded many of the old writings. The Zen Buddhists, for example, of whom there are many in the western world today, are more concerned with meditation as a means of reaching 'enlightenment'.

Help us, O God, to seek after truth;
Help us to learn from the words of others;
Help us to make up our minds what is right;
And when we have decided,
Help us to be true to our beliefs. *Amen.*

Closing prayer No. 63

Buddhism (5)

If you were to go to the Buddhist countries of Asia, you would see many things to remind you of this religion. There are great monasteries, where the Sangha (monks) live, where visitors are made welcome and where many boys are educated, some to become monks themselves and others to take up other occupations.

Buddhist monks are a familiar sight early in the day. They wear their orange robes and come out to collect alms, which the people willingly give. They return for a morning meal and devotions. They have another meal just before mid-day, which is their last for the day. The day is spent in teaching or in some other form of work for the community.

In some Buddhist countries there are huge statues of the Buddha. A worshipper may bow before one and pray, or he may just sit cross-legged and think about any wrong he may have done. He solemnly promises to keep the main Buddhist laws—not to take the life of any creature, to steal, to be immoral, to tell lies or to drink alcohol. Then he may whisper a few sacred words or spend time in meditation.

Devotions may also be held at a stupa (mound) or a pagoda containing the relic of a past Buddha, such as a tooth or some hairs. Although Gautama was *the* Buddha, there have been other Buddhas (enlightened ones). Some forms of Buddhism also have men known as bodhisattvas, or Buddhist saints.

Buddhism in the past spread through parts of Asia. During this century it has reached Europe and America. Buddhist missionaries have been sent to the west where they have set up centres in which people can learn and practise the Buddhist way of life.

We confess to you, O God, that there are times when we have done wrong. We have hurt others by our words and deeds; we have disregarded your teachings; and we have sometimes forgotten you. Forgive us, we pray, and help us to live, speak and act as we should. *Amen.*

Closing prayer No. 88

Judaism (1)

'People of the Book'

Judaism is the religion of the Jews, a group of people who have been more misunderstood than any others in the course of history. They have been persecuted by rulers, herded into ghettos away from other people, killed in their millions and falsely blamed. They have been insulted and ridiculed, yet have remained cheerful, bearing no malice, and accepting suffering bravely rather than be disloyal to their God, whom they praise at all times.

Their story began when Abraham, sick of idolatry around him, left his country. He had a vision of 'the One True God', whose name was too holy to be spoken. It was written down as JHVH, wrongly called Jehovah, possibly Yahweh, but no one really knows.

The story of his descendants, the Israelites or Hebrews, for hundreds of years is recorded in the Hebrew Bible (the Christian Old Testament) so the Jews have come to be known as 'The People of the Book'.

The first five books of the Bible are the Hebrew Torah, or Law. The fifth of these, D'varim (Deuteronomy) sums up many laws and attitudes. Here is one small part.

Bible Reading: Deuteronomy 10: 12–17

Who are the Jews? They are not a nation (although there is now a Jewish nation, Israel), but people of many lands, some of whom were not born Jews but decided to become Jews.

What is most important is that God should have a place in every part of life. The Jews, who have sometimes been called 'a nation of priests', believe that in this way they are helping to build the Kingdom of God on earth.

Unite our hearts, O God, to fear thy name; keep us far from what thou hatest; bring us near to what thou lovest; and deal mercifully with us for thy name's sake. *Amen.*

Talmud

Closing prayer No. 57

Judaism (2)

Christians count their years from the birth of Jesus Christ; Muslims count theirs from the flight of Muhammad; but the Jews go right back to the beginning of time and count theirs from the creation of the world, or when people long ago calculated that to be. The Jewish New Year falls in the autumn, so that in 1979 the Jewish year 5740 began.

The Jewish calendar is based upon the moon. But twelve lunar months, making only 354 days instead of 365 meant that their seasonal festivals came at the wrong time of year. So seven times in every nineteen years an extra month is added. That is why dates of Jewish festivals change from year to year.

The first festival of the Jewish year is Rosh Hashanah (New Year) and begins a period of ten days of deep thought and penitence for anything wrong that has been done, linked with resolutions to do better in the coming year. The tenth day is Yom Kippur, the Day of Atonement, the most solemn day of the year.

Bible Reading: Leviticus 16: 29–34

On this day long ago sacrifices were made and a goat, the 'scapegoat', symbolically bearing the sins of all the people was driven into the wilderness. Today for twenty-four hours the Jew eats and drinks nothing, he spends his day in prayer confessing his sins.

Other Jewish holy days and festivals include Passover, Feast of Weeks, Feast of Tabernacles, Chanukkah and Purim. They are times of thanking God for his goodness in the past.

A prayer of the prophet Habakkuk (Good News Bible)

O Lord, I have heard what you have done, and I am filled with awe. Now do again in our times the great deeds you used to do. Be merciful even when you are angry. *Amen.*

Benediction No. 103

Judaism (3)

From early in the morning until his last thoughts at night a Jew is expected to be mindful of God. As he awakes he should thank God for keeping him through the night. Throughout the day he should thank God for blessings received. Before going to sleep he says the *Shema*, which begins *Hear, O Israel, the Lord our God, the Lord is One: Blessed be His Name, whose glorious kingdom is for ever and ever. And thou shalt love the Lord thy God with all thy heart and with all thy soul and with all they might* . . .

It is the first prayer learned by a Jewish child and the last prayer uttered by a dying person. It is used on many occasions.

Jews pray whenever they wish but there are three periods when prayer is expected in the synagogue and in the home—morning, afternoon and evening. On the Sabbath there are services of prayer and praise in the synagogue.

The Sabbath begins on the Friday evening because the story of the Creation speaks of the 'evening and the morning' being the first day. The Jewish day begins when three stars can be clearly seen by the naked eye.

The Psalms play an important part in worship for they speak of the goodness and the greatness of God. Psalm 92 is the special psalm for the Sabbath. This is how it begins.

Bible Reading: Psalm 92: 1–4 (or 8)

This psalm reflects the joyfulness felt by God's people, who can confidently begin many of their prayers: *Blessed art thou, O Lord our God, King of the universe* . . .

I will proclaim your greatness, my God and king;
I will thank you for ever and ever.
Every day I will thank you;
I will praise you for ever and ever. *Amen.*
                    Psalm 145: 1–2 (Good News Bible)

Closing prayer No. 86

Judaism (4)

The place where Jewish boys and girls begin to learn about their religion is in the home, where it is the responsibility of the parents to provide surroundings in which the children can become familiar with Jewish religious customs.

It has always been up to parents to ensure that they not only teach what they can themselves but send the children to classes after school and on Sunday mornings.

Children have to study their religion. This instruction is called Torah. They also have to learn Hebrew, the language of the Bible and prayer book.

When a Jewish boy reaches the age of thirteen, he is called *Bar-Mitzvah* (a son of the commandment). At a special service in the synagogue he is presented with his Tallith (prayer shawl), which he will wear whenever he stands before God and which will eventually be buried with him. He is now classed as an adult as far as religion is concerned.

Meals in the Jewish household are family occasions, and especially the meal at the beginning of the Sabbath, when there are prayers and singing as well as blessings for the children. Even the food is a reminder of their religion, for there are some foods which may and others which may not be eaten.

Older members of the family, too, are respected and looked after. This was one of the Ten Commandments.

Bible Reading: Exodus 20: 12

Parents, and old folk generally, arc cared foi by the whole family.

Almighty God, giver of all blessings, accept our thanks for our homes and families. Teach us to respect our parents and to show care and affection so that we may enjoy good and lasting relationships with all the family. *Amen.*

Closing prayer No. 60

Judaism (5)

There are various signs, symbols and customs associated with Judaism, most of which have their origin long, long ago.

When you visit a Jewish home, you will find a small cylinder fastened to the right hand door post and on doorposts inside too. This is a *mezuzah* and it contains the first part of the Shema.

Bible Reading: Deuteronomy 6: 4–9

The mezuzah is a constant reminder of God. The other command is observed by wearing tefillin, or phylacteries containing words of scripture. These are worn at prayer on weekdays on the forehead and on the left upper arm.

When praying in the morning, men wear the tallith, or praying shawl. The white cloth stands for purity, the blue stripes for the sky and thoughts of heaven. The tassels at the four corners are a reminder of God's commandments.

Worshippers in the synagogue always cover their heads. They may wear an ordinary hat or a skullcap known as a *copple* or *yarmulka*. This is not decreed in an old law but is a custom which spread from the Middle East about twelve hundred years ago.

There are many other symbols used in the home, especially at festival times, such as the eight-branched candlestick of Chanukkah, but there are also two symbols which are used to represent Judaism. One is the large seven-branched candlestick, or *menorah*, the original of which stood in front of the temple at Jerusalem. The other is the Star (or Shield) of David. Both are symbols of a loyal God-loving religion.

Almighty God, help us to notice those things around us which remind us of you and when we see them to give thanks to you for all your great goodness toward us. For every blessing we praise your holy name, O Lord. *Amen.*

Closing prayer No. 73

Christianity (1)

The Christian Church grew out of the Jewish religion. Jesus Christ was himself a Jew and so were the men he chose to be his disciples. St. Paul, the great leader of the early Christians, was a Jew, brought up and trained as a Pharisee. It is not surprising, therefore, that Christianity has a lot in common with Judaism.

As a boy, Jesus learned a lot about his religion, as this story shows:

Bible Reading: St. Luke 2: 41–47

At the age of thirty, Jesus was baptized by John the Baptist. Then he chose twelve men to help him and he spent three years travelling around, teaching, helping, healing and causing quite a stir one way and another. Some thought he was likely to start a revolution; others saw him as a troublemaker; whilst others said he was the Messiah, the promised one of God, who would bring in a new and wonderful age.

By the end of three years some people were anxious to get rid of Jesus. He was arrested, tried and crucified—as was the fate of most trouble-makers and criminals in those days.

But three days later, the disciples going to his tomb found it empty and the word soon spread that Jesus Christ had risen from the dead. The Bible tells how lots of people saw him afterwards. Some while afterwards, the followers of Jesus were filled with God's Holy Spirit and began teaching as Jesus himself had done.

In the town of Antioch they were nick-named 'Christians' because they spoke and acted as Christ had done. It is by this name that the followers of Christ are known today.

Help us, O God our Father, to learn your teachings and understand the way you would have us to live. Then guide us by your Spirit so that we may serve you faithfully and well. *Amen.*

Benediction No. 104

Christianity (2)

The Holy Trinity

The Scriptures which Jesus had learned, and which he often quoted, were the Jewish scriptures, the Law and the Prophets. Christians believe, as the Jews do, that there is one God, who alone is to be worshipped. Jesus himself said that he did not wish to alter the teachings of the Law but his attitude toward them was quite different from that of the religious leaders of his time.

One day Jesus asked his disciples who people thought he was.

Bible Reading: St. Matthew 16: 13–17

And so people thought of Jesus as a prophet, a great teacher, a Son of David, the Messiah, the Son of God. From some things Jesus said, people believed that he was none other than God himself in an earthly body.

Many years after the time of Jesus, leaders of the Christian Church decided that they should make a statement of what it was necessary for Christians to believe. A statement like this is called a Creed. Two important Creeds are the Nicene Creed and the Apostles' Creed. [*One of these could be read* (p. 425).]

Some people are troubled about the belief in God the Father, God the Son, and God the Holy Spirit, usually known as The Holy Trinity or the 'Three-in-One'. Christians only believe in *one* God. Just as an old-time actor played several characters by wearing different masks or 'persons', so God can be seen in three different 'persons', Father, Son and Holy Spirit.

Almighty God, help us, we pray, to learn the truth about you so that we may worship and serve you as we ought. Take us into your care and keeping so that we may feel secure, and to you, O God, Father, Son and Holy Spirit, be all glory now and forever. *Amen.*

Benediction No. 93

Christianity (3)

Since the main religion of most countries in the Western world is Christianity, it is not surprising that the calendar in those countries is built around the main Christian festivals.

The Christian calendar begins at the end of November with the season of *Advent*, when people begin looking forward to celebrating the coming of Jesus. It is also a time of looking into the future for people remember how Jesus taught that he would come again.

The birth of Jesus is celebrated at *Christmas*. It is not the date when Jesus was actually born, which was almost certainly much earlier in the year, but a pagan festival provided an opportunity for people to remember this. The visit of the Wise men is remembered on January 6th.

The most joyous of the Christian festivals is *Easter*, when Christians celebrate the Resurrection, or rising from the dead, of Jesus. At one time it was kept as a far more important festival than Christmas. In Holy Week, the week leading up to Easter, people remember the events of the last week in the life of Jesus, the Last Supper on Maundy Thursday, the Crucifixion on Good Friday.

Forty days after Easter comes *Ascension Day*, when people recall how Jesus left his disciples and ascended into heaven, leaving them the command to go and teach all nations.

The power to do so came to them on the Jewish Feast of Pentecost. The Holy Spirit of God changed timid men into bold ones and they spoke freely in the city. This is remembered on *Whit Sunday*, the tenth day after Ascension Day.

Bible Reading: Acts 2: 1–4

Hear us, O God, and grant us the guiding power of your Holy Spirit so that we may understand your teachings and be bold to obey them. *Amen.*

Benediction No. 100

Christianity (4)

Christian Denominations

The building in which Christians worship God is called a church, although other names are sometimes given to it instead. Some Christians can say that they meet in a cathedral, an abbey, a tabernacle, a chapel, a meeting house, a citadel, a mission or a gospel hall.

And if you were to go inside some of these buildings you would perhaps be struck by the differences between them. Some are very richly ornamented with carvings, stonework and stained glass, with a fine altar, silverware, candles, tapestries and pictures. Others are very, very plain and have none of these things.

The services, too, are very different. In what are called 'high church' services there is a lot of ritual, incense may be burned and candles lit. In others the service is very simple. In some there is hardly any speaking at all.

This is partly because Christian people have their own thoughts about the way in which things should be done and it is partly because in the past Christians have not been able to agree about this and some of the teachings of the Church. Today there are many branches, or denominations. There are Roman Catholic, Church of England, Methodist, Baptist, United Reformed, Society of Friends and Salvation Army to mention only a few.

In one sense the Christian Church may seem divided, yet the main beliefs about God are the same and the various denominations often work together, united in their desire to help people to understand God, and under the one symbol common to all, the sign of the Cross.

We remember before you, O God, the Christian Church throughout the world and we pray that you will bless all its members as they seek to do your holy will; through Jesus Christ our Lord. *Amen.*

Benediction No. 102

Christianity (5)

The 'Church'

We often think of a church as a building, and yet there is a sense in which the word church refers to people instead. When we speak of The Christian Church, we mean all those people who are called Christians.

We read of a church in Jerusalem in the early days after the disciples of Jesus had preached in the city. This referred to the group of people. There was no church building in Jerusalem. These Christians worshipped God in the Temple and they met in various homes.

Bible Reading: Acts 2: 44–47

We notice how these people not only worshipped and praised God but they were anxious to help one another. Whatever they had they sold and the money was used to help those who were in need. St. Paul, in his letters, often reminded people of their responsibility to help others especially those in need.

So, throughout the history of the Christian Church, we find people who have found ways of serving God in serving other people. Many of the great reforms came about because Christian people saw the desperate needs of others. Many people today, in many lands, are helped through various organizations run by the Christian Church.

Christianity is the religion of those people who believe in Jesus Christ and try to put his teachings into practice by loving and worshipping God, by loving their neighbours and trying to help them in any way they can.

Almighty God, we thank you for the Christian Church throughout the world, for its work and witness through the ages. Guide by your Holy Spirit its leaders and members today and enable them to give of their best in your service. *Amen.*

Closing prayer No. 60

Islam (1)

The youngest of the great world religions is Islam, the religion which was revealed to the prophet Muhammad in Arabia in the year A.D. 610. Arabia, in those days, was cut off from much of the rest of the world by desert and there was little contact with the other great religions. Most of the people worshipped idols.

Mecca was the chief city and it had in the centre a large rectangular stone shrine known as the Ka'aba. People would come to worship there in the courtyard surrounding the Ka'aba.

Muhammad liked to get away from the city at times and go into the desert places where he could think about God, the Creator. Once, while he was thinking an angel appeared to him and gave him a message. It was the first message of what was to become the Holy Qur'ān, the sacred writings of the religion of Islam.

For three years Muhammad shared the secret of his religion with only a few friends. Then God, whom Muhammad knew as Allah, told him that he was to preach about him. So Muhammad preached in Mecca, inviting people to join him.

In Mecca Muhammad made many enemies who saw that if people followed the way of Islam they might lose business from those who came to worship at the Ka'aba. So they plotted to kill Muhammad. But with the help of friends and relatives he was able to escape to Medina, where he joined his friends on 20th September, 622.

The followers of Muhammad are known as Muslims. They do not like to be called Mohammedans because they are followers of Allah, not Muhammad.

A prayer of Muhammad

O Lord, grant us to love thee; grant that we may love those that love thee; grant that we may do the deeds that win thy love. Make the love of thee to be dearer to us than ourselves, our families, than wealth, and even than cool water. *Amen.*

Closing prayer No. 81

Islam (2)

The followers of Muhammad, known as Muslims, call their religion Islam, which means 'submission' or 'surrender' to the will of God, whom they call Allah. This means that a Muslim's whole life is dedicated to the worship of Allah, not just in religious duties and acts but in every action.

A Muslim is expected to believe in one God, his Angels, his Books, his Prophets, the Day of Judgement, good and evil, and life after death. He believes that God is All-knowing, All-just, Loving and Merciful.

The holy book of the Muslims is the Qur'ān, which they believe to be God's last message to man. It is written in Arabic and, although there have been translations into other languages, all services are conducted and prayers said in Arabic.

Muhammad said that Islam was built on five pillars. These are the duties that are expected of anyone who is a Muslim. The first is to bear witness that there is no God but Allah and that Muhammad is his messenger.

The second pillar is the duty of prayer, which is considered of very great importance. The others are the giving of alms to the needy, fasting during the month of Ramadan, and a pilgrimage to Mecca.

It is the duty of every Muslim, once in his lifetime, to make the *hajj*, or pilgrimage to Mecca, where he will pray for forgiveness on Mount Arafat and visit the Ka'aba.

A Muslim daily prayer from the Qur'ān

In the Name of God, the Merciful, the Compassionate. Praise be to God, the Lord of the worlds, the Merciful, the Compassionate, King on the Day of Judgement. Thee do we serve and on thee do we call for help. Guide us on the straight path, the path of those to whom thou hast been gracious, not of those upon whom anger falls, or those who go astray.

Closing prayer No. 63

Islam (3)

Prayer plays a very important part in the life of a Muslim. There are two kinds of prayer. One is simply praying to God for help, which can be done anywhere and at any time. The other is a set form of prayer, which may take place in the mosque (the place of worship and prayer), in the home, or elsewhere.

Each day, at daybreak and on four other occasions during the day, a crier, or *muezzin* climbs to the top of a *minaret*, a tower of the mosque, and cries out in Arabic, *'God is the greatest, I bear witness that there is no God but Allah. I bear witness that Muhammad is the messenger of Allah. Come to prayer. Come to security.'*

Before prayer, the Muslim washes his hands, head and feet and rinses his mouth and nose in a manner that is laid down, saying as he does so, 'In the name of God, the Beneficent, the Merciful.' He then stands on clean ground or on a prayer mat facing Mecca.

The pattern of the prayers includes reciting chapters and verses from the Qur'ān, and making certain movements with the arms and body whilst standing, kneeling, bowing and prostrating on hands and knees with the forehead touching the ground. After the formal prayer is ended, personal prayers may be added.

When Muslims meet together for prayer they are led by a prayer leader or *Imam*. He is not a priest but a leader for the prayers, though on some occasions, such as at midday on Fridays, he may also deliver a sermon in the mosque. Any small group of Muslims can choose one of their number to be prayer leader, and of course, any Muslim can pray on his own.

O God, you are most great, yet we know that you hear the prayers of your people. Hear us now as we bow before you and grant unto us those things that you know that we have need of. *Amen.*

Closing prayer No. 73

Islam (4)

The Muslim Year

Like most people in Eastern lands, Muslims base their year upon the moon. Their calendar has twelve lunar months and so the year is a little shorter than the calendar based on the sun. Each year, therefore, begins a little earlier. Muslims count their dates from the *Hijra* when Muhammad left Mecca for Medina in A.D. 622. So the Muslim year 1399 began on 1st December 1978, while the year 1400 began on 20th November 1979.

Each year the month Ramadan is a month of fasting. Muslims fast from dawn to dusk each day. Two thoughts lie behind the fasting. One is that of self discipline. The other is so that the rich may know how the poor feel when they have to go hungry.

At the end of Ramadan is the great festival of Eid-ul-Fitr. It is celebrated with special prayers in the mosques and delicious meals. Children wear their new clothes and are given presents; gifts are given to the poor; and greetings and Eid cards are sent to friends. In Muslim countries there are great fairs with folk-dancing, music, singing and competitive sports, horse racing and wrestling.

The other big Muslim festival is Eid-ul-Adha. It is celebrated by pilgrims at the end of their pilgrimage to Mecca but also, at the same time, by Muslims all over the world. It is a festival of sacrifice when animals are sacrificed and the meat given to the poor. It is a reminder that one should be ready to sacrifice anything for the glory of God.

Muslim festivals are times for rejoicing but also for expressing thankfulness to God.

Almighty God, we praise you for all those many blessings which you have showered upon us. Help us to remember that all we have is a gift from you to be used for the benefit of those around us and, if need be, sacrificed for the glory of your holy name. *Amen.*

Closing prayer No. 57

Islam (5)

Two things are required of anyone who would call himself a Muslim. One is *belief*; that is belief in God and all that goes to make up the Muslim religion. The other is *action*; that is living a good life and doing whatever is the right thing. One cannot be a Muslim without doing both.

Action means that every person is responsible for his own deeds and that one day, on the Day of Judgement, he will have to answer for what he has or has not done. He must therefore try to help all people, whether they are Muslims or not.

One practical way is to help the poor. One of the Five Pillars is *Zakat*, or almsgiving. In one month of every year a Muslim is expected to give $2\frac{1}{2}$ per cent of his savings to help the poor. He is also expected at all times to do good and offer money, love and sympathy to those in need.

There are certain laws, too, which Muslims are expected to observe. Some foods may not be eaten and all meat must be from animals killed in a certain way. Before meals Muslims will say *Bismillah* (in the name of God), and, after the meal, *Alhamdulillah* (Praise be to God). There are dress regulations, too. Women are expected to dress modestly, hence the wearing of the *shalwar* or trousers.

Devout Muslims neither drink alcohol nor smoke tobacco. Things like gambling, lying, stealing and cheating, as well as more serious offences such as murder, are forbidden by Muslim law.

Muslims are expected to remain true to their faith but also to be friendly toward others, especially Christians and Jews because they also worship the one true God.

Help us, O God, to remember our responsibilities to you and toward other people. Make us thoughtful, considerate, helpful and loving, caring for others more than we care about ourselves, and remembering at all times to observe your commands and praise your holy name. *Amen.*

Closing prayer No. 67

Some other beliefs (1)

Gurus and the Granth

Another religion that had its origin in India is Sikhism, the religion of the people known as Sikhs. These normally strong, well-built Indians, easily recognizable by their turbans and beards, are now to be found in many parts of the world.

The Sikh religion is only about five hundred years old, having been founded in the Punjab region of India by the Guru Nanak, who lived from A.D. 1469 to 1538. Like many others, Nanak wanted to find out the truth about God. Around him were many Hindus and Muslims, but he was not satisfied with either religion.

During the last fifteen years of his life, Nanak settled down to preaching about the One God, who is known to Sikhs as the Name (Näm). Nanak's disciples or Sikhs (the name means 'disciples') were taught to remember the Name every morning in their prayer and meditation.

The Sikhs had ten great teachers or Gurus. Nanak was the first: Guru Gobind Singh, who lived about three hundred years ago, was the last. The great teachings of the gurus had been written down in a holy book called the Granth. There was then no need for more gurus: the Granth would be the only guru or teacher for the future.

It was the fifth guru, Arjun, who put the teachings together in the Granth, and who built the main Sikh temple, the Golden Temple at Amritsar. In that temple the Granth is read continuously all day long by a succession of readers.

The Granth teaches that God is everywhere. He is the great God of Islam, yet the more personal God of Hinduism. 'He dwells in everything; he dwells in every heart; yet he is not blended with everything; he is separated.'

Almighty God, help us to see you in everything; in the beauty of the world around us; in the love of families and friends; in the actions of your faithful servants. And in seeing you, may we love you and glorify your name. *Amen.*

Closing prayer No. 52

Some other beliefs (2)

The Five Ks

It was the last Sikh Guru, Gobind Singh, who formed the Sikhs into the kind of religious community that could be readily recognized. For many years the Sikhs had been persecuted by Muslim and Hindu rulers because they wanted to do things in their own way.

In 1699, Gobind Singh called together a great gathering of Sikhs on the Spring Festival of Baisakhi. This is the beginning of the Sikh New Year and is celebrated now each year on or about 13th April. It is the most important Sikh festival. On this occasion the guru took a sword and asked for a volunteer to give his life in the cause of their faith. Eventually five stepped forward but they were not slain: they were called the *Khalsa*, a word meaning 'pure', and they were given five symbols, the Five Ks, which are the symbols of Sikhs to this day.

Keshas, the uncut hair and beard, is a sign of holiness, and the head is covered with a turban. The *Kanga* is a comb, worn in the hair knot. The *Kirpan* is a sword, to be used only in defence. The *Kara* is a steel bangle worn on the right wrist, a reminder that God has no beginning or end, and also that the hand should not commit any misdeed. The *Kachcha*, a pair of short under-pants was more suitable than loose clothing for 'warrior saints'.

The Sikh place of worship is the Gurdwara. After the Opening of the Book there are hymns, music and prayers including the Anand, a prayer of thanksgiving. A sermon may be given by any member: there are no clergy or priests. All sit cross-legged on the floor, regardless of wealth or position because all are equal in the sight of the one God.

Help us to remember, O God, that all are equal in your sight; that neither position or worldly possessions can bring us nearer to you, only a right attitude of heart and mind. *Amen.*

Closing prayer No. 57

Some other beliefs (3)

Most of the people of the world have a general belief in one of the great religions. The largest religion is the Christian religion. It is difficult to say exactly how many people are Christian because different methods may be used to calculate the numbers but it has been suggested that there are about 850 million Christians in the world. There are nearly half as many Muslims and a similar number of Hindus.

There are also the ancient religions of China, the Confucians and Taoists, and members of the Shinto religion in Japan, numbering many millions.

For most people, the religion in which they are brought up is the religion they keep for the rest of their lives, but there are some who change to another because they find it better. There are also those who, in one way or another, become responsible for starting a new religion. Guru Nanak was one of these, for his thinking developed into the Sikh religion.

During the last two hundred years or so there have been various new religions, or cults, several of which began in America. Some of the best known are Mormons, Jehovah's Witnesses, Christian Scientists, and Seventh Day Adventists but there are others too. They may sometimes be thought of as Christians but they do not accept some of the important Christian teachings and, although they use the Bible, they also have other books and publications which set out their particular beliefs.

How can we decide what is right? Here is some advice:

Bible Reading: II Timothy 2: 14–16

We thank you, O God, for the words of scripture. Help us to study, to meditate, to think, and to decide what we believe to be right: then grant that we may be true to our beliefs. *Amen.*

Closing prayer No. 71

Some other beliefs (4)

Latter-day Saints

One of the fastest growing of the 'new' religions is The Church of Jesus Christ of Latter-day Saints, more commonly known as the Mormon Church.

The story began when an American named Joseph Smith claimed that he had seen an angel named Moroni, who told him to go to a certain hill where there were two golden plates of writing and two stones, known as the Urim and Thummim, through which he would be able to translate the writing on the plates. He did as he was told and translated the writing into the *Book of Mormon*.

On 6th April, 1830, the new Church of Jesus Christ of Latter-day Saints came into being with six members. They were far from popular and Joseph Smith was killed by a mob in 1844. The new leader, Brigham Young, set off westwards with the Mormons until they reached a place where Young said they would build a new city. It became Salt Lake City, the headquarters of the Mormon Church ever since.

Many people have been puzzled about the *Book of Mormon*. Why were the golden plates not available for others to see? Why were they written in a language which no one knew? How could an uneducated man like Joseph Smith translate them? Was it all a big hoax? A lot of people believe it was.

But for the Mormons the *Book of Mormon* is just as important, if not more so, than the Bible itself, which they consider has mistakes in it. Today the Mormon Church has over $1\frac{1}{2}$ million members and Mormon missionaries are sent out to teach others about their religion.

O God our Father, sometimes we are puzzled by the many different things people say about you and the beliefs they hold. Help us to decide what we believe to be right and then remain true to our beliefs so that we may serve you well. *Amen.*

Closing prayer No. 62

Some other beliefs (5)

Groups of people found in many parts of the world are the Jehovah's Witnesses. They meet in a building called Kingdom Hall and spend a lot of time calling from door to door with copies of their *Watchtower* magazine.

The cult began in America in the 1870s, when Charles Taze Russell organized a Bible Class with a few others. Some years later he began publishing a new magazine called *Zion's Watch Tower and Herald of Christ's Presence*. The first issue, on 1st July, 1879, began to spread the ideas of the movement which, on 13th December, 1884, became known officially as Jehovah's Witnesses. The Watchtower headquarters, set up in New York, began to publish books and pamphlets in large numbers and several languages.

Jehovah's Witnesses claim that their beliefs are all based on the Bible but they have their own special *New World Translation* and they emphasize certain passages. The whole interpretation of Bible teachings is directed from Watchtower headquarters.

They also believe that only limited numbers of people are chosen by God. From a passage in the Book of Revelation there will be 144,000 and they will *all* be Jehovah's Witnesses. The Christian Church, and all other religions, they say, belong to the Devil, not to God.

Jehovah's Witnesses are very sincere in their beliefs and they work very hard to persuade other people to accept their teachings, but they are quite sure that they *alone* are right . . . and that always causes bad feelings.

Keep us, O God, from the mistake of believing that we alone are right and that everyone else is wrong. Teach us that there are many ways of reaching you and make us tolerant toward those whose beliefs are different from our own. *Amen.*

Closing prayer No. 78

Religion and life (1)

RELIGION   *Beliefs*

Most people in the world have a religion of some kind. They may
count themselves as members of one of the great religions, Hinduism, Buddhism, Judaism, Christianity or Islam or they may belong
to one of the very small religions found in varous parts of the
world.

The essential part of any religion is to have certain beliefs, the
most important being what one believes about God. Christians,
Jews, Muslims and members of many other religions too, believe
that there is only one true God; Hindus believe in many Gods; and
Buddhists believe in no God. There are many tribal religions in
which people believe in spirits rather than a god.

There are also lots of people such as Atheists, Humanists and
many Communists who do not believe there is a god at all. Yuri
Gagarin, the Russian astronaut and first man in space reported
back to earth that he could not see any sign of a God in space.

So people who believe in God must also make up their minds
what they believe *about* God, and most will agree that he is a spirit,
having no body and not limited to any one place.

Guru Nanak, the founder of the Sikh religion, once fell asleep
with his feet pointing toward the Ka'aba in Mecca. A Muslim told
him that he was insulting Allah. Nanak replied, 'If you think I do
wrong by pointing my feet toward the house of God, then turn
them in some other direction where God does not dwell.'

The Jewish psalmist had no doubts at all. His words tell of a God
who is everywhere and knows everything.

Bible Reading: Psalm 139: 1–12

O God, teach us about yourself and give us understanding, for it is
quite impossible for us to understand you and your nature unless
you yourself show us the way. *Amen.*

Closing prayer No. 59

Religion and life (2)

When we study the religions of the world we find that there is one thing common to nearly all of them and that is the importance of worship. One exception is that there is no worship in some forms of Buddhism, in which there is no God to worship, and meditation takes its place.

Worship, then, is something that goes on in one form or another all over the world and it is an act that is probably as old as man himself. The word 'worship' is a shortened form of 'worthship'. It means paying respect to somebody or something that is worthy of our respect.

Worship is not limited to gods. For some people money can become a god and they think of nothing but getting more. That is a kind of worship. Many young people worship pop groups or sports stars, will go to a lot of trouble to collect pictures or cuttings of them and will travel long distances to see them. That can be a form of worship too. A young man in love may be said to worship his lady-friend . . . or even to worship the ground she walks on! He does not worship her because he wants to get something from her but rather because he loves her so much that he wants to give her everything he can.

So it is when people worship God. True worship is not what we can get out of God but what we can offer to him. We worship God for what he *is*, not for what he *does*. The Jewish psalmist gives an excellent example of this.

Bible Reading: Psalm 95: 1–6

And people worship God in many different ways; in music, singing and dancing; in ritual and prayer; in complete silence; in religious services or in private devotions.

Almighty God, Lord of the universe, Creator of the world and Giver of life; we humbly bow in worship, praising your holy Name and offering our very best as a token of our love. *Amen.*

Benediction No. 103

Religion and life (3)

Prayer and meditation

One very important part of any religion is prayer and meditation. Prayer forms a very important part of worship. For Muslims particularly the act of worship is an act of prayer. For Christians and Jews many of the hymns which are sung are also prayers. In fact the word *Amen*, which comes at the end of many hymns, means 'So be it', and indicates that the hymn ended, at least, on a note of prayer.

But prayers are not kept just for religious services: they are a part of life too. And some of the most important prayers are those which are not organized but come right from the heart. Even people who would not call themselves religious will sometimes offer a prayer when they are in a spot of trouble: 'O God, what am I going to do now?'

Abraham Lincoln, who was one of the great presidents of the United States of America often felt a need to pray to God for guidance. In his own words: 'I have been driven many times to my knees by the overwhelming conviction that I had nowhere else to go; my own wisdom and that of all around me seemed insufficient for the day.'

In the Bible, the psalmist speaks of his love for God because God has heard his prayers.

Bible Reading: Psalm 116: 1–6

And there are countless people since then who have found great help from having prayed to God. There are many forms of prayer, all of them important, but one thing must be remembered. Prayer is only of value if one believes that there *is* a God and that he *hears* and *answers* prayers.

O God, our loving heavenly Father;
Help us to know you as a God who hears our prayers;
Give us faith to believe that you will answer;
Teach us how to pray and what to ask for;
And prepare our hearts to receive your answer. *Amen.*

Closing prayer No. 88

Religion and life (4)

Bible Study schemes

To become learned in or to have a good understanding of any subject, one has to study, whether it be to learn mathematics, or a foreign language, or music. And to help with the learning there are not only books of facts but books that help one to learn.

So it is with religion. All religions have their sacred writings. Jews and Christians have the Bible; Muslims have the Qur'ān; Hindus have the Vedas and Upanishads and Sikhs the Granth. Most religions have other writings, too, the Jewish Talmud, the Muslim Hadith, the Hindu Bhagavad-Gita, the Book of Mormon, the Watchtower, to mention but a few.

The sacred writings of any religion are not just books to be read. They are there to be *studied* and learned, so that people really know what their religion is all about. This is what the psalmist teaches.

Bible Reading: Psalm 119: 97–104

For Christian people there are various organizations which publish daily study notes to provide help in understanding the Bible. One of these, the Scripture Union system of daily readings was started on 1st April, 1879. The Scripture Union claims this as 'the wisest thing ever done on April Fool's Day'. Certainly millions of people have been helped by these notes.

And one of the wisest things that anyone can do, who would wish to understand his religion, is to make good use of these or other study notes and to ensure that a little time for study is set aside every day.

Almighty God, revealed unto us through the words of Holy Scripture; help us to read, to study, to learn, to understand, and to accept the guidance of others, so that we may find your word a guiding light to lead us to yourself. *Amen.*

Closing prayer No. 63

Religion and life (5)

Some people associate religion with church-going and say that a person who attends church must be a good Christian. It is not necessarily so. One may pray to God on one day of the week and forget him on all the other days.

One of the complaints about some people in Old Testament times was that they offered their sacrifices and then did just what they wanted to.

Bible Reading: Isaiah 1: 10b–17

In some countries, Buddhist and Muslim countries particularly, religion is a part of everyday life. Religion is so tied up with the laws of the land that it is impossible to tell where religion ends and other things begin.

In Christian countries the attitude of people to religion varies so much that one can be a good citizen without attending a church. Yet religion is very important because it can affect ones attitude to all sorts of things—to other people, to work and to the use of time. A Christian, for example, who really wants to be true to his beliefs tries very hard to live out the teachings of Jesus Christ and to put everything possible into his service for God and his neighbours.

General Booth, the founder of the Salvation Army, was once asked what was the secret of his success. His reply was, 'I will tell you the secret. God has had all there was of me to have.'

And a person who can say that will certainly find that his religion affects the whole of his life.

Teach us, O God, what to believe and how to live. Help us willingly to offer you all that we have, so that our lives may be in your hands and we may know your guidance and inspiration in everything we think, say or do. *Amen.*

Closing prayer No. 68

How people worship (1)

Have you ever looked at something so wonderful or breath-taking that you are lost for words? It may have been the Crown Jewels in the Tower of London, maybe some lovely scenery or a beautiful work of art or craftsmanship. You felt there was nothing you could do but stand in silence and wonder.

One of the world's famous paintings is a picture called *The Adoration of the Magi*. It was painted by Botticelli, who lived and worked in Florence, where he died on 17th May, 1510. Botticelli was a nick-name meaning 'Little Barrel'. He was a religious man who used his art as an offering to God. This particular painting shows the wise men looking at the baby Jesus and standing in silent worship.

Bible Reading: St. Matthew 2: 1–11

There was no need for words. They had come to find a baby whom they believed to be the Messiah, the Saviour of the people. When they found him they knelt before him, worshipped him and presented their gifts.

People of many religious beliefs have discovered that this is the way to come before God. We think about the mighty power of God, the Creator of the universe and we are filled with wonder. There are not enough words with which to express our feelings about him.

And so we bow before God in silence and humbly adore him. Then we offer the gifts that we know we should—not just gifts of money but the gift of ourselves, our lives, our talents, our service; not because we have to but because we want to.

Almighty God, we bow before you in adoration and worship. We know that we cannot find enough words with which to praise you for your mighty power, nor for your great love in sending Jesus Christ to be our Saviour. Accept the offering of ourselves and use us for your glory, now and for ever. *Amen.*

Closing prayer No. 86

How people worship (2)

We often sing to express our feelings of joy or of sadness and it is only natural that singing should form a part of our worship of God—hymns of joy and thankfulness for God's blessings and hymns of a quieter nature when we remember our sinfulness or our needs.

Such singing may well reflect something of the nature of the singer. Some like to praise God in hymns that are stately or dignified: others prefer rousing hymns with choruses.

Fashions in music for singing change. Long ago much of the singing in worship was in plain-song. This was simple music without any harmony. Then, under Pope Gregory the Great, who died in A.D. 604 and is remembered on 12th March, church men developed the Gregorian chant, still used in some services today.

All of the singing then was by the monks. Most people were uneducated. They met in the nave and just listened. Later, when people could join in the singing, they were often led by a choir of men and boys. Nowadays many choirs have women choristers too. Choirs not only lead other people in worship but they offer their singing as their own special act of worship to God.

Today there are many kinds of hymn and sacred song that can be used in worship and we try to sing them sincerely with meaning. Over two hundred years ago, a leader of the Moravian Church, Peter Bohler, remarked, 'Had I a thousand tongues, I would praise him with them all.'

We can never sing God's praises too highly or too often.

Bible Reading: Psalm 66: 1–4 and 8

O God our heavenly Father, as we remember all that you are and all that you have done for us, our lips are filled with praise and our hearts with singing. Accept our humble act of thanksgiving and worship; and to you be all praise and glory. *Amen.*

Closing prayer No. 68

How people worship (3)

MUSIC *Johann Sebastian Bach*

Bible Reading: Psalm 150

This is one of the psalms which invite people to worship God and it suggests all sorts of musical instruments which could be used. Music has always played an important role in worship, with various instruments to accompany the singing.

The instrument most often associated with church worship today is the organ, which is capable of producing many different sounds. Organs have been used for about 2,000 years. Until recently they were all pipe organs in which sounds were produced by forcing air through pipes of various sizes. A large organ may have over 5,000 pipes.

An organ has keyboards similar in appearance to those on a piano. A large organ may have up to five keyboards, known as manuals, and a pedalboard which the organist plays with his feet. Different tones are obtained by the use of stops, which open or close certain sets, or banks, of pipes. A skilful organist can play very moving music to meet each special occasion.

Many composers have written music for organs, the greatest of them being Johann Sebastian Bach, who lived in Germany and died on 28th July, 1750. He wrote many kinds of music, much of it of a religious nature. Bach was a devout Lutheran who often wrote INJ, the initials of the Latin words 'In the name of Jesus' on his manuscripts.

Through his music, Bach believed he could serve God and the Church. That he certainly did. His music, like that of many others, has helped lots of people in their worship of Almighty God.

We give humble thanks, O God,
For all the music that helps us to worship you;
For the composers who have written it;
And for musicians who play it.
    Praise be to you, O God. *Amen.*

Benediction No. 97

298

How people worship (4)

Lord of the Dance

Dancing has been used as a form of worship for a very long time, often associated with primitive religious beliefs. Some of the earliest dancing on record is that performed in the temples of ancient Egypt, where the dancers expressed their ideas of the harmony of the universe.

Usually the dancing was a kind of offering to God. In history, and in many places today, we have examples of fertility dancing, ceremonial rain dances and the ritual dances before some kind of sacrifice. It is an offering of worship.

Dancing may be a spontaneous offering of joy and happiness. We read in the Bible how King David danced in front of the ark of the Lord.

Bible Reading: II Samuel 6: 12–15

At one time dancing was an accepted part of the worship of the Christian Church. There are many references to dance in worship right up to the twelfth century. In several places in Spain it was the custom until quite recently to dance in front of the high altar of the cathedrals and churches.

There is an English carol in which the Son of God says that he came to call mankind to his dances. This idea is expressed in the modern religious song, *Lord of the Dance*. No doubt you can find the words of this.

There are, of course, many forms of dancing which have nothing to do with religion, just as there are many forms of singing which have not. But dancing, like singing, can be an expression of joy on the part of some people and worship is; after all, offering to God our joy and our love for all that he is.

Help us, O God, to worship you in the offering of whatever we are able to do well, and grant that whatever we feel we can offer in this way will be acceptable to you. *Amen.*

Closing prayer No. 57

How people worship (5)

Holy Communion

One of the most important acts of worship in the Christian Church is that which is known as the Eucharist ('Thanskgiving'), Holy Communion, or The Lord's Supper. It is an act which was started by Jesus Christ himself during the Last Supper.

Bible Reading: I Corinthians 11: 23–26

In this service, Christians eat a small piece of bread or wafer and take a sip of wine, eating and drinking as Jesus commanded and remembering him as they do so.

Roman Catholics believe that after the bread and the wine have been consecrated during the Mass they actually become the body and blood of Jesus. Any bread remaining, which is therefore the body of Christ, is locked in a container on the altar after the service.

Other Christians believe that the bread and wine are symbols which do not change but which remind them of all that Jesus did and taught.

Roman Catholics usually start receiving the Holy Communion about the age of seven but in most other churches it is not until they have been confirmed or become members of the church at a later age.

In some churches there is not an altar but a table and communicants gather 'round the Lord's table' for this special service.

There may be various ways of thinking about the Eucharist or Holy Communion but all who share in this sacrament will agree that it is a very special time for the worship of God and for receiving inspiration from a feeling of closeness to Jesus Christ.

Almighty God, accept our praise and thanksgiving for the life and death and resurrection of our Lord Jesus Christ. Help us to be aware of his presence and to live according to his teachings with the help and guidance of your Holy Spirit. *Amen.*

Benediction No. 91

Where people worship (1)

One of the best known prehistoric monuments in Britain is Stonehenge in Wiltshire. This great circle of stones has stood there for between three and four thousand years. Many people have marvelled at the skill of the builders who set up the great trilithons—two upright stones with another resting on top. It is amazing, too, that some of the stones came from the mountains of Dyfed, in the far west of Wales.

Near Stonehenge is Avebury, a much larger double circle of huge stones with a long approach avenue of stones. Why were such places built? We cannot be sure but it is thought that these were places of worship. This could account for the tremendous amount of hard work that was put into the building of them. People throughout the ages have always wanted to offer their best to their gods.

This was true of the Jews when they were building the temple for the worship of God in Jerusalem.

Bible Reading: I Chronicles 29: 1–5

In eastern lands there are many temples built by people of different religions; the great ziggurat of the Babylonians, huge Hindu temples, the Sikh Golden Temple at Amritsar, and the Jain temple at Dilwara with its magnificent carvings.

These are just a few examples of the work of people who have sincerely believed that only the best was good enough for a place in which to worship the Almighty God.

Almighty God, King of Kings and Lord of Lords, we bow before you in worship and prayer.

We think of your power in creating the world;
We remember your love in sending your Son;
We recall the many gifts you have given us.

Lord, you have given your best to us: help us to give our best to you, offering all our skills and talents for the glory of your holy Name. *Amen.*

Closing prayer No. 89

Where people worship (2)

The building in which most Christian people worship God is a church or a chapel. One does not have to look far to find a church. Most villages have one and towns have several.

Some are very old, dating back hundreds of years. The first churches were wooden ones and these were replaced by churches built of local stone, but at Greenstead in Essex there is still a wooden church with walls made of split tree trunks, most of which are the original ones put there about one thousand years ago.

Most churches have two parts, a nave where the worshippers sit and a chancel for the choir. The sanctuary for the altar is at the eastern end of the chancel so that worshippers facing the altar are also facing Jerusalem.

Between the nave and the chancel there may be a carved wooden screen. There is a pulpit from which the sermon is preached and a lectern on which the Bible is placed. Larger churches and cathedrals have additional sections and probably a lot of ornamental stonework and wood-carving. Often there are memorials in the church to people who have died.

During the past few hundred years some people have wanted to worship in ways different from those of the Church of England. Many wanted, or had only the money to pay for, very simple buildings. These box-shaped buildings with a pulpit, a table instead of an altar and very little decoration are called chapels.

So, in church or chapel, Christian people worship God in the way that they find most helpful, for worship is important to those who trust in God.

Bible Reading: I Chronicles 16: 8–11

Help us to remember, O God, that it is not *where* we worship you that is important but *how* we worship. Help us to find the way that brings us near to you. As we seek you, enable us to find you and to worship with sincerity. *Amen.*

Closing prayer No. 76

Where people worship (3)

Keswick Convention

Temples, cathedrals, churches and chapels are not the only places where God can be worshipped. In fact he can be worshipped anywhere by people who sincerely seek him. Listen to this part of a conversation between Jesus and a Samaritan woman.

Bible Reading: St. John 4: 19–24

Many people in the cities worship God in Mission Halls, built for social work as well as for services. In recent years some groups of people with no church of their own have held services in school halls or other public buildings. There are also religious meetings which are held in large tents, or marquees, when a place is needed only for a short time.

One of the best-known tents is the great marquee put up at Keswick, in the English Lake District, each year for the Keswick Convention. The first Convention, in 1875, was held in a small marquee in a vicarage garden. Today the big tent and a smaller one nearby have room to seat over 6,000 people. Each year they are set up ready for the meetings which are held during the two weeks beginning on the second Saturday in July.

Thousands of people gather in Keswick from all parts of the world to share Christian fellowship and to hear the teachings and testimonies of true people of God. In the tent there is an atmosphere of worship and a sense of the presence of God. There are many who say that they met God for the first time at Keswick.

God is just as much at home in a tent as he is in a temple if people are really seeking him.

O God our Father, we know that you are everywhere. Help us to find the place where we are most able to feel your presence and then to meet you there so that we can worship you and give thanks for all your great gifts. *Amen.*

Closing prayer No. 63

Where people worship (4)

The place where Jewish people worship is called a synagogue. The name comes from a Greek word and means 'assembly' or 'coming together'. Wherever there is a Jewish community there is a synagogue where Jews gather together to pray, to study, and to help one another.

In most synagogues men and women sit separately as has been the custom since the days of the Bible. Services are conducted by the *Chazan*, who may be assisted by a choir. A sermon is given by the Rabbi, or teacher, who is not a priest but one who has studied the Jewish writings, the Torah and the Talmud.

At the end of the synagogue, in front of the congregation is the ark. This is beautifully made of wood and has embroidered curtains in front. The ark in the wilderness held the stone tablets on which the commandments were written: the ark in the synagogue contains five scrolls, the Five Books of Moses, or Torah, written by hand on parchment. Each 'book' is rolled onto two rods to make the scroll. This has a beautiful cover, or mantle, with small bells attached. A pointer in the form of a closed hand with an extended finger is used when reading.

In front of the ark is the perpetual light, a light which never goes out, as commanded in the days when they were in the wilderness.

Bible Reading: Exodus 27: 20–21

The synagogue is a plain building. There may be symbols or stained glass windows but no pictures or images of people or animals—nothing to take the mind of the worshipper away from God and his holy Law.

In these moments together, O God, help us to feel your presence. May nothing now or throughout the day turn us from you but may we thank you for every blessing and praise your holy name. *Amen.*

Benediction No. 107

Where people worship (5)

PLACE OF PROSTRATION   *Mosque*

The building in which Muslims meet together for prayer is called a mosque, meaning a 'place of prostration'. From the outside one can see the main building, a wall which surrounds the courtyard in front of the mosque and the minaret towers from which the faithful are called to prayer.

In the courtyard there is a fountain at which people wash before entering the mosque for prayer. Usually it is only men who meet in the mosque, though nowadays women attend some mosques too, but in a separate room.

In the mosque there is an atmosphere of peace. People of other religions may be struck by the absence of seats. This is because it is for prayer and prayer mats are spread on the floor for this. The floor of the mosque may be tiled with mosaic patterns but at prayer times there is beautiful carpeting on the floor.

On one wall is a recess, known as the Mihrāb. Muslims always face this when they pray for they are then facing in the direction of the Ka'aba in Mecca. Nearby is a Minbar or pulpit from which the Imam may preach, also a lectern holding a copy of the Qur'ān. There are no pictures of people in the mosque but there are decorative patterns and texts from the Qur'ān in Arabic script.

Men remove their shoes for prayer and cover their heads, wearing topis or skull-caps—or even handkerchiefs knotted at the corners. The prayers, all spoken in Arabic, begin at a set time so that Muslims in many places can be united in prayer at the same time.

Almighty God, we bow before you in prayer. May nothing take our minds from you. Hear our prayers for those in need that they may find help, and for ourselves that we may find a blessing in your service, and to you be all the honour and glory for ever and ever. *Amen.*

Closing prayer No. 86

Cathedrals (1)

Sometimes people look at a huge church and assume because of its size and its age that it must be a cathedral. Sometimes, too, we may hear a large church described as 'the Cathedral of the Dales' or 'the Cathedral of the Fens'. It may be a nice description for a large church, but size does not make a building a cathedral. A cathedral is any church building chosen by a bishop as his headquarters.

The name cathedral comes from the Greek word *cathedra*, the bishop's seat or throne, from which he teaches his people and from which he 'rules' over that part of the church which has been given into his care.

The office of Bishop is an old one of the Church. At various times people have expected different things of their bishops. This is what St. Paul had to say about bishops.

Bible Reading: I Timothy 3: 1–7

People have always expected bishops to be good men. But what else? In Saxon times they were expected to spend much of their time in study and prayer. Their cathedrals were often tucked away in country villages, like Dorchester-on-Thames, Oxfordshire.

The Normans, on the other hand, expected their bishops to be scholars and great leaders. So the *See* or headquarters of the Bishop of Dorchester, for example, was transferred to Lincoln, where a great new cathedral was built and consecrated on 6th May, 1092. This collapsed during an earthquake in 1185, after which the present Lincoln Cathedral was built. It was a period when several great cathedrals were purpose-built and when other great abbey churches became cathedrals.

We remember, O God, those who have been called as bishops to lead your people. Grant unto them wise counsel, good judgement and a likeness to Christ, so that they may faithfully lead their flocks in the ways of righteousness and peace. *Amen.*

Closing prayer No. 74

Cathedrals (2)

Cathedral architecture

A visit to a cathedral is always rewarding. There is so much of interest to be seen and so much beautiful workmanship to admire, the work of people who have offered their best to God.

Most cathedrals are several hundred years old and built in the Gothic style with high pointed arches and windows. Liverpool Cathedral, begun in 1904, is a modern Gothic cathedral.

Inside the old cathedrals visitors are immediately impressed by the size of the nave with its huge pillars and vaulted ceiling, all richly decorated. Often the nave is separated from the choir or chancel by a large screen. In days when cathedrals were part of monasteries this separated the monks from the people during worship. Now the church officials occupy the choir seats.

Beyond the high altar in the choir there is usually a Lady Chapel, so named in honour of the Virgin Mary and very useful when a smaller chapel is needed. There are probably small chapels or chantries leading from the nave, rooms for cathedral officials, an organ, tombs and monuments. There may also be a crypt below the cathedral and old monastic buildings and cloisters outside.

On 17th May, 1961, a new cathedral was consecrated at Guildford, Surrey. Building had begun in 1936 on Stag Hill just outside the town. It was different. The architect designed a building of brick and stone, a clear view from the nave to the altar and much better acoustics for speaking and music.

The latest cathedrals, Coventry (Anglican) 1962 and Liverpool (Roman Catholic) 1967 are both of very modern design, planned to meet the needs of the Church in the modern age.

We thank you, O Almighty God for the great cathedrals and churches of our land, reminders of the devoted service of people of long ago and of the work and worship offered in your name. May we follow the example they set. *Amen.*

Closing prayer No. 86

Cathedrals (3)

Cathedral services

If we think of a cathedral just as a building we miss its importance. It is a very beautiful building but it is there for a very important purpose, which is the worship and service of God.

Every few hours of the day the cathedral 'comes to life' as services are held. Matins and Evensong take place every day and so does the Eucharist or Holy Communion. On Sundays this will be at the high altar; on other days it may be in one of the chapels. At other times there may be organ or choir practices and the various officials going about their daily business.

Often a cathedral is used for special celebrations. Coronations are normally held in Westminster Abbey (not a cathedral now) but other national rejoicing or mourning may be in London's St. Paul's Cathedral. At Durham there is an annual miners' service. At Coventry there is an average of one special service a week. At many cathedrals there are music festivals of various kinds.

Then there are special pilgrimages, when people come in their thousands to the cathedrals, to Guildford at Easter, St. Edmundsbury on Whit Monday or to St. Albans for the annual Youth Pilgrimage.

St. Paul gave this advice in one of his letters:

Bible Reading: Ephesians 5: 19–20

In a cathedral you will often see people sitting quietly in prayer; you will find congregations gathered for worship; and you will find celebrations of joy and thanksgiving. And it is a good thing to remember to give thanks to God for every blessing received.

We praise and thank you, O God, for every answered prayer, for every blessing received and for so much that we often take for granted. For all that you have given us we praise your holy name. *Amen.*

Closing prayer No. 87

Cathedrals (4)

Education and service

The acts of worship and the daily services performed in a cathedral are just one side of the activities associated with a cathedral. Look around the main cathedral church and you are likely to find other buildings which are used in the daily life of the cathedral.

Music plays a very important role in the services and it is always the aim that this should be as perfect as possible. Cathedrals therefore have their choir schools in which boy choristers can be trained. Many great British composers began their musical careers in cathedral choir schools.

Cathedrals are linked with other forms of education, too. Some have close ties with local universities; some run adult courses or lectures for those who wish to learn more about the Christian faith. Most have a bookstall at which religious books and materials can be bought. Houses in the cathedral close may be used as training centres for those who will be working in the diocese, for conferences or discussions.

Then, of course, the cathedral is also the centre for various missions and Christian witness in the neighbourhood. We remember, too, that the cathedral is the seat of the bishop, who will often be meeting with people to discuss aspects of that part of the work of the Christian Church for which he is responsible.

Jesus once had this to say to his disciples:

Bible Reading: St. Matthew 5: 14–16

So likewise a cathedral is too large to be hidden and its work is that of bringing the light of Jesus Christ to all within its reach.

We remember before you, O God, the call to your Church to preach the gospel. May it show the way which leads people to understand your ways of love and joy and peace. *Amen.*

Closing prayer No. 55

Cathedrals (5)

Cathedral officers

Since the bishop is the man responsible for a diocese one might be excused for thinking that he is in charge of the cathedral. In fact he has so much to do as bishop that the running of the cathedral is left to a body of men known as the *Chapter*. Each cathedral has a chapter house where they can meet. Many are round or many-sided with seats around the walls—a reminder that though their jobs are of varying importance they are all equal before God.

The leader of the Chapter, and therefore in charge of the cathedral is the Dean or, in some cathedrals, the Provost. Three other members of the chapter have special responsibilities. There is a Precentor (First singer) who directs the music and worship, a Chancellor responsible for the cathedral school and education, and a Treasurer responsible for the cathedral treasures.

There are, of course, many other officials in a cathedral because there is such a lot of work to be done. Many are clergymen, ordained ministers of the church but there are many laymen and women too. There are vergers, who traditionally carry a wand or poker, a useful 'weapon' in days when they had to keep order.

Many laymen too are involved in the cathedral music. The organist is a very skilled musician. So are the lay vicars, lay clerks or choirmen. Bellringers have a very important job too.

These are just a few of the many people whose work is to ensure that the worship and work of the cathedral is as efficient as possible. And just as the builders offered their best for the glory of God, so this team of people offer themselves in his service.

O God our Father, you have invited all people to work for the coming of your Kingdom. Help us to know what we should do and, however, important or humble the task, to do it to the best of our ability. *Amen.*

Closing prayer No. 51

Monasteries (1)

From early times there have been groups of religious people who have liked to live together so that they can help one another and share their religious experiences. We can read of one of these groups in the Bible. They were men known as the Sons of the Prophets and they looked to one of the prophets as their spiritual leader to whom they could turn for guidance. In this case it was Elisha.

Bible Reading: II Kings 6: 1–7

These men were all going to work together to build the new house. When people live together like that they have to share the work so that everyone is doing his fair share.

In the early years of the Christian Church there were certain people who decided to withdraw from the world so that they could think only about God. They lived in simple huts or caves and were known as hermits. People used to go to them for advice on matters of religion.

In time some of those hermits began to live in the same place. They were the first monks and their communities could be regarded as the first monasteries.

It was during the fourth century that some of these groups of monks began to get themselves organized into a set daily routine. If they were unable to work one out for themselves they sought the help of a godly man of their time.

So we find the beginnings of a routine which was commonly found in monasteries with certain times for prayer, work and all the other things that were necessary for themselves and for others.

Teach us, O God, how to spend our day;
Some time for work and some time for leisure;
Some time to meet with you and to pray;
Some time to give help or be of service to others;
And teach us to do all these well. *Amen.*

Closing prayer No. 89

311

Monasteries (2)

St. Gilbert of Sempringham

Monasteries and convents are the homes of monks or nuns who belong to a particular order. That means that they follow the rules laid down by the founder of that order. Benedictines are those who follow the rules laid down by St. Benedict, Augustinians those of St. Augustine and so on.

Only one religious order was founded in England and that was the order of Gilbertines. Gilbert, the son of the lord of the manor of Sempringham, Lincolnshire, became the parson of the church in his own village. It was there that he started a religious community for women under the Benedictine rule in 1131.

To act as chaplains to the nuns, Gilbert had a group of men, canons of the Augustinian rule. The houses of men and women were separated by a wall but they shared the chapel.

The Gilbertine Order grew quickly with many new houses of men and women but also with monasteries for men only, leper hospitals and orphanages. Gilbert remained the head of the order for the whole of his long life. He lived to be over one hundred. The Gilbertine order came to an end in the reign of King Henry VIII, when many of the monasteries including all the Gilbertine ones, were destroyed.

Gilbert himself became known as St. Gilbert of Sempringham and his feast day is kept each year on 4th February.

A prayer of St. Benedict

O Gracious and Holy Father, give us wisdom to perceive you; intelligence to understand you; diligence to seek you, patience to wait for you; eyes to behold you; a heart to meditate upon you; and a life to proclaim you; through the power of the spirit of Jesus Christ our Lord. *Amen.*

Benediction No. 105

Monasteries (3)

The daily round

The daily life of a monastery was arranged long ago to fit in with the services in the church. When St. Benedict drew up his Rule for monasteries he took literally some words from Psalm 119.

Bible Reading: Psalm 119: 57–64

'In the middle of the night I wake up to praise you.' Later in the same psalm it says 'Seven times each day I thank you.' So each day would include such services.

The night office, *Matins* was probably about 2 a.m. *Lauds* was at daybreak, followed by *Tierce*, *Sext* and *None* at three-hourly intervals. *Vespers* were at sunset and *Compline* before retiring for the night. The times of these varied from summer to winter and sometimes several would be taken one after the other.

These services or 'offices' were held in the choir of the abbey. *Tierce* was followed by morning Mass, when local workers could attend this service in the nave of the abbey. Similarly *Sext* was followed by High Mass.

After *None* (about 2 p.m.) the monastery bell was rung. It is from this that we get our expressions 'before noon' and 'afternoon'.

It was after None that the monks took their first and main meal of the day. The only other meal was a light evening meal. At each meal one of them would read something helpful.

Between offices and meals there was the daily business meeting or chapter, work of various kinds, reading and meditation. It was a long, busy day and a very hard one. Life in a monastery has always needed strict self-discipline and a willingness to accept a simple, austere way of life.

Help us, O God, to discipline ourselves;
To be content with what we have;
To make time for all our duties and responsibilities;
And to take time each day for praise and prayer. *Amen.*

Closing prayer No. 88

Monasteries (4)

One of the things that one always associates with monks or nuns is service to the community in one form or another.

Long ago abbeys were founded so that men or women with common religious ideas could live and worship together. There in their religious houses they did various kinds of useful work such as the copying of books in addition to their necessary daily tasks. But the abbeys were also places to which other people would go.

They were the centres of education of their day. Children of royal or noble families were sent there for their education, many of them becoming monks or nuns themselves. There were the celebrations of Mass each day which local people attended. Travellers could be given hospitality and the poor were given alms.

Today there are many religious communities in which monks, friars or nuns live. There are some monasteries run very much along the same lines as the monasteries of long ago. There are many convents too with communities of nuns. Lots of them teach in schools: others, generally referred to as Sisters of Mercy, work amongst the sick, sometimes in hospitals. Many go abroad to work in mission hospitals and schools.

Present day monks and nuns generally follow one of the historic rules, such as Benedictine, Augustinian or Carmelite but each order has its own name, perhaps that given by or named after the founder, such as the Poor Clares, named after St. Clare. Their work of helping others continues.

Bible Reading: Romans 12: 9–13

Hear our prayer, Almighty God:
In meditation help us to know you;
With our whole being help us to worship you;
In all of life help us to serve you;
And in love and service help us to be like you. *Amen.*

Closing prayer No. 54

Monasteries (5)

Community of Taizé

Many of the religious orders and communities were formed a long time ago but there are modern ones too, perhaps the best-known of which is the Community of Taizé in the Bergundy region of France.

Its story began in 1940 when Roger Schultz, a twenty-five-year-old student took an empty house which he hoped might become a centre where Christians of various denominations could meet. Later he was joined by six others who took their vows on Easter Day, 17th April, 1949, having Brother Roger as Prior.

The Rule of Taizé is a summary of what the Brothers accept as the basis of their community. They do not marry, they share things and they accept authority. Some are Catholics and some Protestants. Each day they do various kinds of work but gather three times a day for prayer, when they pray, amongst other things, for Christian Unity.

Taizé has become a centre to which thousands of people from many churches have come to study and discuss many subjects. They enjoy concerts, singing and plays. They join in the community prayers each morning, noon and evening. And they go away with a lot to think about, many of them to continue the work of Taizé in their own countries all over the world.

Bible Reading: Ephesians 4: 1–6

A prayer from The Rule of Taizé

O Lord Christ, help us to maintain ourselves in simplicity and in joy, the joy of the merciful, the joy of brotherly love. Grant that, renouncing henceforth all thought of looking back, and joyful with infinite gratitude, we may never fear to precede the dawn to praise and bless and sing to Christ our Lord. *Amen.*

Closing prayer No. 53

Some Christian Churches (1)

The Church of England

Most towns and villages in England have at least one church referred to as the parish church. It is the church which is part of the organization known as The Church of England or Anglican Church. The clergyman in charge is the parish priest. A number of parishes is grouped to form a diocese which has a bishop in charge. The spiritual head of the Anglican Church is the Archbishop of Canterbury.

The Church of England dates back to before A.D. 314. For a long time it was part of the Roman Catholic Church until King Henry VIII declared that the Pope was no longer head of the English church. There was a lot of unrest in the years that followed.

Today the Church of England is the established or state church in which important official services are held. Any changes in the Church of England would have to be made by an Act of Parliament. It is also accepted as the church of all people in England who do not belong to any other church.

Anglican churches are not all alike. Some are what we would call 'high church', that is similar in ceremonial to the Roman Catholic Church. Others have very little ceremony and may be called 'low church'.

In the Church of England there are set forms of service. These are set out in The Book of Common Prayer. The Prayer Book of 1662 is still commonly used but in recent years services have been printed in a modern form.

There are branches of the Anglican Church in many parts of the world today.

From the Book of Common Prayer:

Lord of all power and might, who art the author and giver of all good things; graft in our hearts the love of thy name, increase in us true religion, nourish us with all goodness, and of thy great mercy keep us in the same. *Amen.*

Closing prayer No. 79

Some Christian Churches (2)

Roman Catholic Church

The Roman Catholic Church can claim to be the oldest of the Christian Churches. Its foundation goes back to Jesus and his disciples, one of whom, Peter, was given special authority.

Bible Reading: St. Matthew 16: 18–19

Roman Catholics believe that this authority as leader has been passed on to others in turn so that the Pope and bishops are the successors of Peter and the other apostles. In early times St. Peter went to Rome, which became the centre from which the church spread. So it became 'Roman' because of its centre and 'Catholic' meaning world-wide or universal. All other Christian churches at some time broke away from the Roman Catholic Church or from churches which had previously done so.

Roman Catholics honour the Blessed Virgin Mary, the Mother of Jesus, much more than do the members of other churches. Many of their prayers are addressed to her and the 'Hail Mary' is the prayer most commonly spoken.

The most important service for Roman Catholics is the Mass, a sacrifice or offering to God which is followed by Holy Communion. Catholics are required to attend Mass every Sunday unless they are prevented from doing so.

There is much more ritual and ceremony in the Roman Catholic Church than there is in other Christian denominations and the priests have a greater authority. Roman Catholicism is much more influential in some countries than it is in Britain other than in Ireland.

A prayer from the Roman Breviary:

Grant, we beseech thee, almighty God, unto us who know that we are weak, and who trust in thee because we know that thou art strong, the gladsome help of thy loving-kindness, both here in time and hereafter in eternity. *Amen.*

Closing prayer No. 62

Some Christian Churches (3)

Various terms are used to describe certain groups of churches or the people who worship in them. We will find, for example, that some are known as *Protestant*. These are churches which are not Roman Catholic—those who, long ago, protested against some of the teachings of that Church.

In England the Church of England became the protestant church. But in later years there were groups of people who broke away from the Church of England because they wished to worship God or organize themselves in different ways. They were known as *Nonconformists* because they did not wish to conform or fit in with the Church of England.

These churches are often referred to today as the Free Churches. It does not mean that one does not have to pay to go to them. One does not pay to go to church anyway. The collection that is taken is a freewill offering to God. They are Free Churches in the sense that they are free to do things in a way that the Church of England cannot because it has some control by the state. They are free churches too in the sense that they have a freer form of service than the set forms of the Church of England.

There are quite a lot of free churches—Baptist, Methodist, United Reformed, Presbyterian and many others. Often they work together through local Free Church Councils and in the national Free Church Federal Council which was founded in 1939. Individually, and working together, the Free Churches have given a lot to the religious life of England, Wales and Scotland, particularly through the faithful preaching of the gospel.

Bible Reading: I Corinthians 1, 17–21

We thank you, O God, for the witness of your Church and the faithful preaching of the gospel which through the centuries has led many to understand your teachings and to walk in your holy ways. *Amen.*

Closing prayer No. 82

Some Christian Churches (4)

The Methodist Church

It was on 24th May, 1738, that an Anglican clergyman, John Wesley, went into a room in Aldersgate Street, London, and came out a different man. He realized then just how much Jesus Christ meant to him, knowing that his sins were forgiven. He determined to let the rest of the world know too. No longer would he stay in one place. He declared, 'The World is my parish'.

So he mounted his horse and set out to save England. In the years that followed he travelled thousands of miles, preaching in towns and villages, by market crosses, at pit-heads and in the open country. He was mobbed, stoned, ill-treated and abused but never stopped.

And wherever he went he left those who would continue his work and preach salvation to all who believed. They were called Methodists—a nickname that had once been given to Wesley and his friends whilst at Oxford University. Methodist chapels were built throughout Britain, in America and elsewhere. By the time Wesley died, on 2nd March, 1791, there were 130,000 full members of the Methodist Church in England and America and nearly a million others attending the chapels.

Today there are few parts of England and Wales where there is no Methodist Church. Most of them share a minister with neighbouring churches and have many services conducted by Local Preachers, people employed in ordinary jobs but who believe that God has called them to preach when needed.

Like other Free Churches, Methodists may not use a printed order of service but they do place a lot of importance on singing and the preaching of the gospel.

Almighty God, we bow before you and confess that we have done those things which are wrong. Grant unto us the sure knowledge that through Jesus Christ our sins can be forgiven if we believe in him; and help us to live in your love. *Amen.*

Closing prayer No. 57

Some Christian Churches (5)

During the Middle Ages, when some people were asking questions about the beliefs of the Christian Church, there lived a man named John Calvin. He was born in France but spent much of his life at Geneva, Switzerland, where he died on 27th May, 1564.

Calvin could not agree with the organization of the church with its Pope and bishops. He believed that each church should have its own ruling body of presbyters or elders, as was done in New Testament times.

Bible Reading: Acts 14: 21–23

Calvin also rejected anything else which could not be found in the New Testament. He demanded a strict self-controlled life from his followers and he warned against such things as lively music, dancing and gay clothing.

The part of Britain where Calvin's teachings were mainly accepted was Scotland, largely because of the preaching of John Knox. The Presbyterian churches of Scotland became the national Church of Scotland.

Other churches which believed that the local churches had no head but Christ himself were the Congregational churches. Each church was independent, having its own minister and a body of officials called deacons. In 1972, many Presbyterian and Congregational churches came together to form the United Reformed Church.

All presbyterian churches stress the importance of the word of God and of preaching.

A prayer of John Calvin:

O Lord, heavenly Father, in whom is the fullness of light and wisdom; enlighten our minds by thy Holy Spirit, and give us grace to receive thy Word with reverence and humility, without which no man can understand thy truth. For Christ's sake. *Amen.*

Benediction No. 104

More Christians (1)

Bible Reading: St. Mark 1: 1–5

The people who took notice of what John the Baptist had to say were led into the River Jordan and dipped in its water to show that their sins were 'washed away'. It was not the water that did this but the belief that God would forgive those who were sorry for their wrong-doings.

In some branches of the Christian Church, babies are baptized by having water sprinkled on them 'in the Name of the Father, and of the Son, and of the Holy Ghost'. When old enough to make up their own minds they are confirmed, accepting what their parents did when they were very young.

But there are some churches in which this is not done. Babies are dedicated to God but baptism is only carried out at a later age when the people themselves are ready to offer their lives to God. The principal churches in which this is done are the Baptist churches but it is the accepted practice in other churches too.

A Baptist Church has a 'baptistry'—a pool of water in which the minister stands and lowers the person to be baptized completely into the water, then raises him out again. It is known as 'baptism by total immersion'. The water covers the whole person to show that he is completely clean because of his belief in Jesus Christ.

The Baptist churches are linked together in the Baptist Union but each church is responsible for its choice of minister, organization and work. The Sunday services are similar to those of other Nonconformist or Free Churches.

Hear our prayer, O God our Father, for we confess that we have sinned in thought, word and deed. Forgive us and cleanse us from all our sin, so that we may approach you freely and know you as our Father; through Jesus Christ our Lord. *Amen.*

Closing prayer No. 79

More Christians (2)

CHRISTIAN SOLDIERS   *The Salvation Army*

The Christian people who are probably most readily recognizable are those of The Salvation Army, for their uniform is well-known in many parts of the world. Salvationists are also well known for their lively singing, their band music and their work of caring.

The Army was founded by William Booth, a former Methodist minister, who began 'The Christian Mission' in London's East-End. The first tent meeting was held on 2nd July, 1865, and the title 'The Salvation Army' was adopted in 1878, It was obvious that there were many battles to be fought against evil and Bible writers had referred to Christian soldiers.

Bible Reading: Ephesians 6, 10–18

So The Salvation Army was born. Its leader was the 'General', its ministers 'officers', its members 'soldiers', its place of meeting a 'citadel' and so on. Hymns are known as 'songs' and the choirs are 'songster brigades'. Music is an important part of Salvationist life and in the various kinds of service held in the citadel.

Above the citadel flies the flag bearing the motto 'Blood and Fire'—a reminder of the blood of Jesus, the crucified Saviour of the world, and the fire of the Holy Spirit. The Salvation Army may have a different approach from that of the churches but its main beliefs are those shared by other Christians—beliefs in God the Father, in Jesus Christ, and in the Holy Spirit.

We look around us, O God, and see much that is evil in the world. Help us to put on the whole armour which you provide so that we may be strong and bold to fight all that is wrong until the whole world acknowledges that you are Lord and God and your kingdom of love and peace reaches to the ends of the earth. *Amen.*

Closing prayer No. 69

More Christians (3)

The Society of Friends

When St. Paul wrote to the people who lived at Corinth, he described a kind of church service which is different from those which most church-goers know today.

Bible Reading: I Corinthians 14: 26–31

There are people today who, when they meet for worship, wait for people to be led by God to speak. One such body of people is The Society of Friends, or Quakers. They do not have a church but a simple Meeting House and their worship of God is in silence unless one of their number feels led by God to say something.

The Society of Friends owes its origin to George Fox, who died on 13th January, 1691. He had left the church, which he disliked, and preached that truth was found when God spoke to man's soul. Several times Fox was arrested and once he said in court that people should 'quake and fear at the word of God'. Hence the nickname 'Quaker' which was given to his followers.

The Friends, as they like to be called, have no time for ceremony, for sacraments, for ministers or for organized services. They are known for their very simple form of life and, in the past, for the plainness of their dress.

Friends are also very well known for the large amount of social work which they do and for their concern for the welfare of others. Many of the important reforms were the work of Quakers and many industrialists who provided fine conditions for their workers were Quakers too. They are known, too, as people who love peace.

Grant unto us, O God, the guidance of your Holy Spirit so that we may know what you would have us to do and be aware of the needs of the world around us: then give us grace to serve you and our neighbours in the ways that are right. *Amen.*

Closing prayer No. 59

More Christians (4)

Some of the liveliest services today are those of the Pentecostal churches. These are churches which have grown up during the present century. British Pentecostals have been mainly in two groups, the Elim Foursquare Gospel Alliance and the Assemblies of God. More recently there have appeared many Pentecostal churches in coloured communities, where West Indians in particular have enjoyed these services.

The Pentecostals take their name from the Day of Pentecost when the Holy Spirit first came to the early Church. They recall how Peter said then that the Holy Spirit would come to all Christians in all times.

Bible Reading: Acts 2: 38–39

Pentecostals are sure that the Holy Spirit is in their meetings, which are times of great joy and often of emotional experiences. Sometimes one of their number will 'speak in tongues'—words which cannot be understood until interpreted by someone else. Nor is it uncommon for someone to interrupt a service if he feels led to do so by the Holy Spirit.

Many Pentecostals also believe in the power of the Holy Spirit to heal, and they have great faith in all the promises of the scriptures. Some would say that their services are noisy; but it is a joyful noise made by people who are filled with the joys of the Holy Spirit of God.

O Holy Spirit, God,
Come into our lives and fill us with your power;
Cleanse us of all that is wrong or unworthy;
Set us aflame with a desire to serve our God;
Make us bold to say and do what is right;
Give us joy in our hearts and praise on our lips;
And keep us in the presence of God. *Amen.*

Benediction No. 95

More Christians (5)

London City Missions

Look around any large city and you will find halls which do not bear the name of one of the main Christian denominations yet, from the name or the notices outside, are obviously places where Christian people meet. Many of them are called Missions and they have probably existed for quite a long time, founded by people who wanted to help others.

David Nasmith, for example, was a Scotsman in London in 1835. Visiting some of the back streets of the city he found things which made his heart ache: squalor, filth, disease, vulgarity, beggars, orphans and people with no hope. If only these people could be helped and at the same time taught about the Gospel of Jesus Christ.

So he gathered together a group of Christians who would help him and the London City Mission was born.

Today the face of London has changed. Many of the evils of Nasmith's day are no longer with us but there are probelms of different kinds and the London City Mission is as active as ever with centres in many parts of London and people who will work wherever they think there may be a need,—in the docks, on building sites, at railway stations, in markets and visiting homes.

These workers are called Missionaries—for that is their real work. They help people in the name of Jesus Christ and they preach the Gospel. And on Sundays, at the hall which has been a centre for many activities during the week, there is a simple Gospel service to teach the way of Christ. It is his example that the missionaries seek to follow.

Bible Reading: St. Matthew 9: 35–38

O God, the Father of our Lord Jesus Christ, who sent him to be the Saviour of the World, grant that your love may be seen today in the lives and service of his servants who seek to lead people to you. *Amen.*

Closing prayer No. 51

The Sabbath (1)

One of the important laws revealed by God to Moses, the fourth of the Ten Commandments, concerned the keeping of the Sabbath day.

Bible Reading: Exodus 20: 8–11

It sounds simple enough. On the seventh day of each week do not work yourself and do not cause anyone else to work. But in time people began to ask questions. What is work?

So the rabbis, the teachers, began to work out the answers to such questions about the sabbath and all the other laws. Their findings were included in the Talmud, a multi-volume encyclopaedia of explanations and opinions about the laws.

It was not long before it became very complicated. In one of the stories of Jesus, for example, we read how the disciples plucked and ate corn as they travelled, only to be told by the religious leaders, the Scribes and Pharisees, that they were doing wrong.

Why? There was nothing illegal about picking and eating the corn, but this was the sabbath day and they were not supposed to work. By plucking the ears of corn they were reaping; by rubbing it in their hands they were threshing; by removing the chaff they were winnowing; and by doing all these things they were preparing a meal, which should have been done the day previous to the Sabbath. So the disciples were guilty four times over! The sabbath laws were difficult to keep.

Was this what the Law originally intended? Jesus thought not. 'The Sabbath was made for the good of man;' he said, 'man was not made for the Sabbath.'

We pray, O Lord, that you will help us to remember your laws and to obey them. In all things help us to see that they are designed for our well-being and our consideration of others; and for this we praise your name, O God. *Amen.*

Closing prayer No. 51

The Sabbath (2)

Jewish days are counted from sunset one day to sunset on the next, so the Sabbath begins on Friday evening. The week's work is done and the day of rest begins. Many of the work restrictions on the Sabbath remain but it is no solemn occasion; the Sabbath is a day to be happy.

So the Jew begins his Sabbath with a service in the synagogue. It is a happy service with psalms of thankfulness and rejoicing, a great and popular hymn which begins, *'Come, my friend, to meet the bride; let us welcome the presence of the Sabbath'*, readings and prayers, and the *Kiddush*, a blessing spoken over a goblet of wine.

At home after the Sabbath eve service it is family night. The table is laid with the best crockery for a special meal. Father blesses the children and then praises his wife in words taken from the Book of Proverbs:

Bible Reading: Proverbs 31: 10–29

The wife then lights the two candles, which recall God's creative power and man's responsibility to others. Father says the Kiddush over the wine and a blessing over the bread. Two loaves are always on the table, a reminder of the way in which God provided two days' food in the wilderness so that there need be no gathering of manna on the Sabbath.

There are special services in the synagogue on the Saturday, ending with the ceremony of *Havdalah* in the synagogue and the home to separate the holy Sabbath from the working week.

We thank you, O Almighty God
For welcome breaks from the weekly work;
For relaxation with our families and friends;
For happy times when we can meet with you.
Grant us your blessing and give us grateful hearts. *Amen.*

Closing prayer No. 53

The Sabbath (3)

For the Jews, the Sabbath has always been a day apart, a day that is different from the rest of the week. It is a way that has been adopted by the Christian and Muslim faiths, too, so that time can be spent with God or at rest from work.

The early Christians, of course, kept the Sabbath. Jesus and his followers were Jews. They worshipped in the temple and in the synagogues. St. Paul did most of his teaching in the synagogues. There came the time, however, when a change was made. Instead of the Sabbath they kept The Lord's Day, the first day of the week, which was the day on which Christ rose from the dead at Easter. From then onwards Christians have kept Sunday as their holy day and day of rest.

Muhammad, too, decided that one day should be different from the other days of the week. Perhaps to be different from Jews and Christians, the day he set apart was Friday. For the Muslims, however, it is a day of prayer when the faithful can gather at the mosque to pray together, but it is not a day of rest. There is nothing to prevent a Muslim from doing whatever work he wishes.

In the Western world, where the Christian calendar is followed, Sunday has long been the day of rest for all. Today things are different from what they used to be. With the kind of life that we know it would be impossible for everyone to have Sunday off work. And so laws have been passed to ensure that all people can have a day of rest from work each week, though for many people it is now a full week-end.

O Lord our God, help us to learn the value of rest from our daily work, so that by rest and recreation we can restore our bodies, and by spending time with you we may restore our souls, making us fit in this life and prepared for the life to come. *Amen.*

Closing prayer No. 55

The Sabbath (4)

As long as there is a day apart there will be differences of opinion as to what should or should not be done on it. In the Old Testament Nehemiah had this to say:

Bible Reading: Nehemiah 13: 15–19

Nehemiah obviously considered this a great evil but apparently the Jewish leaders of his day did not. So today there are people who regard some things which are done on Sunday as wrong, whereas others see no harm in them.

On the one hand we find what is sometimes described as the Catholic attitude, that as long as a person attends Mass on Sunday morning he can then use the rest of the day as he wishes. In the time of Queen Elizabeth I, when Sunday was the only work-free day of the week apart from Holy Days, church-going was followed by sports, noisy amusements and heavy drinking.

During the following century we find the Puritans opposing any form of amusements which they regarded as ungodly and banning most Sunday activities apart from church-going. The Victorian Sunday was also a very strict, sober day when people were expected to do little else. The Lord's Day Observance Society was formed to ensure that Sunday was kept as a day for religious observance and campaigned against Sunday sports or Sunday opening of shops.

Who is right? We have to remember that people have different thoughts on the subject and it is up to each one of us to decide according to our consciences. And having decided for ourselves it does not follow that people who think differently must be wrong.

Almighty God; Guide us in our thinking:
Thank you for giving us one day a week that is different;
Help us to remember your teachings about it;
Keep us mindful of our need to meet with you;
And show us how to use our day of rest. *Amen.*

Closing prayer No. 80

The Sabbath (5)

How should we regard Sunday? There are some very important things that we should remember.

Sunday is the day which is set apart when all people who wish to do so should be able to worship God together. Worship is not just a duty but a way of saying thank you for so much.

Sunday is the day of rest from everyday work. The need for this is a medical fact; it is not just a commandment given by God.

Sunday is a family day which working parents can share with their children. It is also a day when children can learn about God in their Sunday Schools and Christian parents will encourage their children to attend.

There is much to be said for using part of Sunday for recreation and relaxing and to find a little peace and quietness away from the everyday bustle and noise.

If we regard these things as important for ourselves, we should remember that others have a right to them too. We should not *expect* people to work on Sunday unless it is necessary. There are, of course, many people who choose to work on Sunday but that is *their* decision. And if we like peace and quiet ourselves, we should allow others to enjoy their rest.

It is then for us to make up our minds as to what our priorities should be. For a Christian, priority number one must certainly be the worship of God, ideally worshipping as a family. For the other things we must allow ourselves to be guided by the Holy Spirit of God so that Sunday can be used in the most beneficial way for re-creation—the strengthening of body, mind and spirit.

Help us, O God, to get our priorities right;
To value the opportunities to worship you;
To learn the need of recreation and relaxation;
To enjoy the company of family and friends;
And to remember the needs of other people. *Amen.*

Closing prayer No. 90

Prayer (1)

Hot-line to God

Can you imagine a family in which no one speaks? Father never speaks to the children and they never speak to him? Everyone would agree that there would be something very wrong. But are they as ready to believe that something is wrong when God's children never speak to their heavenly Father? Prayer is a conversation with God.

A conversation, of course, is always two-way. We would consider someone very bad-mannered if he kept on talking and did not allow us to say a word. Yet how often are prayers like that? *We* do all the talking and no listening.

In family conversations we would not expect there to be any barriers or restrictions. We would think it most odd if we could only speak to father at certain times in the day. And he would think it peculiar if we could only say thank-you for our pocket money or ask his advice in one particular room at 10.30 on Sunday mornings. Yet there are those who restrict their prayers to God to when they are in church on Sunday mornings. And there are others who never pray at all! The things we accept as normal family life we fail to relate to God.

It is natural too, in a happy family, that those away from home will have a telephone conversation from time to time to speak to parents they cannot see. Many important people and business people have a special telephone hot-line on which they can speak at any time without even having to dial the number.

Prayer is our hot-line to God!

Bible Reading: Psalm 34: 1–8

We thank you, God our Father, that we can speak with you in prayer, knowing that we need no special time or place for prayer and that whenever we turn to you we can be sure you will hear. *Amen.*

Closing prayer No. 58

Prayer (2)

One day the disciples of Jesus came to him and asked him to teach them how to pray. Here are some of his words:

Bible Reading: St. Matthew 6: 7–13

It was only natural that the disciples would want to know how to pray. They wanted to be sure they were right and there are many different customs observed by people who pray. There have been those who have believed that they must keep saying the same prayer over and over again until God answered. Jesus said this is what the heathen do. There are people who believe that they can only pray in a particular place or if they adopt a certain position.

It has long been the custom for people to kneel when they pray—for one is, after all, praying to the Almighty God. Muslims and some others go even further by prostrating themselves on the ground when they pray.

For many, too, prayers are offered with hands together and eyes closed. Hands that are together are not doing other things: eyes that are closed do not see things that would take one's thoughts away from God.

Most people would agree that such things are helpful but not essential. They help us to remember that our prayers are being offered to someone much greater than we are and they help us to be attentive toward him.

What is most important is that we pray sincerely, because we want to, in the way that we find most helpful, and that we *know* that there is a God with whom we can speak.

O God, teach us to pray:
Teach us firstly how to meet with you;
Help us to know what to say and how to say it;
Help us to know the value and importance of prayer;
Then hear us, help us and bless us. *Amen.*

Closing prayer No. 88

Prayer (3)

AIDS TO PRAYER   *Beads and Prayer Lists*

Many people find it helpful to have things which help them with their prayers. Some, for example, have a picture or image which helps them to picture the god to whom they are praying.

There are those, too, who use beads as an aid to prayer, remembering something in particular each time a bead is handled. This is a very old custom and was possibly first used by Buddhists.

For Roman Catholics a treasured part of their faith is The Holy Rosary. It is thought to have been introduced by St. Dominic over seven hundred years ago. The Rosary is a circle of 50 small beads with a larger bead between each ten. It has a pendant with three small beads between two large ones and a crucifix at the end.

When used in prayer, the crucifix is held as the Creed is recited. As each small bead is held a prayer beginning 'Hail Mary . . .' is spoken and each large bead The Lord's Prayer. During each decade, or set of ten Hail Marys one of the mysteries in the life of Christ or the Virgin Mary is meditated upon. The Rosary is usually used in company with other people, after Mass or in the home with the family.

Prayers should never be selfish but should include the needs of others. Sometimes people ask that we pray for them, just as St. Paul did.

Bible Reading: Colossians 4: 2–4

There are many people who like to keep a prayer list as a reminder of all the people and things which they wish to bring before God in their prayers.

O God, in our prayers
We remember your greatness and your love;
We bring before you the needs of other people;
We seek your blessing for ourselves this day.
Hear us and help us. *Amen.*

Benediction No. 92

Prayer (4)

How often should people pray? And for how long? The people of some religions have set times for prayer each day. Those who do not have such times must make up their own minds how much time should be given to prayer. Most people would agree that if one is to pray it is a good thing to do so every morning and every night.

For some people these prayers are brief but for others they are most important and therefore long. John Wesley used to rise early in the morning and pray for two hours before his day's work.

Some would say, 'I haven't time for long prayers.' St. Francis de Sales said, 'Half an hour listening to God each day is essential; except when you are exceptionally busy; then a full hour is necessary.' If we are too busy to pray, we are too busy!

Jesus also gave an example, not just in his regular praying which is characteristic of the Jewish religion but for long periods before doing anything important,—before his ministry began, before choosing his disciples, and in Gethsemane before his trial and crucifixion. Here is one story.

Bible Reading: St. Luke 6: 12–16

But even if we decide that it is a good thing to pray in the morning, in the evening, and before making important decisions, that is still only a small part of prayer.

True prayer is living so closely in touch with God that we can feel free to speak to him and to be aware of his guidance at all times. That is the way the saints of God have learned to live.

We come to you, O God our Father, before we settle down to our day's work and we ask your blessing upon all that we shall do this day. Make us mindful of your presence, help us in our decisions and attend to our needs, so that tonight we may give thanks for many blessings. *Amen.*

Benediction No. 99

Prayer (5)

LIVING BY PRAYER   *George Müller*

There are some people who live by prayer. They believe that God wants them to do a certain work for him and they pray for help. They pray not for themselves but for the work and they have faith to believe that God will hear and answer. They are not surprised when their prayers are answered as some people would be. They would be surprised if they were not. Jesus said, 'Ask and you *will* receive.'

Bible Reading: St. Matthew 7: 7–11

One man who lived by prayer was George Müller. He believed that God wanted him to open a home for orphans in Bristol. So he prayed, believing that God would provide. He prayed for money and it was given. He prayed for helpers and they came. He even prayed for orphans and the first one arrived the very next day. Soon he had several homes. He never asked for money. He just prayed and it came!

One story tells how Spurgeon, the great preacher, went to Bristol and raised £300 for his own work. Then a voice told him to take it to George Müller, which he did. Müller thanked him. 'That is just the amount I have been praying for,' he said.

Spurgeon wondered what he would do without the money but when he went into his office the next day he discovered that someone had sent him a gift of 300 guineas. 'There!' he said. 'The Lord has repaid my money with interest.'

Coincidence? Or two answers to prayer for loyal servants of God who really believed that God would hear and provide?

Grant us the faith, O Lord, to believe that all things are possible with you and that you will do great things for those who trust you. Help us not to pray selfishly but to bring before you the needs we may have for your work and in the service of others. Hear us and help us, O Lord. *Amen.*

Closing prayer No. 53

Make a joyful noise (1)

When we gather together to worship God, singing forms a part of our worship, for singing is one way in which we are able to express our feelings toward God.

Usually when we are singing hymns we use a hymn book which has hymns for many moods and occasions, joyful hymns when we feel happy, solemn hymns for solemn occasions, carols to sing at Christmas and special children's hymns. There are hymns which praise God, hymns which are prayers to God, and hymns in which we make promises to God.

The oldest hymn and prayer book is the Book of Psalms, which we find in the Bible and which is still used today in services in the synagogues. These old Jewish hymns were written by many people, among them David, who was king of Israel some three thousand years ago.

As in modern hymn books, there are songs for all sorts of occasions. In some we feel the sadness of the writer; in others his joy is unmistakable. What wonderful expressions of praise to God we find in Psalm 100.

Bible Reading: Psalm 100

Today in a similar way we sing *All people that on earth do dwell, Sing to the Lord with cheerful voice.* . . . It is the same psalm, translated into English and set to the well-known tune *Old Hundredth* nearly five hundred years ago.

Many of our hymns are based on the psalms. The tunes are different, the language is different, our way of life is different; but God remains the same and we can praise him in the same way that people did all those thousands of years ago.

A prayer from Psalm 139 (Good News Bible)

Examine me, O God, and know my mind; test me, and discover my thoughts. Find out if there is any evil in me and guide me in the everlasting way. *Amen.*

Benediction No. 97

Make a joyful noise (2)

Theodulf of Orleans

Twelve hundred years ago there was a very powerful ruler in Europe named Charlemagne, or Charles the Great. His empire covered almost the whole of western Europe apart from Britain, Spain and Denmark. It was probably toward the end of his reign that he appointed Theodulf to be Bishop of Orleans. Theodulf was a very able and learned man and a respected leader of the church.

But Charlemagne died and his empire was divided. There was some jealousy and plotting against those who ruled and Louis, the son of Charlemagne, suspected that Theodulf was involved in a conspiracy. So Theodulf was removed from office as a bishop and cast into prison.

Not much to sing about, one might think, but the story of the Christian church is a story of a great many people who have been able to sing and be happy in the most difficult or unpleasant situations simply because of the joy in their hearts.

The story is told that King Louis was passing the prison on Palm Sunday, in the year 821, when he heard Theodulf singing with great joy, *'All glory, laud and honour to thee Redeemer, King'*, a hymn which he had written himself. The king was so impressed with Theodulf's devotion to God that he ordered his release.

Whether or not that is true we cannot be sure but the hymn has certainly been sung and enjoyed by many. In its Latin form, 'Gloria, laus et honor' and set to a tune named 'St. Theodulph' it became the great Palm Sunday processional hymn of the Western Church. The translation into English, made during the last century, is found today in many hymn books.

> Thou didst accept their praises;
> Accept the prayers we bring,
> Who in all good delightest,
> Thou good and gracious King.   Amen.
> *Theodulf of Orleans*

Closing prayer No. 86

Make a joyful noise (3)

St. Francis of Assisi will always be remembered as one of the great saints of the Christian Church, a man who gave up his riches and comforts to travel around helping the poor and needy in many different ways.

But even the most helpful people sometimes need help themselves and there came the time when St. Francis did. Toward the end of his life he was ill, blind and lonely. So he made his way to St. Damian, near his home town of Assisi. This was the home of the Poor Clares, a group of nuns whom St. Francis had helped when their order was founded.

There in the courtyard, cared for by the nuns, St. Francis was conscious of the world around him, the warmth of the sun, the presence of wild animals, the song of the birds and all the wonders of creation.

One day at the meal table St. Francis spoke his famous *Canticle of the Sun* which begins, 'Praised by my Lord God, with all his creatures and especially our brother the sun . . .' It was one of his last great works for he died during the night of 3rd October, 1226. (His Feast Day is 4th October.)

The translation of this hymn into English by William Henry Draper, gave us that great hymn of praise:

> *All creatures of our God and King,*
> *Lift up your voice and with us sing:*
> *Alleluia, Alleluia!*

So we join with people of all ages who have praised God and remembered his greatness. Here are some thoughts from long, long ago:

Bible Reading: Psalm 136: 1–9 and 26

Almighty God, whose glory the heavens are telling, the earth his power and the sea his might, and whose greatness all feeling and thinking creatures everywhere herald; to thee belongeth glory, honour, might, greatness, and magnificence now and for ever, to the ages of ages, through Jesus Christ our Lord. *Amen.*

Liturgy of St. James

Benediction No. 103

Make a joyful noise (4)

MY GOD AND KING!   *George Herbert*

Just outside the city of Salisbury is the little village of Bemerton and it was there, between 1630 and 1632, that George Herbert was rector—a man who has been described as a model country parson.

At one time it had seemed that he would have a successful career in Parliament but he decided to leave it to become a minister of the church. There he helped people in lots of different ways, taking medicine to the sick, visiting all the village homes, teaching the children and often giving his own money to help the poor.

Once when going to visit some friends he stopped to help a poor man reload his cart and became very dirty in doing so. His friends told him he should not have done anything so dirty. He replied, 'The memory of it makes music in my heart. If I am to pray for those in trouble I must help them too.'

George Herbert was also a fine poet and musician. He wrote many hymns and verses and also composed hymn tunes. One of the things that St. Paul had to say was certainly true of George Herbert.

Bible Reading: Colossians 3: 16–17

A glance in most hymn books will reveal at least one of his hymns or tunes, perhaps the finest of them being that great hymn of praise:

> *Let all the world in every corner sing:*
> *'My God and King!'*

It is a hymn which reflects something of the joy and praise which was so much a part of the life of this saintly man.

George Herbert died in 1632 when only forty years of age, but his great hymn is immortal.

A prayer from one of George Herbert's hymns:

> *Teach me, my God and King,*
> *In all things thee to see;*
> *And what I do in anything,*
> *To do it as for thee.   Amen.*

Closing prayer No. 61

Make a joyful noise (5)

Bible Reading: Psalm 33: 1–3

When we are happy we like to sing. When something goes well for a person we sometimes say, 'He has something to sing about.' Usually we sing something joyful that means a lot to us. And if we are especially joyful, as the psalmist was, over something God has done, we too, sing our hymns of praise and thanksgiving to him.

Perhaps we sing one of the old hymns to a tune that has been used for a very long time. Or maybe we sing an old hymn to one of the modern tunes or even to the tune of a popular song. And why not? General Booth of the Salvation Army once said, 'Why should the Devil have all the best tunes?'

Nowadays in many hymn books there are new and traditional hymns which have a good beat, a lively chorus or a catchy tune. How better to sing to God than to put heart and soul into singing *Come and praise the Lord our King, Hallelujah!* or *Sing Hosanna!*

There are times, of course, when we are wanting to sing about something else and we are fortunate in having hymns with many different themes. Lots of people have found great help from singing *The Lord's my Shepherd* or *What a friend we have in Jesus*, either of them sung to tunes old or new.

Ask people what are their favourite hymns and you will get a lot of different answers. Some will be old, others new: some will be lively, others much less so. But whatever we sing, let it be a joyful noise to the Lord, sung with sincerity and meaning for this is an offering to God himself.

Accept our praise and thanksgiving, O God our Father, for you have done so much for us and our hearts are filled with joy as we remember the blessings received. Thanks be to you, O God. *Amen.*

Benediction No. 98

Hymns we enjoy (1)

Cecil Frances Alexander

Many of the hymns which children enjoy singing were never really intended for children. It is just that some of them have catchy tunes and often these mean more to the singers than the words do because they are difficult to understand.

There are some hymns, however, which have been written especially for children and which have remained popular for a good many years. *All things bright and beautiful* was written as long ago as 1848 and has been sung by millions of children ever since. Another written in the same year is *There is a green hill far away*.

Both were written by Mrs Cecil Frances Alexander who was born in Ireland in 1818. When she was thirty-two she married a clergyman, the Rev. William Alexander, who was one day to become Archbishop of Armagh, the leader of the Anglican Church in Ireland.

Mrs. Alexander wrote about 400 hymns, most of them for children. She wanted children to be able to understand the scriptures and to appreciate the wonders of God. *There is a green hill* was inspired by a small hill outside Derry, which she passed when going there for shopping. It reminded her of the hill of Calvary outside Jerusalem where Jesus was crucified.

Bible Reading: St. Luke 23: 26 and 32–34

And so she wrote this famous hymn to explain simply what the story was about. [*The hymn or part of it could be read.*] It is sung today as often by adults as by children.

Mrs. Alexander, a faithful Christian all her days, died on 12th October, 1895, but her hymns live on.

We thank you, God our Father for all things bright and beautiful which remind us of your greatness; but we thank you even more for your love in sending Jesus Christ through whom we can come near to you. *Amen.*

Benediction No. 100

341

Hymns we enjoy (2)

SING ALOUD! GOD IS LOVE!   *Percy Dearmer*

One hymn that is very popular with many children and young people is *God is Love* with its rousing chorus of 'Sing aloud, loud, loud! God is good! God is truth! God is beauty! Praise Him!' It was written by a man who has had a great influence on Christian hymns during the present century.

Dr. Percy Dearmer was born on 27th February, 1867 and he attended Westminster School and Oxford University before becoming a clergyman in the Church of England. He became a deacon in 1891 and a priest in the following year, serving in several London churches.

In the years that followed he served the Church in many ways as parish priest, lecturer, Chaplain to the British Red Cross during World War I and as a canon of Westminster from 1931 until his death in 1936. He wrote novels and books on religion but he is especially remembered as an editor of hymn books, the *English Hymnal* in 1906 and *Songs of Praise* in 1925.

He wrote a number of hymns himself and translated others from foreign languages. The carol *Rocking* is one he translated from the Czech language. His own hymns include *Remember all the people who live in far off lands* and *Jesus, good above all other*. But undoubtedly *God is Love* is one of the most popular—a reminder of our relationships with God and with others.

Bible Reading: I John 4: 7–11

Have a look at the words of the hymn again. They tell us a lot. Then sing aloud because God is love . . . and much more besides.

O God our Father, we thank you for all the love and care which you show to us each day. Help us to show our love for you in our attitudes toward others, in helpfulness and kindliness and in a readiness to do your will. *Amen.*

Closing prayer No. 81

Hymns we enjoy (3)

'AMAZING GRACE'   *John Newton*

On 15th April, 1972, a rather unusual recording found its way to the top of the charts and remained in the Top Twenty for no less than 25 weeks. It was a recording of the hymn tune *Amazing Grace*, played by the pipes of the Royal Scots Dragoon Guards and its haunting melody aroused an interest in a hymn written a couple of centuries ago by Rev. John Newton.

Newton was a man who was just about as unpleasant as anyone could be. He had been unfortunate in his early years and his attitude to life was seen most when serving on a slaving ship. His behaviour and language were foul. But after reading a book *Of the Imitation of Christ* he realized that God still cared for him in spite of everything. He became a minister of the Church.

Newton recognized that this was entirely God's doing, not his own. He recognized too the truth of some words of St. Paul which described exactly what had happened to him:

Bible Reading: Ephesians 2: 4–10

From being the kind of man that he had been, Newton was changed by the grace of God, the love which is God's free gift and which draws people to himself no matter what they may have been. So John Newton wrote the hymn which tells of his own experience.

> *Amazing grace, how sweet the sound,*
> *That saved a wretch like me!*
> *I once was lost but now am found*
> *Was blind but now I see.*

We come before you, Almighty God, and confess that we have not been all that we might have been but we know that you can change us by your grace so that we may become truly your children and live in your love. Receive us now, for Christ's sake. *Amen.*

Benediction No. 105

Hymns we enjoy (4)

Many of the hymns which we sing are those which have come to us from other countries, some of them translated into English from the language in which they were first written. Sometimes English hymns have been set to tunes which have come from other lands.

In recent years most collections of hymns have included some which have come from the West Indies. As many people from the West Indies have made their homes in Britain their hymns have come with them. Many are similar to the spirituals sung by the coloured people in the south of the U.S.A., simple Bible stories retold, often with a lively chorus and, of course, the Caribbean rhythm is so often a part of the music.

From the West Indies we have the rousing Christmas hymn *The Virgin Mary had a baby boy*; we have a musical Lord's Prayer with its repeated chorus of *Hallowed be Thy Name*; and we have one of the most popular of hymns today, *Kum ba ya*—a hymn which is really a prayer asking for the presence of God. We do not know who wrote it. It is a traditional hymn that has been sung no doubt by many people who learned it from others without needing the words written down for them in a hymn book.

> *'Someone's crying, my Lord, Kum ba ya . . .'*
> *'Someone's singing, my Lord, Kum ba ya . . .'*
> *'Someone's praying, my Lord, Kum ba ya . . .'*

Sung by folk singers or as a hymn it reminds us of our need for God in all our moods, when we are sad, when we are happy, when we have something to ask for. Kum ba ya, my Lord!

Come to us, O Lord, and let us feel you near:
In our times of sadness grant us your comfort;
In our times of joy accept our songs of praise;
In our times of need hear our humble prayers;
And at all times give us thankful hearts. *Amen.*

Benediction No. 96

Hymns we enjoy (5)

FOLK HYMNS   *Peter Smith*

Peter Smith loved playing the piano and was particularly fond of the classical music of Mozart and other great composers. Then one day he obtained an old guitar and taught himself how to play it. It was not long before he was enjoying music of a different kind—the folk songs that people often sing to guitar music.

Peter changed course in another way, too. He had begun work as an apprentice in the aircraft industry but after five years realized that his work was to be as a Methodist minister. So he went to college and then took a course in youth leadership before going to work in the Liverpool Mission. There he played his guitar, too, in various folk clubs and became known as the 'Singing Minister from the Mission'.

His interest in folk music led him to travel a lot in the United States and other countries, collecting folk hymns and spirituals, then arranging the tunes so that they could be played on the piano or the guitar. In 1967 he edited a book of hymns entitled *Faith, Folk and Clarity*, the first of several collections of folk and modern hymns which have proved popular, particularly with young people.

Some people have made a name for themselves as writers of hymns or composers of hymn tunes. Others, like the Reverend Peter D. Smith, have made their special contribution one of collecting and arranging the kind of hymns that many people find enjoyable and that have a special message for the present day.

Almighty God, we come to say thank-you
For singing voices with which to sound your praises;
For hymns and songs which we so enjoy;
For all who wrote the words and composed the music;
For those who have made them available for us.
For all these blessings we praise your Name. *Amen.*

Benediction No. 94

Sacred writings (1)

Jewish Scriptures

All religions have their sacred books and writings. Some were written down by one person: others were compiled by many people over a long period of time. Some are believed to have been given by God to people who recorded God's words and some the words of great teachers who were inspired by God.

Of these the greatest is undoubtedly the Jewish Bible, which is also the Old Testament of the Christian Bible and was the inspiration for much of the Qur'ān of the Muslims. Bible is a word of Greek origin and simply means 'The Book'. It needs no other title: there is no book that can compare. In fact the Bible is really a library of books made into one.

The Jewish Bible consists of thirty-nine books in three sections, the *Torah* or Law, The Prophets, and The Writings or *Hagiographa*.

The Law, the first five books of the Bible, also known as the Pentateuch or the Five Books of Moses, is the backbone of Jewish religion. The Prophets show how God revealed his purpose in later years through great preachers and teachers. The Writings consist of an assortment of books of poetry, hymns, stories and historical records. There are other books, not included in the Bible which have been grouped under the general title of *Apocrypha* (meaning 'hidden').

The other important Jewish writings are in the *Talmud*, which deals with almost every subject about which a Jew might ask questions. It was written by 2,000 different authors, consists of over 3,000,000 words and is usually printed in twelve huge volumes.

Bible Reading: Psalm 119: 33–38

Almighty God, we thank you for the Bible in which we can learn about you. Help us to read it frequently, study it carefully, learn from it willingly, and live by it faithfully, to the honour and glory of your holy Name. *Amen.*

Closing prayer No. 56

Sacred writings (2)

Dead Sea Scrolls

In the summer of 1947, Muhammad Adh-Dhib, a Bedouin shepherd lad lost a goat. As he climbed the rocks to look for it he spotted a small cave entrance. Idly he threw stones into it and was startled to hear a sound of breaking pottery.

Inside the jars, Muhammad and his friend found linen wrapped round some decayed leather. In the leather was some thin sheepskin with writing on it. The boys took some to Bethlehem to see whether they could get any money for them. They did. Just a few pounds for what was a priceless treasure!

What the boys had discovered were some scrolls of old Jewish writings, some of them books of the Bible.

Once people realized the importance of this discovery, they wondered how many more there might be. Other caves in the region around the Dead Sea were explored. Official excavations of the original cave began on 15th February, 1949 and there have been many since, not only of the caves in Qumran but of the ruins of a monastery.

The importance of the Dead Sea Scrolls is that they helped test the accuracy of the Bible. The scroll of Isaiah was a thousand years older than the oldest known copy, yet it agreed almost word for word.

Long, long ago, Joshua was told to study the scriptures:

Bible Reading: Joshua 1: 6–8

So, today, people study the accuracy and content of the Bible to learn the truth of God's ways.

As we study your word, O God, give us understanding of your commands, so that we may live our lives as you would have us to, and become true children of our Father in heaven. *Amen.*

Closing prayer No. 71

Sacred writings (3)

For Christian people the holy book is the Bible. It consists of the Jewish Scriptures (the Old Testament) and the books about Jesus and the early Church (the New Testament). At one time it was printed in Latin, the official language of the Christian Church, which many people could not read.

Several hundred years ago many people in Europe wanted Bibles in their own language. Several translations into English were made. The principal one, and that which was generally accepted, was the Authorized Version, so called because it was authorized by King James I. It was published in 1611. This has been used ever since and is still widely used today.

The Authorized Version is written in the language of over 300 years ago. Many people like this version: others think it is old fashioned. Some say that it is not easy to understand. So, in recent years there have been many translations of the Bible into modern English.

Perhaps the most important of the modern translations is the one produced by the United Bible Societies of the world. It may be known as *The Bible in Today's English* or as the *Good News Bible*. Parts of it are published as *Good News for Modern Man*. It is written in simple language which can be readily understood by English-speaking people all over the world, who can thus learn the Good News of the Gospel of Jesus Christ.

Bible Reading: Ephesians 1: 11–14

Teach us, O God, to love your word, to study our scriptures and to increase our knowledge of you and your teachings, so that we may learn to live in such a way that we can be recognized as true children of our Father in heaven and know for ourselves the joy that many have found in your holy word. *Amen.*

Closing prayer No. 63

Sacred writings (4)

United Bible Societies

Bible Reading: St. Matthew 13: 1–9

All sorts of things happen to the seed that is sown. Much is lost for various reasons but much of it produces a harvest. And so the sower has been adopted as the emblem of the British and Foreign Bible Society for it knows that, though some of the Bibles it prints will be lost, forgotten or destroyed, many will be read and people helped to understand how to live by its great teachings.

The British and Foreign Bible Society was founded on 7th March, 1804. Its aim was to produce and supply Bibles or parts of the Bible in many different languages at prices which those people could afford. At that time the Bible, or part of it, had been translated into about seventy languages.

In later years other Bible Societies were formed in various parts of the world. In 1946 a meeting of their representatives founded the United Bible Societies. These now work together to produce the books that are needed and they share their various translations.

Today the Bible or part of it has been translated into over 1,520 languages and dialects. Each year the Bible Societies produce over 250 million Bibles, Testaments, Gospels and Selections, many of them illustrated to help those with reading difficulties. Some of these are sold: some are given away. The seed is being sown!

Almighty God, we offer thanks for the Bible in our own language and for those who made it possible. We pray your blessing upon all who translate, print and distribute your word today. May the seed that is sown fall upon good ground and to you be the glory through Christ our Lord. *Amen.*

Benediction No. 100

Sacred writings (5)

The Holy Book of the Muslims is the Qur'ān. It is held in such deep respect that no one would dream of making a sound or of doing anything else whilst it is being read.

The Qur'ān is a record of the word of God as revealed to Muhammad. Muhammad explained how the angel Gabriel appeared to him and told him what to write. He was unable, himself, to read or write but he told others what had been revealed to him and they wrote it down.

The Qur'ān consists of 114 chapters or *suras*, which contain 6,200 verses or *ayyats*. These came to Muhammad a little at a time over a number of years. Much of the Qur'ān is similar to the Jewish Bible and some to the Christian New Testament but there are differences. Muslims believe that God made revelations to other prophets—the Jewish Bible to Moses, the Psalms to David and the New Testament to Jesus—but they say that these have been altered and that only the Qur'ān is accurate. Jews and Christians, of course, would disagree with this.

Muslims also have a collection of the sayings of Muhammad, called the *Hadith*, but the Qur'ān is more important. Although there have been translations of the Qur'ān into modern languages, Arabic is the official language of Islam and is the language used when reading from the Qur'ān.

Muslims use the Qur'ān in their prayers and learn many chapters and verses by heart so that they do not need the written words when they pray. Some Muslims learn the whole Qur'ān by heart and are then known as *Hafiz*. They are very respected men in the Muslim community.

As we study your word, O God, help us to learn of you, as we learn of you to love you, as we love you to serve you, and in our service to find happiness and contentment all our days. *Amen.*

Closing prayer No. 73

7 People of God

The ten themes in this section are all about the lives of people who have made their mark on the community or the world. They are people who may be said to have answered the call of God and to have spent their lives in the service of God. They are grouped under the following headings:

Called by God   *Paying the price*
Teachers and scholars   *Preaching the Gospel*
Into all the world   *Bishops worldwide*
Service   *In the day's work*
Great people of God   *Faithful servants*

Many are Christians but great people of other religions have been included too. Whilst some of the people are historically famous there are many from the twentieth century, some of whom are still living.

There are many other 'People of God' appearing in other sections of the book, notably in Section 5 (pages 187–248). See also the Index of Related Subjects (page 432).

Called by God (1)

Bible Reading: St. Mark 2: 13–17

Many religious people in the time of Jesus were amazed to think that Jesus would choose a man like Levi, or Matthew, to be one of his followers. But no doubt Jesus realized how useful Matthew could be and the gospel that bears his name shows how right Jesus was.

In later years God showed many people ways of serving him in the Church and some of them might have appeared to be strange choices. One was the man who become known as St. Godric, remembered each year on 21st May.

Godric was a young pedlar living near King's Lynn, Norfolk, whose business methods were far from honest and his conduct unruly. Later he became a prosperous sea trader, quite likely a pirate.

But when he was in his forties, after making several pilgrimages, Godric began learning from books. Then he decided to live as a hermit in a hut by the River Wear a few miles from Durham. There he lived to be over one hundred years old.

Godric lived a very hard life as a hermit, trying to make amends for his early life. Many sought advice from him and were given it but perhaps the most remarkable thing about Godric was his ability to write poetry and set verses to music, even though he knew nothing about music. He said that the tunes had been given to him in a vision. So Godric, one of the earliest of English poets and hymn-writers, became of use to God who had led him into a very different way of life.

O God, you know more about us than we know about ourselves. Show us what we ought to do and help us to live our lives in such a way that we may be of service to you and to others in the way that you know we have most to offer. Accept the words of our lips and the works of our hands for your glory. *Amen.*

Closing prayer No. 84

Called by God (2)

When a person knows that something is happening that is wrong, he can do one of two things. He can do or say nothing, which is probably the easier course and will cause him no hardship, except perhaps an uneasy conscience. Or he can take some action which may make him unpopular.

Sometimes Christian leaders have felt that they must speak out against evil things and, if it happened to be the rulers who were at fault that could be a very dangerous thing to do. We know what happened when Jesus spoke out against some of the leaders.

Bible Reading: St. Matthew 21: 33–45

In the year 1565, when Abbot Philip was elected head of the Russian Church, it was quite clear that trouble lay ahead. The Tsar, the ruler of Russia, was Ivan the Terrible, a cruel man who had many people put to death.

Philip knew he must say something. This only made the Tsar more angry and the killing continued. After many protests by Philip, the Tsar had him arrested on false charges and imprisoned in various places. Philip was treated very cruelly and one day smothered to death with a cushion. It was the price that was paid for doing his Christian duty and standing firm for what he believed right.

He later came to be regarded as a saint by the Russian Church, which remembers him as St. Philip of Moscow on 9th January each year.

Make us aware, O God, of all those things around us which are evil or wrong and grant us the courage to do something about them. May fear of the consequences never deter us from doing whatever we believe to be right or make us shelve our responsibilities. *Amen.*

Closing prayer No. 74

Called by God (3)

St. Teresa of Avila

St. Teresa of Avila, whose feast day is on 15th October, was a woman who did not believe in half measures. If she were going to do something it had to be done properly. Even as a girl she had decided to go overseas so that she could be put to death as a martyr for Jesus Christ. But it was pointed out to her that God wanted people to *live* for him, not just to die for him.

When she was about twenty, Teresa entered a convent in her home town of Avila, Spain. It was an easy-going convent with few of the strict rules that applied in many religious houses. Eventually Teresa decided that she would open a convent in which the strict rules of the Carmelite Order would be kept.

Her convent was opened at Avila in 1562. It was the first of many, for Teresa travelled throughout Spain barefoot, founding many convents in which the nuns lived a strict disciplined life, cut off from the world and with much of their day spent in prayer.

Travelling in those days was far from easy and Teresa was often unwell but she would not give in. When back in her convent, Teresa would write books to help other people to know God. Teresa is remembered not only for putting everything she had into her work but for her wisdom, her holiness and the example she set for others to follow.

These words, written by St. Paul, say something about the Christian way of life:

Bible Reading: Philippians 4: 8–9

Help us, O God, to find out how you would have us to live and then give us the courage and determination to live life to the full so that we may live to your glory and have your peace in our hearts. *Amen.*

Benediction No. 99

Called by God (4)

St. Philip Neri

Philip Neri was born in Florence, Italy, in 1515. He was given a good education and apprenticed in a relative's business. But when he was eighteen Philip decided to go to Rome, where he discovered many young men who were in need of help.

Philip found others who were willing to work with him and together they formed a brotherhood which met for worship and ministered to pilgrims and sick people.

When he was thirty-five, Philip Neri became a priest but he still continued to work with young men. Above his church he built a large room or oratory, where people could meet to talk, discuss, sing, or plan their work to help the needy. Several clergymen joined Philip in a society which did not take vows such as those taken by monks but which looked for and found ways of helping the needy. Soon Philip was known throughout Rome and he was able to influence many people by his work and teaching.

Philip often used unusual methods to achieve the results he wanted, which were to get people to live according to Christian teachings. As St. Philip Neri he is remembered particularly on 26th May as a saint whose whole life and especially his joyfulness told of his nearness to God.

St. Paul wrote of this joyfulness and nearness to God in one of his letters.

Bible Reading: I Thessalonians 5: 14–18

We humbly ask you, Almighty God;
Give us a desire to help those around us;
Show us how we can be of service to others;
Help us to live lives that others find pleasant;
Fill us with your spirit of joyfulness;
Teach us to pray;
And be near to us always. *Amen.*

Closing prayer No. 52

Called by God (5)

Wilson Carlile

When Wilson Carlile left school at the age of fourteen he went into business determined to make a fortune by the time he was twenty-five. He worked hard and he saved hard. Although he went to chapel his mind was more on money than it was on God.

Then in 1870 war in Europe put an end to his business there. Soon his fortune was gone and he became ill with worry. It was then that God stepped in. As Wilson said, 'Jesus captured me.' He began working in the Church of England but soon realized that he must give his whole life to the work. He went to college, was ordained and took charge of a church.

But the Reverend Wilson Carlile could not stay inside a church; he had to go outside where he held huge open air meetings. In 1882 he started his Church Army. Notices were posted: 'The Church Army, under the command of the Reverend W. Carlile, declares war on sin. Come if you dare!'

But as he preached the Gospel, Carlile found other things to do. In the slums there were people in need. Soon the Church Army was helping the drunkards and tramps, the prisoners and their families, old folk and children, the unemployed and the homeless. Captains and Sisters were trained and sent to many parts of England. During World War I soldiers were helped from some 2,000 centres. In World War II there was yet more to be done.

It was during that war that Wilson Carlile died on 26th September, 1942 at the age of ninety-five. Called by God for a special task he had done it faithfully to the end. And that work goes on today.

Help us to listen for your words, O God;
Show us what you would have us to do in life;
Make us willing to respond to your calling;
And keep us faithful to the end. *Amen.*

Closing prayer No. 51

Paying the price (1)

One of the famous Jewish teachers after the Jewish Bible had been completed was Rabbi Akiba ben Joseph. He lived in the period shortly after the life of Jesus Christ.

Rabbi Akiba was the head of a school for rabbis (teachers) at Jaffa. One thing for which he is particularly remembered is that he was the first rabbi to write down many of the Jewish sayings. His written work, *Mishnah of Rabbi Akiba* forms part of the Talmud, the collection of Jewish teachings.

At the time when Rabbi Akiba lived, the Romans controlled most of the known world. Jewish leaders longed for the day when their land would be free and they could govern themselves according to their Law.

For many years they had looked for a Messiah—one who had been promised through the prophets who would free his people.

Bible Reading: Micah 5: 1–5a

Many people, but not the Jewish leaders, had believed that Jesus Christ was the Messiah. The leaders still looked. Rabbi Akiba believed that he had found the Messiah, a young man named Simon Bar Koheba. There was a revolt against the Roman Emperor Hadrian in A.D. 135 but it was stamped out by the Romans with much bloodshed.

For his part, Rabbi Akiba was put to death. Today he is one of the ten martyrs mentioned in the Jewish prayer of repentance.

We remember, O God, those people who have been prepared to give everything, even their lives, for those things in which they have really believed. Help us to make up our minds what things are good and true and then grant us the courage to uphold those things even though it may cost us something to do so. Above all, help us to be true to you. *Amen.*

Closing prayer No. 56

Paying the price (2)

To be a Christian in the early days of the Church could be dangerous and many people paid with their lives the price of loyalty to their faith. The Roman authorities had no time for the Christians whom they regarded as troublemakers because they refused to worship the Roman Emperor as a God.

Jesus had warned his disciples that they were likely to suffer for following him.

Bible Reading: St. Matthew 24: 9–14

The leaders of the Church were often the ones to be singled out. So it was that Polycarp, the Bishop of Smyrna, a port of Asia Minor, was singled out at a time when the authorities were persecuting the Christians. He was a great leader and had worked at Smyrna for nearly sixty years.

In the year A.D. 155, soldiers were sent to arrest the old man who was 86 years old. His followers hid him but a servant boy told where he was after being tortured. Back in the city, Polycarp was told that his life would be spared if he offered incense at the emperor's statue. Polycarp refused. 'I have served Christ for eighty-six years,' he said. 'He has never done me wrong. How then can I wrong my king and blaspheme him who has saved me?'

The governor could not persuade Polycarp. The crowds were demanding that he be put in the arena to face the lions. The governor refused as the games where this was done had ended. Not to be outdone, the crowds demanded that he should be burned and they saw to it that he was.

Polycarp, who remained faithful to the end is now remembered as St. Polycarp each year on 26th January.

We remember with thankfulness those who have given their all for Christ, for it is through their sacrifice that we have our church today. Make us faithful as they were faithful. *Amen.*

Benediction No. 91

Paying the price (3)

FOR OPPOSING A DICTATOR   *Dietrich Bonhoeffer*

On 9th April, 1945, as World War II was drawing to a close, a German pastor was led into a prison yard and hanged. It was the final curtain for a man who had spoken out against Hitler and his regime and had spent the last two years of his life in prison.

Dietrich Bonhoeffer was a clever young man who thought deeply about religion. He was a member of the Lutheran Church, which was often ready to speak out against any laws and acts which were contrary to their Christian beliefs. In fact, on the day after Hitler came to power Dietrich Bonhoeffer made a broadcast which was cut off the air by the authorities before he had finished speaking.

Bonhoeffer was a marked man! He knew that every move he made would be watched. He was anxious to let other people know what was happening inside Germany, so he took charge of a church in London for two years. He returned to Germany, watched very closely by the authorities, yet he was allowed to leave again for London and America. He chose, however, to return to Germany just before war broke out. He wrote, 'I will have no right to participate in the reconstruction of Germany after the war if I do not share in this time with my people.'

He never did, of course. His work finished in prison. His *Letters from Prison* and his books on religion have helped many. Like St. Paul he was still able to help even though it was from prison.

Bible Reading: Ephesians 3: 7–13

We give thanks, O God, for those who have remained faithful in prison and even to death, so giving courage to others. We pray for those imprisoned or facing death for their beliefs today. Grant them your strength we pray. *Amen.*

Closing prayer No. 72

Paying the price (4)

THE VOLUNTEER   *Maximilian Kolbe*

One day in July, 1941, a prisoner escaped from Block 14 of
Auschwitz Concentration Camp in Poland. The Commandant
replied by saying that twenty other prisoners from that block
would die in a starvation cell. By the evening he had decided to
make it only ten and the ten were picked out. One, a married man
with two children, pleaded to be allowed to live.

Then another man stepped forward, asked if he could take the
place of the married man and was led away with the other nine to
an airless underground cell.

He was Maximilian Kolbe, a Franciscan priest who had been
taken on 28th May, 1941, to Auschwitz after imprisonment and
ill-treatment in Warsaw because of his Christian belief and witness.

For many years Maximilian had worked faithfully for God as a
Franciscan. As a young man he had organized missionary groups
all over Poland. He had published a monthly Christian magazine.
He had started what was to become one of the biggest Franciscan
houses in Poland. He had worked in Japan for six years. But when
the German armies invaded Poland the Franciscans came under
suspicion. Maximilian was arrested because of his plain speaking
against the evil around him.

In the underground cell Maximilian led the others in prayer.
One by one they starved or were beaten to death until Maximilian
alone was left. He was given an injection of poison. Maximilian
Kolbe had died willingly to save the life of another.

Bible Reading: St. John 15: 12–14

'Greater love hath no man than this, that a man lay down his life
for his friends.' Grant unto us, O God, that love which leads us to
think more of others than we do of ourselves. *Amen.*

Closing prayer No. 79

Paying the price (5)

Jesus warned his followers of the dangers of being his disciples. Many would be put to death for their beliefs, he told them. And many were. Throughout history there have been thousands who have suffered and died as they tried to teach the Good News. We read many stories of missionaries killed in far away places and think perhaps these things belong to the past. Yet they still happen.

Only a few years ago some young Americans were working in the jungle of Ecuador. Ed McCully, Jim Elliot and Peter Fleming were missionaries working among the Quichua Indians. Nathaniel Saint was one of the pilots who lowered supplies into small clearings or landed on small strips of ground to take people to hospital.

These four decided they would like to go to the Auca Indians, a fierce war-like tribe living to the south. They learned the Auca language, flew over their village, and called out 'We are your friends'. They dropped gifts and the Aucas sent gifts back on the line which they lowered. All seemed to be well.

On 3rd January, 1956 the four, together with Roger Youderian, landed a few miles away to set up a base by the river. They made contact with a few Aucas. On Sunday 8th January they told their wives by radio that ten Auca men were coming to them. That was the last call they made. A search party found their bodies, speared and knifed by the Aucas.

But that was not the end. Many young men went to take their place. So did Jim's wife and Nat's sister, showing that Christian love can overcome even personal tragedy and distress.

Bible Reading: I Corinthians 13: 1–7

Almighty God, who showed your love for the world in Jesus Christ, grant to us that love for you which will overcome all things as we seek to live our lives in your service. *Amen.*

Closing prayer No. 70

Teachers and scholars (1)

St. Bonaventure

When we think of the people who have been called by God to serve the Church, we discover that there have been some who would be regarded as clever, intelligent or wise but there are many more who were very ordinary people. St. Paul referred to this in one of his letters:

Bible Reading: I Corinthians 1: 26–31

One of the wise and intelligent people whom God chose was St. Bonaventure, whose feast day falls on 14th July. He was one of the great scholars and teachers of the Church. Born in Italy, he went to the University of Paris and remained in that city for many years as a teacher and preacher.

Bonaventure became a friar in the Franciscan order which had been founded by St. Francis of Assisi. In 1257 he was chosen to be their leader and he did this so well that he has come to be regarded as the most important leader after St. Francis himself. In time, too, there were others who recognized his abilities and he was appointed a bishop and cardinal of the Church.

But for all his learning and wisdom, St. Bonaventure is regarded as a man who liked a simple life and one who recognized that it was not necessary to be clever to be near to God. Indeed he often taught that a simple person could have a much greater love and knowledge of God than an intelligent person. A person does not need intelligence to believe in God but a simple faith that with God all things are possible.

Grant unto us, O God,
A simple faith to accept your teachings;
An understanding of your holy ways;
A love for you that is strong and deep;
A readiness to accept your guidance;
And a very real sense of your presence. *Amen.*

Closing prayer No. 76

Teachers and scholars (2)

Moses Maimonides

One of the greatest thinkers and teachers of the Middle Ages was Moses Maimonides, born in A.D. 1135 into a Jewish family living in Cordova, Spain. When he was thirteen his family was forced to leave Spain because of their devout Jewish faith. Maimonides lived in North Africa and Palestine before settling in Egypt at the age of thirty.

There Maimonides studied medicine and became a most successful doctor, working at the court of the Sultan, Saladin. But for Maimonides, medicine was his profession and not as important as his study of religion. He spoke with many outstanding scholars and collected information on every possible subject.

Jews, Christians and Muslims were then all becoming puzzled. Scholarly thinking, religion and science often seemed to contradict each other. What should they believe? So Maimonides wrote his famous book *Guide for the Perplexed* to help them. It was a masterpiece, used by great Christian teachers as well as by Jews. It was translated later into other languages and has been studied by many, many people.

The *Guide* ends with the thought: 'God is near to all who call upon Him if they call upon Him in truth and turn to Him. He is found by everyone who seeks Him, if he always goes towards Him, and never goes away.'

Maimonides, otherwise known as Rabbi Moses ben Maimon, died at the age of seventy in 1204. His body was taken to the Holy Land and buried near the Sea of Galilee, where his tomb became a place of pilgrimage.

O God, our Father, give us wisdom to seek after you and find you, to call upon you and know that you answer prayer, to study your teachings and live according to them, to learn what you would have us do and then do it faithfully and well. Hear us and help us. *Amen.*

Closing prayer No. 82

Teachers and scholars (3)

William Caxton

William Caxton was an intelligent and well-educated man. In his day few people were able to read or write but Caxton could speak several languages very well and had a good knowledge of English. He was born about 1422 in Kent and was apprenticed to a London mercer on 24th June, 1438.

Three years later his master died and Caxton went to Bruges in Belgium where he became very prosperous. While in Europe he learned of the work of a German named Gutenburg, who had made the first printed book in Europe, the Bible, using movable type. Before that all books had been written by hand.

Caxton realized what an important discovery this was. He set up a small printing press in Bruges and made his first books. Then he decided to go back to his homeland and, with the help of some important people, he set up a printing press at the Almonry in Westminster. There he printed over eighty books before he died aged about seventy. One of the most famous of these was Chaucer's *Canterbury Tales*. Many were religious books.

But Caxton's work was very important for another reason too. When he came to translate books into English for printing, he discovered that there were very many forms of the English language. So he printed his books in a form of English that would be acceptable to as many people as possible. This proved to be very useful later when people wanted to translate the Bible into English.

William Caxton was one man who put his talents to very good use.

Thank you, O God
For all useful discoveries and inventions;
Especially for printed books to read and enjoy
And for the opportunities we have of learning.
May we use them wisely and be thankful. *Amen.*

Closing prayer No. 77

Teachers and scholars (4)

Desiderius Erasmus

Desiderius Erasmus was born in Rotterdam about 1467. Within a few years both his parents had died of the plague and he was brought up by a guardian who wanted him to become a monk. After a good education he entered a monastery but did not find it to his liking. He wanted to study and spend his life in a world of books.

Erasmus became a very good Latin scholar and he then decided he should learn Greek too. He studied all the Greek manuscripts he could find until he became an expert in that language.

During his lifetime he travelled to many countries of Europe—France, England, Belgium, Germany, Switzerland—settling for a few years to study, to meet other scholars and pore over ancient documents. It was while he was in England that he was persuaded to translate the Bible into Greek. It took him sixteen years to complete the New Testament.

Erasmus wrote other books too. A very popular one was *In Praise of Folly* in which he poked fun at all sorts of people and especially of things that he believed were wrong in the Church. Those were the days of the Reformation, when people were having new ideas about the Church. Erasmus refused to take sides. He had studied to better himself and he wanted his learning to benefit everyone. He died on 12th July, 1536, having sought the truth and stuck firmly to his beliefs.

Bible Reading: II Timothy 3: 14–17

A prayer of Erasmus:

O Lord, Jesus Christ, who art the Way, the Truth, and the Life, we pray thee suffer us not to stray from thee, who art the Way, nor to distrust thee, who art the Truth, nor to rest in any other thing than thee, who art the Life. Teach us by thy Holy Spirit, what to believe, what to do, and wherein to take our rest. *Amen.*

Closing prayer No. 74

Teachers and scholars (5)

Dr. William Barclay

When we want to learn all we can about a subject that interests us, we usually ask someone who knows about it or we read books on that subject by people who are experts. So it is with the Bible. We can read it for ourselves but we can understand it better with help from the experts.

One man who is regarded today as one of the greatest modern experts on the Bible is Dr. William Barclay. His knowledge is so great that he can discuss with the greatest Bible scholars, yet he is able to explain so simply that ordinary people can be helped tremendously by listening to his broadcasts or reading his books.

William Barclay was born in Wick in the far north of Scotland but his parents moved to Motherwell when he was five. After attending University, he became a minister in the Church of Scotland with the charge of a church in Renfrew. In 1946 he became a Lecturer at Trinity College and in 1963 a Professor at Glasgow University.

One thing that William Barclay did was to make his own translation of the New Testament. Then he wrote notes about each passage and had them published as the *Daily Study Bible*. He has written over sixty books, regular articles in newspapers and journals, notes for Boys' Brigade Bible Class courses and books of prayers for young and old. He has also appeared on television.

Dr. Barclay has never spared himself but has used much of his spare time to write helpful things. And there are many who have cause to be grateful to him for this.

A prayer of Dr. William Barclay:

O God, our Father, grant to us, not only to know your truth with our minds, but also to experience it in our hearts, and to translate it into our lives. So grant us to know, to love, and to live the truth: through Jesus Christ our Lord. *Amen.*

Closing prayer No. 59 (also by Dr. Barclay)

Preaching the gospel (1)

A CALL TO PREACH   *Stephen Grellet*

Bible Reading: St. Luke 9: 1–6

In this story the disciples were sent out to preach the Gospel of the Kingdom of God. The last command which Jesus gave his disciples was also to preach to all people. Since then many people have felt that God wanted them to preach in a particular place and have felt compelled to go.

Stephen Grellet was one of these. Born at Limoges, France in 1773, he went to America in 1795 and became a minister of the Society of Friends (Quakers). He died in Burlington, New Jersey in 1855 but in the meanwhile went on missionary journeys over practically the whole of Europe and the U.S.A.

One story tells how he felt a call to preach in a lumber camp in the United States. He arrived at this particular camp only to find it deserted. He was puzzled and decided to go back home. But the voice inside him said, 'Preach'.

So he went into the dining hut, tidied it up, took out his Bible and preached to the empty room just as though he had a full congregation there. Then he closed his Bible and left for home, wondering whether that was about the daftest thing he had ever done.

It was some years later that he met a man who reminded him of this. How did he know? He was the foreman, who had gone back for something the gang had left behind. Hearing Grellet's voice, he sat outside and listened. And Grellet's words struck home. The foreman went, bought a Bible and started a Bible study group from which three men became missionaries.

Grellet may have *thought* his preaching that day was wasted. But who knows what God has in mind when he calls someone to preach?

Some words usually attributed to Stephen Grellet:

I shall pass through this world but once. If, therefore, there be any kindness I can show, or any good thing I can do, let me do it now; let me not defer it or neglect it, for I shall not pass this way again.

Closing prayer No. 82

Preaching the gospel (2)

Catherine Booth

For a very long time there have been people who have said that women should not preach. It may be that they remember what St. Paul had to say.

Bible Reading: I Corinthians 14: 33b–35

But there have been, and there are today, some very able women preachers. The Rev. William Booth was a very courageous man when, in 1860, he not only allowed his wife to 'say a word' in the morning service at his Methodist Church in Gateshead, but also announced that she would be the preacher that evening.

But Catherine Booth was a very able preacher and when her husband began his work which led to the founding of the Salvation Army, she proved just how able she was, leading revival campaigns and preaching to those who might be able to support their work amongst the poor.

There was much that was wrong in those days and Catherine went into battle alongside her husband to try to put it right. But she once wrote to her husband, 'Let us make up our minds to win souls whatever else we leave undone.' And this was the theme of her preaching often to large audiences.

Up and down the country Catherine travelled with her husband, sometimes exhausted by her work, often in pain, yet preaching in a way that led vast numbers of people to accept Jesus Christ as Lord.

Catherine Booth died of cancer on 4th October, 1890. Over thirty-six thousand people attended her funeral service at Olympia and many others mourned the loss of the 'mother of the Salvation Army', faithful worker and preacher of the gospel.

O God, you have shown us the way of salvation through Jesus Christ. Help us to recognize what is wrong and turn away from it, accepting the way that you have shown us, and living as true children of our Father God. *Amen.*

Closing prayer No. 76

Preaching the gospel (3)

POWERFUL PREACHING   *William Edwin Sangster*

Every Sunday thousands of preachers enter the pulpits of our churches to preach the Christian gospel. They preach because they believe it is what God would have them to do, just as people have done since the early days of the Church.

Bible Reading: II Corinthians 4: 5–6

Of these preachers a few are outstanding, men and women who might be described as 'born preachers'. These are the ones who are able to hold people spellbound as they preach.

One of the really great preachers of not so long ago was Dr. W. E. Sangster, remembered especially for his fine preaching and for other work which he did at the Westminster Central Hall, London.

William Edwin Sangster was ordained a minister of the Methodist Church on 27th July, 1926. Only twenty-five years later he was to hold the most important office in the Methodist Church, the President of Conference. Meanwhile in various places he had helped a great many people to know God, some through his pastoral work of caring and loving, and some through his powerful preaching.

Those who heard him preach will never forget the experience. Sangster believed in preaching and he put everything God gave him into it. He preached as long as he was able until he was silenced by an illness which took away his voice.

But even then he was not really silenced, for when he died on 24th May, 1960, he left behind many writings, not the least of which were books to help other preachers to improve their preaching.

We thank you, God our Father, for great preachers who have helped people to understand your ways. Help us to listen to the words of your servants so that we may know you better. *Amen.*

Closing prayer No. 78

Preaching the gospel (4)

OPEN AIR PREACHING   *Lord Soper*

On 23rd February, 1977, an elderly gentleman climbed on to a grey stone wall at Tower Hill, opposite the Tower of London. Soon he was surrounded by a group of people who wondered what he would have to say. A number of them were regular Wednesday visitors to Tower Hill for they enjoyed listening to Lord Soper.

It was exactly fifty years previously that as a young Methodist minister, the Rev. Donald Soper had taken his stand on Tower Hill and during those fifty years he allowed nothing, if it were humanly possible, to interfere with his Wednesday lunch-time sessions.

His first appointment as a minister in 1925 had been to a church in the Old Kent Road. People did not seem anxious to come into his church and so he decided to go out to them. Tower Hill seemed the most likely spot for an audience and so that was where he set up his pitch.

Christians have always laid emphasis on preaching the word of God. Hear what St. Paul had to say:

Bible Reading: II Timothy 4: 1–4

Donald Soper certainly had a mixed reception. He did not mince his words but said what he thought needed to be said. His audience did not mince their words either. They heckled and argued, scoffed or cheered, sometimes angrily and sometimes good humouredly.

For over forty years he ministered to people at the West London Mission in Kingsway Hall. In 1953 he was President of the Methodist Conference. In 1965 he took his seat in the House of Lords as Lord Soper. But Tower Hill remained a most important pulpit.

Hear our prayer, O Lord, for all who are called to preach your word, that their words may be inspired by your Holy Spirit and the ears of their hearers opened to receive; in Christ's name. *Amen.*

Closing prayer No. 71

Preaching the gospel (5)

WORLD EVANGELIST   *Billy Graham*

Some preachers are known as evangelists. An evangelist is one who preaches the gospel with a view to getting people to commit themselves fully to the Christian way of life or, as is often said, to give themselves to Jesus Christ.

One of the best known present-day evangelists is Dr. Billy Graham, who has preached in major cities all over the world. Billy Graham was born on 7th November, 1918, on a farm near Charlotte, North Carolina. He recalls how a visiting evangelist prayed that 'out of Charlotte the Lord would raise up someone to preach the Gospel to the ends of the earth'.

How well that prayer was to be answered! Before the evangelist left Charlotte, Billy Graham, then nearly sixteen, had begun thinking. God had called him: he had responded.

In the years that followed he went to college, studied his Bible, accepted invitations to preach and took part in evangelistic meetings. Within a few years he was part of a team and a great organization which planned and held great campaigns throughout the world. Thousands of people came to the meetings in huge halls, tents or stadia. At some meetings over 100,000 people have been present.

Billy Graham sometimes recalls how God spoke to Ezekiel:

Bible Reading: Ezekiel 2: 1–7

Ezekiel was to speak God's words, not his own. Billy Graham preaches God's word from the Bible. Before each meeting much prayer is offered. At the end of each meeting many people are nearer to God. That is the work of the evangelist.

Open our ears, O Lord, so that we may hear what you would tell us to do. Make us ready to respond to your call and offer our lives in your service; through Jesus Christ our Lord. *Amen.*

Closing prayer No. 63

Into all the world (1)

St. Martin of Tours

The Christian Church has always been a missionary church with its
members taking the Gospel message to people of other lands. This
was what Jesus told his disciples to do.

Bible Reading: St. Matthew 28: 16–20

Today we think of missionaries as those who go from countries
such as those in Europe which may be regarded as Christian
countries. But long ago it was necessary for missionaries to be sent
to them.

One of the early Christian missionaries was a soldier named
Martin who was born in Hungary. As a young soldier he became a
Christian and asked to be discharged from the army because as a
soldier of Jesus Christ he did not want to kill people.

After a while he went as a clergyman to found the first monastery to be set up in Gaul, as France was then called, and, in A.D.
370, was made Bishop of Tours. From there he travelled far and
wide, often on foot or on a donkey, sometimes by boat but always
ready to help people to know the Christian way of life.

Sometimes Martin destroyed heathen places of worship and
often he spoke out forcibly so that even cruel rulers took notice of
his words. His influence spread not only throughout Gaul but to
Ireland, Africa and other lands. After his death he became known
as St. Martin of Tours and he is remembered each year on 11th
November.

It was through people like St. Martin that the people of lands
such as the present day Britain, France and Germany accepted
Christianity as their religion.

O God our Father, we remember with thankfulness your servants
of old who faithfully carried your word to people of other lands.
May your Kingdom continue to grow until all people walk in your
holy ways. *Amen.*

Benediction No. 92

Into all the world (2)

When Mary Slessor arrived in Duke Town in the Calabar region of Nigeria, the senior missionary there was amazed to think that a young woman should be sent to this wild part of Africa. He was soon to discover that Mary Slessor was no ordinary young woman. In fact she was one of the most remarkable people ever to become a missionary.

Mary had a hard life as a child because her father was a drunkard. At the age of eleven she had gone to work in a mill and later had worked amongst some pretty tough characters in the slums of Dundee. She was twenty-six when she sailed for West Africa, where she believed God wanted her to work.

After twelve years at Duke Town she obtained permission to go up-country to work amongst a fierce, warlike people who lived in Okoyong. Her friends believed that Mary would be killed but she had a fearless determination which won over even the hardest of men. We can imagine what they must have thought when they first saw this white woman with five black children—all of whom were orphans whom Mary had adopted and regarded as her 'family'.

To the Africans, Mary Slessor was the white 'Ma'. Ma was the name given to an influential woman. And influential she certainly was. She was able to persuade the people to give up some of their evil ways; she fought a never ending battle against drunkenness; she saved the lives of lots of children; she even managed to prevent a war by telling the warriors not to behave like fools.

Mary Slessor died in 1915 at the age of sixty-six, having worked in Calabar for half her life-time.

Almighty God, Father of all people, we give thanks for those people whose courage has enabled them to uphold what is right in face of many difficulties. Inspire us by your Spirit to follow their example. *Amen.*

Closing prayer No. 61

Into all the world (3)

Evangeline French

When St. Paul wrote to the Romans he told them how anxious he was to travel where he could teach people about the Christian way of life.

Bible Reading: Romans 15: 14–21

By the end of the nineteenth century there were few parts of the world where Christianity was unknown or where missionaries had not been but there were many people who felt that God wanted them to go to far away places.

It was in 1893 that Evangeline French set out for China to work at Shansi. She was about to return home on leave when the Boxer Rising broke out in which many missionaries and Chinese Christians were killed. Evangeline French was lucky to escape with her life. When she returned soon afterwards it was with a friend, Mildred Cable. The two were joined some short time later by Evangeline's sister Francesca.

Together the three worked in Shansi until 1923, when they felt they must move on to become pioneers in the Gobi Desert. With a cart and a team of mules they became travelling evangelists, talking to people of various nationalities and religions, or, as Evangeline described it, 'gossiping the Gospel'. After they had talked to people they would hand them copies of the scriptures provided by the Bible Society.

In 1936 they had to leave the Gobi. War had broken out between China and Japan and missionaries were told to leave the country. They had done what they had set out to do. They had preached the gospel to those who had not heard it before and who knows how many people may have been helped to know God better through these faithful servants of his?

O Lord Jesus Christ, who commanded your servants to preach the gospel, grant that today there may be those who will answer your call to teach the people of the world of your ways of love. *Amen.*

Closing prayer No. 79

Into all the world (4)

A LIFETIME IN INDIA   *Ethel Tomkinson*

Bible Reading: II Timothy 4: 7–8

On 11th December, 1967, an old lady died who could have echoed those words of St. Paul, for her life had been spent totally in the service of God and of people who needed her help.

Ethel Tomkinson was greatly interested in missionary work when she was a child and it was hardly surprising that she decided to spend the greater part of her life overseas, helping the poor and needy people of India. She trained firstly as a Deaconess of the Methodist Church and then as a nurse before joining the staff of a hospital belonging to the Methodist Missionary Society at Mysore, South India.

After eighteen years, she was asked to undertake some special work outside the hospital, helping women and girls who were in need. Many were undernourished and diseased; many were prostitutes; many were outcasts. Always she told them about Jesus Christ and how he had been sent to save those who were lost.

In those days there were three Christian Churches in India, Anglican, Methodist and the United Church. After many years of talking they united on 27th September, 1947 to become the Church of South India. Ethel Tomkinson became one of the first Sisters in the new church.

At last the time came for her to retire and return to England. It was not long before she was involved in other forms of service. Her last work was helping to comfort women who were dying in a home for old people in London. It was there that she herself died, having served God faithfully all her life.

All around us, O God, there are people in need. Show us which of them we can help and how best to do it. We think of old folk for whom we can do things, lonely people we might visit, other children who might need a friend, people overseas who need our prayers. Teach us to give a smile, a cheery word, a helping hand— things which cost us little but mean so much to others; for Jesus Christ's sake. *Amen.*

Closing prayer No. 81

Into all the world (5)

WHERE GOD DIRECTS   *Howard Souster*

Bible Reading: Genesis 12: 1–4a (or 5)

Abram had no idea where he was to go but he trusted God and was prepared to leave home and go where God directed. Many since then have done likewise and have been blessed in doing God's will.

Howard Souster, who was born in Forest Gate, East London on 9th November, 1919, was training to be a dentist in 1935, when he heard a missionary speak about his work. Howard realized that God wanted him overseas and he changed from dental to medical training.

Having offered to serve the Methodist Missionary Society in China, he was sent to Nigeria instead. So he was neither a dentist, nor a missionary where he had desired, but looking back he realized God's wisdom in overruling both desires.

For ten years, from 1943 to 1953, Dr. Souster served as Medical Officer and then Acting Medical Superintendent in Uyo, Eastern Nigeria, where he performed over 6,000 surgical operations. He also served for a while in Sierra Leone.

In 1968 Dr. Souster was invited to become Medical Secretary of the Methodist Missionary Society, now the Overseas Division of the Methodist Church. Its Mission Hospitals are now run by the churches of the countries concerned but they welcome many kinds of assistance. Dr. Souster helps to recruit staff for them, to offer advice and to help in all sorts of ways. In his first ten years as Medical Secretary he travelled over half a million miles, visiting every continent except South America.

He regards it a privilege to be able to use his Christian and professional qualifications in the service of God's people in many places.

We thank you, O God, for the example of those who have heard your call and have answered it. Help us to listen, to respond, and to do what you would have us do. Grant us your blessing. *Amen.*

Closing prayer No. 76

Bishops worldwide (1)

George Selwyn

Living at peace with one's neighbours is not always easy. James offered this advice in his letter.

Bible Reading: James 3: 14–18

Jesus once said, 'Happy are those who work for peace; God will call them his children.'

When George Selwyn arrived in New Zealand in 1842 to take up his appointment as first Bishop of New Zealand, he discovered that he had to be a peacemaker on many occasions.

Some years before, British settlers had gone to New Zealand to make their homes there. Some were more friendly toward the native people, the Maoris, than others were. Sometimes the British clergymen were called upon to protect the Maoris from those who would cheat and steal from them. In 1840 a treaty was made by which all New Zealanders, the Maoris and the white settlers, became subjects of Queen Victoria. But the trouble did not end.

As he travelled around the country there were times when the Maoris suspected that he was helping the settlers. Sometimes it was the other way round. But Bishop Selwyn was there to care for all of them. The only side he would take was God's side, the one which proclaimed that the white men and the Maoris were all God's children and equal in His sight.

By the time he returned to England in 1867, the Christian Church had been well organized in New Zealand and the Pacific islands, with bishops, clergymen and lay leaders, both Maori and white, working side by side as children of God.

Hear our prayer, O God;
For those today who live in fear of others;
For all who try to understand the views of others;
For all who seek to bring peace where there is strife;
For all who teach your ways of love.
Let your peace be within them. *Amen.*

Closing prayer No. 55

Bishops worldwide (2)

Samuel Azariah

Samuel Azariah was born in 1874 into a good Christian home in the south of India. His father had been a Hindu but had become Christian and he sent his son to school, then to a Christian college.

For thirteen years after leaving college, Samuel worked among Indian students in schools and colleges. Soon he had persuaded some of his friends that they ought to form a missionary society to send Indian missionaries to their own people in other parts of India. They decided to work in the Telugu district, where most of the people were outcastes. To Samuel Azariah they were all children of God, for Christianity has no barriers between groups of people.

Bible Reading: Galatians 3: 26–28

The English Bishop of Madras knew that one day there would be Indian bishops and he saw that Samuel Azariah had many qualities. He ordained him as a clergyman and he went to work at Dornakal, where he taught the uneducated outcastes to sing and pray in their own Telugu language. Three years later, in 1912, he became Bishop of Dornakal.

The lives of many of the people were changed. Their lives of misery became lives full of joy. They were really children of God.

But Azariah was also concerned with the unity of all Christian people and churches and he worked tirelessly to that end, pleading for unity at church conferences. He died in 1945, only two years before part of his dream had come true, the forming of the United Church of South India.

We pray, O God, for the unity of all your people. We thank you that we are all your children, regardless of wealth or position, colour or creed and that we are all equal in your sight. Help us to work together for the good of all people and the glory of your holy name. *Amen.*

Benediction No. 104

Bishops worldwide (3)

Archibald Fleming

Archibald Fleming worked in a shipyard by the River Clyde in Scotland. He worked hard during the day, studied in the evenings and taught in a Sunday School in Glasgow on Sundays.

One day he read in a magazine a letter from a Canadian Bishop asking for someone to go and preach the Gospel to the Eskimos in the Arctic, many of them still believing in the old tribal spirits and Sedna the goddess who lived under the ice.

So, in 1908, when he was twenty-five Archibald Fleming sailed for Canada where he studied for a year before going to Baffin Land to work among the Eskimos. For part of the year he lived in a mission hut and for part in the Eskimos' igloos. He travelled by sledge from one settlement to another.

He was very sorry to leave them when he had to go to Toronto to complete his training as a clergyman but he was soon back and warmly greeted by his Eskimo friends. The Eskimos who accepted the Christian way steadily increased in numbers and Eskimos themselves became leaders. The Reverend Archibald Fleming was appointed Archdeacon of the Arctic, to supervise all the Christian missions to the Eskimos. In 1933 he was appointed the first Bishop of the Arctic and spent much of his time travelling in small aeroplanes to the isolated communities.

Bishop Fleming died in 1955, having lived bravely and adventurously in the service of God and resolutely upheld the Christian faith, following the advice offered by St. Paul.

Bible Reading: Titus 1: 7–9

We thank you, God our Father, for all who have lived bravely and adventurously in your service, remaining true to their high calling. Grant that we may follow their example and become faithful servants of our heavenly Father. *Amen.*

Closing prayer No. 51

Bishops worldwide (4)

Joost de Blank

Joost (*yoast*) de Blank was born in Rotterdam on 14th November, 1908 but before he was a year old his parents moved to London and it was there that he was brought up and spent much of his life as a clergyman in the Church of England.

It was in 1952 that he was consecrated Bishop of Stepney, responsible for all the Anglican churches in East London. It was a time of challenge. The area was being developed after wartime destruction. But the new bishop made a great impression. He was a hard worker; he had the kind of humour that the people loved; he was down to earth in his thinking and speaking; and he was a great preacher.

Then came the bombshell! In 1957 he was invited to go to South Africa to become Archbishop of Cape Town, head of all the Anglican churches in South Africa. This was an even greater challenge than Stepney had been, for the South African government had adopted a policy known as *apartheid* by which white and coloured people were separated with the coloured people very much second-class citizens. Joost hated this. At his enthronement in Cape Town he deliberately preached on these words:

Bible Reading: I John 4: 7 and 19–21

He soon became very unpopular with the government and some of the white South Africans but he openly said what he believed. His stand was a dangerous one but one from which he refused to be moved.

Ill-health forced him to leave South Africa in 1963 and it was back to London, where he became a Canon of Westminster Abbey, and where he died on 1st January, 1968. He is remembered as an indomitable fighter for human rights.

O Lord God, the father of all men, grant that people the world over may remember that all are equal in your sight. May issues of race and colour be set aside as we learn the ways of brotherhood and peace and love, as children in the family of God. *Amen.*

Closing prayer No. 79

Bishops worldwide (5)

David Sheppard

David Sheppard was born in Surrey on 6th March, 1929. He was a good scholar and his education took him to the University of Cambridge. He was also an outstanding cricketer. He played for the university, for Sussex and for England, being captain of each. He was described by a well-known sports writer as 'one of the sporting heroes of his generation'.

But whilst David enjoyed his sport, he was also thinking of the important work which he had in mind, which was to be a clergyman in the Church of England and minister to those who were in need. This, of course, was the example which Jesus had set.

Bible Reading: St. Matthew 11: 2–5

It was to the poorer people that Rev. David Sheppard went after he had been ordained in 1957. He was Curate of a church in Islington, North London for two years and then Warden of the Mayflower Family Centre, Canning Town, in London's dockland. He still played cricket for England at times and was capped no less than twenty-two times but his work was concerned with helping people with problems and particularly the kind of problems to be found in inner city areas. The story of this early part of his life was published in his book *Parson's Pitch*.

In 1969 he left the Mayflower Centre to become Bishop of Woolwich in South London, where he remained for six years until he was appointed Bishop of Liverpool in 1975, an appointment in which his knowledge of inner city work would again be of great benefit to the people who live there.

Help us, O God, to be aware of the needs of those around us, the poor, the sick, the aged, the lonely and all who need a helping hand. Grant that we may be aware of these needs and do what we can to help. *Amen.*

Closing prayer No. 64

Service (1)

St. John the Almsgiver

If we keep our ears open it is not long before we hear of someone who is in need, for the world is full of hungry people and homeless people, old folk, sick folk, sad ones and lonely ones.

We may say, 'What a shame!' or 'Someone ought to do something!' It is a good thing to feel sorry for other people, but often feeling sorry isn't enough and we need to ask, 'Is there something *I* can do to help?'

The Bible tells how Peter and John were able to help someone in a very special way.

Bible Reading: Acts 3: 1–10

Not everyone can help like that but there are many stories of people who have done a lot to help. One who is remembered for the help he gave is St. John the Almsgiver, whose very title tells of his works.

John was born in Cyprus about A.D. 560 and he died there on 11th November, 619. He spent his life in Cyprus and in Egypt. He was determined to show that the Christian Church was a caring church. He helped many poor people; he founded hospitals; he started homes for old and sick people and lodgings for travellers; and he offered his advice quite freely.

His last words were that he had found the treasury of his church full and he left it empty. 'I have done my best to render to God the things that were God's.'

St. John the Almsgiver is remembered on 23rd January as a saint. He is remembered as the original patron saint of the Order of St. John at Jerusalem but also as one who saw a need and did something about it.

Help us, O God, to be aware of the needs of people around us. Whatever we can do to help may seem small but grant that we may never leave things to others if there is something practical that we can do. *Amen.*

Closing prayer No. 75

Service (2)

BUILDING BETTER HOMES   *Octavia Hill*

'Do you know what I would do if I had some money?' Octavia Hill, a young woman who had come from Wisbech to live in London, was talking to John Ruskin, the art critic and writer. 'What would you do?' Ruskin replied.

Octavia Hill then told him of the urgent need to do something about the dreadful conditions in which some people in London lived. In some cases whole families lived in single rooms, their water had all to be carried upstairs in buckets and the dirty water carried down again to be thrown away. Rooms were damp, smelly and in some cases unbelievably filthy. Octavia Hill had a plan to change some of this.

It so happened that she couldn't have mentioned it to John Ruskin at a more appropriate time. He had just been left a large sum of money and he agreed to let her have some for her housing ideas if she would make them pay and give him 5 per cent interest on his money.

Soon Octavia was working with a will. She was remarkably successful. Slum houses were improved. Others were pulled down and new pleasant buildings put up in their place. Soon others were taking notice of Octavia Hill's methods. This was not just a question of helping people but of teaching them to help themselves.

For Octavia Hill it was a means of putting her Christian beliefs into practice. Her work was recognized by the Church as being of such great importance that, when she died in 1912, she might have been buried in Westminster Abbey, had she not expressed the wish to be buried close to her sister in Kent.

We thank you, God our Father, for those who plan better homes for people to live in. We remember those who pioneered the way and we are thankful for the blessings that are ours today. *Amen.*

Closing prayer No. 56

Service (3)

When a baby girl was born in India in 1858, her father gave her the name Ramabai—'Giver of Delight'. He was a Hindu religious teacher, or Pandit, and he was determined to give his daughter the best education he could, even though it was not normally the custom to educate girls.

Ramabai's father died whilst she was still young, but by that time she was well educated and even knew the sacred Sanskrit language which was never taught to girls.

But Ramabai was becoming unhappy in the Hindu religion. She did not like the way in which girls and women were treated. Widows especially were treated very badly and led a very unhappy life. Then she was introduced to some Christians and she began reading the scriptures. Soon she was a widow herself, her husband dying after they had been married for only two years.

Ramabai was puzzled at the way in which Christian nuns cared for women who had lived bad lives. She was told that this was what Jesus had done.

Bible Reading: St. John 8: 1–11

Ramabai became a Christian herself and spent the rest of her life in helping the Hindu widows. In 1889 she set up her first Widow's Home in Bombay. A few years later she started a new settlement in the country. Before long it had become a Christian village with 700 girls in it.

Ramabai, who had been given the title of Pandita—'Lady Teacher'—used her knowledge, too, to translate the Bible into an Indian language but she died on 5th April, 1922, before it was printed.

O God, Father of all, we are thankful for those who have seen the needs of others and have done something to help. Make us aware of anything we can do to be of service and willing to put ourselves out in the service of others. *Amen.*

Closing prayer No. 66

Service (4)

John Ashley

It was while the Reverend John Ashley was on holiday in Somerset in 1835 that he made a most important decision and one which would bring help to a great number of people. He visited some fishermen who lived on some islands in the Bristol Channel and spoke about the seamen on the ships that lay off the Welsh coast.

'No one ever visits them!' he was told. So John Ashley hired a boat and went to see them. They gave him a warm welcome and John realized what he must do. If these people could not go to church, the church must go to them. He resigned his church living, bought a small ship and converted it into a floating chapel.

Wherever he found ships, John Ashley went. Soon he had formed the Bristol Channel Seamen's Mission and during the next fourteen years visited over fourteen thousand ships, helping the seamen and giving out Bibles and Prayer Books. In 1850 ill-health caused him to resign.

But his work continued. Missions were started in other places and these became united in an organization called Missions to Seamen. Its flag, the 'Flying Angel' was seen in more and more ports until it flew in ports all over the world.

Life at sea can be lonely, difficult and dangerous. Hear what the psalmist had to say.

Bible Reading: Psalm 107: 23–32

The Missions to Seamen helps seamen in many ways. Chaplains visit men on ships or in hospital. They serve seamen whatever their race or religion. In Mission buildings men can find accommodation, friendship and a place to worship together. Many a seaman has been thankful for help received at the 'Flying Angel'.

Almighty God we commend into your hands all who sail the seas, that they may be protected from harm and danger, storm and shipwreck. Bless all who help them, especially the Missions to Seamen and grant that many may find comfort and help through these your servants. *Amen.*

Benediction No. 96

Service (5)

Mother Theresa

One of the best known missionaries of the present century is Mother Theresa of Calcutta. The daughter of an Albanian grocer, she was born in Skopje in 1910. By the time she was twelve she knew that she must devote her life to the service of God. At eighteen she joined an order of missionary sisters, the Loreto nuns. After training, she taught in a school in Calcutta from 1929 to 1948, becoming the principal of the school.

Then one day in a train she felt that God wanted her to give up teaching and work amongst the poorest of the poor in Calcutta. In parts of that city there is unbelievable poverty with people dying in the streets from starvation and disease and these were the people Mother Theresa went to help on 8th August, 1948. No doubt she recalled these words of Jesus:

Bible Reading: St. Matthew 25: 31–40

In these poor people, Mother Theresa saw Christ himself. Each one was a person to be touched and loved. Only love could make these people feel wanted. Many of course were past help and about half of those taken into the converted Hindu temple that she used for her work died very shortly afterwards. In Calcutta alone Mother Theresa and her Sisters of Charity care for ten thousand lepers; elsewhere they care for another thirty-seven thousand.

The Sisters of Charity now work in many parts of the world and Mother Theresa visits them from time to time, but Calcutta is 'home' and the poor people of that city are her special care.

Part of Mother Theresa's morning prayer:

Lord grant that I may seek rather to comfort than to be comforted, to understand rather than be understood; to love than to be loved; for it is by forgetting self that one finds; it is by forgiving that one is forgiven; it is by dying that one awakens to eternal life. *Amen.*

Closing prayer No. 52

In the day's work (1)

JOURNALISM   *Hugh Redwood*

On the morning of 7th January, 1928, the daily newspaper *News Chronicle* carried a story which was a scoop. The Thames had broken its banks at Westminster, flooding many of the slum houses and drowning a number of people. The night editor, Hugh Redwood made his way homeward to Kent when he suddenly felt an urge to go to help the homeless. So he turned round and went back.

There he found the Salvation Army busily at work and he gave a hand. It was the work of that day which inspired Hugh Redwood to write a book which was to become a best-seller, *God in the Slums*.

Hugh had once been a member of the Salvation Army but had left and had little time for religion for many years until one day he heard a radio programme which made him think. As he said later, he 'took the hand that God offered him'.

Friends of his in the Fleet Street offices noticed that he was a different man. Prayer became an important power in his life.

In the years that followed, other books were written but Hugh Redwood's contribution to help many people was through his everyday work as a journalist. Each day the *News Chronicle* had 'Today's Parable'—a single-sentence sermon by Hugh Redwood. Each Saturday he wrote a 'Lay Sermon'. On his desk was an index of people who had asked him to pray for them. Hugh Redwood's Christianity was right at the centre of his everyday world and it remained so until the end of his life.

Here is some advice given by St. Paul:

Bible Reading: Ephesians 5: 1–2 and 15–17

Help us to realize, O God our Father, that religion is not for one day a week but a part of our everyday life; and help us to do all our work as though we are doing it for you so that others may be able to see something of you in us. *Amen.*

Closing prayer No. 72

In the day's work (2)

INSURANCE   *T. Arthur Chester*

True religion is not just a one day a week affair but something that is a real part of life, as many will testify. T. Arthur Chester is one of these. He went to work as a clerk in an insurance broker's office in the city about 1911. Then, after service in the army during World War I, he was elected in 1919 to Lloyd's as an underwriting member, becoming a respected figure in the world of insurance.

Born on 8th June, 1893, he came from Methodist stock. Grandfather on his father's side had been a minister of the United Methodist Free Church. Arthur's parents had settled in Manor Park, East London and Arthur attended Sunday School there from the age of 6 or 7. In later years he became a Sunday School teacher, helper in other church activities and holder of many offices in the Manor Park church and London North-East District of the Methodist Church.

Of his daily work he said: 'the influence of my parents and work in the Sunday School and church contributed in a large measure to my outlook on life, both at home and in my daily working with other people, and showed me the best and truest way of Christian living. It gave me a code of behaviour and a standard which has stood me in good stead in all aspects of life.'

Those who have worked with T. Arthur Chester in the office, in the church or elsewhere have known a kindly, generous and helpful Christian gentleman.

There are some who think of religion as a kind of insurance policy—keeping in with God just in case something goes wrong! Real Christianity is far more than that. It is a whole way of life, a life lived with God and for God, every day.

Help us, O God, to come to you because of what you are and not for anything we may get from you; to learn from you those things in life which are of lasting value; and to live our lives every day and in every way in your service. *Amen.*

Closing prayer No. 64

In the day's work (3)

SOCIAL WORK   *Sir Basil Henriques*

One of the most respected names in the east end of London during this century is that of Sir Basil Henriques, whose life was spent in helping others.

Born on 17th October, 1890, into a Jewish family, he was brought up to love God and his religion. This was to influence his whole life. It was while at university at Oxford that he decided on a career in social work. He had become very interested in work that was being done in Boys' Clubs and he determined to start a Jewish Club in the east end of London. It opened in 1914 in a house in the parish of St. George.

It was a beginning. Gradually the work expanded. Basil was engrossed in his work with the boys: his wife Rose ('Bunny') looked after the girls. In 1930 they moved into a fine new building, the Bernhard Baron St. George's Jewish Settlement, of which Basil remained warden until 1947. In the following year he was awarded the C.B.E. and in 1955 a knighthood.

But Sir Basil was not just concerned with his Settlement. He encouraged other work with clubs and was a Vice-President of the National Association of Boys' Clubs for 25 years. He was also a magistrate, chairman of a juvenile court and an authority on delinquency. He served on hospital and charity committees. He visited prisoners and helped solve the problems of very many people.

In all this he lived out his religious beliefs. The sermons he preached in the synagogues were put into practice every day. Sir Basil Henriques, who died on 2nd December, 1961, was a loyal servant of God, whose deep feeling for God and his religion were so readily recognizable.

Help us, Almighty God, to know you and to be ready to offer ourselves in your service so that day by day we may show our love in our relationships with others. Make us kind, helpful and generous, thinking more of others than we do of ourselves. *Amen.*

Closing prayer No. 81

In the day's work (4)

There are many people who have had roads or buildings named after them but very few who have given their name to a town. Peter Lee, who gave his name to Peterlee, County Durham, is one.

Peter Lee was the son of a miner who lived in those parts and Peter became a miner himself. After a while he went to America but returned, a tough fighting man yet with qualities that others came to respect. After a while he went to South Africa but stayed only a year.

When he returned this time he was a different man. He had done some deep thinking about God and about people. He began to work in the Methodist Church, where his wife worshipped and soon he was a Local Preacher, taking services regularly in neighbouring Methodist Churches.

But Peter Lee wanted to work for better things for the benefit of the community. In turn he became Parish Councillor, District Councillor and County Councillor, serving for a time as Chairman. He was also a trade union official. In 1930 he was elected General Secretary of the Durham Miners' Association and three years later President of the Miners' Federation (now the National Union of Mineworkers).

All this meant that Peter Lee was a very busy man but, whenever possible he kept Sunday free for his preaching. Sunday, he believed, was not a day for work but the gospel he preached on Sunday was something to put into practice in all his weekly activities so that the people around him could have better conditions. It was, perhaps, appropriate that he should die on the Lord's Day, Sunday, 16th June, 1935.

Hear our prayer, O Lord, for those who work for their fellow men and women, especially those who give their spare time to work on local or district councils, that you will guide them into making wise decisions for the good of all. *Amen.*

Benediction No. 103

In the day's work (5)

IN PARLIAMENT   *George Thomas*

One very important Member of Parliament is the Speaker of the House of Commons, an office which dates back to the fourteenth century. He is responsible for seeing that the business of the House is conducted in a proper manner. Although the Speaker is elected, as are all Members of Parliament, he does not belong to one of the political parties because he must not favour one or the other.

The Rt. Hon. Thomas George Thomas, who became The Speaker on 3rd February, 1976, was formerly a Labour M.P. and had been Deputy Speaker for a couple of years. As an elected Member for Cardiff he remained the M.P. to whom people turned for help but at Westminster he became Mr. Speaker.

In the Commons he sometimes has to shout, 'Order! Order!' if it becomes noisy. That may remind George Thomas of his days as a teacher, but in the Commons he has a 'class' of over six hundred.

George Thomas is a Methodist and has conducted many services as a lay preacher. In 1960–61 he was the Vice-President of the Methodist Conference. His sincere Christian belief is evident in Parliament. It was his strength of character and fine qualities which caused his fellow M.P.s to elect him as The Speaker. He is a man with a big heart and a warm nature who whispers a prayer each day before entering the House, asking for wisdom, patience and humour, trusting God to guide him in all that he has to do.

In one of his letters, St. Paul advised his readers to seek and accept the guidance of God.

Bible Reading: I Thessalonians 5: 16–23

Guide us, O God, in all the affairs of this day.
In our work, our play and our varied activities;
In all our relationships with other people;
In everything we do in your service;
Grant us wisdom, patience and humour;
And inspire us by your Holy Spirit. *Amen.*

Closing prayer No. 52

Great people of God (1)

Rabbi Hillel the Elder

One of the most important Jewish leaders and scholars was Rabbi Hillel the Elder, who lived about two thousand years ago from about 70 B.C. to A.D. 10.

Hillel, who was born in Babylonia and could trace his family history back to King David, made his home in Palestine, where he was soon recognized as a great scholar and teacher of Jewish Law. Thousands of students travelled to Jerusalem so that they could study under him.

Because of his learning, Hillel was made one of the princes of the Sanhedrin, the supreme Jewish court. In 30 B.C. he became its leader and he held this office for forty years until he died.

One very important thing he did was to rearrange the Jewish laws so that they could be studied more easily under six main subject headings. He said that the whole of the Jewish way of life could be summed up simply in a few words: 'What is hateful to thee, do not unto thy fellow man; this is the whole Law; the rest is mere commentary.' Christians will notice the resemblance between this and what Jesus had to say a little later:

Bible Reading: St. Matthew 7: 12

Rabbi Hillel the Elder was an important leader, a great scholar and a good teacher but he is also remembered as a very humble man who had a great love for his fellow men.

We thank you, God our Father
For all the good gifts you have given us;
For knowledge and learning and the art of study;
For teachers who help us to understand;
For wisdom to know what we should do.
Help us
To make the most of our opportunities;
To become the best that we are able;
To use our knowledge and talents to help others;
And to be humble, considerate and kind. *Amen.*

Closing prayer No. 66

Great people of God (2)

Ramakrishna

Bible Reading: Proverbs 3: 5–8

'Remember the Lord in everything you do, and he will show you the right way.' Throughout the centuries those people who have been willing to let God show them the right way have been the ones who have led the holiest and the most contented lives.

A great holy man of last century was Ramakrishna. Born on 18th February, 1836, in Hooghly, Bengal, he came from a poor Brahmin family. He had very little schooling and all his life he spoke a coarse dialect of Bengali with no English or Sanskrit. But at a very early age he decided that he wanted to know God and, when he was given a chance of an education he turned it down. He did not want to know God from books: he wanted to find God for himself, to experience God through the way he lived and worshipped.

Ramakrishna was brought up a Hindu; at the age of 30 he followed the way of Islam; and later he studied Christianity. He discovered that each religion had much to offer but knew that God must be at the centre of everything. Ramakrishna saw God in everyone and everything.

And because he saw God in everyone he rejected any ideas of caste or of social divisions. All people were God's children. Ramakrishna became one of India's foremost teachers and preachers. Thousands gathered near his Calcutta home to hear him speak, for however crudely his ideas may have been expressed they were regarded as gems of wisdom.

It was at Calcutta that he died on 16th August, 1886 and it is at Calcutta today that a religious order bearing his name has its headquarters and sends missionaries throughout the world.

Help us, O God, to seek you, to find you and to follow you; to see you in all people and all things; to know what you would have us to do; and to live our lives fully in your service. *Amen.*

Closing prayer No. 82

Great people of God (3)

One might think that the daughter of a Brahmin priest at the court of the King of Nepal would have had an excellent start for a full life. But her parents arranged for her to marry when she was only seven years old and her husband died two years later. So Chundra Lela was expected, according to her Hindu religion, not to remarry but to spend the rest of her life in mourning.

More tragedy was to follow. Her mother had died. At the age of thirteen she went on a pilgrimage with her father to the shrine of Jagannatha at Puri and there her father died. Chundra Lela was now a widow and an orphan. And her faith taught that tragedy was a result of sin.

So she began a series of pilgrimages and religious acts to try to find peace with God. The pilgrimages took her to many parts of India, to an island near Sri Lanka and to the snow-covered Himalayas. She tortured her body with extremes of heat in summer and of cold in winter, after twenty years she was still no nearer to finding God.

Then she discovered some Christian books, which led her to buy a Bible for herself. For some years she had been a Hindu guru, teaching that faith. Now she became a Christian, travelling without possessions, much as St. Francis had done, and teaching the Christian faith.

To the end of her life, on 26th November, 1907, there was nothing that would stop her teaching about the God who had come to mean so much to her. People of various faiths acknowledged that hers was a holy life which had brought help to lots of others.

Help us, O God, to find that deep peace in our hearts which comes when we have found you for ourselves; and when we have found the way, grant that we may follow it faithfully, helping others to know you too. *Amen.*

Closing prayer No. 55

Great people of God (4)

A CHRISTIAN SADHU   *Sundar Singh*

Sundar Singh was born into a Sikh family on 3rd September, 1889. Even as a boy he had thought he would like to be a Sadhu or holy man. He attended a Christian school but left it when he was expected to read the Christian scriptures. To show how he felt about this religion he publicly burned a copy of the Gospels.

But one day he had a vision of Jesus Christ and he realized that though he was very religious he was not doing things as God would have him do them—much as Saul, later St. Paul, was given a vision on his way to Damascus.

Bible Reading: Acts 9: 3–8

Sundar Singh was immediately disowned by his family but he found his way to a Christian school where he was baptized. For a time he joined a Franciscan community but he could not settle. He went to college but decided against becoming a priest. Instead he became a Christian sadhu travelling through many parts of India and across the Himalayas to Tibet, a land where preaching was forbidden.

But Sundar Singh often preached, using parables much as Jesus had done so that people could understand what he had to tell them. Nothing would stop him from preaching even though he was imprisoned for a while as a result. He preached faithfully to the end, which probably came about mid-1929. He had set off once again for Tibet at a time when he was not in very good health and he was never seen again. He had no doubt died in the Himalaya mountains.

Grant, O Heavenly Father, that you will give us a vision of what we should believe and how we should live; and then, by the guidance of your Holy Spirit, help us to do your perfect will. *Amen.*

Closing prayer No. 52

Great people of God (5)

Pope John Paul II

When Cardinal Karol Wojtyla (*Voytilla*) was elected Pope on 16th October, 1978, it was a historic occasion, for it was the first time for 455 years that a man who was not Italian had been chosen. At 58 he was also the youngest Pope for many years. He took the name of Pope John Paul II.

Pope John Paul II was born in Wadowice, Poland on 18th May, 1920, the son of a factory worker. As a young man in German occupied Poland during the war he decided to become a priest and risked his life by studying in secret. If caught he would have been imprisoned. He completed his studies after war had ended and became a priest in 1946.

Life was never easy as a priest, for Poland was by then a Communist country, where Christianity was regarded with suspicion and church leaders considered enemies of the state. But many people in Poland are Roman Catholics and their leaders have sometimes had to stand firm against the government. Cardinal Wojtyla, Archbishop of Cracow was one who was never afraid to do so.

The Cardinal was held in great respect in Poland. His background helped him understand ordinary people. Students and young workers appreciated the way he spoke out for their rights and freedom. Intellectual people warmed to the man who had studied hard and was able to speak fluently in several languages. For a long time he has helped keep the torch of the Christian faith burning.

His choice as Pope meant that Christians in the Communist countries had an even more powerful champion, and not just Roman Catholics but people of other religious denominations too would be encouraged.

Almighty God, we remember the people of many lands who have remained true to their beliefs in face of difficulty or danger. Grant that they may be encouraged today to maintain a true witness and keep their lamps of faith burning brightly. *Amen.*

Benediction No. 91

Faithful servants (1)

Abbé Michel Quoist

Michel Quoist was born in Le Havre, France, on 18th June, 1918. His was a working class home and he grew up amid poverty and suffering. He knew that something had to be done to help such people. At eighteen he began his studies to become a Roman Catholic priest and once he had been ordained went on to further studies.

But the Abbé's studies were about people and their problems. And there is no better way to find out about such things than to live amongst them. So that was what he did, living for several months amongst the very poor people.

Then it was back to Le Havre, where the Abbé Michel Quoist served as a pastor in a city parish, spending much of his time amongst the young and the poor. He became well known for his work as chaplain to various youth groups and clubs.

But Michel Quoist is probably better known by many people for the books he has written. His *Prayers of Life* sold over two million copies in a couple of dozen languages. It is a book of prayers about everyday situations, and people, and problems. And he believes that prayer is a part of life itself.

The title of another of his books is *Meet Christ and Live!* It sums up what he believes, that if we will only spend time in prayer and meet Christ ourselves, problems will gradually disappear and we shall know what it means to live a really full life in close communion with God.

Part of a prayer of Michel Quoist

Thank you for all the time you have given me.
Thank you for life. Thank you for grace.
Thank you for being there, Lord.
Thank you for listening to me, for taking me seriously, for
    gathering my gifts in your hands to offer them to your
    Father.
Thank you, Lord. Thank you. *Amen.*

Benediction No. 99

Faithful servants (2)

Pastor Martin Niemoller

The strength of many Christians lies in their belief that there is nothing whatever in this world that can separate them from the power and the love of God. Hear the words of St. Paul:

Bible Reading: Romans 8: 35–39

It was that belief, no doubt, that enabled Pastor Niemoller, the Pastor of one of the churches in Berlin, to stand up to Adolf Hitler, the German dictator, and tell him he was wrong. Hitler wanted all the churches to do what he said and set up a new Church organization. Niemoller nailed notices to the trees of Wittenberg, calling on all Pastors to be faithful.

It was a dangerous thing to do but Martin Niemoller refused to back down. Courage was not lacking where he was concerned. As a young man he had served in U-boats in the German Navy and often his life was in danger. In fact it was his experience in seeing loss of life at sea that made him want to save life and persuade people to change their ways. It was this that led him to become a Pastor. Now he wanted to protect people from the evil ways of the Nazi regime.

Soon after his stand against Hitler, on 1st July, 1937, he was arrested by the secret police. Seven months later he was tried but there was no evidence for his conviction. But instead of being freed he was sent to a concentration camp near Berlin. In 1941 he was transferred to another camp at Dachau.

Much of the time he was kept apart from other prisoners but later he shared a room and was allowed books to read. He was freed in 1945 when the war ended and became President of his Church two years later. Nothing had separated him from God!

Almighty God, we thank you for the example of those who have remained faithful to you at all times. May we know your guidance, protection and sense of your presence all our days. *Amen.*

Benediction No. 93

Faithful servants (3)

LOVE GOD: LOVE YOUR NEIGHBOUR *Corrie ten Boom*

Bible Reading: St. Mark 12: 28–31

Corrie ten Boom lived in Haarlem in the Netherlands with her family. They were devoted Christians who had a strong faith in God and great desire to help others. Many came to their home for Bible study or turned to them for help and advice.

Then came World War II. German armies overran the country and the ten Booms found themselves giving help of a different kind. All Jews were in great danger and tried to escape. Corrie's home was one of many in which they could find a hiding place. There was always danger but they were thankful they could help in this way.

At last the dreaded moment came. On 28th February, 1944, the Gestapo arrived and arrested everyone in the house, including many who had come for Bible study. Soon they were on their way to prison and some dreadful experiences. For father the imprisonment was short. The old man died after ten days in prison.

Corrie was taken before an officer who questioned her. At the end of his report he wrote, 'She plans to continue in the future what she has done in the past because she wants to help all those who appeal for her aid regardless of their race or creed. She is determined to do this because she is obedient to the command of Christ to love God and her neighbours.'

In the years that followed she suffered greatly—cruel guards, solitary confinement, cold, hunger and vermin. She witnessed torture, death and misery both in the prison and later in the concentration camp at Ravensbruck, where her sister Betsie died in the hospital. Throughout this time until she was eventually freed she found strength and comfort in her faith in God and did what she could to comfort others.

O God, help us to love you with our whole being and to have faith in you at all times. Grant us strength in time of weakness, comfort in our distress and help when in need. May we show our love for you by loving others so that they too may know your love; for Jesus Christ's sake. *Amen.*

Closing prayer No. 70

Faithful servants (4)

POPE FOR A MODERN AGE   *Pope John XXIII*

When a new Pope was needed in 1958, few people gave much thought to Cardinal Roncalli, the Patriarch of Venice. He was seventy-seven years old, whilst his fat, good-natured face gave the impression of a wise peasant rather than the leader of a powerful church.

Yet when the elections were over, Angelo Roncalli was the new Pope, taking the title of John XXIII. And, in the four years and seven months that he held office, great changes took place in the Roman Catholic Church.

The new Pope was a man of wide experience, which helped him form his ideas. He was, in fact, the son of a poor peasant living in the north of Italy. His first appointment as a priest was as secretary to a bishop. Part of World War I was spent as chaplain in military hospitals. Then he served as Bishop in Bulgaria, Turkey and Greece until 1944 when he moved to France.

No doubt his background helped keep him in touch with ordinary people; his work in Eastern Europe gave him connections with the Eastern Orthodox Church. He soon made it clear that he welcomed personal contacts with all sorts of people and wanted to talk with leaders of other churches.

Pope John XXIII was most anxious to see greater co-operation between the Christian Churches and to break down some of the barriers which existed between them. He remembered especially some words of Jesus:

Bible Reading: St. John 17: 20–22

'That they all may be one' became his frequent prayer and was the last one he prayed. It sums up the work of the man who died on 3rd June, 1962, and has been regarded by many as a modern day saint.

Almighty God, we cannot understand all your ways but we know that you are the great Father of us all and we are your children. We may think of you in different ways and we ask you to help us to know that there are many paths that lead to you. Give us an understanding of each other's form of worship and bless all who work for the unity of your people. *Amen.*

Closing prayer No. 80

401

Faithful servants (5)

100TH ARCHBISHOP OF CANTERBURY   *Dr. Arthur Michael Ramsey*

Since St. Augustine brought Christianity to England in A.D. 596, Canterbury has been a great centre of Christianity in England. The Archbishop of Canterbury, also known as The Primate of All England, is the leader or spiritual head of the whole of the Church of England.

On 27th June, 1961, in a moving ceremony in the historic cathedral, the 100th Archbishop of Canterbury was enthroned. He was Arthur Michael Ramsey, who had been Archbishop of York for five years and previously Bishop of Durham.

Born at Cambridge in 1904 and educated at Cambridge University, Dr. Ramsey spent the whole of his life in the service of the church in a variety of appointments as parish priest, and in various colleges where he lectured in theology. He was recognized as a Bible scholar and author of a number of books.

But for many people he will be remembered for his great wish for closer links and unity between the various Christian denominations. He was the President of the World Council of Churches from 1961 to 1968 and this brought him into close contact with the leaders of churches from all over the world. He used these and many other opportunities to discuss ways in which Christians could work more closely together. St. Paul had urged this when he wrote to the people of Corinth:

Bible Reading: I Corinthians 1: 10 (or 10–13)

Dr. Ramsey retired as Archbishop of Canterbury in 1974 and was created a life baron, becoming known as Lord Ramsey of Canterbury and quietly continuing his work as a faithful servant of God.

Almighty God, we praise you for all your faithful servants who have worked for the unity of your Church and the good of your people. Bless all who follow in their footsteps. *Amen.*

Benediction No. 102

Prayers and Bible Readings

Prayers for opening worship

These prayers are suitable for use as part of the opening act of worship. They should be regarded as supplementary to the many which can be found in anthologies of prayers in order to provide a wider selection which will give variety in this part of the service.

PRAYERS OF PRAISE AND THANKSGIVING

1 Almighty God, at whose command all things were created, we bow before you in thankfulness and praise. Accept our thanks for all your blessings and keep us mindful of every mercy, that we may ever worship you and praise your holy Name. *Amen.*

2 Almighty God, Creator of all things visible and invisible, we your children come before you to praise your holy Name. With thankfulness we remember every blessing received and every joy that has come to us. Accept our praise and thanksgiving; make us worthy to be called your children; and to you be all the praise and glory for ever. *Amen.*

3 At the beginning of our school day we stand before you, O God, and remember your great power and your great love for us. Thank you for all you have done for us and for all you have given us. Keep us mindful of your presence, fill us with your Spirit, and give us thankful hearts. *Amen.*

4 O God our Father, we come to you this morning to say thank you for all the blessings you have given us.
Thank you for our homes, our parents and all whom we love.
Thank you for our school, our teachers and all who help us to learn about your world.
Thank you for our friends, our neighbours and all people who mean a lot to us.
Help us to show our thanks to you by being thoughtful and considerate to others in the name of our Lord Jesus Christ. *Amen.*

5 O Lord our God, we stand before you in silence and remember
   that you are the great God of Creation. (*Pause*)
   We remember that you loved the world so much that you sent
   your Son, Jesus Christ, to help us. (*Pause*)
   We remember how Jesus taught us that you are our Father and
   that we should pray to you.(*Pause*)
   Hear our morning prayers and help us
   To feel your presence now;
   To remember you all through the day;
   To know that you can help us.
   And teach us to be true children of our heavenly Father;
   through Jesus Christ our Lord. *Amen*.

6 Praise be to you, O God:
   For the blessings of the past night and our safe awakening this
       morning;
   For the joys and security of our homes and the love of our
       families;
   For the work and play in our school and for all who help us
       here;
   For the friendships we enjoy and the companionship of others;
   For the world around us—sunshine and rain, animals and
       birds, trees and flowers;
   For these and all your blessings, Praise be to you, O God.
       Amen.

7 We praise you, God our Father, for the joys of our world and
   every blessing received from you. We remember with thankfulness that you are the great Creator, yet we can call you our
   Father; we remember how you loved the world so much that
   you sent your Son to be our Saviour; we remember how you
   have sent your Spirit to help people to understand your ways.
   Keep us mindful of your presence today, and help us to do only
   that which pleases you; through Christ our Lord. *Amen*.

8 We thank you, God our Father for all your many blessings; for
   food and clothing, for health and strength, for families and
   friends, for work and play; and for all those gifts which so often
   we take for granted. Keep us mindful of all these things and
   help us to show our thankfulness by sharing our blessings with
   others and seeking to do your will. *Amen*.

9 RESPONSE: *We thank you, God our Father.*

We thank you, O God, because you are the great Creator of the universe and of all things seen and unseen.
We thank you, God our Father.
We thank you because you have given us so many gifts and have shown us how to enjoy our world.
We thank you, God our Father.
We thank you because you sent Jesus Christ to help us to understand your great love for us.
We thank you, God our Father.
Help us to enjoy our world and to live our lives as you would have us to live as your children; through Jesus Christ our Lord. *Amen.*

10 RESPONSE: *We praise and thank you, Lord.*

For creating the world and all the beautiful things around us;
We praise and thank you, Lord.
For helping us to learn about you through the words of your servants;
We praise and thank you, Lord.
For giving us so much that helps us live a full and happy life;
We praise and thank you, Lord.
For blessings so numerous that we cannot count them;
We praise and thank you, Lord.
Help us to use our gifts wisely in your service and in the service of others; through Jesus Christ our Lord. *Amen.*

11 RESPONSE: *Praise be to you, O God.*

For the world in which we live and for all the beautiful things which are around us;
Praise be to you, O God.
For our homes, our families, our friends and all whom we love;
Praise be to you, O God.
For animals and birds, flowers and trees, the town and the open country;
Praise be to you, O God.
Accept our thanks for all your gifts and keep us mindful of your love, now and always. *Amen.*

12 *Open spaces*

O Lord, our God, we thank you for the enjoyment of open spaces:
For parks and gardens with lovely flowers, shrubs and trees;
For recreation grounds where we can take exercise and enjoy our sports;
For open country where we can walk or play, have picnics and enjoy the sunshine;
For hills to climb and woods to explore.
Help us to enjoy these things and to be thankful to you for every blessing. *Amen.*

13 *The animal world*

O God our Father, we thank you for all the living creatures around us:
For animals, birds and many small creatures;
For those that come from other lands and for places where we may see them;
For those animals and birds, our pets, which share our homes.
May we, and all who are entrusted with the care of animals, have patience with them and look after them, just as we should care for everything with which you have entrusted us. *Amen.*

14 *Spring*

Lord of all lovely things, we praise you for springtime with all its signs of new life:
For the brightness and gaiety of spring flowers;
For the first green of leaves and catkins;
For birds beginning to build their nests;
For lambs and all new life on the farm;
For brighter weather and longer days.
As we see the new life around us and the brightness of our world, help us to remember the new life that Jesus offered to those who follow him and seek that way for ourselves. *Amen.*

15 *Eastertide*

At Eastertide, O God, we give thanks for the message that Jesus died and rose again, so that we might know your great love for us and be able to call you Our Father. *Amen.*

16 *Summer*

We give you thanks, O God, for all we can enjoy in summer:
For hot sunshine and cooling breezes;
For shady trees and rippling streams;
For country walks and picnics;
For sports and games to play;
For recreation in the open air;
For holidays by the sea or in the country;
Accept our thanks and give us grateful hearts. *Amen.*

17 *Autumn*

Almighty God, Creator of all things, we thank you for all the
joys of autumn:
For misty mornings and bright warm sunshine;
For falling leaves which rustle under our feet;
For fruits and nuts appearing on the trees;
For autumn flowers in parks and gardens;
For cosy homes when the day's work is done;
For these and all your blessings we say 'Thank-you, God.'
Amen.

18 *Winter*

O God we thank you for all that we can enjoy in winter: the
cold winds that make our faces glow; our fun and games in ice
and snow; the beauties of snowflakes and icicles, snow-
covered trees and snow-capped mountains; the warmth and
comfort of our homes; hot drinks, good food and warm
clothes; and for all other blessings that are ours to enjoy. Hear
our prayer for those not as fortunate as ourselves and help us
to help them in your name. *Amen.*

19 When skies are grey and the day is gloomy, we come to you, O
God, and thank you for the bright things of life now hidden
from our sight—bright sunshine, clear skies, pretty flowers
and gay colours. We thank you that every cloud has a silver
lining and that brighter days lie ahead. Help us in all things to
trust your goodness and feel your guidance so that we may
always have brightness in our lives. *Amen.*

Other prayers of praise and thanksgiving may be found on pages
15, 42, 43, 81, 116, 180, 292, 297, 308, 338, 340, 411

20 We thank you, O God, for the town in which we live with its many houses, busy streets, offices, factories and shops. Thank you for all the people who live and work here and who help to make our town what it is today. Help us to remember our responsibilities toward others and to be good neighbours to all around us; through Jesus Christ our Lord. *Amen.*

21 O God our Father, thank you for the open country, the hills and valleys, moors and meadows, farmland and forest. Thank you for the many hamlets, villages and towns [especially the one where we live], and for all the interesting things in them. Open our eyes that we may enjoy our world. *Amen.*

22 O God our Father, as we look around us we see many people who are different from ourselves but we know that all are your children. We thank you for all the people of the world with their differing gifts and customs, and especially for those who have learned to live at peace with others. May your Spirit come into the hearts of all people and give peace in the world; through Jesus Christ our Lord. *Amen.*

23 RESPONSE: *O Lord, hear our prayer.*

We thank you, O God, for all the peoples of the world and for the knowledge that we are all your children. Hear our special prayers

For all who are hungry or homeless,
                O Lord, hear our prayer;
For all who live in fear or danger,
                O Lord, hear our prayer;
For all who suffer because of war,
                O Lord, hear our prayer;
For all who are ill or in hospital,
                O Lord, hear our prayer;
For all who are sad or lonely,
                O Lord, hear our prayer;
Bless your people everywhere and help us all to live together in peace and love, thinking more of others than we do of ourselves, in the name of our Lord Jesus Christ. *Amen.*

Prayers for the school

24 O Lord, bless our school: that working together and playing together, we may learn to serve thee, and to serve one another; for Jesus' sake. *Amen.*

The Daily Service

25 We thank you, God our Father, for this school and all that it means to us:
For the opportunities of learning and for all the books and equipment we use;
For our teachers who make our work interesting and enjoyable and who patiently help us to learn;
For caretakers and cleaners, for meals staff and playground ladies, and for all who attend to our comfort;
For all the children with whom we share our work and play, and especially for our friends:
For these and every blessing received, praise be to you, O God. *Amen.*

26 We give you thanks, O God, for this school and all who work in it. We are all very different and we worship and serve you in different ways, but we come together this morning to praise you for all your blessings. Grant that we may be mindful of your presence throughout the day and that you will help us to work together for the good of our school, the happiness of each other and the glory of your holy Name. *Amen.*

27 We come before you, O Lord our God, before we begin our day's work and we ask your blessing upon our school and all that shall be done in it today.
Help us to concentrate on the work we shall do;
Guide us when we find things difficult to learn;
Teach us to play fairly and unselfishly;
Make us thoughtful and considerate toward others;
Help us to do only what we know to be right;
So bring us to the end of the day, having done nothing to tarnish the good name of our school and thankful to you for all your blessings. *Amen.*

Prayers of penitence and confession

28 Grant, we beseech thee, merciful Lord, to thy faithful people pardon and peace; that they may be cleansed from all their sins, and serve thee with a quiet mind; through Jesus Christ our Lord. *Amen.*

Gelasian Sacramentary (Eighth Century)

29 Hear us, Almighty God, as we bow before you.
We confess our many failings:
Unkind words, thoughtless deeds, selfish attitudes;
Discourtesy, jealousy, pride, prejudice, hatred;
A disregard for the feelings of others;
And our failure to follow in your holy ways.
We are sorry for all that has offended you,
And we ask your forgiveness.
Grant us your peace in our hearts. *Amen.*

30 O most merciful Lord, we come to you knowing that you will forgive all those who confess their sins. Pardon us for all our offences and make us more worthy to be called your children; through Jesus Christ our Lord. *Amen.*

31 We confess, O God, that we have not been all that we might have been; we have hurt other people in things we have said and done; and we have been disloyal to you in thought, word and deed. Forgive us for all our sins and grant us the guidance of your Holy Spirit so that we may be more faithful in the days to come; through Jesus Christ our Lord. *Amen.*

See also the following pages:
72, 230, 319, 321

Prayers for special occasions

32 *The beginning of term*

At the beginning of our new term we come to you, O God, to say thank-you for the holiday we have just enjoyed, for all the pleasure it has given us, for rest, relaxation and renewed strength for our daily work. Now as we face a new term with fresh opportunities for learning we pray for the help we shall need, for patience and understanding when tackling new work, for a right attitude in all our dealings with others and for a determination to make this our best term ever. *Amen.*

33 *End of term or half-term*

We thank you, God our Father, for all that we have been able to do since this term began. Now as we look forward to this break from our work we pray that you will be with us. Help us to enjoy ourselves without displeasing others, to be helpful to those around us, and to build ourselves up through rest and recreation so that we come back to school renewed in body, mind and spirit, ready to do your holy will. *Amen.*

34 *End of the school year*

We gather together today, O God, for the last time in our present school year and we look back with thankfulness on all the joys and blessings it has brought us.
Thank you for lessons learned and enjoyed.
Thank you for special achievements and pleasures.
Thank you for all who have helped us this year.
Thank you for your help and inspiration.
We ask now that you will bless all who are leaving school today and help them wherever they go: and bless those who are returning that they may do so with renewed strength and vigour. Grant that all we have learned this year may be remembered; and help us so to live that we shall be true children of yours and a real blessing to others. *Amen.*

35 *Before a school journey*

We commend into your hands, O God, those of our number who will be going today on a school journey [*to* . . . . .]. Be with them in all their activities and grant that theirs will be a memorable and happy experience from which they will receive much benefit. Keep them in your care, we pray, and bring them safely home at the end. *Amen.*

36 *After a school journey*

We offer thanks, O Lord, for the safe return of our school journey party [*from* . . . . .], for the enjoyment of their time together and for everything seen and done. May the lessons learned and the experiences gained be of lasting benefit and may many happy memories remain. *Amen.*

37 *On sports day*

Almighty God, we give our humble thanks for healthy bodies and for the pleasures of sporting activities. Help us to enjoy our sports, to put everything we can into our efforts, and to be fair and open in all we do. Teach us that it is not the winning that is important but the spirit in which we participate. Grant that we may be humble winners, good losers or loyal supporters. *Amen.*

38 *On Open Day*

Almighty God, our Heavenly Father, we thank you for all the work and activities of this present school year and for the opportunity to show our parents what we have done. We are thankful for all those who have helped us; our parents who have done so much for us through the years; our teachers who have helped us to increase our knowledge; and many other people who have meant a lot to us in all sorts of ways. We thank you, too, O God, for all your love and care and for every blessing you have given. *Amen.*

39 Serious illness of children or staff

Almighty God, Comforter of all who are in distress in body, mind or spirit; grant your blessing today upon all who suffer or are in need [*and especially* . . . . .]. Watch over *him/her/them* in this time of need; comfort *him/her/them* while in pain or discomfort; restore *him/her/them* to health and strength; and if it be your will reunite us soon. *Amen.*

40 Death of a member of staff

O God of the spirits of all men, we praise your holy Name for the courage and faithfulness of your servant who, having fought a good fight, has passed from his life on earth; and we beseech you that, encouraged by *his* example and strengthened by *his* fellowship, we with *him* may be found ready to share in the life eternal, through the power of Jesus Christ our Lord. *Amen.*

(Source unknown)

41 Death of a child

O God, the Father of us all, we thank you for the life and friendship of . . . . . who has been taken from us [and no longer has to suffer pain]. Receive *him* into your holy keeping and grant your fatherly comfort to the family which mourns; through Jesus Christ our Lord. *Amen.*

42 For those who mourn

Grant, O God our Father, that you will look down in love upon those who mourn the loss of their dear ones. Comfort them in their time of sorrow and help them to see beyond their present distress to the joys of the world beyond; through Jesus Christ who himself is the Resurrection and the Life. *Amen.*

43 A wedding in the school

O God, whose nature is love, we thank you for that love which can unite a man and a woman in a bond which can last as long as life itself. Today we rejoice with . . . . . and . . . . . as they make their promises to each other and before you; and we ask your blessing upon their marriage; praying that every joy might be theirs in their life together and that they may know your richest blessings; through Jesus Christ our Lord. *Amen.*

44 *Confirmation of pupils*

Almighty God, by whose Son we were taught the need through baptism to show that we desire to be changed and lead a new life; we thank you for those whose parents brought them to you as children and who now wish to confirm this action by offering themselves for your blessing. Let your Holy Spirit enter their lives to inspire them to serve you faithfully all their days: in the Name of the Father and of the Son and of the Holy Ghost. *Amen.*

45 *After an accident or disaster*

Today, O God, we remember . . . . . who has been hurt in a [*street*] accident. Be with *him/her* while in pain and grant that *he/she* may soon be well enough to return to school. *Amen.*

Today, O God, we think of all those who have lost their lives and all who suffer as a result of the *disaster* at/in . . . . . We pray for all who are injured or in pain and ask that they may find relief in their sufferings. We pray for those who mourn the loss of loved ones and ask that you will comfort them. We pray for all who tend the suffering or help in other ways and ask you to give them strength. Hear us, O God, for Jesus's sake. *Amen.*

46 *Before an election*

Tomorrow, O God, many people will be voting for those who will represent them in the government of our *country/town /community* . . . . . and we ask your guidance and blessing upon all that shall be done. May those who are elected be those who will serve us faithfully and well. *Amen.*

47 *Those responsible for our school*

Hear our prayer, Almighty God, for all who are concerned
with the well-being of this school; the Council and the Education Committee Members; The School Governors/Managers;
the Education Officers and their staff; [our Parent Teacher
Association] and friends of the school. Guide them in every
decision they make, so that our school may prosper and meet
the needs of this neighbourhood. *Amen.*

48 *Former pupils*

Heavenly Father, we thank you for all those teachers and
pupils who have made this school what it is today. We thank
you for those who have remained interested in the school and
its welfare since they left to go their several ways. Grant that
we, like them, may enter whole-heartedly into our school life
so that for us, as for them, our school may hold many treasured
memories. *Amen.*

49 *School neighbours (differences of opinion)*

O God our Father, we pray that we may be good neighbours to
those who live near our school. Forgive us if sometimes we do
things which annoy them or if we speak rudely or unkindly
when they complain. Grant that they may have patience with
us and that we may be considerate toward them, so that a
happy relationship may exist between us; through Jesus Christ
our Lord. *Amen.*

50 *A special event*

Almighty God, we commend into your hands the [*event which
should be named*] for which we have been working. We thank
you for all the enjoyment which we have had in preparing for it
and we pray that it may be a success, bringing pleasure to all
who attend and satisfaction to all taking part; through Jesus
Christ our Lord. *Amen.*

Closing prayers

51 Almighty God, whose service is perfect freedom; grant us
    so to follow the example of thy Son Jesus Christ, that we may
    find our joy in service all the days of our life. *Amen.*

The Daily Service

52 Dear Father God, help us day by day to grow in the love of the
    Lord, so that others may love us because of your likeness.
    Amen.

Beryl Bye

53 Father, we pray for your presence this day so that in all the
    rush and bustle of our comings and goings we may know your
    peace in our hearts. *Amen.*

54 Father, we thank you for all those whose company we enjoy.
    Help us to know the love of others for us, and to be loving and
    kind in all our ways: for Jesus Christ's sake. *Amen.*

55 For joy and peace and quiet minds, praise be to you, O God.
    Amen.

56 God grant me the serenity to accept the things I cannot
    change, the courage to change the things I can, and the wisdom
    to distinguish the one from the other. *Amen.*

Reinhold Niebuhr

57 Grant, Lord, that what we have said with our lips we may
    believe in our hearts and practise in our lives; and of thy great
    mercy keep us faithful unto the end. *Amen.*

John Hunter

58 Grant, O God, that these few minutes with you may send us
    out again more kind to others; more honest with ourselves;
    more loyal to you; through Jesus Christ our Lord. *Amen.*

Dr. William Barclay

59 Grant to us, O God, the seeing eye, the hearing ear, the understanding mind and the loving heart, so that we may see your glory, and hear your word, and understand your truth, and answer to your love; through Jesus Christ our Lord. *Amen.*

Dr. William Barclay

60 Guide me, teach me, strengthen me, till I become such a person as thou wouldst have me be; pure and gentle, truthful and high-minded, brave and able, courteous and generous, dutiful and useful. *Amen.*

Charles Kingsley

61 Help us, O God, to do some little thing today that will make the world a better place because we have been here. *Amen.*

62 Help us, O God, to know what is right and to do nothing but the right; for Jesus Christ's sake. *Amen.*

63 Help us, O Lord, to seek you, to find you and to follow you, so that we may walk in wisdom now and all our days. *Amen.*

64 Into thy hands, O God, we commend ourselves this day;
Let thy presence be with us to its close.
Enable us to feel that in doing our work we are doing thy will
And that in serving others we are serving thee;
  Through Jesus Christ our Lord. *Amen.*

Prayers in use at Uppingham School

65 Lord have mercy upon all who suffer in body, mind or spirit and let your healing hand rest upon them; through Jesus Christ our Lord. *Amen.*

66 Lord, make me gentle and unselfish.
Help me to strive manfully for that which is right.
Make me merciful to all that are broken or bowed down.
Create in me a clean heart.
Teach me the way of peace: and let me be of them that make
  peace.
For Jesus Christ's sake. *Amen.*

The Daily Service

67 O God, be our strength and inspiration, so that we may be bold to resist temptation and to stand up for all those things which we believe to be right. *Amen.*

68 O God, come and dwell in our hearts so that we may be like you in all our ways; and to you be the glory for ever. *Amen.*

69 O God, give us humility and meekness, make us long-suffering and gentle, help us to esteem others better than ourselves, and so, O Lord, teach us to follow more closely in the steps of our Divine Master, Jesus Christ our Lord. *Amen.*

A Chain of Prayer

70 O God, give us the kind of love that cares more about others than ourselves. *Amen.*

Beryl Bye

71 O God, give us wisdom to know what is right; strength to do it; and courage to declare it; for the sake of Jesus Christ our Lord. *Amen.*

72 O God, make us to be all that we ought to be, so that your Name may be glorified through us. *Amen.*

73 O God! O God! We ask that thou wilt turn away our faces from any goal than thyself, and grant us to gaze toward thy noble countenance until we see thee in everything. *Amen.*

A Muslim prayer

74 O God of truth and love, make us strong and courageous so that we may ever uphold your truth and live in your love; for Jesus Christ's sake. *Amen.*

75 O God, open our eyes to the wants of our fellow men and open our hearts and purses to meet those needs. *Amen.*

Beryl Bye

76 O God
   Open my ears that I may hear you speaking to me;
   Open my eyes so that I may see how to do your will;
   And open my heart so that I may think more of you than I do of
      myself;
   For Jesus Christ's sake. *Amen.*

77 O God our Father, give us work to do, patience to keep at it
   and perseverance until it be finished; through Jesus Christ our
   Lord. *Amen.*

78 O God, teach us your ways of wisdom, truth and love, so that
   we may grow more like you in all our ways. *Amen.*

79 O Heavenly Father, we pray thee to send into our hearts and
   into the hearts of all men everywhere, the Spirit of our Lord
   Jesus Christ. *Amen.*

   (Source unknown)

80 O Lord, help us to understand that there are many paths that
   lead to thee, and that *our* way isn't necessarily the only one.
   Amen.

   Beryl Bye

81 O Lord, may others see that we love you, by the way we live
   every day. *Amen.*

   Beryl Bye

82 Open my eyes that I may see
   The work that thou hast set for me;
   And help me daily by thy grace
   Thy will to do, thy steps to trace. *Amen.*

83 Open our eyes, O God, to the beauties of the world around us.
   May nothing we do spoil it for others; through Jesus Christ our
   Lord. *Amen.*

84 Teach us, good Lord, to use our gifts in the service of others.
   Make our feet willing, our hands useful, our minds active and
   our hearts pure in your service; for Jesus Christ's sake. *Amen.*

85 The things, good Lord that we pray for, give us grace to labour for; through Jesus Christ our Lord. *Amen.*

St. Thomas More

86 Thine, O Lord, is the greatness, and the power, and the glory, and the victory, and the majesty; for all that is in the heaven and in the earth is thine; thine is the kingdom, O Lord, and thou art exalted as head above all. Now, therefore, our God, we thank thee and praise thy glorious name. *Amen.*

I Chronicles 29: 11–13 (A.V.)

87 Thou hast given so much to us, give us one thing more, a grateful heart; for Christ's sake. *Amen.*

George Herbert

88 Throughout this day, O Father, let us walk with you and talk with you. May your presence be known and your will be done. We ask it for Jesus Christ's sake. *Amen.*

89 We thank you, O God, for all that you have given us. May we use these gifts wisely in the service of others and so prove good stewards of all that has been entrusted to us. *Amen.*

90 We thank you, O God, for all your blessings. Help us to share them with others, knowing that as we do so we are serving you; for Christ's sake. *Amen.*

Benedictions

(An asterisk * denotes traditional benedictions or source unknown.)

---

91 Into the faithful hands of our God we commit ourselves now and always. O Lord, let us be thine and remain thine for ever; through Jesus Christ, thy Son, our Lord. *Amen.**

92 May God the Father bless us and all men everywhere and fill our hearts with his peace and goodwill. *Amen.*

93 May God the Father bless us.
May Christ the Son take care of us.
The Holy Ghost enlighten us all the days of our life.
The Lord be our defender and keeper of body and soul both now and forever. *Amen.*

Bishop Aedelward (Ninth Century)

94 May God the Father of our Lord Jesus Christ, bless, direct and keep us, and give us thankful hearts, now and for evermore. *Amen.**

95 May grace, mercy and peace from the Father, the Son and the Holy Spirit, be with us all this day and always. *Amen.**

96 May the blessing of God Almighty, the Father, the Son, and the Holy Spirit, rest upon us and upon all God's people everywhere, now and for ever. *Amen.**

97 May the grace of courage, gaiety, and the quiet mind, and all such blessedness as cometh from the Father to his children, be ours now and ever. *Amen.**

98 May the Lord grant us his blessing and fill our hearts with the spirit of truth and peace, now and evermore. *Amen.**

99 May the Lord lead us when we go, and keep with us when we sleep, and talk with us when we wake; and may the peace of God, which passeth all understanding, keep our hearts and minds; through Jesus Christ our Lord. *Amen.**

---

100 May the Spirit of the Lord Jesus Christ direct our thoughts and help us to learn of him with honest hearts, now and always. *Amen.**

101 May the strength of God pilot us. May the power of God preserve us. May the wisdom of God instruct us. May the hand of God protect us. May the way of God direct us, and may the shield of God defend us, now and evermore. *Amen.*

St. Patrick

102 Now may God bless us and keep us: may he give us light to guide us, courage to support us, and love to unite us, this day and for evermore. *Amen.**

103 Now unto the King, eternal, immortal, invisible, the only wise God, be honour and glory for ever and ever. *Amen.*

St. Paul (I Timothy 1: 17–A.V.)

104 Our God and Father himself, and our Lord Jesus Christ, direct our ways; and the Lord make us to increase and abound in love towards one another, and towards all men, now and ever. *Amen.*

St. Paul (I Thessalonians 3: 11–12 adapted)

105 The grace of our Lord Jesus Christ and the love of God, and the fellowship of the Holy Spirit, be with us all, evermore. *Amen.*

St. Paul (II Corinthians 13: 14 adapted)

106 The peace of God, which passeth all understanding, keep your hearts and minds through Christ Jesus. *Amen.*

St. Paul (Philippians 4: 7–A.V.)

107 Unto God's gracious mercy and protection we commit ourselves. The Lord bless us and keep us. The Lord make his face to shine upon us and be gracious unto us. The Lord lift up the light of his countenance upon us, and give us peace, both now and evermore. *Amen.*

Numbers 6: 24–26 (adapted)

Creeds

Two Creeds are commonly used in services in the Christian Church, the Apostles' Creed and the Nicene Creed the latter being longer. Both will be readily available in the traditional wording. This version of the Apostles' Creed is that of the International Consultation on English Texts.

The Apostles' Creed

I believe in God, the Father almighty,
  creator of heaven and earth.

I believe in Jesus Christ, his only Son, our Lord.
He was conceived by the power of the Holy Spirit
  and born of the Virgin Mary.
He suffered under Pontius Pilate,
  was crucified, died, and was buried.
He descended to the dead.
On the third day he rose again.
He ascended into heaven,
  and is seated at the right hand of the Father.
He will come again to judge the living and the dead.

I believe in the Holy Spirit.
  the holy catholic Church,
  the communion of saints,
  the forgiveness of sins,
  the resurrection of the body,
  and the life everlasting. *Amen.*

Sources of prayers

Bible readings linked to stories

Index of Related Subjects

This index does not include subjects readily found in the general index nor those for which there is little outside the general theme heading given in the Table of Contents. In this index the main theme headings are given first, followed by additional related pages.

433

Index of Prayer Subjects

439

Sick, 190, 194, 207, 382, 410
Simplicity, 128, 315
Sin, 319, 321
Singers, 112
Singing, 297, 345
Skills, 89, 258, 301
Slaves, 227
Snow, 409
Space, 179
Speaking out, 136
Spoiling things, 38
Sport, 78, 408, 409, 414
Springtime, 79, 408
Stars, 172
Stockbreeders, 19
Storms, 56
Straying from God, 366
Strength, 111, 400
Strife, 378
Studies, 236, 364
Study, Bible, 214, 288, 294, 346, 347, 348
Suffering, 55, 190, 192, 195, 196, 207, 217, 227, 410, 415, 416, 419
Summer, 409
Sun, 85, 409
Sunday, 329, 330

Talents, 81, 89, 108, 152, 153, 154, 205, 240, 258, 301, 407
  use of, 33, 89, 108, 139, 143, 152, 161, 163, 166, 169, 176, 178, 181, 236, 421, 422
Tapestries, 134
Teachers, 94, 236, 393, 405, 411, 414
Teachings, 20, 262, 276, 278, 300, 318, 364
Teamwork, 119, 239
Television, 115
Temptation, 60, 253
Term—beginning and ending, 413
Thankfulness, 35, 37, 65, 81, 85, 96, 128, 162, 171, 195, 199, 227, 344, 405, 413
Thanks, 15, 66, 178, 203, 273, 275, 300, 304, 398, 407
Theft, 144
Thoughtfulness, 12, 73, 104, 285, 405
Thoughtlessness, 412
Thoughts, 336
Time, 24, 25, 235, 258, 311
Tolerance, 7, 184, 185
Town, 407, 410

Town planning, 46
Translators, 349
Transport, 57, 88
Travellers, 144
Trees, 39, 48, 406, 407
True to beliefs, 95, 221, 251, 269, 288, 289, 358, 380, 397
Trust in God, 22, 60, 254, 260, 317
Truth, 142, 262, 263, 266, 269, 277, 320, 367

Understanding, 36, 66, 177, 193, 262, 278, 291, 347, 363, 387, 401, 419
Unfaithfulness, 232
Unity, Church, 243, 379, 401
Universe, 171, 172, 174, 175, 180
Unkindness, 234, 412
Unknown, The, 178
Unselfishness, 51, 80, 104, 114, 132, 419
Untruths, 62
Unwanted, 190, 200
Upholding the right, 62, 374
Use of talents (see *Talents*)
Usefulness, 163

Veterinary surgeons, 218
Views of others, 184, 378
Violence, 185
Vision, 125, 156, 396
Voices, 345
Voting, 416

War, 92
Waste, 49, 50, 51, 52, 87
Water of life, 27, 48
Weather, 85, 86, 408
Well-being of others, 61
Wild flowers, 35
Wild life, 13, 29, 31, 39, 40
Wind, 409
Winter, 68, 409
Wisdom, 66, 169, 175, 193, 214, 246, 251, 312, 364, 392, 393, 418, 420
Witness, 280, 318
Wonders of the world, 41, 170
Word of God (see *Bible*)
Words, 123
Work, 4, 17, 66, 245, 311, 327, 388, 392, 406, 411, 419, 421
Workers, 85, 88

General Index

Aberdeen, 15, 49
Abraham, 259
Accidents, 57, 58, 91
   Road, 208
Achievements, 157
Adoration, 292, 296
Advent, 278
Aesop fable, 244
Africa, 87, 374
Aggrey, Dr. James Kwegyir, 232
Agni (Hindu God), 261
Agricultural research, 18
Air disaster, 57, 184
Aircraft, 57, 237
Akiba, Rabbi, 358
Albert, Prince, 97, 167
Aldrin, 'Buzz', 178
Alexander, Mrs. Cecil Frances, 341
Alhamdulillah, 285
Alice in Wonderland, 131
All Creatures Great and Small, 218
All Creatures of our God and King, 338
All Glory, Laud and Honour, 337
All Hallows, 90
All Saints' Day, 90
All Souls' Day, 90
All things bright and beautiful, 80, 341
Allah, 282
Alps, 157
Altars, 259
Amazing Grace, 343
Ambulance brigades, 217
Amen, 293
America, 55
Amulets, 256
Ancestors, 67
Anderson, Elizabeth Garrett, 205
Anglican Church, 316, 318
Angling, 125
Animals, 28–32, 218
   farm, 12, 19, 20, 21, 22, 218
   preservation of, 31
Animism, 252
Apartheid (South Africa), 230, 381
Apocrypha, 346
Apologies, 232

Apostles' Creed, 277, 425
Appeals, 191
   (See also under *Charities* on page 432)
Aqualung, 160
Archbishop of Canterbury, 402
Archers, The, 8
Architecture, 142, 307
Arctic, 380
Arjun, Guru, 286
Armstrong, Louis, 116
Armstrong, Neil, 178
Art, 133–7
Art galleries, 137
Ascension Day, 278
Ash Wednesday, 72
Ashbourne, Derbyshire, 71
'Ashes, The', 118
Ashley, Jack, M.P., 192
Ashley, John (Rev.), 386
Asia, 7, 87
Assemblies of God, 324
Association, 209
Astronauts, 176, 177, 178
Astronomy, 171–5
Atheists, 291
Attitudes, 229–33, 295
Auca Indians, 362
Augustine, St., 402
Augustinians, 312
Australia, 118, 207
Australian Inland Mission, 207
Authorized Version, 348
Autumn, 90–4
Avebury, 301
Ayrians, 261
Azariah, Bishop Samuel, 379

Babylonians, 259, 301
Bach, Johann Sebastian, 298
Baden-Powell, Lord, 239
Baker, Sir Benjamin, 170
Bakewell, Robert, 19
Ballingdon Hall, 44
Balloonists, 147
Ballot, 221
Bamangwato tribes, 247
Bangladesh, 87

446

Miners, 61, 391
Miracle plays, 108, 110
Miser, 238
Mishnah of Rabbi Akiba, 358
Misjudging, 238
Mission halls, 197, 303, 325
Missionary, 203, 204, 270, 325, 362, 368, 373–7 (see also p. 434)
Missions to Seamen, 386
Mistakes, 182
Mistletoe, 97
Model village, 45
Mona Lisa, 135
Monasteries, 267, 268, 270, 311–15
Monks, 267, 268, 270, 313, 314
Monti, Eugenio, 69
Moon, 178
Mormons, 288, 289
Morris dancing, 82, 106
Morris, William (Lord Nuffield), 235
Morse, Samuel, 213
Mortimer, Harry, 114
Mosque, 283, 305
Mothering Sunday, 73
Motor cars, 59, 145, 146, 235
Motorways, 146
Mountains, 156, 157
Moving house, 44
Muezzin, 283
Muhammad, 281, 284, 327, 350
Müller, George, 335
Mummers, 108
Music, 84, 110, 113–17, 151–5, 264, 298
Muslims, 281–5, 288, 291, 295, 305, 327, 350
Mystery plays, 108

N.A.S.A, 176
Nanak Guru, 286, 288, 291
Nasmith, David, 325
National Association of Boys' Clubs, 390
National Brass Band Championships, 114
National Children's Home, 191
National Gallery, 137
National Health Service, 206
National Parks, 41
National Playing Fields Association, 127
National Trust, The, 42, 130
Nature, World of, 9

Navigation, 164, 212
Nazi Party, 183
Need, 194–8
Negro spirituals, 117, 344, 345
Neighbourliness, 190, 202
Netherlands, 400
New Towns, 47
New Year, 65
  Celtic, 90
  Chinese, 67
  Jewish, 272
  Muslim, 284
  Sikh, 287
New Zealand, 378
Newcastle-upon-Tyne, 61, 90
Newspaper, 388
Newton, Sir Isaac, 173
Newton, John, 343
Nicene Creed, 277
Niemoller, Pastor Martin, 399
Nigeria, 377
Nine lessons and carols, 98
Nirvana, 263, 265, 266
Nobel Prizes, 165, 184, 185, 228, 229
Noble Eightfold Path, 266
Nonconformists, 318–25
Nonsense, 128
North Sea Oil, 15, 49
Northern Ireland, 185
Norway, 248
Nottingham, 236
  Goose Fair, 104
Nought for your comfort, 230
Noye's Fludde, 110
Nuffield Foundation, 235
Nuffield, Lord, 235
Nuns, 314, 338
Nursing, 207, 245, 376

Observatories, 175
Oceans, 160
Offices, Church daily, 308, 313
Oil, 15, 38, 49, 234
Old and New, 43–7
'Old Clem', 94
Old Vic, 109
Olney, Bucks, 71
Olympic Games, 120, 121
Opera, 110
Orbit, 177
Orchestra, 113, 151
Organs, 298
Orienteering, 126

450